PLANET INTERNET

What Is It All About?

First, just what is the Internet? The Internet, sometimes called simply "the Net," is a vast global network of computers that are connected. Technically, rather than one network, the Internet is a loosely organized collection of thousands of networks. It is accessed by students, business people, scientists, computer professionals, hobbyists, and anyone else who can tap into the Net's extraordinary resources.

It seems to me that one day I have never heard of the Internet, and then the next day I see it everywhere. That's true for a lot of people, even computer professionals. Part of the confusion is that the Net started out with a different name: Arpanet. The military created Arpanet in the 1970s to scatter their computers so that no single nuclear bomb could wipe out their computing capabilities. The network evolved and spread to other organizations, especially universities and libraries. Eventually, a more generic name was adopted: the Internet.

Why has it become so popular recently? The main reason is that it became easy to use. It is especially easy when compared to previous access methods, some of which required sophisticated technical knowledge.

OK, let's assume that it's easy enough even for me. Why should I jump in? The one answer that fits everyone is that you dare not risk being left behind. Futurists predict that networking of some kind will be as necessary to work and to living as technologies such as the telephone or computers. After that, the answer to this question depends a lot on the individual. Are you curious? Would you like to connect with people around the world? Would you like an amazing library at your fingertips? Would it amuse you just to see what other folks are up to?

Give me some for-instances. OK. Do you plan a job search in the near future? The Internet offers job boards and online help. Having a problem with your dog? Veterinary specialists answer individual questions from Net users. If you forget a birthday and thus need to send a gift quickly across the country, shopping on the Internet rivals any mall you have ever seen. Finally, consider some screens that could show up during your Internet travels. The White House image shown here signals your ability to ask questions of the president or even take a picture tour inside the White House.

Is this going to cost money? Maybe. Free Internet access is common in schools and libraries and other government organizations. Your employer may offer free access. If you want to hook up from your own personal computer, you will have to pay some sort of monthly charge and perhaps extra charges based on usage. Your local computer store could offer advice.

What's coming up later in the Internet discussions? For the most part, we'll examine various offerings on the Internet, some serious, some less so. Information about using the Internet will be tucked in here and there, so your knowledge will grow. In the next discussion of *Planet Internet,* we'll start traveling on the most popular part of the Internet, the World Wide Web. As we said, it's easy.

PLANET INTERNET

Getting Around

Is anyone in charge here? Not exactly. Unlike a commercial product, the Internet is not owned or managed by anyone. One consequence of this is that there is no master table of contents or index for the Internet. However, several organizations have produced ordered lists that can be used as a helpful starting place.

How do I start? We said we'd do it the easy way. Briefly, you need an URL for the Web. Translation: you need a starting address (*URL*, for *Uniform Resource Locator*) to search the Net by using the *World Wide Web*, also called *WWW* or just "*the Web*."

What is the Web? The Web is a way of searching the Net that lets you move from place to place. Each place on the Web is called a *site*. Each site has a *home page*, the first page you come to on the site. The key to the Web is that each site contains embedded *links* in the text to sites that have related information; those sites probably have further links to other sites, and so on. For example, a site discussing fine dining might have links to different cities, which in turn might have links to types of ethnic restaurants, which then link to individual restaurants. This simple dining example has an end, but many links go on and on, leading a user to unanticipated places on the Net. Links are readily identifiable within the site, probably a different text color and underlined (so it will show as a link when printed), or perhaps a graphics icon (small picture). You simply click your mouse on the link and you are transported to that site.

What does an URL look like? It's often pretty messy—a long string of letters and symbols. The good news is that once you get started, you can just click on a link rather than typing more URLs. Since everything on the Net, including URLs, is subject to change, in this text we supply only the Benjamin/Cummings Publishing Company (B/C) URL, which will not change. The B/C web site, in turn, supplies up-to-date links to all the sites we mention in these discussions. Once you link to a site, its URL will show on the screen, and you can save it so you can go there directly in the future if you like. A good starting site is The Whole Internet Catalog. It has links to major topics such as Entertainment, Business, Health, and Travel. Each major category has links of its own, as do the topics at the next level, and so on.

What other starting points are there? Well, of course, you can begin anywhere with an URL of your choosing. Users often favor Planet Access and Yahoo as comprehensive starting places. Special favorites are the Cool Site of the Day (including links to prior cool sites) and The Top 25 (the busiest 25 sites for the week).

THE WHOLE INTERNET CATALOG

But I need to get to the Web first. Yes. To access the Web you need special software called a *browser.* You need to ask your instructor, lab personnel, or designated employee how to use the Web browser at your location. If you are using a browser purchased for your personal computer, or have access to the Internet via some online service, then these suppliers will provide instructions.

Internet Exercises

In each chapter we offer two exercises. The first exercise is called a *structured exercise* because once you are on the B/C web site we can make sure that the sites you visit remain current. No wild goose chases. Use the URL supplied here to get started. If you are feeling adventurous, try the *freeform exercise.* We start you out but make no guarantees.

1. **Structured exercise.** Go to the B/C site using the URL: http://www.aw.com/is/planet/essentials.html Link to The Whole Internet Catalog, and then link to The Top 25. From there choose three Top 25 places to link to.
2. **Freeform exercise.** At the B/C site link to Netizens, a changeable list of individuals who maintain their own sites.

PLANET INTERNET

Global Village

The Internet is big, really big. Some say that working on the Internet gives new meaning to the word infinity. One way to grasp the vastness of the Net is to start linking to sites overseas.

So far away. As intriguing as these faraway sites may be, it may take some time to access them. An option that may be available is a *mirror site*, a nearby site that has the identical offering. The WebMuseum site in Paris, for example, which offers paintings from the Louvre on your screen, urges you right away to switch (link) to one of the mirror sites on their list; California has a mirror site for the Louvre. Using a mirror site dramatically improves the speed of data access.

The CERN site. It is entirely appropriate that we mention the CERN site, a laboratory for particle physics in Geneva, Switzerland. CERN is the birthplace of the World Wide Web. The architect of the Web, Tim Berners-Lee, perceived that his work would be easier if he and his far flung colleagues could link to each other's sites. He saw the set of links from site to site as a web; hence the name. This site includes a link to the history of the relationship of CERN with the Web.

English or not English. Many foreign sites offer an English version of their site to present to visitors whose language is English; you could as easily be in Kansas. Other sites offer a choice: Would you prefer English or Swedish? Others simply launch into their native tongue. You either speak it or just go along for the pictures. It is intriguing to see the Russian alphabet come on the screen as you tour the Kremlin.

Worth the trip? You decide. A good place to begin is the World Communities site, where you can hop from country to country. Be prepared for the fact that some developing countries have relatively primitive offerings at this point; in fact, some cannot be reached at all. But many sites are fascinating. The sites are as diverse as those of the three home page logos shown here: Japan's Hottest Links, the Egypt Interactive Home Page, and The University of Bristol Philosophy Department. If you check out the Australian National University site you'll find a Mediterranean art and architecture exhibit, complete with sight and sound, that won an award for its multimedia presentation.

Internet Exercises

1. **Structured exercise.** Begin with the B/C URL http://www.aw.com/is/planet/essentials.html and use the link supplied to go to the Canadian site.
2. **Freeform exercise.** Beginning with the World Communities site, compare the home pages you find for countries in Europe, Asia, the Pacific, and South America.

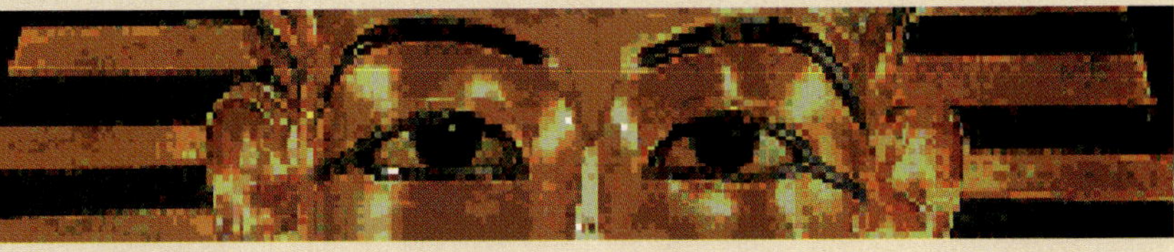

PLANET INTERNET

Just the FAQs, Please

When people begin to learn something new, they usually have many questions. In fact, beginners on the same subject often have the same questions. Rather than answer each question individually, it makes sense to keep the most Frequently Asked Questions—FAQs—in a handy place that anyone can access. FAQs are a long-standing tradition on the Internet. We will answer a few FAQs here and also refer you to online FAQs that you can check at your convenience.

Why do URLs all begin with http? Most do, but not all. HTTP stands for Hyper-Text Transfer Protocol, the means of communicating using, among other things, links. The html you often see at the end of an URL stands for HyperText Markup Language, a language to make pages that take advantage of multimedia—pictures, sound, and even film clips. And, while mentioning Web software, we should note that it was software called Mosaic, invented by Marc Andreessen when he was a college student, that made Web page multimedia possible. Today there are many competitive browsers, but it was Mosaic that got the Web off the ground.

How can I avoid typing URLs? The easy way, of course, is to simply click links from one site to another. But, inevitably, there will be a site to which you want to return without going through a chain of links. Most browsers offer a *hot list* where you can store your favorite sites and their URLs. Then, in another session, simply go to the hot list and click the site without typing the URL.

So far we have used just the Web. Is that all there is to the Internet? No. The Web is one way to access the Internet. The Web uses links to go from site to site, but Gopher, named for the mascot at the University of Minnesota, where it was developed, lets you "go fer" a certain file through a series of menus that zero in on your choice. For example, when a region on the world map shown here is clicked, the screen switches to a Gopher menu, from which you select a country, then a smaller geographical area such as a state, which lists all the WWW servers in that area. Another possibility is FTP, for File Transfer Protocol, which lets you transfer files from a remote computer to your computer. These and other Net access methods came before the Web and many have been incorporated into the Web. However, since non-Web sites are textual only, no graphics, the Web is becoming dominant. You can tell which access method is being used by the first part of the URL: http, ftp, and so forth.

I know there is no "top" of the Internet, but what are some good starting places? A good place to begin is Where to Start, a site that has a directory of directories. Many directories feature "What's new" so you can take off in a new direction. Also, we can't resist The Awesome List, featuring not only the Awesome but also the Truly Awesome, and World Wide Web Must-Sees.

What help sources are online? A helpful FAQ list for the beginner is the World Wide Web FAQs. Several sites offer lists of definitions, including The World Wide Web Starter Kit. A favorite for beginners is The Newbie Adoption Agency, which will match a beginner with a seasoned user.

Internet Exercises

1. **Structured exercise.** Begin with the B/C URL http://www.aw.com/is/planet/essentials.html and link to the World Wide Web FAQs.
2. **Freeform exercise.** If you are a "newbie," we suggest that you put yourself up for "adoption."

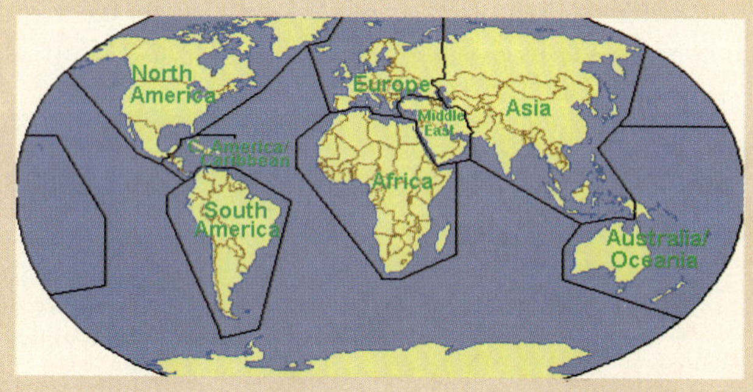

PLANET INTERNET

Shopping Tour

Shopping conveniences have existed since catalogs were invented. Convenience is at a high point today because computer shopping offers goods and services handily bundled together. The variety of available goods is stunning. What would you like to buy? Fishing tackle? An ergonomic chair? A gift box of fruit? Mexican pottery? (The images shown here are from the home pages of the stores.) All these products are available from companies that sell their wares on the Internet. As for the service, with a few clicks of a mouse and taps on the keyboard an order can be on its way to you.

So many stores. The term *electronic mall* refers to a group of Internet stores that rivals physical malls in size and variety. A good place to start is the Hall of Malls, which lists dozens of malls, each of which has many stores. Many shoppers find that, in a rather short time, they have stumbled on favorite stores. We offer these from our list: Net Sweats and Tees, The Plastic Princess (Barbie!), and the Chocolate Lover's Page. You can use the B/C URL to check these out, but you will soon make your own list.

Finding what you want. It is all well and good to know the names and the URLs of several shopping sites. And, although more convenient than traipsing around by car and foot, you are still faced with the prospect of searching for what you want, store by Internet store. What if there was a better way? What if you could just say what you want and have the computer search through the stores for you? One possibility is a *search engine,* a site that allows you to key in a request and then returns locations that you can click on. The only problem with search engines is that they are often busy. If you get a busy response, you can simply click your browser's Reload button to try again. If you repeatedly get a busy response, switch to a different search engine. We offer several search engines at the B/C site so you have a choice. Search engines, by the way, are not just for shopping; they can come in handy any time you need to find something specific on the Net.

What if I don't want to buy anything? No problem. It's just like old-fashioned window shopping, where you are welcome to look to your heart's content. Of course, as do retailers in real stores, they hope you will see something you want to buy.

Charge it? Standards for secure transmission of transactions through the Internet are still evolving. For this reason, some people prefer to do their shopping on the Net but place the actual order by telephone or some other secure means.

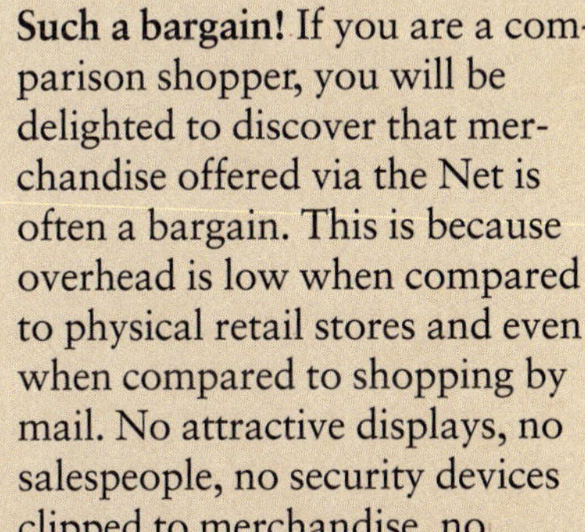

Such a bargain! If you are a comparison shopper, you will be delighted to discover that merchandise offered via the Net is often a bargain. This is because overhead is low when compared to physical retail stores and even when compared to shopping by mail. No attractive displays, no salespeople, no security devices clipped to merchandise, no printed catalogs, and possibly even no advertising. And, of course, a successful business has a potential worldwide audience and can thus purchase in high volume and pass the savings on to consumers.

Internet Exercises

1. **Structured exercise.** Begin with the B/C URL http://www.aw.com/is/planet/essentials.html and go to one of the search engine sites. Choose an object to purchase, and see what stores the search turns up.
2. **Freeform exercise.** This is obvious: Head right down the Hall of Malls.

PLANET INTERNET

Career in Gear

Many people, whether college students or experienced employees, dread the prospect of facing the world and begging for a job. Resources for this onerous task are often limited to the classified ads and perhaps a placement center. You have no such resource limitation if you have the Internet. A number of services, both commercial and nonprofit, specialize in matching employers with job seekers. However, although assistance is available for first-time job seekers, it would be fair to say that the jobs posted on the Internet lean toward experienced people in the computer field.

More schooling. Perhaps your career move requires further schooling before you are ready to enter the job market. You may seek help in taking the tests required as part of the application process. One informative site on the Internet is the Kaplan Education Center.

Online help for students. The Online Career Center is a nonprofit site that offers career support services, such as which keywords to use to search for jobs from thousands of companies. For a modest fee you can place your resume online for 90 days. Career Mosaic, whose on-screen logo is shown here, lists high-powered employers and offers a variety of support for job seekers. The Interactive Employment Network also features a searchable list of jobs and, in addition, lets job seekers key in a location and get the advertisements for that geographic area. If you are seeking a job in the Midwest, an attractive option is the Jobweb, which permits a job seeker to fill out a form online to create a listing on its pages. Most interesting of all, at least from a graphics point of view, is the Job Monster Board, whose logo is also shown here. Guided by amusing monster graphics characters, you can examine employer profiles, check out career events and information, or even submit your resume. The Monster Board lets you search its employer database by location, industry, company, discipline, and job title.

Your home page résumé. Some job seekers have taken advantage of Web exposure by developing their own home page résumés. This goes so far beyond the traditional résumé that a new name should be invented for it. To see what we mean, check the résumé home pages listed at the B/C site. You will find, typically, that the candidate includes a nice photo and then offers perhaps a 10- to 15-line résumé. Why so short? Each résumé line has links! For example, one line may refer to classes taken, with classes being a link. A potential employer merely clicks on the word *classes* to pop up a list of classes the job seeker has taken. Similarly, links can be made to intern work, laboratory assignments, work experience, extracurricular activities, and so forth. A person developing such a home page from scratch can make the résumé as variable as desired.

Internet Exercises

1. **Structured exercise.** Hooking up to the B/C site with URL http://www.aw.com/is/planet/essentials.html take a look at the Monster Board. Check out the Cyberzone link especially designed to provide college students with opportunities and discussion groups.
2. **Freeform exercise.** To expand your set of resources, begin with the Whole Internet Catalog. Find and click on a careers link.

PLANET INTERNET

Images, Icons, and Flags

Since many people are interested in colorful graphics, it is not surprising that the subject is well covered on the Internet. A good place to begin is the site called Images, Icons, and Flags. This site has dozens of links to nature and travel scenes, medical images, and museum archives. Shown here is a fractal artwork (art generated by variations on an original pattern—the fractal) done by pioneer Benoit Mandelbrot. You can find this by linking to a site called the Fractal Art Gallery.

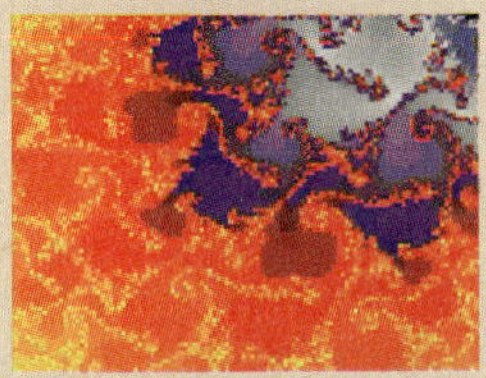

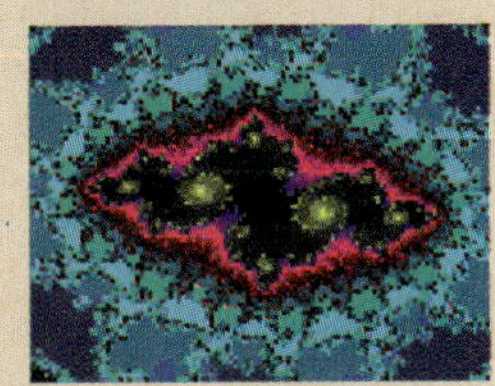

Images. Graphics images may be art or photos or some combination of the two. Art may be produced entirely on the computer. A photo or artwork devised externally may be shown on a computer screen once it has been input to the computer in some form.

Icons. An icon is a small symbolic picture, usually artwork but possibly a photo. Icons are everywhere, especially in advertising—think of the Pillsbury Doughboy or the swoosh that identifies Nike running shoes. On the Net, people use icons on their home pages. Many users like to use icons in computer-produced newsletters, advertising, and even correspondence. A large collection of icons is on the Net, and most of them are freely available for your use.

Flags. The Net supplies broad flag coverage, including colorful depictions of the flags themselves. The original site we referenced (Images, Icons, and Flags) has links to international flags, maritime flags, and semaphore flags.

Keeping it for yourself. Many files, including graphics images, can be downloaded—moved—from the source computer to your computer. Also, we'll mention briefly that you may have available, or can purchase, screen capture software. Using this software, you can save anything that you can see on your screen to a disk file.

Permission. Many artists and photographers put their works on the Internet to be shared freely by all. Others, usually professionals, state that their works are copyrighted and may be used only with permission. An example is The Stock Solution, whose logo is shown here. The Stock Solution is an agency that represents professional photographers whose works can be seen right on your screen. But you must agree to a lease fee before you can make any further use of the photos.

Waiting and waiting. Anyone who wants to explore images on the Net needs to understand that it is a time-consuming process. This could be a problem if you use shared computer resources. Unlike text, which is mostly white space with occasional black markings, color images are made up of tiny tightly-packed dots, sometimes hundreds of thousands of them for a single image. Moving an image from the source computer to your screen takes time. Your best defense is a speedy modem. Also, consider getting on the Net at odd hours when there are fewer users.

Internet Exercises

1. **Structured exercise.** Begin with the B/C URL http://www.aw.com/is/planet/essentials.html and click on semaphores; look up the semaphore alphabet.
2. **Freeform exercise.** From the starting point of Images from Various Sources, choose three links and bring images to your screen.

PLANET INTERNET

Not Quite Perfect Yet

The Internet has been heaped with well-deserved praise. But still there are concerns. To begin with, no one really knows exactly who is out there on the Net and what they are doing online. No one can truly compile statistics, much less establish content standards or control behavior. It's a little worrisome. On the other hand, many users find the freewheeling, no-controls aspect of the Internet appealing. Some fear that eventually the government, or perhaps a liaison of governments, will try to tame the Internet.

There really are some behavior problems. True. But there are behavior problems in any aspect of society, from the playground to the boardroom. Those who abuse the Net are, relatively speaking, small in number. Besides, the community of users monitors behavior on the Net. *Netiquette* refers to appropriate behavior in network communications, such not typing in caps (IT'S LIKE SHOUTING) and sticking to the subject at hand in a discussion group. Netiquette rules are published in various places on the Net and in every book about the Net. Users who commit serious sins may be subjected to flaming. *Flaming* refers to angry e-mail, sometimes by the hundreds or even thousands, directed to someone on the Net who has done something egregious, such as mass advertising. Meanwhile, some user/philosophers have occasionally produced statements of principle about the Internet. The Cyber Rights Home Page, sponsored by an organization called Computer Professionals for Social Responsibility, focuses on a variety of Net-related social issues, including online privacy and free speech.

Uselessness. Some people consider some home pages useless. In fact, there is a site called Useless Pages that maintains a listing of pages the site manager deems useless. However, many people are willing to pay for the connection to a Web server in order to promote a home page they fancy, such as Pete's Pond, shown here. Others put out birth or wedding announcements, complete with photos. One useless page does nothing except count the number of times the page is accessed. If you are not interested, simply skip such pages. No harm done.

Overburdened. It is just a matter of time before exponential user growth overwhelms the most popular sites. What's New and Cool Site of the Day are two of the most heavily accessed Web sites; they may soon be almost inaccessible. In addition to access problems, some individuals on the Net become overburdened by input from other Net users. You may see poignant messages on sites pleading for no more e-mail or, at least, explaining that they get so much e-mail that they cannot respond to it.

No guarantees. The Internet is full of misinformation. Just because something is on the Internet does not mean it is true. If someone steps up to announce that the government uses black helicopters to spy on us or that tapes sound better if you soak them in water first, you need not accept such information as fact. It's not that people intend to be wrong, it's just that they sometimes are. If you are doing serious research on the Internet, be sure to back it up from other sources, especially non-Internet sources.

Internet Exercises

1. **Structured exercise.** Begin with the B/C URL http://www.aw.com/is/planet/essentials.html and read the Cyber Rights manifesto.
2. **Freeform exercise.** Beginning with the Useless Pages site, spend a few minutes checking out pages you will never have to visit again.

PLANET INTERNET

Free and Not Free

Many people, especially those associated with schools and government organizations, have free access to the Internet. But is the information available on Internet sites also free? Often the answer is yes. This means that the average citizen could go to, say, the local library, get on the Internet for no charge and then also pick up information from the Net free of charge. Free and free. Even users who have to pay for Internet access can get free Net information.

What information is free and what isn't? There are no uniform rules to guide you. Although some information providers make a blanket "help yourself" statement, much information is unaccompanied by a proprietary statement. However, business people and others who do not want their works copied can post clear notices on their pages, using phrases such as *copyrighted, online access only,* and *all rights reserved.*

Freebies. Several categories of information tend to be free. Categories of such information include health care, the environment, science, government agencies, humor, lists of events, family issues, social sciences such as philosophy and religion, the weather, anything to do with space, and most topics found on individual home pages. The heart shown here is the logo for a site that does a serious job of exploring the heart. The planets are from the popular and educational Nine Planets site. The multicolor shot is from a NASA volcano exhibit; this shot was taken from the space shuttle.

Not free. Noticeably missing from the list of freebies are business activities. Although there is always free advice on any topic, businesses by nature want to make a profit, so business products and services are likely to have a fee. What's more, businesses are running, not walking, to the Net, so the proportion of for-a-fee offerings can only increase. Even information on sites related to sports and entertainment may not be freely available. For example, the MTV site cautions, in case anyone wants to borrow their cool logos for an individual home page, that "all logos are trademarks" and "all rights are reserved."

Free forever? Probably not. Generally, when a product or service is offered free, its use may be abused. Users may be charged something, however nominal, just so they will recognize the value of the Internet and use it wisely. The most serious problem, however, is overload. The number of users of the Net is doubling worldwide every few months. In short order, critical mass will demand that some scheme be devised to limit usage in some way, and that approach may include access fees.

Internet Exercises

1. **Structured exercise.** Begin with the B/C URL http://www.aw.com/is/planet/essentials.html and examine the free (save frog lives!) computerized Frog Dissection Kit.
2. **Freeform exercise.** Beginning with the EINet Galaxy directory or your own your favorite online directory, find the maps to track the weather in your home state.

PLANET INTERNET

Resources for Living

Need information? Need information fast? Whether commonplace or rare, any information you may need is probably somewhere on the Internet.

Government resources. The government had a head start and has made excellent use of the Internet. We have already mentioned the White House, but you can also use the resources of the Library of Congress, whose opening screen is shown here, or contact the United States House of Representatives or even the CIA. You may peruse recent Supreme Court decisions by topic or by case name. And, although you may have little inclination, you can access the Internal Revenue Service site to get forms or advice. Finally, how would you like a crack at reducing the deficit? The site called Balance the Budget lets you do just that.

News you can use. Consider bits of information you might need in any given week. Weather forecast for your travel destination? Every sort of weather information is available, for regions and individual cities. Buying a new or used car? Pricing information is available just a computer away. As you would expect, consumer information is available on just about any topic. Want to plan ahead for natural calamities? You can get serious advice on food supplies and survival in the event of an emergency from sources on the Net. Would you just like a good book? Project Gutenberg makes books available online.

Finding like-minded folks. *Usenet,* a network intertwined with the Internet, offers *newsgroups,* special groups set up by people who share a common interest. Usenet computers store messages sent by users and periodically forward them to other Usenet computers. Using your browser software, you can access Usenet to read messages contributed by others and perhaps add some of your own. Usenet newsgroups are arranged in topical hierarchies, with focus shifting from broad to narrow. The major categories are quite general, for example, computers or business. Categories are subdivided by topic, which is further subdivided into newsgroups and then subjects. The broadest category by far is the Alternative category, which has hundreds of topics ranging from aromatherapy to Elvis to Rhodesia. Your browser will let you single out newsgroups in which you have a particular interest and then, on command, pick up new messages from just those newsgroups.

Different kinds of people participate in newsgroups. Some are experts who dispense wisdom, and others are neophytes who are there to soak it up. Some users, called *flamers,* like to respond to messages with personal insults. New users are often *lurkers,* people who read messages but want to learn about the group dynamics before contributing anything of their own.

Reaching out. Nonprofit organizations such as Impact Online, whose screen is shown here, use the Net to send their messages. Impact Online helps people get involved with nonprofits nationwide through the use of technology. One advantage of a truly *worldwide* web is the possibility of addressing worldwide issues. The site for Friends of the Earth, an environmental group, is in Britain.

Internet Exercises

1. **Structured exercise.** Begin with the B/C URL http://www.aw.com/is/planet/essentials.html and take your turn at balancing the budget.
2. **Freeform exercise.** Venture into Usenet. Use your browser to access newsgroups and read messages from topics that interest you.

PLANET INTERNET

Internet on the Internet

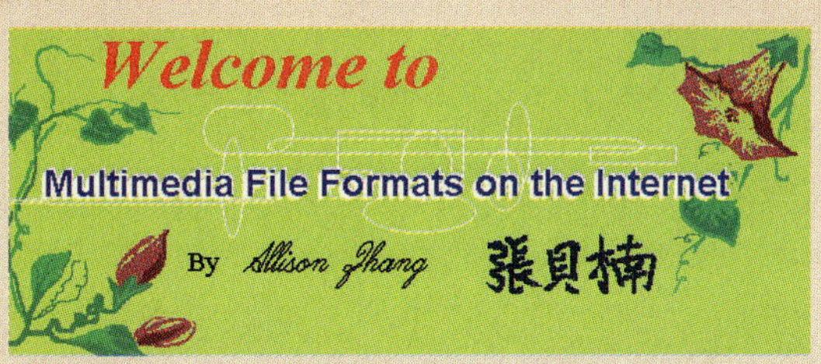

Magazine articles about the Internet usually supply a list of attractive Web sites, but little else of substance. Internet books usually have not caught up with the latest developments, which may have happened yesterday. But Net users have a ready source of current information: the Internet itself.

What kind of help is available? All kinds, from free online help navigating the Internet to the services of private paid consultants who advertise on the Net. You can even get the latest advice on choosing browser software; a good listing is at the WWW Client Software site.

Can I get help setting up my own Web site? Yes, but you need to make some arrangements yourself. To set up your own site, you need (1) to have access to a server and (2) to make your own home page. A *server* is a computer whose owner agrees to offer some hard disk space and also access to your link. Computer resources in educational, government, and business settings may be available to appropriate personnel. If you are an individual or a small business, however, you will probably use a private server and pay a monthly fee for the services provided.

A home page is prepared by you, possibly with some assistance, and then transferred to the server. You are then, theoretically, in business. But how will anyone know your site exists? You need to pass the word so that other sites will link to yours. Friends and colleagues who have sites may link to each other, but that is small potatoes. You need to request being added to some of the major directories. The Yahoo directory, for example, has an Add link that supplies an application form online. In general, once the existence of your link has been verified, your page is added. We assume that you also have browser software, with which to view your own home page and, of course, the rest of the Web.

Where can I get assistance to make a home page? There are several possibilities. Many colleges include home page creation as part of an Internet course. Private firms advertise courses to teach you the basics in a few hours. Resources to help you are right on the Net; our B/C site lists several references.

You can make a simple home page with word processing software that offers page preparation as an option. Since multimedia is a key aspect of the Web, you probably want to use attractive fonts and graphics, and possibly even sound or film clips. The Multimedia File Formats site, whose home page logo is shown here, was prepared specifically to assist beginners.

Serious business users often engage the services of consultants who can create a sophisticated home page. Such consultants usually offer a wide range of services related to the Internet. For example, the Open Business Markets consultants, whose Internet home page logo is shown here, combine technical expertise with business savvy to facilitate electronic commerce on the Internet. Many consulting firms also offer seminars.

Internet Exercises

1. **Structured exercise.** Begin with the B/C URL http://www.aw.com/is/planet/essentials.html and link to the WWW Client Software site. Compare the features mentioned for the browsers you find there with browsers you have used.
2. **Freeform exercise.** Investigate the private consultants listed at the B/C site. You can probably leave e-mail messages with your questions. Compare services and prices for help with a home page or with server access or the total package.

PLANET INTERNET

Eye on Business

The Internet was started by the military and long remained the province of the government and educational institutions. Businesses wondered if commercial enterprises were even permitted on the Net. The answer, a resounding yes, has lead to an explosion of activity. As the throbbing new center of the computing universe, the Net is attracting the brightest technical talent, the sharpest marketers, and the most ambitious entrepreneurs.

Who's out there? Good question, to which enterprising business people have responded with business directories. For example, the Commercial Site Index, whose logo of a world with stars representing sites is shown here, lets you peruse alphabetic listings of companies who have sites on the Net. If you prefer, you may request a search by company name. Formal directories, however, are not likely to include the very small businesses, the folks who go into business for themselves on the Internet.

A game anyone can play. And we do mean anyone, from agriculture to real estate to finance. In particular, even the smallest entrepreneur can get in on the act. Individuals can gain access to people and markets—even global markets—not readily available or even affordable elsewhere. For a minimum investment, far less than that needed for a physical store or office, you can have a server link and a smashing home page that exactly expresses the nature of your business. You can even alter the page as your business grows and changes.

But this isn't television. Despite the fantastic opportunities for sales of products and services, some commercial folks, especially retailers, do not take advantage of the Web's multimedia nature. If hawkers simply transfer their hype from traditional media such as television and magazines, the result may be hardly more than a bunch of print ads or boring catalogs. Furthermore, business people may continue to direct their pitch to a mass audience, failing to recognize Internet users as unique individuals who chose to look at their site. Savvy business users approach the Net with the idea of adding an interactive entertainment component to their pitch.

Taking care of business. Business people on the Net have special opportunities for customer service. FedEx, shown here, for instance, offers a home page where users can personally track a package they sent. But the big change for everyone is same-day response. When inquiries or orders are received over the Internet, the company should respond by e-mail, even just to acknowledge the order, within hours.

Investing. Money matters are taking a whole new turn as investors bravely go online. Since the Net is available any time from any place, the world's financial markets are never further away than the personal computer. Leaving behind what the major players can do, the individual investor can investigate markets, compare mutual funds, get up-to-date stock quotes, and more.

Internet Exercises

1. **Structured exercise.** Begin with the B/C URL http://www.aw.com/is/planet/essentials.html Choose a business directory to see what kinds of sites are on the Net.
2. **Freeform exercise.** Assume that you want to start your own business using the Internet as your forum. Using a search engine, choose words related to that business to find sites that you can use as a source of information and inspiration.

PLANET INTERNET

Downloading Files

You already know that you can access files that reside on remote computers through the Internet and view them on your own computer screen. But what if you wanted to keep a file; that is, what if you wanted your own copy of a file on your own computer? It may be possible to download—get—the file from the distant computer and place it on the hard disk of the computer you are using. A bit of a warning first: You are wading into deeper waters here. Copying files is more complicated than just viewing a web site. We can get you started, but you may need to supplement this information with your browser documentation or perhaps assistance from your lab personnel.

Can I get any file for myself? Maybe. Whether or not you can depends on two things: (1) whether you are allowed to download files to the hard disk of the computer you are using, and (2) whether the file you want is available for taking. By this time you should know whether or not you are permitted to download files to the computer you are using. Disk space is at a premium in some locations. Of course, if you are using your own personal computer, you may do whatever you like.

Why are files on other computers available to be taken? All kinds of files—programs, text, graphics images, even sounds—are indeed available to be taken. We must first acknowledge that many computer files are proprietary, and a user who wants them must have an account on that computer and a password. The files you can take are not proprietary. The free files are public archives, often associated with an educational institution or the government. The CyberSpace site, whose logo is shown here, is a private consulting firm that offers FTP files.

Why would I want other people's files? Lots of reasons. Perhaps a colleague in another city has just written a 150-page grant proposal and wants to send it to you; it is not convenient to send large files via e-mail. Perhaps you want some NASA space photos or some game software. Perhaps you have nothing particular in mind but, knowing the free stuff is out there, simply go to a popular FTP site and look around. You can also upload—send your own files to another computer—but most people do a lot more downloading than uploading.

How do I go about this? Computers on the Internet have a standard way to transfer copies of files, a program called *FTP,* for *file transfer protocol.* The term has become so common that FTP is often used as a verb, as in "Jack F-T-P-ed that file this morning." Most downloading is done by a method called *Anonymous FTP.* This means that instead of having to identify yourself with a proper account on the remote computer, you can simply call yourself Anonymous. Also, instead of a password, just use your e-mail address. This is just background information; your browser will do all this work for you when you indicate you want to transfer to an FTP site to select a file and download it. Prepare yourself for an occasional rejection message such as "Sorry, too many anonymous users at this time. Limit is 50. Please try again."

What do I do when I get to the site? The first thing you will see on the screen is an opening statement telling you about the site and recommending that you click and read certain files—usually named README—before you begin. An FTP site, by the way, may be rather "bare bones" compared to what you may be used to seeing on Web sites. An FTP site arranges files hierarchically by subject matter, but the various layers are linked so you need only click repeatedly in your area of interest to narrow down to a specific file name.

Once you are ready to copy a file, you need to know its type—text or binary. A text file is straight text. Everything else is a binary file. However, knowing which is which is not this straightforward. There are various ways to determine file type; the explanation is lengthy and beyond the scope of this discussion. Once you have identified the file, you can click its name to download it.

No exercises. Although we do offer FTP sites at the B/C site, the information offered here is merely introductory and probably insufficient to support follow-up exercises.

PLANET INTERNET

Life and Living

As in every other category, the Net has much to offer to enrich our daily lives. Let's begin with art.

Artworks. Begin on the ArtWeb site to see both original physical works—oil, watercolor, and so forth—or computer graphics artworks. Would you like to display your own artwork on the Net? Join other artists in the OTIS Project. Many graphics images are available for viewing and, with permission, perhaps downloading. The Lightscape Technologies site will be of particular interest to those interested in the use of light effects in computer graphics images.

A family affair. Check out the Kids' Web site, which has links to sites of interest to children so parents and kids can explore together. The Cartoon Arts Network, whose page logo is shown here, offers access to cartoons of interest to children and adults. Also, the whole family will enjoy the Electronic Zoo and the Comics and Stuff sites. Everyone can participate in the birthday site: Just input your name and birthday and it will show up on a list on your special day. If you mention an e-mail address, expect felicitations to roll in. Time to try a new mealtime experience? There are many cooking and recipe sites, but we chose the Chile-Heads site, whose home page logo is shown here.

The stay-at-home tourist. If you'd like to take an electronic field trip, then check the sights and sounds of The JASON Project, a scientific expedition to rain forests, caverns, and coral reefs. Another must-see site is Sobek Mountain Travel, whether or not you enjoy trekking. It features fascinating locations and exquisite graphics. The United States of America site has a coast-to-coast map that can be clicked at a particular location to show more detailed information. If you are curious about New York City, visit the charming Central Park site. Finally, how would you like to send a postcard—on the Net, of course. The Postcard Store site offers several attractive cards; you can write your own message and send it off to a fellow Net user.

A walk on the wacky side. You've heard about all the weird stuff on the Net—usually the strange offerings of individuals on their own pages. Want to find some? Just pick up a search engine and search on words such as *strange*, *weird*, *odd*, *wild*, and so forth. These are the very words people often include in their home page titles, so you may come across some dandies. Don't bother doing this if you have good taste or are sensitive to trash.

Getting isolated. Arguments about the good or bad aspects of computers have raged since their inception. When personal computers came along, the discussion focused on individuals. Sociologists worried that users would substitute the computer for in-person social interaction. Today that concern has a new dimension. Since users can take care of much interaction via the Internet and other connections, will we become a society of isolated individuals? Here, we only raise the questions. The answers will become clear in time.

Internet Exercises

1. **Structured exercise.** Begin with the B/C URL http://www.aw.com/is/planet/essentials.html and link to the United States home page site. Click on your own home state to see what this site has to say about it.
2. **Freeform exercise.** Travel is just the thing to send you off in different directions worldwide. Begin with your favorite directory, click the travel menu, and link from site to glorious site.

PLANET INTERNET

Entertainment

In this section on entertainment, we will stick to that topic. No little lessons, just site seeing. The topics include sports, games, music, television, movies, and humor—especially humor. The Net has been a veritable hotbed of humor from the beginning. For a classic humor piece, see the purported news story of Microsoft acquiring the Vatican in exchange for stock. The Web's most famous cartoon humor is on the Doctor Fun site, where you can see a new cartoon each day and also check archives of previous cartoons. The Humor Archive is a good place to start for everything else.

Sports and more sports. You can follow any sport that captures your interest. The many sport sites compete with each other to offer the most complete account of scores, player statistics, schedules, standings, and even player injuries. Most cover both professional and amateur sports. Into cycling? The Tour de France is a huge deal in Europe and its page gives full coverage, including team colors, TV schedules, detailed course maps, and the latest race results.

Music, music, music. Everything you could possibly want to know about music is on the Net. Keep in mind that the multimedia capability of the Web means the potential for hearing as well as seeing the subject matter. The RockWeb site, whose screen is shown here, has band information and photos of bands. Would you like to learn a bit about classical music? See the Allegro Music page, a site that offers sound samples accompanied by text explanations. Whatever your taste—rock, classical, jazz, whatever—it's all on the Net.

The big guys. Conglomerates, especially those with an entertainment connection, are flocking to the Net to display their wares. Sony, for example, whose screen is shown here, offers an interactive screen to encourage users to link to related information on their myriad offerings. You can even see what the famous BBC—British Broadcasting Corporation—is up to.

Arm-chair entertainment. Ever wondered if your phone number spells something interesting? For example, 929-2665 spells WAY-COOL. Stop by the Phonetic site to check yours out. Speaking of cool, check out the Celebrity Hotlist for the latest about your favorites. Do you dabble in math puzzles? The Mathpro site offers a puzzle of the week. If you like kitchen table games, the Games Domain site has every kind of game—board, card, and (of course) computer games. If you follow Star Trek, you will probably not be surprised to learn that Trekkies have their own site. There are lots of books and CD-ROMs that provide movie information, but they cost money. The Cardiff University movie database has details and reviews of thousands of movies, plus downloadable graphics and sound. If, in the end, you want to be a couch potato, the Net can help you with television information on the Ultimate TV site.

Go look. We have discussed many aspects of entertainment on the Internet. We have assembled—for your viewing pleasure!—a long list of entertainment links at the B/C site.

Internet Exercises

1. **Structured exercise.** Beginning with the B/C URL http://www.aw.com/is/planet/essentials.html go to the Phonetic site, and get a new name for your telephone number.
2. **Freeform exercise.** Pick an interest, say music or sports, and compare offerings from the competing Web sites.

ISBN: 0-8053-1605-1

Essentials of Computing

Second Edition

June
July
800
600
400
Scenarios:
Flat Numbers
High Numbers
Weird Scenario
Add...
Delete
Edit...
Summary...
Help
Changing Cells:

Essentials

H. L. Capron

The Benjamin/Cummings

Publishing Company, Inc.

Redwood City, California

Menlo Park, California

Reading, Massachusetts

New York

Don Mills, Ontario

Wokingham, U.K.

Amsterdam

Bonn

Singapore

Tokyo

Madrid

San Juan

# of Computing

SECOND EDITION

Sponsoring Editor	Maureen A. Allaire
Developmental Editor	Sue Ewing
Associate Editor	Nancy E. Davis
Editorial Assistant	MaryLynne Wrye
Senior Production Editor	Jean Lake
Production Editor	Adam Ray
Design Manager	Michele Carter
Marketing Manager	Melissa Baumwald
Senior Promotions Specialist	James Fisher
Text Designer	Mark Ong
Cover Designer	Yvo Riezebos
Illustrations	Illustrious, Inc.
Photo Editor	Kelli d'Angona-West
Photo Researcher	Sarah Evertson
Copy Editor	Barbara Conway
Film	York Graphic Services
Manufacturing Coordinator	Janet Weaver
Printing and Binding	R. R. Donnelley and Sons

Library of Congress Cataloging-in-Publication Data

Capron, H.L.

Essentials of Computing/H.L. Capron, —2nd ed.

p. cm.

Includes index.

ISBN 0-8053-1380-X, —ISBN 0-8053-1381-8

1. Electronic data processing. I. Title.

QA76.C359 1994

004—dc20 94-23445

CIP

SE	ISBN 0-8053-1380-X
AIE	ISBN 0-8053-1381-8
MC	IBSN 0-8053-0812-1

2 3 4 5 6 7 8 9 10 DO 99 98 97 96 95

The Benjamin/Cummings Publishing Company, Inc.
390 Bridge Parkway
Redwood City, CA 94065

Dedicated to

- *Nancy*
- *Bill*
- *Wendy*
- *Robin*

The Capron

Supplements to the Text

- **Interactive multimedia packages.** Through two completely interactive tutorial packages, your students can explore the inner workings of computer components, chart the history of computers, and examine related topics such as artificial intelligence, virtual reality, and programming. Benjamin/Cummings offers CD-ROMs for the Macintosh and PC. The PC version is also available on disk. Contact your Benjamin/Cummings sales representative for more information.
- **Instructor newsletter: *BC Link*.** Benjamin/Cummings is now offering an instructor-oriented newsletter for teaching introductory computing. This useful resource includes articles on the use of computer technology in education, teaching strategies, and a section designed for use with students in the classroom.
- **Instructor's Edition with Annotations for *Essentials of Computing, Second Edition*** by S. Langman with H. L. Capron. This special edition contains annotations for lecture preparation and includes supplementary material not found in the Instructor's Guide. The annotations include Learning Objectives, Lecture Activities, Discussion Questions, Lecture Hints, Class Projects, test bank references, transparency references, and Key Terms.
- **Test bank for *Essentials of Computing, Second Edition*** by H. L. Capron. The test bank contains multiple choice, true/false, matching, and completion. Each question is referenced to the text by page number, and the answers are provided. The test bank is available both in printed form and in a computerized format for the IBM PC and compatibles, and Macintosh computers.
- **Color transparency acetates.** The 100 full-color transparency acetates include artwork and diagrams taken directly from the text.
- **Instructor's Guide for *Essentials of Computing, Second Edition*** by H. L. Capron. For each chapter there are Learning Objectives; a Chapter Overview; a detailed Lecture Outline; and a list of Key Words. The Instructor's Guide also includes a reference guide to the CD-Rom offerings, the lecture support software screens, and to the videotape offerings.
- **Videotapes.** Benjamin/Cummings makes available to qualified adopters free videotapes from our library of commercially produced tapes. Use this valuable resource to enhance your lectures on concepts presented in the text. Your Benjamin/Cummings sales representative has details about this offer.

Collection
A Complete Supplements Package

- **Lecture support software** by J. Huhtala. This seven-disk package for the IBM PC and compatibles or the IBM PS/2, provides 280 color screens containing animation and text that summarize key concepts for each section of the book. The accompanying student workbook (300 pages) supports the software with additional text, learning objectives, key terms, review questions, and completion questions. The software and workbook can be used in lecture or lab. The Instructor's Guide contains a reference guide to help you incorporate these materials.
- **University Gradebook.** This class record-keeping software is available for the IBM PC and compatible computers.

Of Related Interest

The Student Edition of Lotus 1-2-3, Second Edition (509 pages); *The Student Edition of dBASE IV* (704 pages).

Brief Table of

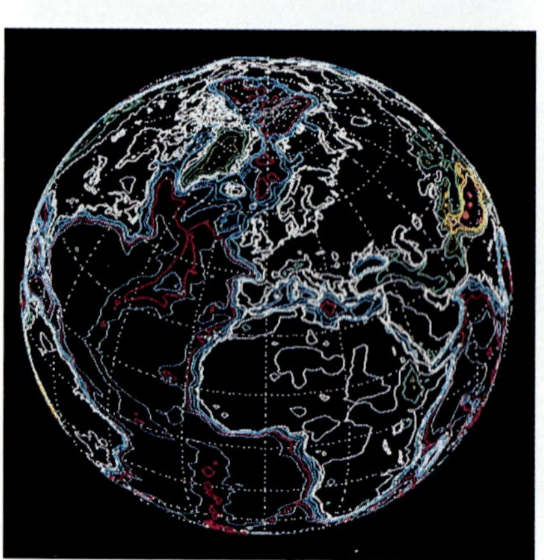

Contents

Detailed Table of

Contents

Chapter 4
Input and Output: The User Connection 64

Chapter 5
Storage Devices: Electronic Filing Cabinets 88

Chapter 10

Security, Privacy, and Ethics: Protecting Hardware, Software, and Data 194

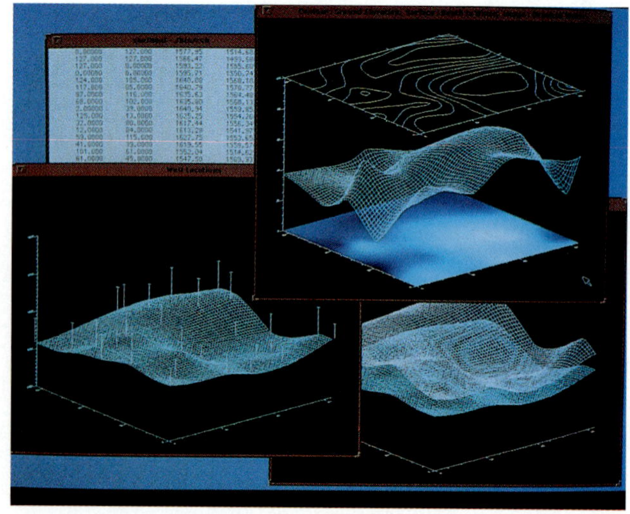

JURASSIC PARK
MICHAEL CRICHTON

The Buyer's Guide and Galleries

Buyer's Guide (follows page xxxii)

How to Buy Your Own Personal Computer

This special eight-page section presents an overview of points to consider before buying a personal computer and software. If you are thinking about buying a personal computer now or in the future, read this section carefully.

Gallery 1 (follows page 96)

Multimedia

The New Sight and Sound

This section describes the hardware/software combination that supports multimedia, and presents a sample of popular multimedia programs. Such programs offer text, photos, art, sound, and—best of all—the opportunity to participate interactively.

Gallery 2 (follows page 224)

Color Graphics

Computers at their Best

The computer is an artistic virtuoso. In this colorful montage, the computer's talents are shown in a spectrum from art to whimsy to photo manipulation.

Preface

The SELECT System

The Benjamin/Cummings Publishing Company is pleased to announce an innovation in publishing that will change the way you think about teaching computing concepts and microcomputer applications. We put technology to work to provide you with one convenient, affordable text that can meet the changing nature of your course. Now you can get a concise introduction to computing by the best-known author in computer information systems, plus a customized selection of applications modules for the software packages you teach. The plan is simple. Here's how it works:

The SELECT Edition of *Essentials of Computing, Second Edition*

A Text with Concepts and Customized Application Coverage

You choose the SELECT Edition of *Essentials of Computing, Second Edition.* Next, you choose any combination of the following modules.

Application Modules

	Windows	DOS
Word Processing	WordPerfect 6 Projects for Windows	WordPerfect 6.0 Projects for DOS
	WordPerfect 5.2 Projects for Windows	Projects for WordPerfect 5.1
	Word 6 Projects for Windows	
Spreadsheets	Lotus 1-2-3 Rel. 4 Projects for Windows	Projects for Lotus 1-2-3, Rel. 2.3/2.4
	Excel 5 Projects for Windows	Projects for Lotus 1-2-3, Rel. 2.2
	Excel 4.0 Projects for Windows	Projects for Quattro Pro 4.0/5.0
	Projects for Excel 3.0	
	Quattro Pro 1.0/5.0 Projects for Windows	
Database	Access 2 Projects for Windows	Projects for dBASE IV
	Paradox Projects for Windows	Projects for dBASE III PLUS
		Projects for Paradox 3.5

Integrated Packages		Microsoft Works 3.0 Projects for Windows
		Projects for Microsoft Works 3.0 for PCs
		Projects for Microsoft Works 2.0 for PCs
DOS/Windows	Projects for DOS 6.0 and Windows 3.1	
	Projects for DOS 5.0 and Windows 3.1	
	Projects for DOS 2.0/3.3 and Windows 3.0	
Programming	Structured Basic for Beginners	
	QBasic for Beginners	

Once you place your order with your bookstore manager or your sales representative, your choice of modules will be bound together into one convenient, durable text with *Essentials of Computing, Second Edition.* We will then send the bookstore your SELECT Edition. Your students will learn from a textbook that has been tailored to match the objectives of your course. Sound easy? It is.

We introduce new modules regularly, so call the SELECT Hotline at 800-854-2595 or contact your sales representative for the most current information.

Complimentary Review Copies

We have prepared the following materials for review and adoption consideration.

The Instructor's Edition with Annotations of *Essentials of Computing, Second Edition*

This edition contains the complete contents of the student text plus eight types of margin annotations to support instruction.

Custom complimentary copies of *Essentials of Computing, Second Edition*, bound with your choice of SELECT modules, can be ordered upon request. Contact your Benjamin/Cummings sales representative if you wish to see a preview of a SELECT Edition.

Ordering and Pricing Information

We believe our SELECT System offers unprecedented opportunity for educators to evaluate flexible text components and build them into a customized teaching support system suitable for individual course configurations. Your Benjamin/Cummings representative will be happy to work with you and your bookstore manager to outline the ordering process, and provide pricing and delivery information. To take advantage of the SELECT System, you may also call Benjamin/Cummings Publishing Company at 800-854-2595. This special hotline is attended by service representatives ready to answer inquiries and to provide you with additional complimentary or desk copies.

The SELECT Edition of *Essentials of Computing, Second Edition*

The concepts portion of the SELECT Edition is *Essentials of Computing, Second Edition*. For those students taking an introductory course who are just beginning to discover computers, this textbook makes the process of discovery both enjoyable and educational. For those who are not entirely comfortable with computers, the concepts portion of this textbook provides blocks of information presented within the framework of the user's environment. This introduction to computers is written in a friendly and engaging style that sparks the reader's interest. When students enjoy what they read, they remember it.

Most introductory computer books are comprehensive in scope. *Essentials of Computing, Second Edition* is too, but we want to offer you more than just the basics of computing. We want to engage you and draw you into the text without detracting from the seriousness of the material. We want to present a book that sounds and feels like everyday living. To do that we offer part opening interviews with real people who use computers in a wide variety of businesses. Each chapter opener is a life-with-computers vignette that correlates chapter content with a story about computing. Real examples are sprinkled throughout the text to show how computers actually affect the lives of people who use them.

The everyday living theme also shows up in our extensive photo collection. Rather than standard shots of people in front of computers, we have chosen photos showing computers being used in a variety of settings. In fact, photos are a prime way of drawing readers into the text.

The second edition retains all of the elements that made the first edition a best-seller. We have updated material and added new features. Our hope is that this book and its related learning materials offer students everything they need to make computers a part of their own everyday living.

New and Updated in the Second Edition

The entire manuscript has been updated to reflect current technology. New topics, such as the Internet and the PENTIUM chip, have been added. A significant addition to this edition is the Multimedia Gallery. Although the technology of multimedia is described in Chapter 5, "Storage Devices," the flavor of the multimedia phenomenon is presented in a gallery of eight glorious color pages.

For those of you who used the first edition of this book, you can note these changes. The CPU is now in its own chapter. There is expanded coverage of networking, systems analysis and design, and Windows. The Buyer's Guide has been upgraded to indicate current offerings and buying trends. All part-opening interviews and the Macintosh boxes have been rewritten. Computing Highlights boxes have been replaced with the more significant Computing Trends boxes.

If you are not in a lab environment, note that the three personal computer software chapters (Chapters 12, 13, and 14 on word processing, spreadsheets, and database management, respectively) have been rewritten generically to present the core ideas on these topics. And, finally, a small matter that loomed large, the answers to the built-in study guide are now included in the book.

Organization of the Text

The text is divided into four parts.

- Part 1 offers an overview of computer systems and their uses in our society, and an introduction to the personal computer.
- Part 2 explores computer hardware, including coverage of the central processing unit, input/output, storage, and communications.
- Part 3 looks at software, including programming, programming languages, and operating systems.
- Part 4 examines personal computers in the workplace: management of information systems; security, privacy, and ethics; and artificial intelligence, expert systems, robotics, and virtual reality.
- Appendices include a discussion of the history of computing and information on number systems.

Key Themes

- **Extensive personal computer coverage**. We place a strong emphasis on personal computers, reflecting their continuing prominence in people's business and personal lives. Each chapter features a *Personal Computers in Action* box. One chapter focuses specifically on business issues related to the personal computer: Chapter 9, "Computers on the Job: Action and Power." In addition, we have incorporated a wide variety of personal computer examples throughout the text.
- **Focus on computers in business settings.** We provide several features that focus on the uses of computers in the business environment. Each of the five parts of the text begins with a personal interview, in which individuals from a variety of situations discuss how they use computers on the job. Part 4, Computers and Business, is devoted to issues of current interest in business computing. Topics include the use of personal computers, the role of the information systems manager, security, privacy, and ethics, artificial intelligence, expert systems, robotics, and virtual reality.

Special Features

- **Appealing style.** When students enjoy what they read, they remember it. The text's friendly style encourages the reader and increases students' comprehension and confidence. For example, each chapter begins with an engaging story that leads the student into the material. The real-world applications included throughout the text pique student interest as well as illustrate key points from the chapter.

- **Buyer's Guide**. Students and their families are making important economic decisions about the purchase of a computer for their educational, personal, and business needs. This concise eight-page guide offers students information to aid hardware and software purchases.
- **Multimedia gallery.** This color photo essay provides a more in-depth look at multimedia and what it has to offer.
- **Graphics gallery**. A color photo layout on computer graphics vividly shows the sophistication of computer graphics.
- **Computing Trends**. To give students a glimpse of the new directions computer technology is taking, each chapter provides a brief essay that focuses on issues and trends in the world of computing. Examples include electronic résumés, courtroom computers, "wearable" computers, and the lack of privacy in office electronic mail.
- **Personal Computers in Action**. Each chapter includes a feature article on personal computers that demonstrates the range of tasks personal computers perform. The articles include a broad range of topics, from saving the whales to handling diskettes to making online connections.
- **Built-in Study Guide.** To allow students to review concepts and to confirm their comprehension of the material, each chapter concludes with a study guide. The Chapter Review provides an end-of-chapter summary of core concepts and key terms, followed by a Student Personal Study Guide that includes true/false, multiple-choice, and completion questions. In response to suggestions from current users, the answers to all questions now are provided for the student at the end of the study guide.
- **Margin notes**. To further engage the student, margin notes are carefully placed throughout the text. The margin notes extend the text material by providing additional information and highlighting interesting applications of computers.
- **The Macintosh computer** is highlighted in six chapters through brief discussions of Macintosh applications and procedures. Topics covered include the wise use of disk space, America Online, GUI interface, desktop publishing software, graphics, and HyperCard.

In-Text Learning Aids

Each chapter includes the following pedagogical support:

- A chapter **preview** outlines key concepts.
- **Key terms** are boldfaced throughout the text.
- A **Chapter Review** offers summaries of core concepts and boldfaced key terms. The **Student Personal Study Guide** gives students three types of questions (true/false, multiple choice, and completion) that they can answer to check their comprehension of essential concepts. All answers are provided for the student at the end of the Chapter Review.
- An extensive **glossary** and comprehensive **index** are included.

The Applications Modules in the SELECT Edition of *Essentials of Computing, Second Edition*

Learning software applications is easy when students practice skills in the context of problem solving. By completing these modules, students gain realistic preparation for their future careers when software skills will be an important component of their jobs. These modules are designed to teach Windows/DOS and popular software applications packages for personal computers in an introductory computer literacy/microapplications course. These modules are intended for the first-time computer user with basic typing skills.

Each module is written by an experienced author and instructor and follows a consistent, pedagogically sound format. The modules begin with an overview of basic concepts for each software application—concepts such as starting the program, getting help, and an explanation of the conventions the modules use. Then, within the context of seven or more increasingly challenging projects, students learn problem-solving techniques that enhance and reinforce comprehension of the specific software applications package.

Applications Modules: The Philosophy of the Project Approach

The projects are the core of the student's learning process. They motivate the student reader by offering both general-interest and business-related examples. Each project title identifies a functional task in which specific commands are mastered. Students gain an appreciation of both the conceptual and keystroke levels of a software application. The modules are intended for the first-time computer user but contain selected advanced topics for the more experienced student.

Applications Modules: Pedagogy and Learning Aids

- **Learning objectives** define in practical terms what the student will be able to do after completing each project.
- Six to eight **projects**, increasingly challenging in nature, teach students important concepts and commands in a real-world context.
- **Case studies** lay out problems or situations that students will address in the projects. The **Designing the Solution** section analyzes each Case Study and then helps students develop problem-solving strategies.
- **Numbered steps** guide students through the projects. A computer icon cues students as to when to begin working on the computer.

- **Screen captures and margin figures** visually reinforce key concepts and help students check their work.
- **Key terms** appear in boldfaced italics throughout the text.
- Special features, such as **Tips, Reminders, Quick Fixes, and Cautions,** highlight specific material in a project that is particularly helpful, important, or pertinent to what students are learning in the project. **Exit Points** indicate places where students can save a file and temporarily stop work.
- **The Next Step** extends the material presented in the project and make students think about other applications for the skills.
- Each project concludes with a **Summary** and a list of **Key Terms and Operations**.
- Each project also includes **Study Questions** (multiple choice, short answer, and discussion) that may be used as a self-test or as a homework assignment. End-of-project **Review Exercises** present hands-on tasks with abbreviated instructions to build on skills learned in the project.
- **Assignments,** found at the end of each project, draw upon the skills introduced in the projects, and require synthesis, integration, analysis, and critical thinking to complete.
- Each module has its own **Operations Reference**, extensive **Glossary of Key Terms,** and an **Index**.

SELECT Authors

Hans-Peter Appelt, Corning Community College
William J. Belisle
Gary R. Brent, Scottsdale Community College
J. Patrick Fenton, West Valley College
James A. Folts, Oregon State University
Marianne B. Fox, Butler University
Ahmer S. Karim, University of San Diego
Marcy Kittner, University of Tampa
Philip A. Koneman, Colorado Christian University
Tony Lima, California State University, Hayward
Lawrence C. Metzelaar, Purdue University at Indianapolis/IUPUI
James T. Perry, University of San Diego
Eugene J. Rathswohl, University of San Diego
Carl A. Scharpf, University of Southern California
Jane Whittenhall, Corning Community College

To develop these project-based applications modules we went one step beyond the traditional publishing model and added a consulting team of developmental editors. The team, Evelyn Spire, Nancy Canning, Shelly Langman, and Rebecca Johnson extensively analyzed the most effective teaching philosophies to create the project approach. They carefully prepared a logical presentation of the application software. They combined their business acumen with the academic perspective of the authors and the instructors who reviewed the material. They scrutinized the modules from the standpoint of pedagogical consistency, tone, level, and writing style. They gave considerable thought to the conventions used and chose those that were easiest to use in the laboratory environment. The end result is a set of projects that will stimulate learning and prepare students for their careers.

Supplements for the SELECT Edition of *Essentials of Computing, Second Edition*

Instructors can take advantage of the complete instructional package that has been developed to support *Essentials of Computing, Second Edition.* We also have designed individual instructor's manuals with transparency masters and test bank that support the modules. The complete list of supplements for both the text and the modules follows.

- **Interactive multimedia packages.** Through two completely interactive tutorial packages, students can explore the inner workings of computer components, chart the history of computers, and examine related topics such as artificial intelligence, virtual reality, and programming. Benjamin/Cummings offers CD-ROMs for the Macintosh and PC. The PC version is also available on disk. Contact your Benjamin/Cummings sales representative for more information.
- **Instructor newsletter: *BC Link.*** Benjamin/Cummings is now offering an instructor-oriented newsletter for teaching introductory computing. This useful resource includes articles on the use of computer technology in education, teaching strategies, and a section designed for use with students in the classroom.
- **Instructor's Edition with Annotations for *Essentials of Computing, Second Edition*** by S. Langman with H. L. Capron. This special edition contains annotations for lecture preparation and includes supplementary material not found in the instructor's guide. The annotations include Learning Objectives, Lecture Activities, Discussion Questions, Lecture Hints, test bank references, transparency references, Key Terms, and Class Projects.
- **Test Bank for *Essentials of Computing, Second Edition*** by H.L. Capron. The test bank contains multiple choice, true/false, matching, and completion. Each question is referenced to the text by page number, and the answers are provided. The test bank is available both in printed form and in a computerized format for the IBM PC and compatibles, and Macintosh computers.
- **Instructor's Guide for *Essentials of Computing, Second Edition*** by H. L. Capron. This guide supports the concepts portion of your customized package. For each chapter, you will find lecture preparation material such as Learning Objectives, a Chapter Overview, a detailed Lecture Outline, and a list of Key Words. The instructor's guide also contains a reference guide to the CD-Rom offerings, the lecture support software screens, and the videotape offerings.

- **Color Transparency Acetates.** The 100 full-color transparency acetates illustrate key diagrams and artwork from *Essentials of Computing, Second Edition.*
- **Instructor's Manuals for the modules**. Each module has a corresponding Instructor's Manual with a test bank and transparency masters. For each project in the module, the Instructor's Manual includes Expanded Student Objectives, Answers to Study Questions, and Additional Assessment Techniques. The test bank contains two separate tests (with answers) consisting of multiple choice, true/false, and fill-in-the blank questions that are referenced to pages in the module. Transparency masters illustrate 25 to 30 key concepts and screen captures from the module.
- **Instructor's Data Disk for the modules.** The Instructor's Data Disk contains student data files, answers to selected Review Exercises and Assignments and the test files from the Instructor's Manual, which are in ASCII format.
- **Videotapes.** Benjamin/Cummings makes available to qualified adopters free videotapes from our library of commercially produced tapes. Use this valuable resource to enhance your lectures on concepts presented in Chapters 1 through 11 of *Essentials of Computing, Second Edition*. Your Benjamin/Cummings sales representative has details about this offer.
- **Software for the SELECT Edition of *Essentials of Computing, Second Edition* Lecture support software** by J. Huhtala. This seven-disk package for PCs and PS/2s provides 280 color screens containing animation and text that summarize the key concepts for each section of *Essentials of Computing, Second Edition.* Also available is *Computer Concepts* (300 pages), a student workbook that supports the software with additional text, learning objectives, key terms, review questions, and completion questions. The software and workbook are suitable for either lecture or lab. A reference guide for this software will be found in the instructor's guide.

Special Note to the Student

We welcome your reactions to this book. It is written to open up the world of computing for you. Expanding your knowledge will increase your confidence and prepare you for a life that will be influenced by computers. Your comments and questions are important to us. Write to the author in care of Computer Information Systems Editor, Benjamin/Cummings Publishing Company, 390 Bridge Parkway, Redwood City, California 94065. All letters with a return address will be answered by the author.

Acknowledgments

Many people contributed to the success of this project. Although a single sentence hardly suffices, we would like to thank some of the key people: The Consulting Team of Evelyn Spire and Nancy Canning created our model and went the extra step to make the SELECT Edition and its applications modules into a seamless instructional tool. Developmental

Editor Sue Ewing executed a multi-faceted role with enthusiasm and ingenuity. Jean Lake, as production editor, skillfully coordinated the efforts of many people, keeping the book on the accelerated schedule that contributes to its currency. Michele Carter, as art and design manager, patiently refereed endless discussions relating to the needs and desires of artists and nonartists. Kelli d'Angona-West showed early enthusiasm for the photo research task and was persistent in tracking down outstanding pictures. Editorial Assistant MaryLynne Wrye provided able assistance, on matters large and small, on a daily basis. Sponsoring Editor Maureen Allaire's vision placed the project on the right track, and her steadying hand kept it there.

Reviewers and consultants have provided valuable contributions that improved the quality of the book. Their names are listed in the following section, and we wish to express our sincere gratitude to them.

Essentials of Computing, Second Edition Reviewers

Tom Affholter
Spokane Community College
Spokane, Washington

Ann Ban
Skyline College
San Bruno, California

Roger R. Bossert
State University of New York
College at Brockport
Brockport, New York

Patricia L. Clark
North Seattle Community College
Seattle, Washington

Jill L. Davis
State University of New York at
Stony Brook
Stony Brook, New York

Fredia F. Dillard
Samford University
Birmingham, Alabama

Laura I. Doig
Embry-Riddle Aeronautical University
Daytona Beach, Florida

William J. Dorin
Indiana University Northwest
Gary, Indiana

Joyce M. Farrell
McHenry County College
Crystal Lake, Illinois

Darrell Z. Gobel
Catonsville Community College
Catonsville, Maryland

Ananda Gunawardena
University of Houston, Downtown
Houston, Texas

Margaret Jamison
Ferrum College
Ferrum, Virginia

John W. Krogman
Albuquerque Vocational Technical Institute
Albuquerque, New Mexico

Della Y. Lee-Lien
Quinnipiac College
Hamden, Connecticut

Jean L. Lutt
Wayne State College
Wayne, Nebraska

Linda Lynam
Central Missouri State University
Warrensburg, Missouri

Barbara J. Maccarone
North Shore Community College
Danvers, Massachusetts

J. Michael McGrew
Ball State University
Muncie, Indiana

Walter Merrick
Johnson County Community College
Overland Park, Kansas

Vincent J. Motto
Asnuntuck Community-Technical College
Enfield, Connecticut

Lucy Parakhovnik
California State University-Northridge
Northridge, California

E. Raydean Richmond
Tarrant County Junior College,
South Campus
Fort Worth, Texas

Ingrid Russell
University of Hartford
West Hartford, Connecticut

Patricia A. Stans
University of New Mexico
Albuquerque, New Mexico

Larry Stroud
Edgecombe Community College
Tarboro, North Carolina

Matthew Tucker
University of Iowa
Iowa City, Iowa

Lloyd C. Vaught
Modesto Junior College
Modesto, California

P. Lynn Wermers
North Shore Community College
Lynn, Massachusetts

Deborah Wheeler
University of Arkansas at Little Rock
Little Rock, Arkansas

SELECT Reviewers

We would like to thank the following reviewers who have provided valuable input in various stages of these books.

Joseph Aieta, Babson College
Tom Ashby, Oklahoma City Community College
Bob Barber, Lane Community College
Robert Caruso, Santa Rosa Junior College
Robert Chi, California State University, Long Beach
Jill Davis, State University of New York at Stony Brook
Fredia Dillard, Samford University
Peter Drexel, Plymouth State College
Ralph Duffy, North Seattle Community College
David Egle, University of Texas, Pan American
Jonathan Frank, Suffolk University
Patrick Gilbert, University of Hawaii
Maureen Greenbaum, Union County College
Sally Ann Hanson, Mercer County Community College
Sunil Hazari, East Carolina University
Bruce Herniter, University of Hartford
Lisa Jackson, Henderson Community College
Cynthia Kachik, Santa Fe Community College
Bennett Kramer, Massasoit Community College
Charles Lake, Faulkner State Junior College
Ron Leake, Johnson County Community College
Randy Marak, Hill College
Charles Mattox, Jr., St. Mary's University
Jim MCommunity Collegeullough, Porter and Chester Institute
Gail Miles, Lenoir-Rhyne College
Steve Moore, University of South Florida
Anthony Nowakowski, Buffalo State College
Gloria Oman, Portland State University
John Passafiume, Clemson University
Leonard Presby, William Paterson College
Louis Pryor, Garland County Community College
Michael Reilly, University of Denver
Dick Ricketts, Lane Community College
Dennis Santomauro, Kean College of New Jersey
Pamela Schmidt, Oakton Community College
Gary Schubert, Alderson-Broaddus College
T. Michael Smith, Austin Community College
Cynthia Thompson, Carl Sandburg College

Marion Tucker, Northern Oklahoma College
JoAnn Weatherwax, Saddleback College
David Whitney, San Francisco State University
James Wood, Tri-County Technical College
Minnie Yen, University of Alaska, Anchorage
Allen Zilbert, Long Island University

Buyer's Guide

HOW TO BUY YOUR OWN PERSONAL COMPUTER

We cannot choose your new computer system for you any more than we might select a new car for you. But we can tell you about various features to look for or avoid. We do not mean that we can lead you to a particular brand and model—so many new products are introduced every month that doing so would be impossible. If you are just starting out, however, we can help you define your needs and ask the right questions.

Where Do You Start?

Maybe you have already done some thinking and have decided that owning your own personal computer offers advantages. Now what? You can start by talking to other personal computer owners about how they got started and how to avoid pitfalls. Or you can read some computer magazines, especially ones with evaluations and ratings, to get a feel for what is available. Next, find several dealers. Most dealers are listed in the yellow pages of the phone book, and many advertise in the business section of the local newspaper. Visit several dealers. Don't be afraid to ask questions. You are considering a major purchase, so plan to shop around.

Finally, you may consider buying a computer system by direct mail. You can find advertisements in any computer magazine. Call a company's listed 800 number and ask them to send you a free brochure. Some reputable companies that sell heavily by direct mail are Dell Computer, Gateway 2000, Compaq, and even IBM.

Questions to Ask the Salesperson at the Store

- ❑ Can I expand the capabilities of the computer later?
- ❑ Whom do I call if I have problems configuring the machine at home?
- ❑ Does the store offer or recommend classes on how to use this computer and software?
- ❑ What kind of warranty comes with the computer?
- ❑ Does the store or manufacturer offer a maintenance contract with the computer?

Analyze Your Needs and Budget

Begin with a wants-needs analysis. Why do you want a computer? Be realistic: Will you use it mostly for games or for business applications? People use personal computers for a variety of reasons. At some point you will have to establish

What to Look for in Hardware

The basic personal computer system consists of a central processing unit (CPU) and memory, a monitor (screen), a keyboard and a mouse, a storage device—probably a 3½-inch diskette drive and a hard disk drive—and a printer. Unless you know someone who can help you out with technical expertise, the best advice is to look for a packaged system—that is, one in which the hardware components (with the exceptions of the mouse and the printer) are assembled and packaged by the same manufacturer. This gives you some assurance that the various components will work together.

Central Processing Unit

If you plan to purchase an IBM or compatible machine, many software packages run most efficiently on computers using at least an 80486—also called a "486"—microprocessor. Many 486 processors are upgradable to the more powerful Pentium chip. If you want the most powerful machine, Pentium computers are available and are becoming more affordable.

a budget ceiling. After you have examined your needs, you can relay them to the sellers who will help you select the best hardware-software combination for your budget.

An Early Consideration

Although many brands of computers are available, the business standard is an IBM or IBM-compatible machine. If you will be using your computer for business applications and, in particular, if you need to exchange files with others in a business environment, consider sticking with the standard. However, the Apple Macintosh is an attractive alternative. The Macintosh is noted for ease of use, especially for beginners.

Memory

Memory, or RAM, is measured in bytes, with each byte representing a character of data. The amount of memory you need in your computer is determined by the amount of memory required by the applications programs (like word processing or spreadsheets) that you want to use. The minimum memory threshold keeps rising, as software makers produce sophisticated products that run efficiently only with ever larger amounts of memory. Some people buy 2 or 4 megabytes with their first personal computer, but we recommend 8 megabytes (8MB) or even more. However, most machines have expandable memory, so you can add more later if you need it.

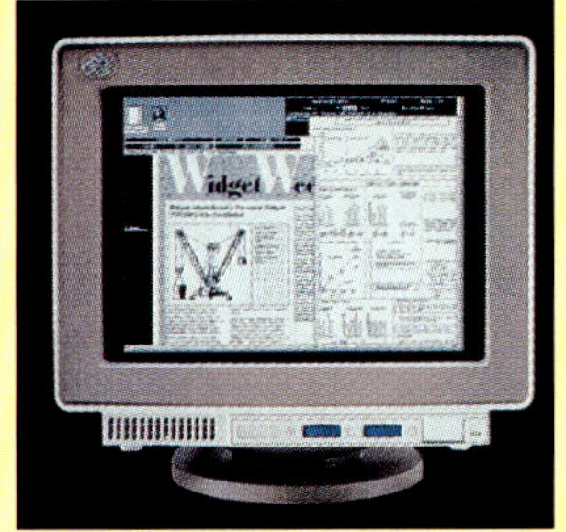

Monitor

Sometimes called a video display screen, the monitor is a very important part of your computer system—you will spend all your computer time looking at it.

Color or Monochrome

Monochrome (usually green or white on a black background) monitors are a possibility when a computer will be used almost exclusively for simple word processing applications. However, a color monitor is strongly suggested. Most software, even for business use, makes impressive use of color. You will certainly want color if you want to create graphics on your screen or if you plan to run entertainment programs on your computer.

Screen Size

Monitors usually have a screen display of between 12 and 15 inches, measured diagonally. Generally, a larger screen provides a display that is easier to read, so most monitors sold today have at least 14-inch screens.

Screen Readability

Be sure to compare the readability of different monitors. First, make certain that the screen is bright and has minimum flicker. Glare is another major consideration. Harsh lighting nearby can cause glare to bounce off the screen, and some screens seem more susceptible to glare than others.

A key factor affecting screen quality is resolution—a measure of the number of dots, or pixels, that can appear on the screen. The higher the resolution—that is, the more dots—the more solid the text characters appear. For graphics, more pixels means sharper images. Color monitors most commonly available are—in ascending order of good resolution—enhanced graphics adapter (EGA), video graphics adapter (VGA), and super VGA (SVGA).

Ergonomic Considerations

Can the monitor swivel and tilt? If so, this will reduce your need to sit in one position for a long period. The ability to adjust the position of the monitor becomes an important consideration when several users share the same computer, particularly people of different sizes, such as parents and children. Another possibility is the purchase of add-on equipment that allows you to reposition the monitor. Furthermore, if you expect to type for long periods of time, you would be wise to buy a wrist pad to support your hands and wrists.

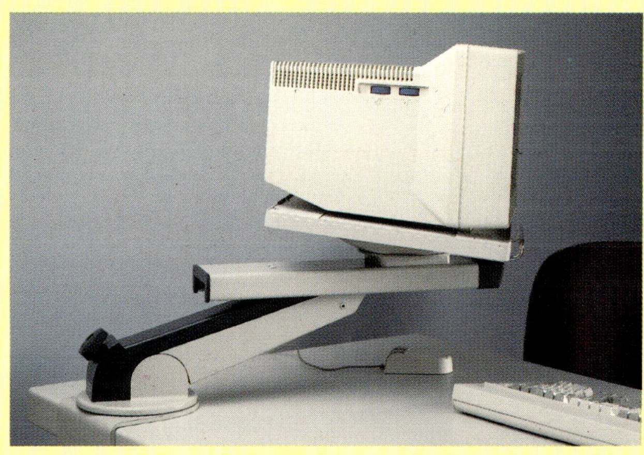

Input Devices

There are many input devices. We will mention only the two critical ones here: a keyboard and a mouse.

Keyboard

Keyboards vary in quality. To find what suits you best, sit down in the store and type. Consider how the keys feel. You may be surprised by the real differences in the feel of keyboards. Make sure the keys are not cramped together; you will find that your typing is error-prone if your fingers are constantly overlapping more than one key.

A detachable keyboard—one that can be held on your lap, for example—is the norm. You can move a detachable keyboard around to suit your comfort. This feature becomes indispensable when a computer is used by people of different sizes.

Most keyboards follow the standard QWERTY layout of typewriter keyboards. Many have a separate numeric keypad. In addition, most keyboards have separate function keys that simplify applications software commands.

Assess the color and layout of the keyboard. Ideally, keys should be gray with a matte finish. The dull finish reduces glare.

Mouse

A mouse is a device that you roll on a tabletop to move the cursor on the screen to make selections. A mouse was, until recently, considered a convenient option. However, since many applications software packages and even operating systems are designed to be used with a mouse, a mouse has become a necessity.

Secondary Storage

You will need disk drives to read programs into your computer and to store programs and data that you wish to keep.

Diskette Drive

Most personal computer software today comes on diskettes, so you need a diskette drive to accept the software. Further, many users keep backup copies of their software and data files on diskette. Most computer systems today come with a 3½-inch diskette drive, with a 5¼-inch diskette drive as an option. If you have no need to be compatible with 5¼-inch diskettes, either from your old computer system or from someone else's computer, you probably do not need a 5¼-inch diskette drive.

Hard Disk Drive

Although more expensive than a diskette drive, a hard disk drive is fast and reliable and holds more data. Once merely an attractive option, a hard disk drive is now considered a necessity. Modern software comes on a set of several diskettes; it would be unacceptably unwieldy to load all of them each time the software is used. Instead, the software on the diskettes is stored on the hard drive, where it is conveniently accessed from that point forward.

Most computer systems offer a built-in hard disk drive, with variable storage capacity—the more storage, the higher the price. Storage capacity is measured in terms of millions of bytes—characters—of data. Keep in mind that software, as well as your data files, will be stored on the hard disk. Since even a simple word processing program can fill up ten million bytes or more, you can understand why most users elect a minimum of 100 million bytes on a hard disk. Some users buy many times that capacity.

Printers

A printer is probably the most expensive peripheral equipment you will buy. Although some inexpensive models are available, you will find that those costing $400 and up are the most useful. When choosing a printer, consider speed, quality, and cost.

Until recently the **dot-matrix printer** was the standard for everyday printing. A dot-matrix printer forms each character with a series of closely spaced dots. But dot-matrix printers are being phased out in favor of affordable ink-jet and laser printers; each type produces high-quality output and is much quieter than a dot-matrix printer.

Ink-jet printers, in which ink is propelled onto the paper by a battery of tiny nozzles, can produce text and graphics that surpass that of dot-matrix printers. In fact, the quality of ink-jet printers approaches that of laser printers. The further attractions of low cost and quiet operation has made the ink-jet printer a current favorite among buyers. **Laser printers**, which use technology similar to copying machines, are the top-of-the-line printers for quality and speed. The price of a low-end laser printer is now within the budget of most users. Laser printers are particularly favored by desktop publishers to produce text and graphics on the same page. For years, standard laser printers have printed text and graphics at 300 dots per inch, a resolution that produced crisp, professional documents. Now, powerful—and expensive—laser printers produce output at 600 dots

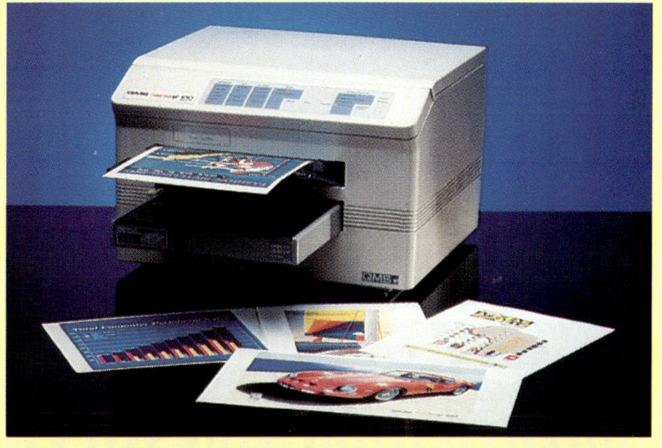

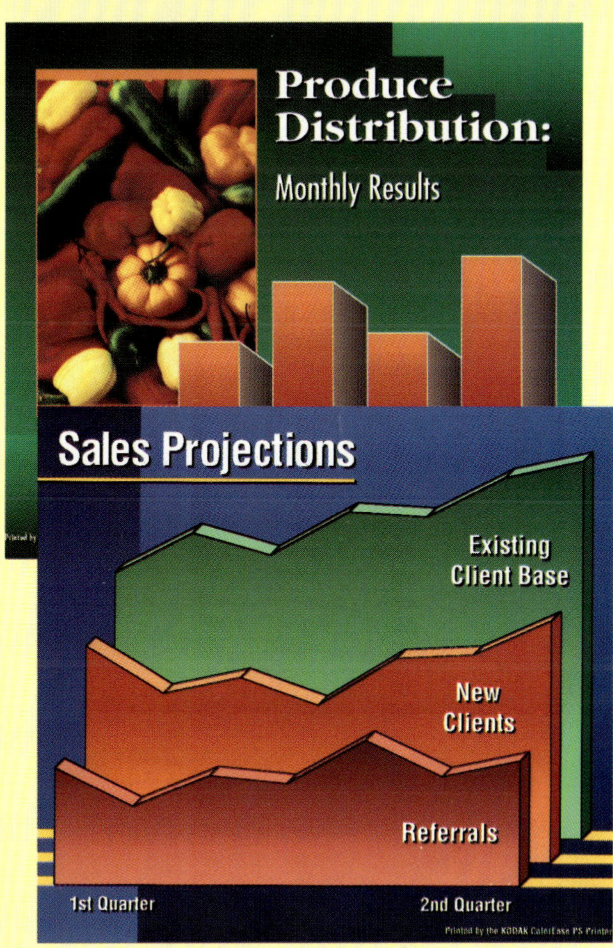

per inch, giving graphic images a sharpness that rivals photographs. However, this rich resolution may be of little value to a buyer who plans to produce mostly text.

Although a few **color printers** are available for less than $500, most are priced at well over $5000. Even at this price, color printers are not perfect. The color seen on the computer screen is not necessarily the color that will appear on the printed output. Furthermore, color printers often have high operating costs for staples such as special coated paper and color ink cartridges. Still, color printers, once prohibitively expensive and slow, are approaching affordable prices and speeds.

Portability

Do you plan to use your computer in one place, or will you be moving it around? Portable computers have found a significant niche in the market, mainly because they are packaged to travel easily. A laptop computer is lightweight (often under 8 pounds) and small enough to fit in a briefcase.

Generally, you should look for the same hardware components in a portable computer as you would consider in a desktop computer: a fast microprocessor, plenty of memory, clear screen, and a diskette drive and hard drive. You will have to make some compromises on input devices. The keyboard will probably be attached and the keys more cramped than a standard keyboard. Also, traveling users often do not have a handy surface for rolling a mouse, so you may want to consider an attached trackball to move the cursor on the screen.

Other Hardware Options

There are a great many hardware variations; we will mention a few here.

Communications Connections

If you wish to connect your computer via telephone lines to electronic bulletin boards, mainframe computers, or information utilities such as America Online or Prodigy, or if you wish to send and receive electronic mail, you need a modem. This device converts computer data into signals that can be transmitted over telephone lines. The Hayes family of products has become the industry standard; most new modems claim some degree of Hayes compatibility.

You may choose an external modem that can be used on different computers. But most buyers prefer an out-of-sight internal modem that fits inside the computer.

Other Input Devices

If you are interested in games, you may wish to acquire a **joystick**, which looks like the stick shift on a car. A joystick allows you to manipulate a cursor on the screen. A **scanner** is useful if you need to store pictures and typed documents in your computer. Scanners are frequently purchased by people who want to use their computers for desktop publishing.

Multimedia Access

A fast-growing area is multimedia: sophisticated software that offers text, sound, photos, graphics, and even movie clips. To take advantage of multimedia, which is presented on optical disks, you need a **CD-ROM disk drive**. Furthermore, you will probably want to invest in a sound card to be installed in your computer and a set of speakers.

Surge Protectors

These devices protect against the electrical ups and downs that can affect the operation of your computer. Some of the more expensive models provide up to 10 minutes of full power to your computer if the electric power in your home or office is knocked out. This gives you time to save your work on disk (so that the work won't be lost if the power fails) or to print out a report you need immediately.

Plotters

These output devices draw hard-copy graphics: maps, bar charts, engineering drawings, overhead transparencies, and even two- or three-dimensional illustrations. Plotters often come with a set of six pens in different colors.

What to Look for in Software

The first software decision is made by the choice of an IBM-compatible or Macintosh computer: you will use the operating system that matches that machine. In the case of an IBM-compatible machine, the operating system called MS-DOS can be overlayed with a software shell called Microsoft Windows. Since so much software is being written for the Windows environment, we recommend that you make Windows part of your purchase.

Hardware Requirements for Software

Identify the type of hardware required before you buy software. Under the heading "system requirements" right on the software package, a list will typically include a particular kind of computer and operating system, and a certain amount of memory and hard disk space.

Brand Names

In general, publishers of well-known software offer better support than lesser-known companies. Support may be in the form of tutorials, classes by the vendor or others, and the all-important hot-line assistance. In addition, makers of brand-name software usually offer superior documentation and upgrades to new and better versions of the product.

Where to Buy Software

Not very long ago, computer users bought their software at small specialty stores where they hoped they could understand the esoteric language of the sales staff. In contrast, buyers now go to enormous stores and pile software packages into their shopping carts like so many cans of soup. The choices of software vendors have expanded considerably.

Computer Superstores

The superstores, such as CompUSA, sell a broad variety of computer hardware and software. Although their primary advantages are a vast inventory, they also offer on-site technical support.

Warehouse Stores

Often billed as clubs, such as Wal-Mart's SAM's, these giant stores sell all manner of merchandise, including computer software.

Mass Merchandisers

Stores such as Sears sell software along with their other various merchandise.

Software-only Stores

These stores, such as Egghead Software, offer a wide selection of software. Furthermore, in marked contrast to the larger stores, these stores are

System Requirements

Make sure your hardware is compatible with the requirements of the software you are buying. You can find the requirements by reading the fine print on the software package. Here is a typical blurb from a software package: Requires an IBM or compatible PC with one diskette drive, a hard drive, Windows 3.1 or higher, and a minimum of 4MB RAM.

staffed with people who are familiar with the software.

Computer Dealers

These smaller retail stores, such as MicroAge or CompuAdd, sell hardware systems and the software that runs on them. Such a store usually has a well-informed staff, and may be your best bet for in-depth consulting.

Mail Order

Users who know what they want can get it conveniently and reasonably through the mail. Once an initial contact is made, probably from a magazine advertisement, the mail-order house will send catalogs of software regularly.

Now That You Have It, Will You Be Able to Use It?

Once the proud moment has come and your computer system is at home or in the office with you, what do you do with it?

Documentation

Computer systems today come with extensive documentation—the written manuals that accompany hardware. Installation procedures, however, is often largely (and conveniently) on a diskette. Usually, a simple brochure with detailed drawings will help you plug everything together and then help you invoke the software on the diskette. The computer configures itself, largely without any assistance from you.

Software documentation usually includes a user's guide—a reference manual for the various commands available with the software. Many software packages also include a workbook of some sort to help you train yourself. Software tutorials are also common, and useful for the novice and experienced user alike. Software tutorials usually come on a separate diskette, which guides you as you work through sample problems using the software.

Training

Can you teach yourself? In addition to the documentation supplied with your computer, numerous books and magazines offer help and answer readers' questions. Consult these sources. Other sources are classes offered by computer stores and local colleges. These hands-on sessions may be the most effective teaching method of all.

Maintenance Contract

Finally, when purchasing a computer, you may wish to consider a maintenance contract, which should cover labor and parts. Such contracts vary in comprehensiveness. Some cover on-site repairs; others require you to pack up the computer and mail it in. Another option is that the replacement part, say, a new monitor, is sent to you and then you return the old monitor in the same packaging.

Essentials of Computing

Second Edition

Interview: Growing Gardens for AIDS Patients

Joe Mondello (above) and Bruce Detrick (below), founders of the Tamarand Foundation, talk about how computers helped them get started.

Tell us about the foundation and why you started it.

Joe: In 1987, when my 6-month-old niece Tamara and her mother died of AIDS, I wanted to do something personal to help AIDS sufferers. Bruce saw a way that we could do something that would directly affect the quality of their lives—bringing nature and the arts to them.

Bruce: Institutional money was just barely enough for the basics—medicine, care, and education. We found that we could make a difference by bringing joy and beauty and a *garden*—the things that really nurture human beings—into institutions. Since we were starting out with no money, we networked with landscape architects, organizations, volunteers who love to garden, and schools that had school children who wanted to do something for sick children. The response was wonderful.

Joe: We began with small things, like going into an AIDS ward with bulbs and gravel and water and little plastic trays, and having a January planting day. We helped create little minigardens with paper whites and narcissus bulbs that would bloom in a few weeks and create a wonderful fragrance. The patients get to nurture their own bedside garden and watch it grow.

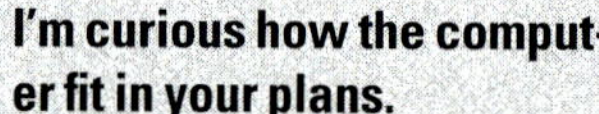

I'm curious how the computer fit in your plans.

Joe: Right off the bat the computer gave us a look of legitimacy. We started without any money, even though we put *Foundation* after our name to make it sound like we were something. We could make a very nice-looking letter on the computer to send to organizations such as the Parks Department and the World Health Organization.

The computer gave us the flexibility to create our own posters, flyers, leaflets. It is like having a graphic arts studio right there in the apartment. I knew if we had to do it on the outside, it could take weeks or months to get people to volunteer to do that stuff for us.

Before. The Tamarand foundation coordinated landscape architects, New York landlords, and an army of volunteers to tackle this Manhattan wasteland.

A First Look

PART 1

The plan. The design firm Arca Terra used computer graphics software to generate this design, which includes a play area, cedar playhouse, lawn, wooden bridges, fountain, murals, and plenty of flowers.

What else do you use the computer for?
Joe: We do our own mailings, and we keep track of all of our regular business stuff on the computer. You know, it even goes beyond that. We're just two guys with a phone and a Macintosh who decided to create a charity. Having the computer, I think, gave us the courage to try it.

What about the gardens?
Joe: Some of the gardens are designed on the computer by landscape architects. Bruce has an overall design concept, and the designers work under his guidance.
Bruce: We work with a team of landscape artists and horticulturists and volunteers to create gardens at health-related facilities throughout the New York area. Sites are selected to provide outdoor therapy for people living with AIDS. Horticultural therapy is the dream.

After. The new garden is a safe haven for sick children at Variety House, a transitional home for sick toddlers. The garden is maintained by the Association to Benefit Children, which also created the home.

We're just two guys with a phone and a Macintosh who decided to create a charity. Having the computer, I think, gave us the courage to try it.

at Computers

Chapter Overview

When Lashalla Richards began college, she was fairly sure that she wanted to be a journalist. Her college counselor advised her to get a little experience along the way, so Lashalla decided to seek a part-time job at the local newspaper. Although she envisioned herself pursuing hot stories, she was actually hired to key in the classified advertisements on the newspaper's computer.

The Ongoing

Lashalla knew her way around a computer keyboard and quickly picked up the procedures for entering the customer's name and billing address and the advertisement message. She also learned how to pick the correct code for the type of advertisement. But that was just the beginning. Lashalla also learned that the computer could sort the ads by code, so that advertisements of the same type, such as apartment rentals, would appear together. The customer data, of course, was used for computer-prepared bills and mailing labels.

Lashalla was surprised to learn that the newspaper used the customer data for a variety of purposes not related to the original advertisement. The newspaper staff extracted from the computer certain customer names and addresses and placed them on lists to be sold to other interested customers. For example, customers who advertised fishing gear or sports equipment might be placed on a list to be conveyed to sports magazines.

When she eventually did some reporting for the paper, Lashalla discovered that reporters have computer access to stored background information. For example, when she reported that a city council member was going to run for mayor, she fleshed out her story with computer-collected material about the candidate, such as the candidate's past employment and current philanthropic activities.

Lashalla was impressed with her computer savvy but knew she had a lot to learn about how computers worked and what they had to offer. To broaden her knowledge, she included a computer literacy class in her college schedule. As it turned out, Lashalla ended up with a career in publishing, where her computer skills serve her very well.

Revolution

Computers in Your Life

The Computer Revolution

It is hard to remember a time, just a few years ago, when computers were not everywhere. They were not on desks or sales counters or bank walls. They also were not *in* everything, from watches to ovens to cars. The Computer Revolution has come upon us with amazing speed. You could compare this revolution to the Industrial Revolution.

The Industrial Revolution changed human society on a massive scale, introducing electricity, telephones, radios, automobiles, and airplanes. The Computer Revolution also is bringing dramatic shifts in the way we live, but it is happening a great deal more quickly than the Industrial Revolution.

The Computer Revolution is unfinished; it will probably roll on into the next century. Nevertheless, perhaps we can glimpse the future now. Let us see how far we have come, first in society and then on a more personal level.

The Information Age: Forming a New Society

Computers have gone beyond acceptance; they are shaping society in fundamental ways. Traditionally, economics courses taught that the cornerstones of an economy were land, labor, and capital. That tenet is now being challenged, and we speak of *four* key economic elements: land, labor, capital, and information. We have converted from an industrial society to an information society. We are moving from physical labor to mental labor, trading muscle power for brain power. Just as people moved from farms to factories when the Industrial Revolution began, so must we adjust to the information age. You have already taken that first step by taking a computer class and reading this book. But how will computers become a part of your life beyond the classroom? Let us look at some ways in which we're already adjusting to this information age.

How You Will Use a Computer

Personal computers have moved into many facets of our lives. In our homes we use them for a variety of purposes, including keeping track of bank accounts, writing term papers and letters, learning foreign languages, designing artwork, turning on lawn sprinklers or coffeemakers, monitoring temperature and humidity, presenting math and reading skills to children, and organizing mailing lists or directories.

Many people are also using computers on the job, whether they sit at a desk in an office or run a farm. Personal computers are now used for writing memos and reports; forecasting and updating budgets; creating and maintaining files; searching for information; and producing charts, graphs, and newsletters. Almost any job you hope to obtain in the future will involve a computer in some way. A relatively new wrinkle in the job arena is a concept called skill-based pay. Instead of the old idea of across-the-board raises, companies are rewarding employees who have more job skills. It should not come as a surprise that computer skills are among the most prized.

Clearly, the computer user no longer has to be a scientist or mathematician. We are all computer users (Figure 1-1).

Figure 1-1 Personal computer users.
All these people—whether at home, at work, or at school—are making use of the personal computer.

Computer Literacy for All

Why are you reading this book? Why are you studying computers? In addition to fulfilling a course requirement or satisfying your curiosity, you probably recognize that it will not be easy to get through the rest of your life if you know nothing about computers.

We offer a three-part definition of computer literacy:

- **Awareness.** As you study computers and their uses, you will become aware of their importance, their versatility, their pervasiveness, and their potential for good and ill in our society.
- **Knowledge.** You will learn what computers are, how they work, and their functions. This requires learning some new terminology that will help you deal with computers and the people who work with them.
- **Interaction.** Computer literacy also means learning to use a computer for some basic tasks. Many courses include a hands-on component; after such training you should feel comfortable sitting down at a computer and using it for some suitable purpose.

Climb Aboard

Is it really that important to be computer literate? Yes. But people have not always thought so. In the early days of the Computer Revolution, the average person worried about the disadvantages of computers but failed to recognize the advantages. The situation was similar to that in the early 1900s, when cars were first introduced. Historians tell us that the reaction to that newfangled contraption was much the same as people's reactions to computers. Today's traffic crush, however, is a good indication that attitudes changed somewhere along the way.

The analogy between cars and computers is illuminating. In the very near future, people who refuse to have anything to do with computers may be as inconvenienced as people who refuse to learn to drive.

Note that no part of this definition suggests that you must be able to write the instructions that tell a computer what to do. That would be akin to saying that everyone who plans to drive a car should become an auto mechanic. Someone else can write the instructions for the computer; the interaction part of the definition merely implies that you should be able to make use of those instructions. For example, a bank teller should be able to use a computer to see if an account really contains as much money as a customer wants to withdraw. Computers can also be used by an accountant to prepare a report, a farmer to check on market prices, a store manager to analyze sales trends, or a teenager to play a video game. We cannot guarantee that these people are computer literate, but they have at least grasped the hands-on component of the definition—they can interact with computers.

Since part of the definition of computer literacy is awareness, let us now look at what makes computers so useful. We will then turn to the various ways computers can be used.

Everywhere You Turn

It seems that everywhere you turn these days, you see computers—in stores, cars, homes, offices, hospitals, banks. What are some of the features of computers that make them so useful?

The Significance of Computers

The computer is a workhorse. It is generally capable of laboring 24 hours a day, does not ask for raises or coffee breaks, and will do the 10,000th task exactly the same way it did the first one—without complaining of boredom.

Computers have become an indispensable part of our lives for six key reasons. The first three are key reasons because they are inherent to computers; the last three are valuable by-products.

- **Speed.** We all appreciate fast service, whether we are waiting in line at the supermarket or waiting for grades to come in the mail. More often than not, the computer is a key element in providing fast service. So unless we are prepared to do a lot more waiting—for paychecks, grades, telephone calls, travel reservations, bank balances, and many other things—we need the split-second processing of the computer. The speed of the computer also makes the machine ideal for processing large amounts of data, as in accounting systems and scientific applications.
- **Reliability.** Computers are physically reliable and can thus be counted on to be accurate. Of course, you might not think this from hearing stories about "computer errors." Unfortunately, what these stories almost never bring out is that most mistakes are not the fault of the computers themselves. True, equipment sometimes fails. But most errors supposedly made by computers are really human errors, often caused by someone hitting a wrong key when giving data to the computer. Although the phrase *computer error* is quite common, the blame usually lies elsewhere.
- **Storage capability.** Computer systems are able to store tremendous amounts of data, which can then be retrieved quickly and efficiently. This storage capability is especially important in an information age.

Personal Computers In Action

Saving the Whales

Pieter Folken's "desk" is a craggy cliff along the coast of Alaska. A committed environmentalist, Pieter uses his perch to observe humpback whales and make immediate notations of sightings using his portable laptop computer. For environmentalists trying to save the whales, part of the difficulty is that too little is known about their behavior to take appropriate action. Pieter's hands-on research will help change all that. The on-site data collected on size, movement, and range of whale populations eventually will be used to help make global decisions on their conservation.

- **Productivity.** Unfortunately, computers sometimes eliminate jobs, most notably in factories, but computers also free human beings for other work. Although a learning curve can cause an initial slow-down, most users will notice increased productivity. In particular, office workers using computers do their jobs better and faster.
- **Decision making.** Because of expanding technology, communications, and the interdependency of people, we suffer from an information deluge. This overload is in part brought on by the computer, but the computer will also help solve it. To make essential business and governmental decisions, managers need to take into account a variety of financial, geographical, logistical, and other factors. Using problem-solving techniques originally developed by humans, the computer helps decision makers sort through and organize this vast amount of information and make better choices.
- **Reduction in costs.** Finally, because it enhances productivity and the decision-making process, the computer helps reduce duplication of effort and hold down costs for labor and energy. Thus, computers help reduce the costs of goods and services. Trend watchers who study the impact of computers on the overall economy have hedged their bets for years, noting the increased level of competition but the still-stagnant economy. Although they are usually reluctant to make robust predictions, some experts seem to agree on a mid-1990s productivity burst, due largely to the impact of computers.

Getting Older Via Computer

The Hollywood special-effects folks call it morphing—the gradual computerized transformation of one image to another. Here is a demonstration of the aging process.

With all these wonderful features to its credit, it is no wonder that computers have made their way into almost every facet of our lives. Let us look at some of the ways computers are being used to make our workdays more productive and our personal lives more rewarding.

Some Applications of Computers

The jobs that computers do are as varied as we can imagine, but the following are some of the principal uses:

- **Graphics.** There is no better place to get a sense of the computer's impact than in the area of computer graphics—computer-produced visual images. The computer as artist is evidenced in medicine, where brain scanners produce color-enhanced "maps" to help diagnose mental illness. Biochemists use computers to model, in three dimensions, the structure of molecules. Architects use computer-animated graphics to give clients visual walk-throughs of proposed buildings, to show possible exteriors, and to subject buildings to hypothetical earthquakes.

  Business executives play artist, making bar graphs and pie charts out of tedious figures and using color to convey information with far more impact than numbers alone can create. Finally, a new kind of artist has emerged who uses computers to create cartoon animation, landscapes, television logos, action sketches, print commercials, and still lifes (Figures 1-2 and 1-3).
- **Commerce.** Products from meats to magazines are now packaged with zebra-striped symbols that can be read by scanners at supermarket checkout stands to determine the prices of the products. These stripes, called the Universal Product Code (UPC), are part of one of the most highly visible uses of computers in commerce; however, there are numerous others. Modern warehousing and inventory management could not exist without computers. Take your copy of this book, for instance. From printer to warehouse to bookstore, its movement was tracked with the help of computers.
- **Energy.** Energy companies use computers and geological data to locate oil, coal, natural gas, and uranium. Meter readers use hand-held computers to record how much energy is used each month in homes and businesses. The utility companies also use computers to monitor and analyze their vast power networks. Building managers use computers to control lighting, heating, and cooling in skyscrapers and warehouses. In addition, computers can analyze the efficiency of the insulation in your home and the fuel consumption in your car.
- **Transportation and travel.** Computers are used to help run rapid transit systems, load cargo ships, keep track of what trucks and railroad cars have been sent where and with what cargo, fly and land air-

Figure 1-2 Computer-generated action art.
This fanciful art work was produced by a computer artist, using special graphics software.

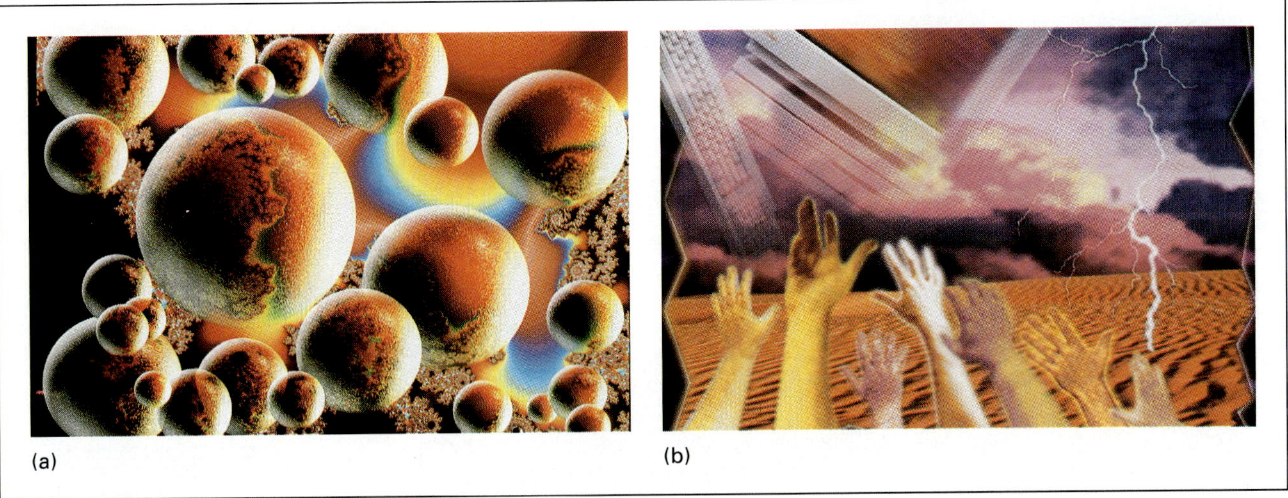

Figure 1-3 Computer-generated still life.
(a) This stunning artwork is called Glass Planets. (b) This dizzying rendition was prepared to convey the variety of offerings on multiple-channel cable television.

planes and keep them from colliding, schedule airline and hotel reservations, and monitor traffic.

- **Paperwork.** There is no doubt that our society runs on paper. In some ways the computer contributes to this problem—as in adding to the amount of junk mail you find in your mailbox—but in many other ways it reduces paper handling. The techniques of word processing, for example, let you prepare documents in draft form and place them in computer storage. If the document needs to be changed, it can be retrieved, edited, and saved again or printed without retyping. Even Supreme Court justices use word processing, storing their opinions for future reference. Computerized bookkeeping, record keeping, and document sending have also made paperwork more efficient.
- **Money.** Computers have revolutionized the way money is handled, and nowhere is this more obvious than in banking (Figure 1-4). Once upon a time it was possible to write a check for the rent on Tuesday and cover it with a deposit on Thursday, knowing it would take a few days for the bank to process the rent check and debit it against the account. With computers, however, the recording of deposits and withdrawals is done more quickly. Computers have also brought us the age of do-it-yourself banking, with automated teller machines (ATMs) available for simple transactions. Furthermore, in many grocery stores you can use your ATM card to transfer money from your account to pay for your groceries—with no cash changing hands. Computers have helped fuel the cashless economy, enabling the widespread use of credit cards and instant credit checks by banks, department stores, and other retailers. Some oil companies are now using credit-card-activated, self-service gasoline pumps.
- **Communications.** Users have the potential to link up one computer with another through a communications system such as telephone lines. Most businesses use computer communications systems to send memos and reports and messages, transfer computer data files, and even have "meetings" among people in dispersed locations. In fact, computer networking is the fastest growing area in the industry.

COMPUTING TRENDS

Your Resume: Untouched, Unseen

You send out dozens of copies of your resume, knowing that it will sit in stacks with hundreds of others or, even worse, be placed "on file" in a deep drawer. The waiting begins; you know that this is the tough part of a job search. But wait: a phone call, just two days later. You are interviewed and you are hired.

Has something changed in the hiring process? Yes. A computer is checking the resumes. Instead of human eyes, the computer reviews the current resume collection, looking for particular job qualifications. Resume preparers must make some adjustments for this latest trend in corporate hiring.

Many time-honored methods of getting attention no longer work. A flashy resume meant to catch a recruiter's eye may not be helpful. Skip all the flourishes—fancy typefaces, underlining, graphics, colored paper. Do use a good printer, with easily readable print. Send an original rather than a copy. Use standard-size paper, but do not fold the resume because the words on a crease may be hard for the computer to read. And, for once, technical jargon is a good idea; the computer may search for those words.

Of course, we must add a disclaimer: not *all* companies are scanning resumes by computer. Try to find out what would be appropriate for the companies to which you are applying.

RESUME

L. Banfield Harrison
5738 East Green Lake Way North
Redmond, WA 98052
(206) 634-9808

SYNOPSIS — College faculty and department head, Computer Information Systems department. Author of college textbooks. Consultant, reviewer, lecturer, systems analyst, attorney.

EDUCATION — JD, University of Washington School of Law (Honors)
MSE, Seattle University
BA, University of Notre Dame, Mathematics

COMPUTER EXPERIENCE
- Machines — HP 3000, IBM and CDC mainframes, PRIME, IBM PS/2, Macintosh.
- Software — Lotus 1-2-3, dBASE, Rbase, WordPerfect,
  - Languages — Pascal, FORTRAN, BASIC, others.
  - Applications Areas — Industrial relations, marketing, sales, food brokerage, cattle registration, accounts payable, aircraft design, terminal reservations, marketing, personnel, political organizations, mass mailing, customer surveys.
  - Positions — Instructor, department head, author, consultant, lecturer, project lead. Major responsibilities in feasibility, analysis, design, and development of large-scale computer systems.
  - Courses Taught — Database management, systems analysis and design, operating systems, data communications, logic, PC applications, computer literacy.

MANAGEMENT — Department manager, 30 employees, computer systems
Division head, 18 college professors

Figure 1-4 Computers where you expect them: in banks.
The employees of Louisiana's Hibernia National Bank can concentrate their time and attention on their customers because the bank contracted with IBM for a service agreement to manage the bank's computing resources.

Figure 1-5 A farmer's computer. This farmer uses his laptop computer to enter crop data from the field.

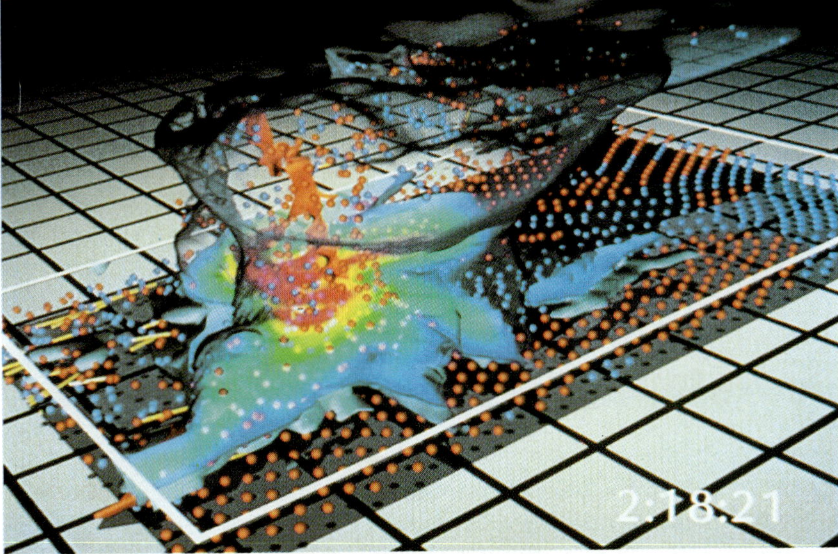

Figure 1-6 When will the storm get here? To improve the science of weather forecasting, researchers program various weather conditions into a computerized global weather model. In this graphic, different colors represent different water densities.

- **Agriculture.** High tech down on the farm? Absolutely. Farming is big business, and computers can help with billing, crop information, cost per acre, feed combinations, and automatic irrigation. A Mississippi cotton grower, for example, boosted his annual profit 50 percent by using a computer to determine the best time to fertilize. Cattle breeders use computers to generate information about livestock breeding and performance. Some farmers even take along computers as they check their crops (Figure 1-5).
- **Government.** The federal government is the largest single user of computers. The Social Security Administration, for example, produces millions of benefit checks each month, with the help of computers. Computers are also used for forecasting weather (Figure 1-6), for admitting vacationers to parks, for processing immigrants, for meting out justice, and yes, for collecting taxes. The FBI keeps track of suspected criminals by compiling separate bits of information into elabo-

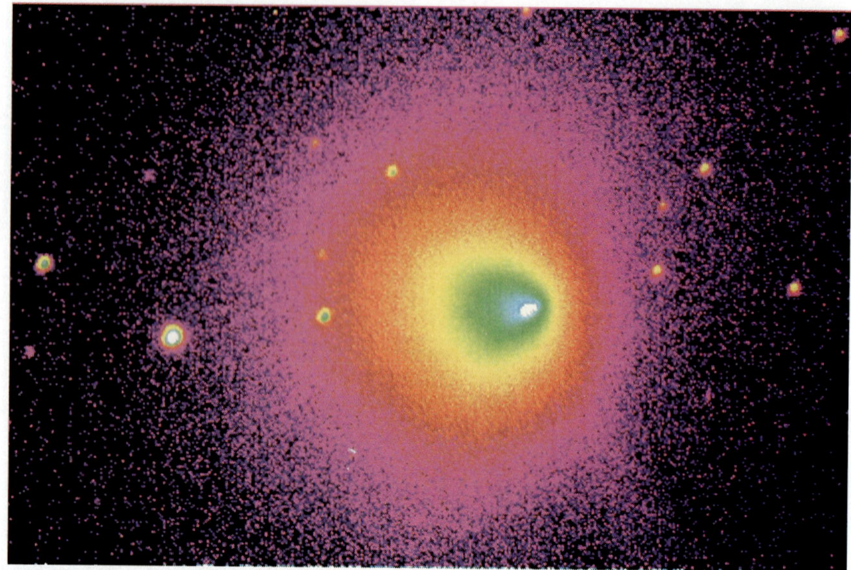

Figure 1-7 The Swift-Tuttle comet. Space is filled with objects that threaten the earth, notably the so-called Swift-Tuttle comet, seen with powerful telescopes on October 22, 1992, and enhanced by computer. The comet is a six-mile-long frozen dirt ball, which astronomers give a 1-in-10,000 chance of colliding with the earth on August 14, 2126.

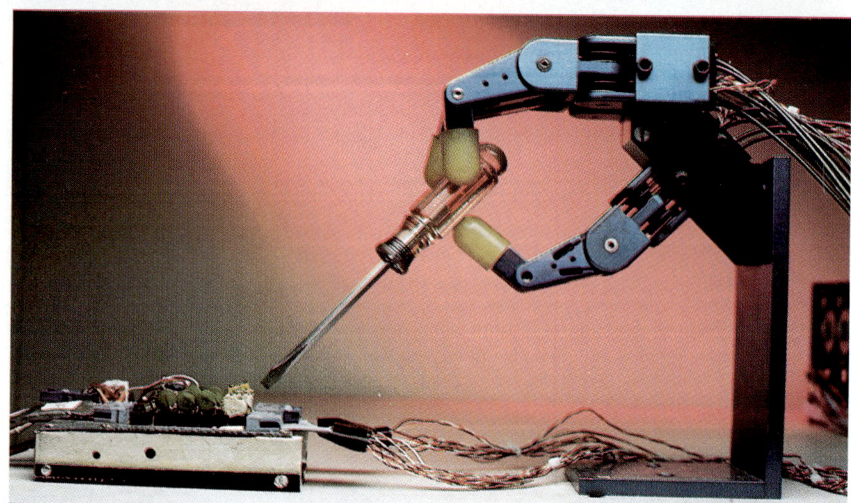

Figure 1-8 The tactile robot. Robot chores require delicate maneuvers such as those required of this robot "hand," which has the dexterity to use a screwdriver.

rate dossiers, including computer-produced mug shots, that have already helped put several organized crime lords behind bars. On a more positive note, computer technology is the basis of the technology that has provided information about space (Figure 1-7).

- **Robotics.** With the age of the computer has arrived the age of the robot (Figure 1-8). Robots are information machines with the manual dexterity to perform some tasks too unpleasant, too dangerous, or too exacting to assign to human beings. Examples are robots used by the military for bomb removal; robots used in defense to perform underwater military missions; robots used by fruit growers to pick fruit; and even robots that patrol jail corridors at night and report any persons encountered. Especially controversial are the robots that do tedious jobs better than human beings do, jobs such as welding or paint spraying in factories. Clearly, these robots signal the end of those jobs for some factory workers—a troublesome social problem. However, improved technology has always meant some workers must be retrained, as blacksmiths did with the advent of the automobile.
- **Health and medicine.** Computers have long been used on the business side of medicine for record keeping, but the most impressive

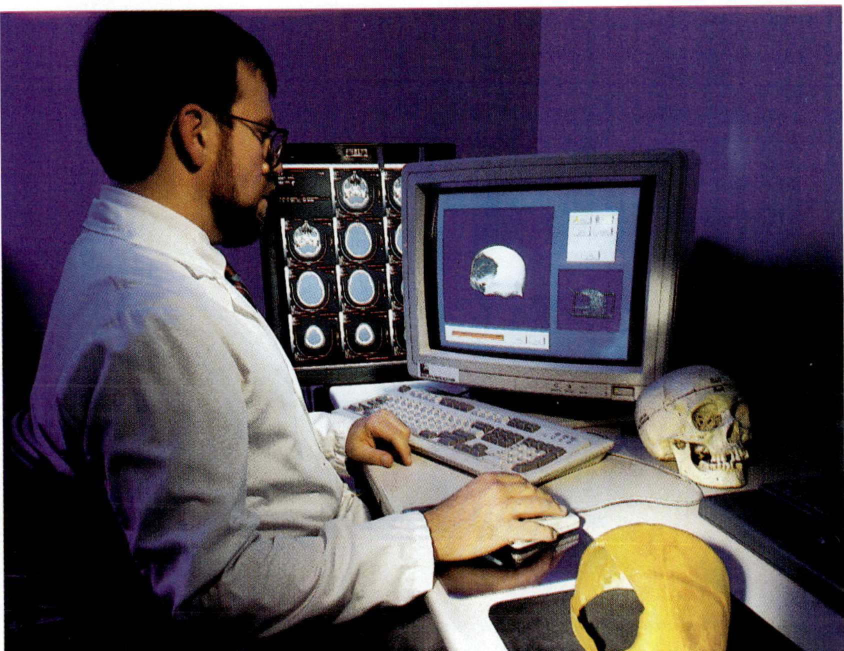

Figure 1.9 Surgeon planning operation. A patient with a gunshot wound to the head was given a computer-assisted tomography (CAT) scan of the internal damage. The pictures are then assembled into the three-dimensional view shown here on the screen, which the surgeon can use to plan the operation.

advances have been in the diagnostic and healing processes. A key application of computers is to produce cross-sectional views of the body that physicians can study before proceeding with treatment (Figure 1-9). It is estimated that computers make disease diagnoses with 85 percent accuracy. (Doctors, of course, make the final diagnoses.) Another application helps pharmacists test patients' medications for drug compatibility. If you are one of the thousands who suffer one miserable cold after another, you will welcome the news that computers have been able to map, in exquisite atomic detail, the structure of a human cold virus; this is a big step on the way to a cure for the common cold (Figure 1-10). Computers are also being used to monitor everything from weight loss to heart rates.

- **Education.** Computers have been used behind the scenes for years in colleges and school districts for record-keeping and accounting purposes. Now, of course, they are rapidly coming into the classrooms—elementary, secondary, and college. At the college level, many students realize that they need at least a fundamental grounding in computers. Some colleges require that incoming students purchase computers because many of their class assignments will be done directly on the computer. At the high-school and elementary-school levels, many parents and teachers feel that computer education is a necessity. Parents want to be sure their children are not left behind in the computer age (Figure 1-11).
- **The home.** Are you willing to welcome the computer into your home? Many people already have, often justifying it as an educational tool for their children. But that is only the beginning. Adults often keep records, write letters, prepare budgets, draw pictures, prepare newsletters for volunteer organizations, and communicate with other computer users—all with their own computers at home. The adventurous make their homes "smart" by using computers to control heating and air conditioning, water their yards, turn lights on and off, and even "watch" for burglars.

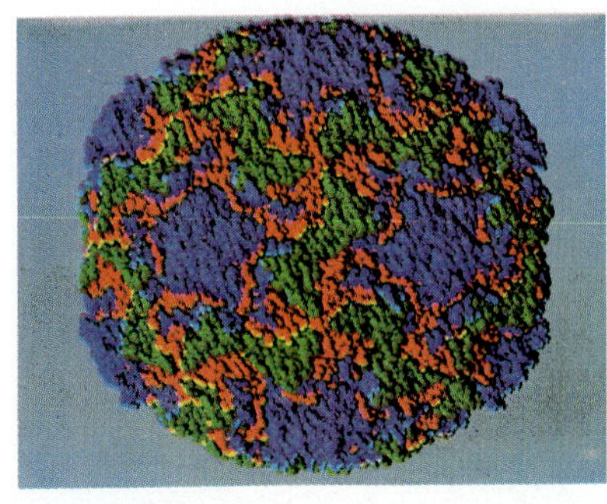

Figure 1-10 Cold virus. This computer-produced model of a cold virus raises hope that a cure for the common cold may be possible after all. With the aid of a computer, the final set of calculations for the model took one month to complete. Researchers estimate that, without the computer, the calculations would have required ten years of manual effort.

Figure 1-11 Painting for kids. Elementary schoolchildren love to learn how to make pictures on the computer. This splashy high-seas scene was made by a 6-year-old.

- **The sciences.** Computers are used extensively in the sciences. For example, the Food and Drug Administration uses a computer to replace live subjects, such as mice, in experiments. Computers are also used to generate models of DNA, the molecule that houses the genetic instructions that determine the specific characteristics of organisms. Aerospace engineers use computers to design and test airplane parts (Figure 1-12). In England researchers have used computers to invent a "bionic nose" that can distinguish subtle differences in fragrance—an invention that could have major benefits for the food, perfume, and distilling industries. Academicians can be graphically creative even as they study mathematical relationships (Figure 1-13).
- **Training.** Computers are being used as training devices in industry and government. To teach aspiring sea captains to navigate, for instance, it is much cheaper (and, of course, safer) to use computerized training simulators rather than real ships. Likewise, novice engineers or pilots can get the experience of running a train or flying a plane with the help of a computerized device (Figure 1-14). Computer-based training simulators are also used in medical schools, environmental agencies, science labs, and business schools.
- **The human connection.** Do computers seem cold and impersonal? Look again. The disabled don't think so. Neither do other people who use computers in very personal ways. Computers can be used to assist humans in areas in which we are most human. Can the disabled walk again? Some can with the help of computers. Can dancers and athletes improve their performance? Often they can by using computers to monitor and analyze their movements. Can we learn more about our ethnic backgrounds and our cultural history with the aid of computers? Indeed we can.

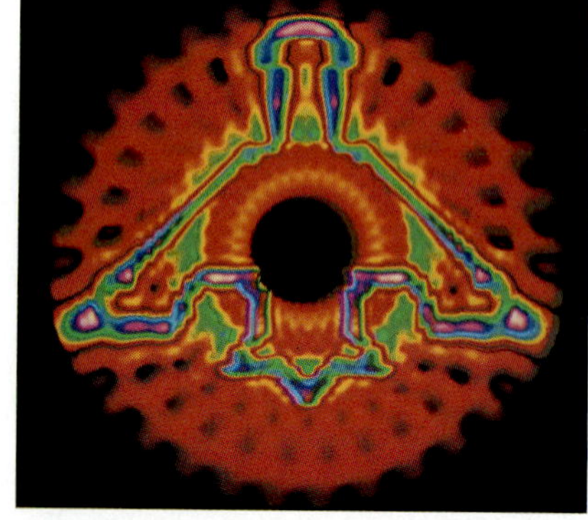

Figure 1-12 Airplane design. The precise design of this plane has yet to be determined, but this computer-generated image of a delta-wing craft suggests one possible shape.

Try making an early assessment of your computer literacy at this point. You probably know more than you think you do. Even though you may not know a lot about computers yet, you have been exposed to computer hype, computer advertisements and discussions, and magazine articles and newspaper headlines about computers. You have interacted

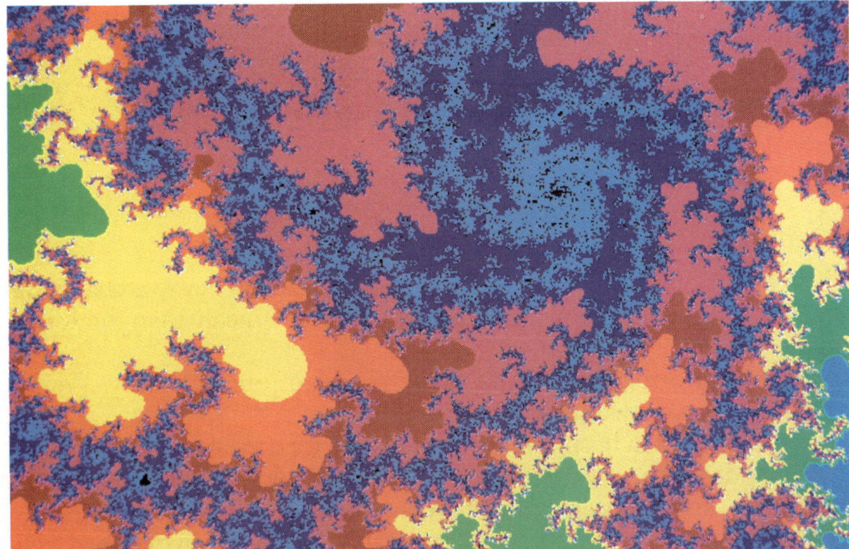

Figure 1-13 Fractals.
Each point on a screen is assigned a color, depending on its behavior under a series of simple repeated mathematical operations.

Figure 1-14 Pilot training.
Pilots practice airplane handling in a computer-controlled simulator. The computer alters instrument readings and the appearance of the runway as the pilot maneuvers from a ground-based cockpit.

with computers in the various activities of your life—at the grocery store, your school, the library, and more. The beginnings of your computer literacy are already apparent.

▼ ▼ ▼

Most careers involve computers in some way. This book will provide you with the foundation you need in computer literacy. If the computer is to help us rather than confuse or threaten us, we must assume some responsibility for understanding it.

Chapter Review

Summary

- Like the Industrial Revolution, the Computer Revolution is making massive changes in society. However, the Computer Revolution is happening more quickly than the Industrial Revolution did.
- Land, labor, capital, and information are the cornerstones of our economy. We are changing from an industrial society to an information society.
- Personal computers can be used in business and in the home for a variety of purposes.
- Computer literacy includes (1) an awareness of computers, (2) knowledge about computers and their functions, and (3) interaction with computers.
- Three key characteristics make computers an indispensable part of our lives: speed, reliability, and storage capacity. By-products of these characteristics include increased productivity, enhanced decision making, and reduced costs.
- Computers are used in many areas, including graphics, commerce, energy, transportation and travel, paperwork, money, agriculture, government, education, the home, health and medicine, robotics, the sciences, and training.

Student Personal Study Guide

Review Questions

1. In what ways are the Industrial Revolution and the Computer Revolution similar? In what ways are they different?
2. What are the four cornerstones of today's economy?
3. List four uses of personal computers in the home.
4. List four uses of personal computers in business.
5. What are the three components of computer literacy?
6. List three characteristics that make computers indispensable.
7. Name one use of computers in each of the following areas: graphics, commerce, energy, transportation, paperwork, money, agriculture, government, education, the home, health and medicine, robotics, the sciences, and training.

Discussion Questions

1. Do you believe that computers make life easier and better? Explain.
2. Why are you taking this class? What do you expect to learn from this class?
3. Some people are afraid of computers because they think they might somehow break something or, even worse, appear stupid. Can you think of other reasons that people might be afraid of computers?
4. How will you, individually, be part of the Computer Revolution?

True/False

T F 1. The Computer Revolution will take about the same amount of time as the Industrial Revolution.

T F 2. The Computer Revolution is almost complete.

T F 3. Jobs assigned to robots often are those that are too unpleasant, dangerous, or exacting for humans to do.
T F 4. Computers have had a significant impact on cutting down on junk mail.
T F 5. Computer literacy means being able to write instructions to tell the computer what to do.
T F 6. The federal government is the largest single user of computers.
T F 7. Three key reasons why computers have become indispensable are speed, reliability, and storage capability.
T F 8. A "computer error" is usually the result of a breakdown in the computer.
T F 9. Computers are generally used only in office settings.
T F 10. Computers can help reduce waste and hold down costs.

Fill-In

1. The four cornerstones of today's economy are ____________________, ____________________, ____________________, and ____________________.
2. The three components of computer literacy are ____________________, ____________________, and ____________________.
3. The Computer Revolution is happening more quickly than the ____________________.
4. Computers are used in the home to ____________________, ____________________, ____________________, and ____________________.
5. Three much-valued by-products of computers are ____________________, ____________________, and ____________________.

Answers

True/False: 1. F, 2. F, 3. T, 4. F, 5. F, 6. T, 7. T, 8. F, 9. F, 10. T
Fill-In: 1. land, labor, capital, information; 2. awareness, knowledge, interaction; 3. Industrial Revolution; 4. (any four of the following) keep records, write letters, prepare budgets, draw pictures, prepare newsletters, communicate with other computers, control heating and air conditioning, water yards, turn lights on or off, watch for burglars; 5. productivity, decision making, reduction in costs.

Chapter Overview

Curtis Burbank had been the division office manager for 21 years, and his knowledge of the company was encyclopedic. He knew everything from the broad company mission statement to the new product development plans and the routes of new sales employees. He even had a general understanding of the computer-produced reports that came from the headquarters office. However, when Curtis learned that the company was planning to bring personal computers to the division office, it caused him to pause. Computers might be a part of everyday life to his teenage children, but to Curtis they were still a mystery.

Overview of a

CHAPTER 2

Computer System

Hardware and Software

At Curtis's suggestion the company sent him to a three-day seminar on the role of computers in the office. He knew the seminar alone would not make him computer savvy, but it did increase his comfort level somewhat. The instruction was very basic, beginning with the difference between hardware and software: Hardware is the computer itself, and related equipment, while the software is a set of instructions to tell the computer how to do a task. Curtis was determined to learn more.

Back in the office Curtis gathered the staff together to explain the impact of the impending new equipment. He began with a homey example, describing the functions of the new computers in terms of already-familiar equipment. Each computer, he noted, took on the roles of several old systems. Word processing software let the computers and printers behave as sophisticated typewriters. Spreadsheet software turned the computer into a flexible accounting system. Database software let the computer's storage act as a super-convenient filing cabinet. Furthermore, the wires that linked all the computers let the staff exchange mail via computer, reducing the amount of paper memos and alleviating the company's problem with "telephone tag."

For the next two weeks, Curtis and a dozen other staffers spent their afternoons at a hands-on class provided by the computer vendor. Each of them acquired a passing acquaintance with the computers and how they could be used in the office.

The arrival of the computers at the company was quite an event. Typewriters were, for the most part, stowed away. New wiring was installed to link the computers together. Gleaming new computers were set up on each desk. Most work came to a halt. But gradually, with the temporary help of an on-site instructor sent by the vendor, Curtis and the staff began to pick up speed. Eventually, Curtis and four other staffers enrolled in an evening computer literacy class, paid for by the company, at a local college.

All this happened a year and a half ago. Now Curtis routinely uses the computer on his desk, just as he does other office equipment. He has joined the people who cannot imagine how they ever got along without computers.

The Computer As a Tool

When most people think of tools, they think of hand tools such as hammers and saws, or perhaps lug wrenches and screwdrivers. But think of a tool in a broader sense, as anything used to do a job. This expands the horizon to include stethoscopes, baseball bats, kettles, shovels, and yes, computers.

The computer is a sophisticated tool, but a tool nonetheless. Who would use such a tool? Carrying our analogy further, would you buy a baseball bat if you had no intention of hitting a ball? Probably not. You probably would not purchase a computer either, or learn how to use it, unless you had some use in mind. Business people are not interested in buying useless tools. Instead, they have a plan in mind. Businesses purchase computers because they have problems to solve or tasks to perform.

The Beginning: Some Basic Terminology

Knowing just a few basic concepts will prepare you for meeting a computer for the first time, whether at school, at home, or on the job. If you are a beginner, you may have heard of hardware and software but still have only a vague notion of what they are.

The computer and its associated equipment are called **hardware.** The instructions that tell a computer what you want it to do are called **software.** Software is also referred to as programs. To be more specific, a **program** is a set of step-by-step instructions, written in a language a computer understands, that directs the computer to do the tasks you want it to do and to produce the results you want. A **computer programmer** is a person who writes programs. But most of us do not write programs; we *use* programs written by someone else. This means we are **users**—people who use computer software. In business, users are sometimes called **end-users** because they are at the end of the "computer line," actually making use of the computer's capabilities.

As we continue the chapter, we will examine first hardware and then software. Along the way we will note how these components work together to turn raw data into useful information. Then we will return to look at the personal computer in more detail. As the title of this chapter indicates, what follows is an overview, a look at the "big picture" of a computer system. Thus, many of the terms introduced in this chapter are defined only briefly. In subsequent chapters we will discuss the various parts of a computer system in greater detail.

Hardware

What is a computer? A **computer** is a machine that can be programmed to accept raw data (input) and process it into useful information (output). For example, a computer in a company's payroll department could be programmed to accept input data about an employee's rate of pay and hours worked and process that data to create the employee's paycheck. The processing is directed by the software but performed by the hardware, which we will examine in this section.

To function, a computer system requires four main areas of data handling: input, processing, output, and storage (Figure 2-1). The hardware responsible for these four areas operates as follows:

- *Input devices* accept data in a form that the computer can use and send the data to the computer's processing unit. These devices allow you to get data into the computer.
- The *central processing unit (CPU)* has the electronic circuitry that manipulates input data into the information wanted. The central processing unit actually executes computer instructions. *Memory* is associated with the central processing unit. Memory consists of the electronic circuitry that temporarily stores the data and instructions (programs) needed by the central processing unit.

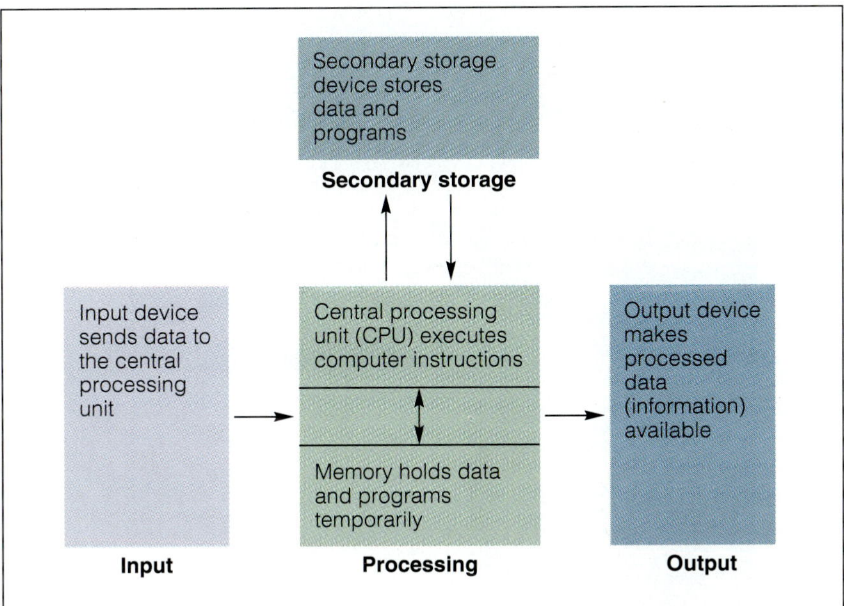

Figure 2-1 The four primary components of a computer system.
To function, a computer system requires input, processing, output, and storage.

- *Output devices* show you the processed data, or information, in a form that is useful to you.
- *Secondary storage devices*, such as disk drives, can store additional data and programs permanently. These devices, which may or may not be physically attached to the computer, supplement the computer's memory.

Now let us consider the equipment making up these four parts in terms of what you would find on a personal computer.

From a Personal Computer Perspective

Suppose you want to do word processing on a personal computer, perhaps writing a letter or memo, using the hardware shown in Figure 2-2. Word processing software allows you to input data such as a letter, save it, revise and resave it, and print it whenever you wish. The *input device*, in this case, is a keyboard, which you use to type, or key in, the original letter and any changes you want to make to it. All computers, large and small, must have a *central processing unit* (on a personal computer it is within the personal computer housing). The central processing unit uses the word processing software to accept the data you input through the keyboard. Processed data from your personal computer is usually *output* in two forms, on a screen and on a printer. As you enter the letter on the keyboard, it appears on the screen in front of you. After you examine the letter on the screen, make changes, and determine that the new version is acceptable, you can print the letter on a printer. Your *secondary storage device* could be a disk drive, which accesses the diskette that stores the letter until it is needed again. The personal computer is a convenient vehicle for examining the overall hardware configuration. We will return to the personal computer in more detail later in the chapter.

Now we will take a general tour of the hardware needed for input, processing, output, and storage. All computer systems—whether small,

Figure 2-2 A personal computer system.
In this IBM PS/2 personal computer system, the input devices are both a keyboard and a mouse, which feed data to the central processing unit. The central processing unit is an array of electronic circuits on a piece of silicon in the computer housing. The two output devices in this example are the screen and the printer. Secondary storage is on both diskettes and hard disk. These four components of the system operate together to make the computer work for you.

medium, or large—are composed of these same components. These topics will be covered in more detail in subsequent chapters.

Input: Raw Data

Input is the data put into the computer system for processing. Some of the most common ways of feeding input data into the system are by

- Enterring on a **keyboard.** The layout of a computer keyboard is similar to that of an electric typewriter keyboard. The computer responds to what you enter; that is, it "talks back" to you by displaying on the screen what you type (Figure 2-3a).
- Moving a **mouse** over a flat surface. As the ball on its underside rotates, the mouse movement causes corresponding movement on the computer screen, so the user can use the mouse to point to commands on the screen. Buttons on the mouse let the user invoke commands (Figure 2-3a).
- Reading with a **wand reader,** which can be used to scan the special letters and numbers on price tags in retail stores (Figure 2-3b). Wand readers can read data directly from the source, such as a price tag, into the computer. Thus, they significantly reduce the cost and potential error associated with manually entering data on a keyboard.
- Moving a product over a **bar code reader,** which scans **bar codes,** the zebra-striped symbols now carried on nearly all products (Figure 2-3c). Like wand readers, bar code readers collect data at the source, reducing errors and costs.

An input device may be part of a **terminal** connected to a large computer. A terminal includes (1) an input device—a keyboard, wand reader,

Figure 2-3 Input.
(a) The most widely used input device is the keyboard. The mouse, under the user's right hand, is a common substitute for some keyboard functions. Movement of the mouse on a flat surface causes corresponding movement of a pointer on the screen. (b) To input data, this wand reader scans special letters and numbers on price tags. Wand readers are often found in department stores. (c) Bar code readers are used in supermarkets to input the bar codes found on product labels.

(a)

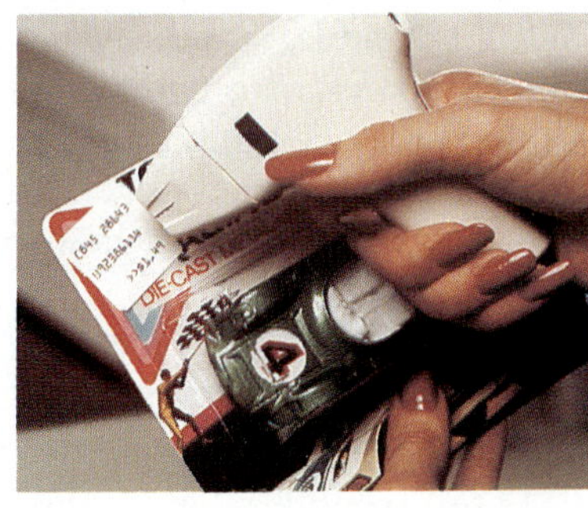

(b)

(c)

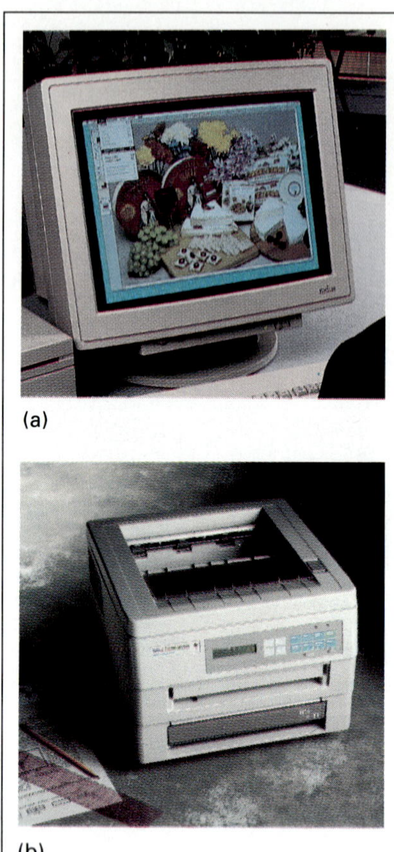

▲
Figure 2-4 Output.
Screens and printers are two types of output devices. (a) The graphics displayed on this screen are one form of output. (b) This laser printer produces output in the form of printed documents.

or bar code reader, for instance; (2) an output device—usually a television-like **screen;** and (3) a connection to the main computer. The screen displays the data that has been input. After the computer processes this data, the screen displays the results of the processing—the information you wanted. In a store, for instance, the terminal screen displays the individual prices (the data) and the total cost (the desired information).

The Central Processing Unit and Memory: Data Manipulation

The **central processing unit,** or **CPU,** is the computer's center of activity. The central processing unit consists of electronic circuits that interpret and execute program instructions as well as communicate with the input, output, and storage devices.

It is the central processing unit that, using software, actually transforms data into information. **Data** is the raw materials to be processed by a computer. Such materials can be letters, numbers, or facts—such as grades in a class, baseball batting averages, or light and dark areas in a photograph. Processed data becomes **information**—data that is organized, meaningful, and useful. Data that is very uninteresting to one person may become very interesting information to another. The raw facts—the *data*—of births, eating habits, and growth rates of calves, for instance, may mean nothing to most people. But the computer-produced relationships among feed, growth, and beef quality are critical pieces of *information* to a cattle breeder.

Computer **memory,** also known as **primary storage,** is closely associated with the central processing unit but not actually part of it. Memory holds the data after it is input to the system but before it is processed. It also holds the data after it has been processed but before it has been released to the output device. In addition, memory holds the programs (computer instructions) needed by the central processing unit. Memory consists of electronic circuits, just as the CPU does.

Output: Information

The results produced by the central processing unit are, of course, a computer's whole reason for being; **output** is usable information. That is, raw input data has been processed by the computer into relevant and useful information. Some ingenious forms of output have been devised, such as music and synthetic speech, but the most common forms are words, numbers, and graphics. Words, for example, may be the letters and memos prepared by office workers using word processing software. Other workers may be more interested in numbers, such as those found in formulas, schedules, and budgets. As we will see, numbers can often be understood more easily when they are output in the form of computer graphics.

Two common output devices are screens and printers. You already read about screens when you read the description of input. Screens can show lines of text, a numerical display, or color graphics (Figure 2-4a).

Printers are machines that produce printed documents at the instruction of a computer program (Figure 2-4b). Some printers form typed images on paper as typewriters do; they strike a character against a rib-

COMPUTING TRENDS

Wearable Computers

Can it really be true? Will we soon be *wearing* our personal computers around our waists or necks, or perhaps slung over our shoulders? According to industry spokespersons, the personal computer is about to become such an integral part of our daily lives that we will indeed add it to our wardrobes. For those who need a keyboard on hand at all times, a notebook personal computer with a shoulder strap is underway. As for all the rest of the computer wardrobe accessories, we will have to wait a bit longer.

bon, which makes an image on the paper. Other printers form characters or graphics by using lasers, photography, or sprays of ink.

Secondary Storage

Secondary storage is additional storage that can hold data and programs permanently (recall that primary storage can hold data only temporarily). Secondary storage has several advantages. For instance, it would be unwise for a college registrar to try to house student records in computer memory; if this were done, the computer probably would not have room to store anything else. Also, memory holds data and programs only temporarily—hence the need for permanent secondary storage.

The two most common secondary storage media are magnetic disk and magnetic tape. A **magnetic disk** is a flat, oxide-coated disk on which data is recorded as magnetic spots. A disk can be a diskette or a hard disk. A **diskette,** usually 3½ inches in diameter (or perhaps 5¼ inches), is used with a personal computer and looks something like a small stereo record, although it is housed in a square container (Figure 2-5a). A **hard disk** is inflexible and is often in a sealed shell. Used by both small and large computers, hard disks hold more data and can store and retrieve data faster than diskettes. Hard disks usually hold the programs users need to perform tasks. Users in a public setting, such as a school lab or business office, usually keep their own data on diskettes they can take with them. Disk data is read by **disk drives** (Figure 2-5b).

Magnetic tape, which comes on a reel or in a cassette-like cartridge, is similar to tape that is played on a tape recorder. Magnetic tape reels are

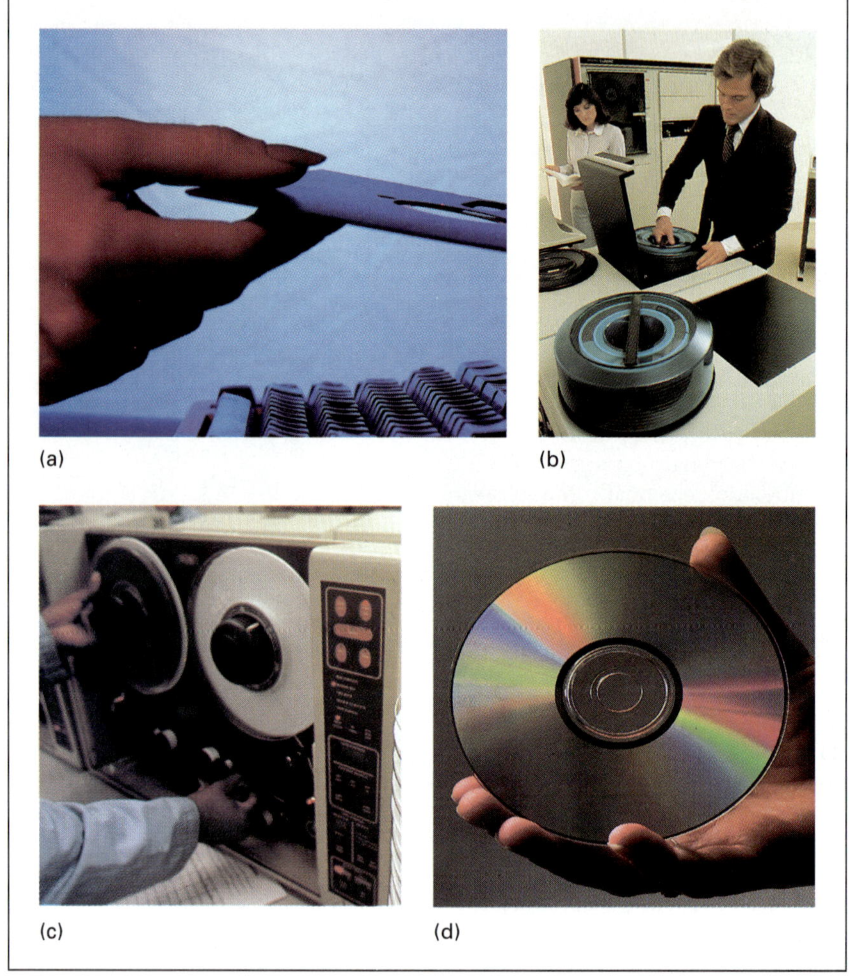

Figure 2-5 Secondary storage. (a) A 5¼-inch diskette is being inserted into a disk drive. (b) Hard disks are contained within the round disk pack shown on the top of the cabinets, which contain the disk drives. When it is to be used, a disk pack is lowered into the open compartment. (c) Magnetic tape, shown here being mounted on a tape drive, travels off one reel and onto another. (d) Optical disk technology uses a laser beam to store large volumes of data.

mounted on **tape drives** when the data on them must be read by the computer system or when new data is to be written on the tape (Figure 2-5c).

The most recent storage technology, however, is **optical disk,** which uses a laser beam to store large volumes of data at low cost (Figure 2-5d). This interesting medium, and its fascinating applications, will be explored in more detail in Chapter 5, which focuses on storage devices.

The Complete Hardware System

The hardware devices attached to the computer are called **peripheral equipment.** Peripheral equipment includes all input, output, and secondary storage devices. In the case of personal computers, some of the input, output, and storage devices are built into the same physical unit. In the personal computer we saw in Figure 2-2, for instance, the CPU and disk drive are contained in the same housing; the keyboard and screen are separate.

In larger computer systems, however, the input, processing, output, and storage functions may be in separate rooms, separate buildings, or even separate countries. For example, data may be input on terminals at a branch bank and then transmitted to the central processing unit at the bank's headquarters. The information produced by the central processing unit may then be transmitted to the bank's international offices, where it is printed out. Meanwhile, disks with stored data may be kept in the bank's headquarters, and duplicate data may be kept on disk or tape for safekeeping in a warehouse across town.

Although the equipment may vary widely, from the simplest computer to the most powerful, by and large the four elements of a computer system remain the same: input, processing, output, and storage. Now let us look at the various ways computers are classified.

Computer Classifications: Diminishing Differences

Computers come in sizes from tiny to monstrous, in both appearance and power. The size of a computer that a person or an organization needs depends on the computing requirements. The National Weather Service, keeping watch on the weather fronts of many continents, has different requirements from those of a car dealer's service department that is trying to keep track of its parts inventory. The requirements of both of them are different from the needs of a salesperson using a small hand-held computer to record client orders on a sales trip.

Supercomputers

The mightiest computers—and, of course, the most expensive—are known as **supercomputers** (Figure 2-6a). Supercomputers process *billions* of instructions per second. If you ever work for the federal government in an area such as worldwide weather forecasting, oil exploration, and weapons research, you might use a supercomputer. Supercomputers are now moving toward the mainstream for activities as varied as creating special effects for movies and analyzing muscle structures. Supercomputers can also produce super graphics (Figure 2-7).

Mainframes

In the jargon of the computer trade, "ordinary" large computers are called **mainframes** (Figure 2-6b). Mainframes are capable of processing data at very fast speeds—several million program instructions per second, for example—and they have access to billions of characters of data. The price of a mainframe varies from several hundred thousand to many millions of dollars. With that kind of price tag, you will not buy a mainframe for just any purpose. The principal use of such a powerful computer is for processing vast amounts of data quickly. You will be most likely to use a mainframe if you work for a bank, an insurance company, a government agency, a utility company, or a manufacturer. This list is not all-inclusive; you might also use such a computer if you ever work for a large mail-order house, an airline with a sophisticated reservations system, an aerospace company doing complex aircraft design, or the like.

Minicomputers

The next step down from mainframe computers are **minicomputers** (Figure 2-6c). Minicomputers are generally slower than mainframes and are less costly. In fact, when minicomputers first appeared on the market,

(a) (b) (c) (d)

Figure 2-6 Computer classifications.
(a) The Cray-2 supercomputer has been nicknamed Bubbles because of its bubbling, shimmering coolant liquids. You can own it for a mere $17.6 million. (b) Shown here is the Control Data 7600 mainframe computer. Despite the sterile look of this staged photo, it does show that a mainframe computer has many components. (c) The VAX, a popular minicomputer made by Digital Equipment Corporation (DEC). (d) This personal computer is made by Macintosh.

their lower price fell within the range of many small businesses, greatly expanding the potential number of computer users.

Minicomputers were originally intended to be small and serve some special purpose. However, in a fairly short time they became more powerful and more versatile, and the line between minicomputer and mainframe has blurred. In fact, the appellation *mini* no longer seems to fit very well. The term **supermini** has been coined to describe minis at the top of the speed/price scale. If you ever work in a retail business, a small college, or a state or city agency, you may use a minicomputer. However, the market for minicomputers, and for mainframes, too, is diminishing as buyers choose computers that are less expensive and nearly as powerful: microcomputers.

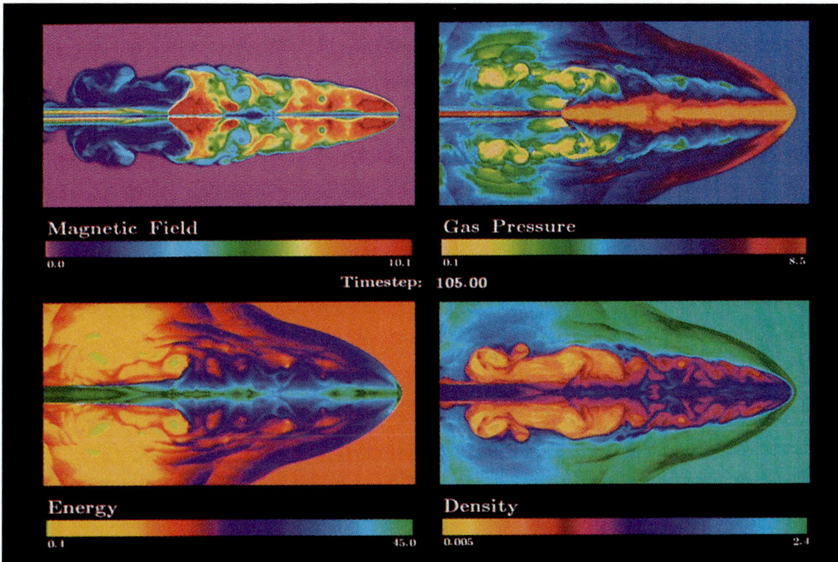

Figure 2-7 Super supercomputers. These graphics, prepared on a supercomputer, represent a magnetic field, gas pressure, energy, and density.

Microcomputers

Computers that are the next step down in size are called **microcomputers** (Figure 2-6d). Microcomputers are often called by other names, such as desktop, home, or personal computers; we will use the common name **personal computer (PC)** in this book. For many years, the computer industry was on a quest for the biggest computer; the search was always for more power and greater capacity. Prognosticators who timidly suggested a niche for a smaller computer were subject to ridicule by people who, as it turned out, could not have been more wrong. Now, for a few hundred dollars, anyone can have a small computer. (Most people, however, are more likely to choose a computer that costs a few *thousand* dollars.) **Supermicros**, generally faster and more powerful than other personal computers, are found in offices that use the top of the line. Supermicros have significantly increased memory and hard disk storage capacity.

Laptop computers

A computer that fits in a briefcase? A computer that weighs less than a newborn baby? A computer you do not have to plug in? A computer to use on your lap on an airplane? Yes, to all these questions. **Laptop computers,** also called **notebook computers,** are wonderfully portable and functional, and popular with travelers who need a computer that can go with them (Figure 2-8). Most laptops accept diskettes, so it is easy to move data from one computer to another. Laptops are not as inexpensive as their size might suggest; many carry a price tag equivalent to a full-size personal computer for business.

Getting smaller still

Using a pen-like stylus, **pen-based computers** accept handwritten input directly on a screen (Figure 2-9). Users of the hand-held pen-based computers, also called **personal digital assistants (PDAs),** are mainly people in companies who want to automate the work of their clipboard-carrying workers, such as parcel delivery drivers and meter readers.

(a)

(b)

(c)

Figure 2-8 Laptops
All these users, whether in the office or working outdoors, find it convenient to use laptop computers.

Other potential users are workers who cannot easily use a laptop computer because they are on their feet all day: nurses, sales reps, real estate agents, and insurance adjusters.

Software

When you first interact with a computer system—whether at school, at home, or on the job—you will probably be captivated by the hardware.

Figure 2-9 Pen-based computers.
Workers on the job sometimes prefer lightweight pen-based computers, which will accept handwritten input.

But you will soon discover that it is really the software—the planned, step-by-step instructions required to turn data into information—that makes a computer useful.

Categories of Software

Generally speaking, software can be categorized as system software or applications software. **System software,** also called **operating systems,** is the underlying software found on all computers. **Applications software** is software that is *applied*, or put to use, to solve a particular problem or perform a particular task. Applications software may be either custom or packaged. Many large organizations pay programmers to write **custom software**—software that is specifically tailored to their needs. The average person is most likely to deal with **packaged software,** also called commercial software—the software that is literally packaged in a container of some sort, usually a box or folder, and sold in stores or catalogs. Packaged software for personal computers often comes in a box as colorful as a Monopoly game. Inside the box you will find one or more diskettes holding the software and an instruction manual, also referred to as **documentation** (Figure 2-10). To use the software, you begin by inserting the diskette in the disk drive. Then,

Personal Computers In Action

But What Would I Use It For?

In addition to the general categories we have mentioned in the text, there are some very specific—and idiosyncratic—software packages that find their way into home computers. See if any of the offerings in this sampler appeal to you.

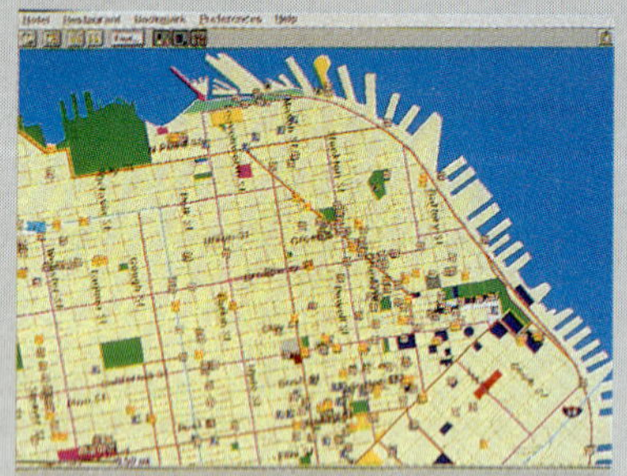

- **Taxis.** If you are a frequent traveler to—or live in—a big city, you will appreciate what the New York Times calls "one of the hottest new guidebooks of the decade." The software provides a unique combination of mapping ability and ratings of hotels and restaurants. Cities currently available are New York, Chicago, Los Angeles, San Francisco, and Washington, D.C. (from Zagat-Axxis)
- **Calendar Creator Plus.** Create your own customized calendar, a whole month at a time, to hang on the refrigerator. You can list single or recurring events and include graphics icons for drama. Try these icons: a gift box (birthday), football (the big game), or a tooth (dentist appointment). (from Power Up!)
- **Auto Insight.** Learn how a car works with software that takes you on a journey through the inner workings of a car. Check out the braking system, cooling system, engine, steering, suspension, fuel injection system, transmission, emission control, and more.
- **Design and Build Your Deck.** This software lets you lay out a simple deck just by manipulating an image on the screen, using a mouse. You can view your design from the top, the side, or in a realistic 3-D view. As you change the deck's size and shape, and add stairs and railings, the program automatically creates the necessary structural underpinnings and updates a list of materials needed and a cost estimate. (from Books That Work)

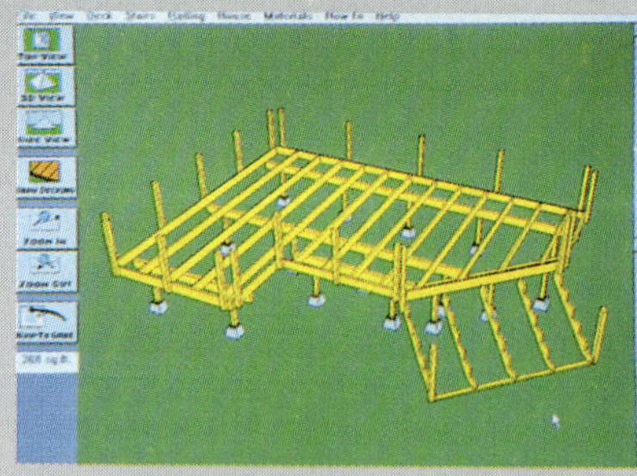

- **Roots.** If you have studied your family's history, you know how much fun—and how confusing—it can be. Easy enough for amateurs but powerful enough for professionals, Roots provides an organizational framework to help you untangle the family data. Its

depending on the hardware and software, you either type specified instructions on the keyboard or give a command with the click of a mouse to begin running the software on the computer.

There is a great assortment of software to help you with a variety of tasks—writing papers, preparing budgets, drawing graphs, playing games, and more. The wonderful array of software available is what makes computers so useful.

Most personal computer software is planned to be user friendly. The term **user friendly** has become a cliché, but it still conveys meaning. It usually means that the software is supposed to be easy—perhaps even intuitive—for a beginner to use or that the software can be used with a minimum of training. Even so, such software may seem overwhelming at

searching and sorting capabilities let you note relationships among newly discovered ancestors. You can look up family members by name, date, location, and more. (from Commsoft)

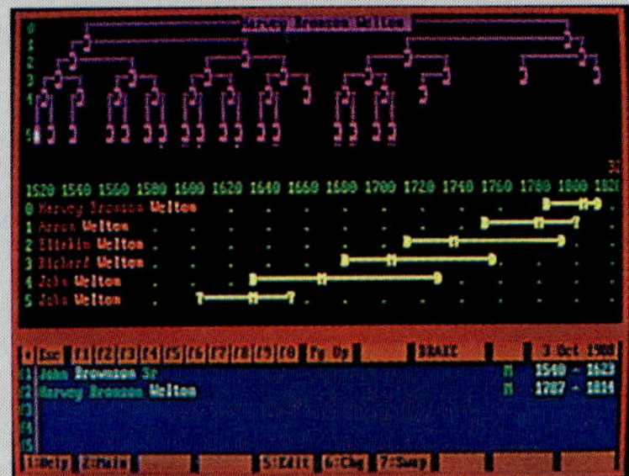

- **Print Shop.** Design cards, posters, banners, or invitations that use a built-in art library of ready-made pictures and symbols and a dozen backgrounds and borders. Choose type style and size, all with optional outline and three-dimensional effects. You cannot produce cards that are as nice looking as those you buy in a store, but you can say, "Look Mom, I made it myself." (from Broderbund)
- **Orbits: Voyage Through the Solar System.** Explore the mountains of the moon, the rings of Saturn, the coronas of the sun, and other worlds through full-color animation and 3-D graphics. (from Software Marketing Corporation)

- **The Running Program.** Take just a few minutes each day to input your running data so that the program can produce graphs of how you performed over different distances at different paces. It also has screens full of advice—from warm-up exercises (including graphic demonstrations) to remedies for knee pains to what you should wear. About the only thing it does not do is get you out of bed in the morning. (from MECA Software)
- **World Atlas.** It's an atlas, an almanac, and a fact book all in one. The screen maps are especially useful with a mouse: just point and click on a country, state, or city and be supplied with facts such as population and an array of climatic information. (from Power Up!)
- **Personal Physician.** Mindful of soaring medical costs, ordinary folks are using their personal computers as supplements to MDs. This software quizzes you on-screen about symptoms, suggests treatment, and (dubiously) comes with a real stethoscope. (from FamilyCare Software)
- **Personal Law Firm.** Write your own will, leases, contracts, or prenuptial agreement. Just answer simple on-screen questions. The forms are valid in all states except Louisiana. (from BLOC Publishing)
- **Flight Simulator.** Climb into the cockpit of a Cessna 182 and get ready for almost anything in a flight simulation so realistic that even licensed pilots have their hands full with it. More than a game, this approaches training and is a real challenge. (from Microsoft)

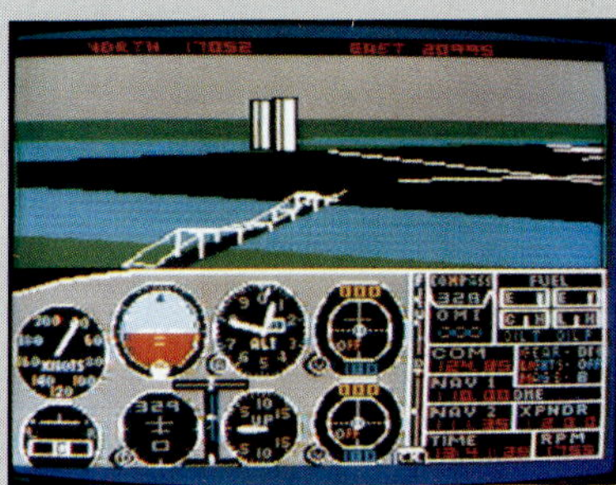

first. Although software is usually generalized enough to be marketed to a broad audience, it is possible to set up the features of the software to match a particular user's needs.

Some Task-Oriented Software

Most users, whether at home or in business, are drawn to task-oriented software, sometimes called productivity software, that can make their work faster and their lives easier. The collective set of business tasks is limited, and the number of general paths toward performing these tasks is limited, too. Thus, the tasks and the software solutions fall, for the most part, into just a few categories that can be found in most business environments. These major categories are word processing (including

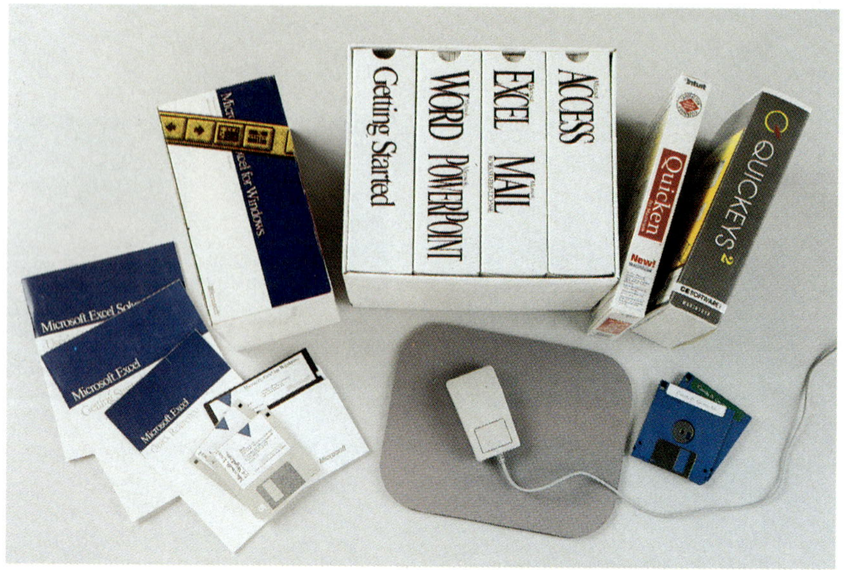

Figure 2-10 Packaged software. Each of the software packages shown here includes one or more disks containing the software needed to run the program and an instruction manual, or documentation, describing how to use the software.

desktop publishing), spreadsheets, database management, graphics, and communications. We will present a description of each category here.

Word Processing

The most widely used software is for **word processing.** This software lets you create, edit, format, store, and print text. From this definition, it is the three words in the middle—*edit*, *format*, and *store*—that make word processing different from plain typing. Since you can store on disk the memo or document you type, you can retrieve it another time, change its content or appearance, save it again, and reprint it. The timesaving factor is that the unchanged parts of the saved document do not need to be retyped, and the whole document can be reprinted as if new. Businesses use word processing for every conceivable type of document—in fact, for everything that used to be typed.

In the task called **desktop publishing,** users employ software and a high-quality printer to produce printed materials that combine graphics with text. The resulting professional-looking newsletters, reports, and brochures can improve communication and help organizations make a better impression on the outside world (Figure 2-11). Although sophisticated users invoke software specifically designed for desktop publishing, many users produce similar results with the desktop publishing features inherent in their word processing software. Since publishing in one form or another typically consumes up to 10 percent of a company's gross revenues, desktop publishing has been given a warm welcome by business. Home users are becoming just as captivated by this technology, as evidenced by the improved look of club newsletters and other "homemade" publications you may find in your mailbox.

Spreadsheets

Used to organize and analyze business data, a **spreadsheet** is a worksheet divided into columns and rows. For example, the simple expense spreadsheet in Figure 2-12a shows time periods (months) as columns and

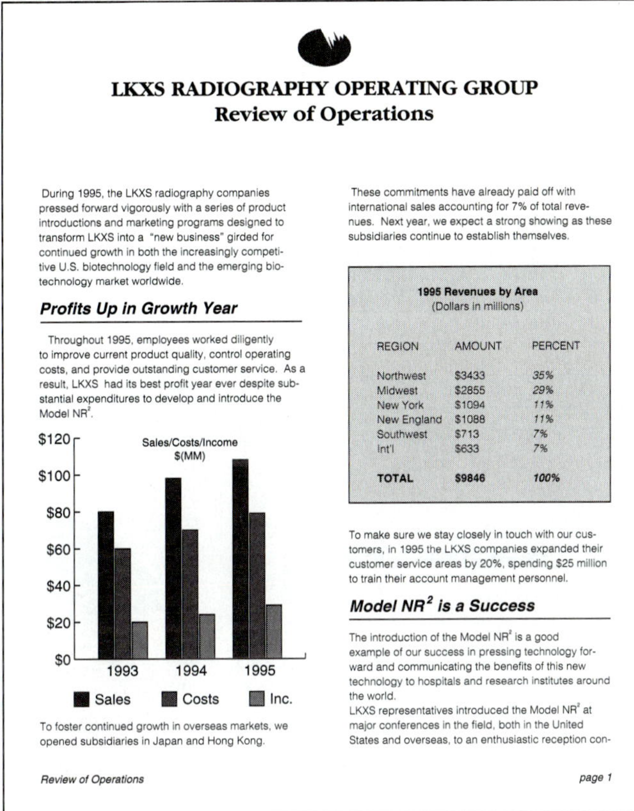

LKXS RADIOGRAPHY OPERATING GROUP
Review of Operations

During 1995, the LKXS radiography companies pressed forward vigorously with a series of product introductions and marketing programs designed to transform LKXS into a "new business" girded for continued growth in both the increasingly competitive U.S. biotechnology field and the emerging biotechnology market worldwide.

Profits Up in Growth Year

Throughout 1995, employees worked diligently to improve current product quality, control operating costs, and provide outstanding customer service. As a result, LKXS had its best profit year ever despite substantial expenditures to develop and introduce the Model NR^2.

To foster continued growth in overseas markets, we opened subsidiaries in Japan and Hong Kong.

These commitments have already paid off with international sales accounting for 7% of total revenues. Next year, we expect a strong showing as these subsidiaries continue to establish themselves.

1995 Revenues by Area
(Dollars in millions)

REGION	AMOUNT	PERCENT
Northwest	$3433	*35%*
Midwest	$2855	*29%*
New York	$1094	*11%*
New England	$1088	*11%*
Southwest	$713	*7%*
Int'l	$633	*7%*
TOTAL	**$9846**	***100%***

To make sure we stay closely in touch with our customers, in 1995 the LKXS companies expanded their customer service areas by 20%, spending $25 million to train their account management personnel.

Model NR^2 is a Success

The introduction of the Model NR^2 is a good example of our success in pressing technology forward and communicating the benefits of this new technology to hospitals and research institutes around the world.
LKXS representatives introduced the Model NR^2 at major conferences in the field, both in the United States and overseas, to an enthusiastic reception con-

Review of Operations *page 1*

Figure 2-11 Desktop publishing. Desktop publishing software lets users produce attractive output that combines text and graphics.

various categories (rent, phone, and so forth) as rows. Notice the calculations: the figures in the rightmost column are the sums of the items in that row—the expense total—and the figures in the last row are the sum of the items in that column—the month total. Manual spreadsheets have been used as business tools for centuries. But a spreadsheet can be tedious to prepare by hand, and when there are changes a considerable amount of work may need to be redone. An **electronic spreadsheet** (Figure 2-12b) is still a spreadsheet, but the computer does much of the work. In particular, spreadsheet software automatically recalculates the results when a number used in calculations is changed. The ability to automatically recalculate lets businesses experiment with numbers based on different forecasts or predictions—a kind of experimentation called "What-if" analysis—and obtain the results quickly. Many spreadsheet programs will also convert the spreadsheet into a graph or chart (Figure 2-12c).

Database Management

Software used for **database management,** a variation on old-fashioned record keeping, is the management of a collection of interrelated facts. The software can store data, update it, manipulate it, and create reports in a variety of forms. A concert promoter, for example, can store and change data about upcoming concert dates, seating, ticket prices, and sales. The promoter can then use the software to retrieve information such as the number of tickets sold in each price range or the percentage of tickets sold the day before the concert. The promotor could list events

EXPENSES	JANUARY	FEBRUARY	MARCH	APRIL	TOTAL
RENT	425.00	425.00	425.00	425.00	1700.00
PHONE	22.50	31.25	17.00	35.75	106.50
CLOTHES	110.00	135.00	156.00	91.00	492.00
FOOD	280.00	250.00	250.00	300.00	1080.00
HEAT	80.00	50.00	24.00	95.00	249.00
ELECTRICITY	35.75	40.50	45.00	36.50	157.75
WATER	10.00	11.00	11.00	10.50	42.50
CAR INSURANCE	75.00	75.00	75.00	75.00	300.00
ENTERTAINMENT	150.00	125.00	140.00	175.00	590.00
TOTAL	1188.25	1142.75	1143.00	1243.75	4717.75

(a)

	A	B	C	D	E	F	G
1							
2		JAN	FEB	MAR	APR	TOTAL	
3							
4	EXPENSES						
5	RENT	425.00	425.00	425.00	425.00	1700.00	
6	PHONE	22.50	31.25	17.00	35.75	106.50	
7	CLOTHES	110.00	135.00	156.00	91.00	492.00	
8	FOOD	280.00	250.00	250.00	300.00	1080.00	
9	HEAT	80.00	50.00	24.00	95.00	249.00	
10	ELECTRICITY	35.75	40.50	45.00	36.50	157.75	
11	WATER	10.00	11.00	11.00	10.50	42.50	
12	CAR INSURANCE	75.00	75.00	75.00	75.00	300.00	
13	ENTERTAINMENT	150.00	125.00	140.00	175.00	590.00	
14							
15							
16	TOTAL	1188.25	1142.75	1143.00	1243.75	4717.75	
17							
18							
19							
20							
21							

02:39 PM

(b)

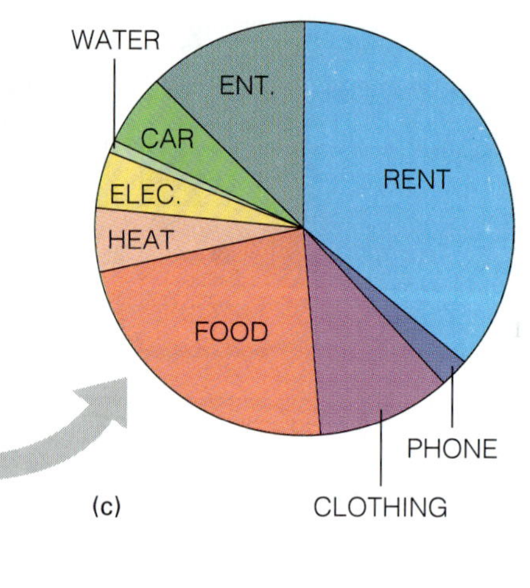

(c)

Figure 2-12 A simple expense spreadsheet.
(a) This expense sheet is a typical spreadsheet of rows and columns. Note the calculations needed to generate the values in the rightmost column and the bottom row. (b) This spreadsheet summarizes the same information, but now the computer is doing the calculations. (c) Here the same information has been transformed into a simple computer-generated pie chart.

in order of data or ticket price. Database software can be useful to keep track of and extract subsets from large amounts of data.

Graphics

Maps, charts, and other **graphics** help people compare data, spot trends easily, and make decisions quickly (Figure 2-13). Six pages of numeric

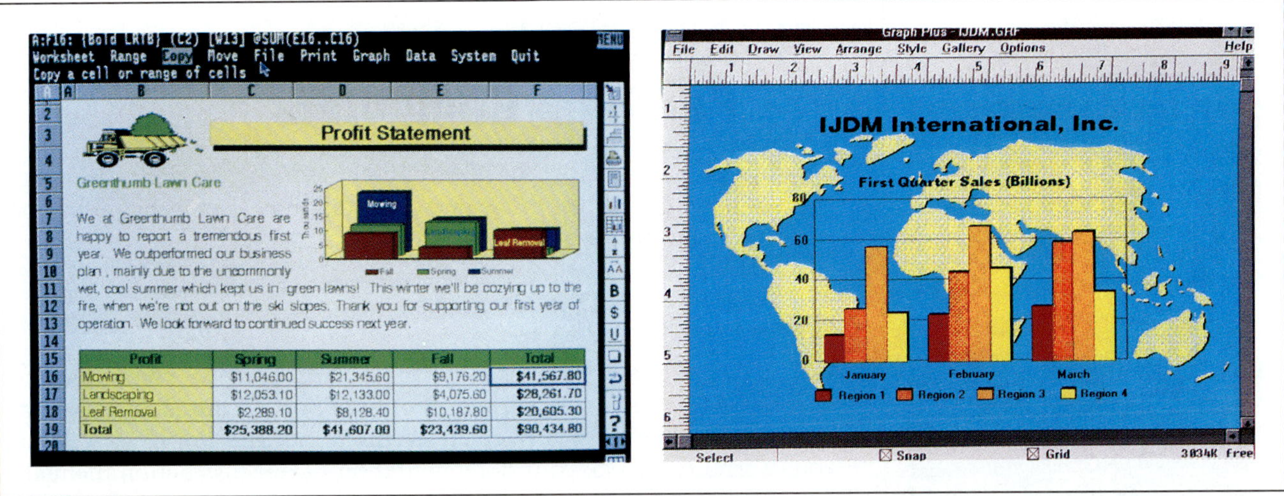

Figure 2-13 Business graphics.
These colorful computer-generated graphics can help people compare data and spot trends.

confusion can be made into a single chart that anyone can pick up and understand.

Communications

From the viewpoint of a worker with a personal computer, data communications means—in simple terms—that he or she can link up the computer with the phone system or some other communications link and send data to or receive data from a computer in another location. Business users send memos, exchange project data, leave messages, send data to the headquarters office, access stock quotes, and on and on. Home users send greetings to friends and family who have computers, transfer bank funds, buy stocks, make airline reservations, access data banks such as encyclopedias, and even order products.

People and Computers

We have talked about hardware, software, and data, but the most important element in a computer system is people. Anyone nervous about a takeover by computers will be relieved to know that computers will never amount to much without people—the people who help make the system work and the people for whom the work is done.

As we noted earlier, computer users now are simply called users, a nickname that has persisted for years. Whereas once computer users were an elite breed—high-powered Ph.D.s, research-and-development engineers, government planners—the population of users has broadened considerably. This expansion is due partly to user-friendly software for both work and personal use and partly to the availability of small, low-cost computers.

So, I Don't Have to Be a Techie

To be computer literate, you do need to have some knowledge of the terminology. But, to put it in the vernacular, you do not have to become a professional "techie." Just what computer-related skills *are* desirable to take to the job world? Here is one person's list of the subjects you should know something about, no matter what career you pursue: word processing, desktop publishing, spreadsheets, graphics, databases, communications, interfacing with operating system software, getting on and off a computer network, using electronic mail, using fax software, buying a computer and peripherals, evaluating and buying software, and computer security and ethics.

It is too soon in your course of study to have even a passing acquaintance with all these concepts. But it is not too soon to set goals and begin meeting them.

A Closer Look at Personal Computers

We have taken a general tour of computer hardware, but for most people the computer of interest is the personal computer. Let us begin by considering what is inside a personal computer.

Basic Components

It is really pretty easy to have a look inside most personal computers; you may not even need a screwdriver. (Caution: Some manufacturers are *not* interested in having you peer under the hood, and doing so will void your warranty. Check your documentation—your instruction manual—first.) You will find an impressive array of electronic gear. If you look inside your personal computer, part of what you see before you is the central processing unit and memory.

A miniaturized central processing unit can be etched on a chip smaller than a thumbtack (Figure 2-14), hence the term *computer on a chip.* A central processing unit on a chip is called a **microprocessor.** The type of microprocessor in your personal computer depends on the computer you purchased. In addition to the microprocessor, a personal computer has two kinds of memory chips: random access memory (RAM) and read-only memory (ROM). **Random access memory (RAM)** chips hold the data and instructions currently being used. **Read-only memory (ROM)** stores programs that you cannot alter. We will explore microprocessors and memory components in some detail in Chapter 3.

External computer components vary. You need a keyboard, of course, so you can interact with the computer. Also, you need a video screen to display input and output. Most personal computers have a separate screen (or monitor) and a detached keyboard, so the positions of these components can be adjusted for individual comfort.

For secondary storage purposes, you need a disk drive to read and write on diskettes and, in particular, to load software into the computer. In addition, hard disks are available for most personal computers.

Basic personal computer hardware consists of memory, a central processing unit, a keyboard, a screen, and a storage device. In addition, most systems have a printer; paper is a communication medium that is hard to do without. The printers most often used with personal computers are dot-matrix and laser printers. Printers are described in more detail in Chapter 4 and in the "Buyer's Guide."

Additional Equipment

You have seen people buy every kind of gadget for their boat or car or camper. For computer users, the story is no different. In this discussion *add-ons* refers loosely to any device that attaches to the computer so that it can participate in the computer's work. An example is a mouse or an extra disk drive. *Accessories* are convenience items—such as dustcovers, lockup cables, and diskette trays—that are not directly related to the

Chapter Review

Summary and Key Terms

- The equipment in a computer system is called **hardware.** The **programs,** or step-by-step instructions that run the machines, are called **software. Computer programmers** write programs for **users,** or **end-users**—that is, people who use computer software.
- A **computer** is a machine that can be programmed to process data (input) into useful information (output). A computer system comprises four main categories of data handling—input, processing, output, and storage.
- **Input** is data put into the computer. Common **input devices** include a **keyboard;** a **mouse;** a **wand reader,** which scans special letters and numbers such as those on specially printed price tags in retail stores; and a **bar code reader,** which scans the zebra-striped **bar codes** on store products.
- A **terminal** includes an input device; an **output device,** usually a television-like **screen;** and a connection to the main computer. A screen displays both the input data and the processed information.
- The **central processing unit (CPU)** uses software to organize raw **data** into meaningful, useful **information.** It interprets and executes program instructions and communicates with the input, output, and storage devices. **Memory,** also called **primary storage,** is associated with the central processing unit but is separate from it. Memory holds the input data before and after processing, until the data is released to the output device.
- **Output,** raw data processed into usable information, is usually in the form of words, numbers, and graphics. Users can see output displayed on screens and use **printers** to display output on paper.
- Computer memory is limited and temporary. Therefore, **secondary storage** is needed, most commonly in the form of magnetic disks and magnetic tape. **Magnetic disks** can be diskettes or hard disks. **Diskettes** are usually 3½ inches (or perhaps 5¼ inches) in diameter. **Hard disks,** often contained in disk packs, hold more data than a diskette. Disk data is read by **disk drives. Magnetic tape** comes on reels that are mounted on **tape drives** when the data is to be read by the computer. **Optical disk** technology uses a laser beam to store large volumes of data relatively inexpensively.
- **Peripheral equipment** includes all the input, output, and secondary storage devices attached to a computer.
- Computers can be loosely categorized according to their capacity for processing data. The most powerful and expensive computers are called **supercomputers.** Large computers are called **mainframes. Minicomputers** were originally intended to be small but have become increasingly similar to mainframes in capacity. Therefore, the largest and most expensive minicomputers are now called **superminis.** The next step down in size are **microcomputers** or **personal computers (PCs). Supermicros,** generally faster and more powerful than other personal computers, have significantly increased memory and hard disk storage capacity. **Laptop computers,** also called **notebook computers,** are small portable computers. **Pen-based computers,** also called **personal digital assistants (PDAs),** accept handwritten input directly on a screen.
- **System software,** also called **operating systems,** is the underlying software found on all computers. **Applications software** solves a particular problem or performs a particular task. Applications software may be either custom or packaged. **Custom software** is

specifically tailored to user needs. **Packaged software,** also called commercial software, is packaged in a container and sold in stores or catalogs.

- Software is accompanied by an instruction manual, also called **documentation.** Software that is easy to use is considered **user friendly.**
- Task-oriented software falls, for the most part, into just a few categories: **word processing, desktop publishing, spreadsheet (or electronic spreadsheet), database management, graphics,** and **communications.**
- The main components of a personal computer are the microprocessor, random access memory (RAM), and read-only memory (ROM). A keyboard is used for inputting data, and a video screen displays input and output. A disk drive is used for reading and writing diskettes.
- A **microprocessor,** also called a computer on a chip, contains the computer's central processing unit. **Random access memory (RAM)** chips hold the data and instructions currently being used. **Read-only memory (ROM)** stores programs that cannot be altered by the user.
- *Add-ons* refers to devices that attach to the computer so that they can participate in the computer's work. *Accessories* are convenience items that are not directly related to the computer's work. *Supplies* are necessary consumable goods, such as printer paper.
- Expandable computers allow users to insert additional circuit boards into **expansion slots** inside the computers. Nonexpandable computers limit add-ons to those that can be plugged into the back of the computers.

Student Personal Study Guide

True/False

T F 1. The processor is also called the central processing unit, or CPU.
T F 2. Secondary storage units contain the instructions and data to be used immediately by the processor.
T F 3. Desktop publishing software is used primarily to store and retrieve information.
T F 4. Processed data that is organized, meaningful, and useful is called information.
T F 5. *User friendly* refers to a special kind of terminal.
T F 6. To use a computer, you need not know its internal functions.
T F 7. PDAs are also called mainframes.
T F 8. Mainframes are also called notebook computers.
T F 9. Computers can be classified, smallest to largest, as mainframes, microcomputers, or minicomputers.
T F 10. Custom software may be purchased off the shelf.

Multiple Choice

1. Holds instructions and data for processing:
   a. CPU c. RAM
   b. slot d. microprocessor
2. The storage technology that uses laser beams:
   a. optical tape c. magnetic tape
   b. magnetic disk d. optical disk
3. Another name for programs:
   a. software c. data
   b. RAM d. storage

4. Storage and retrieval of data is a key function of:
   a. desktop publishing   c. graphics
   b. database management   d. documentation
5. Software that prints high-quality combined text and graphics:
   a. spreadsheets   c. word processing
   b. desktop publishing   d. graphics
6. A "computer on a chip":
   a. RAM   c. optical disk
   b. microprocessor   d. primary storage
7. The zebra-striped identifier on a store product:
   a. key   c. bar code
   b. magnetic tape   d. wand
8. One type of secondary storage:
   a. RAM   c. wand reader
   b. mouse   d. optical disk
9. The computer converts raw data into:
   a. input   c. custom software
   b. processor   d. information
10. Another name for memory:
   a. primary storage   c. diskette
   b. hard disk   d. secondary storage

Fill-In

1. After it is input but just before it is processed, data is held in ____________________.
2. The input, output, and secondary storage devices attached to a computer are called ____________________.
3. Another name for laptop computers is ____________________.
4. Another name for personal digital assistants is ____________________.
5. Software to help people compare data and spot trends at a glance is called ____________________.
6. Computers linked together are said to be part of a ____________________.
7. Software that is easy to use is said to be ____________________.
8. Software created for a specific user is called ____________________.
9. The planned step-by-step instructions required to turn data into information are ____________________.
10. The most powerful computers are called ____________________.

Answers

True/False: 1. T, 2. F, 3. F, 4. T, 5. F, 6. T, 7. F, 8. F, 9. F, 10. F
Multiple choice: 1. c, 2. d , 3. a , 4. b, 5. b, 6. b, 7. c, 8. d, 9. d, 10. a
Fill-In: 1. memory, 2. peripheral equipment, 3. notebook, 4. pen-based computers, 5. graphics, 6. network, 7. user friendly, 8. custom , 9. software (or program), 10. supercomputers

Interview: The Information Superhighway

Randy Katz, who works for the Advanced Research Projects Agency (ARPA) of the Department of Defense, talks about the information superhighway.

Can you start with a little bit about your background?
I'm a professor of computer science at the University of California at Berkeley. After the 1992 election, I got excited about a bunch of young guys coming to Washington who seemed to have high technology as part of their agenda. I took a leave from the university to become a program manager at ARPA, which has a long tradition of being the federal government's lead agency in technology research and development.

Is it possible to give a simple explanation of the information superhighway?
OK. Everyone understands what a highway is. Before we had the interstate highway system, just about everything you purchased was grown or built locally. It would have been pretty unusual for someone in Florida to be eating apples that were grown in Washington state. But once the highway system was in place, in the 1950s, it opened up new markets. It really didn't matter where the stuff was produced; it could be sold anywhere in the country.

Now we'll do the same thing for information services. It doesn't matter where the information is located. The Library of Congress may have fabulous collections of ancient books and, if I am in Nebraska, I don't have to get on an airplane and fly to Washington, D.C., to gain access to those reference materials. The information is available by tapping into the information superhighway. Any information that is available anyplace can be accessed anywhere in the country if I'm on the information superhighway.

How does the information superhighway differ from the online services that we already have available, such as America Online or Internet?
Those services are early versions of the information superhighway. The problem is that they must be accessed through a computer, and computers are not in every home. But most homes in the United States do have a telephone and a television set, and almost

Exploring

PART 2

Hardware

everyone knows how to use them. These are the sort of components to consider for the information superhighway.

But what will the people connection to the information superhighway actually look like?

The truth is no one really knows. For one approach, industry is making major investments to incorporate the television system as part of the information superhighway. Your television will be like a computer screen, but it doesn't have a keyboard or anything like that. You would have some sort of remote control device, sort of like the one you use with your television now, that you would use to make selections from menus of services and information. A good example is a movie-on-demand service. You turn on your television set, then use a remote control device to make your selection. The fact that there might be a computer embedded in that television set is pretty much immaterial to the person who is using the television set.

How does the federal government fit into the development of the information superhighway?

Consider this true story. In the mid-1800s, Samuel Morse, with government research funding, put in the first telegraph link between Washington, D.C., and Baltimore. So the idea came from an entrepreneur in the private sector, but the money came from the government. People thought it was incredible that you could send a message 50 miles. So Morse said to the government, "Well, give me more money and we'll build this all around the country." But the government said, "No, if this is such a great idea, you should be able to provide your own backers to build a private sector system to do this," which is exactly what he did. And that's the basis of Western Union.

So the United States has a long tradition of a partnership in the early stages between the private sector and the federal government to demonstrate a concept, and then the private sector takes over. That's the model the government would like to have now for the information superhighway.

Any information that is available anyplace can be accessed anywhere in the country if I'm on the information superhighway.

When will we have an information superhighway in place?

I firmly believe that the information superhighway is a ten-year, if not longer, development process. However, in the next few years, from the government's perspective, I think there will be a complete revolution in the regulatory environment for telecommunications. They will open things up so there will be much greater competition.

Chapter Overview

Sue Ewing, an accounting major, worked with spreadsheets on a computer as part of her summer job. She decided that it would be helpful to have a personal computer of her own when she went back to college in the fall. But she felt unsure of how to make a purchase. In fact, she felt she did not even know what questions to ask. She discussed this with an office colleague, who casually noted that any computer setup comes with the "standard stuff"—processor, keyboard, screen, disk drives—and that all she had to do was go to a computer store and pick one that fit her price range. Sue was not satisfied with this approach, especially in light of the advertisements she had seen in the local newspaper and in computer magazines.

CHAPTER 3

Processing

What Goes On Inside the Computer

Most advertisements displayed photos of personal computers, accompanied by cryptic descriptions of the total hardware package. A typical ad was worded this way: *486DX, 50MHz, 8MB RAM, 128K cache, 1.44MB diskette drive, 320MB hard drive.* The price for this particular machine was pretty hefty—over $2000. Sue noticed in the ads that machines with lower numbers—for example, only 25MHz—also had lower price tags. Similarly, higher numbers meant higher price tags. Although she did recognize the term *disk drives*, she had no idea what the other items were or why the numbers mattered. Clearly, there was more to a purchasing decision than selecting a system with the "standard stuff."

Sue tore out some of the ads and marched to a nearby computer store. After asking a lot of questions, she learned that *486* is a type of microprocessor, that *MHz* stands for megahertz and is a measurement of the microprocessor's speed, that *RAM* is the computer's memory, that *cache* is a kind of handy storage place for frequently used data and software instructions, and that *MB* is an abbreviation for megabytes, a measurement of the capacity of some parts of the computer. All this was somewhat understandable, but she remained confused about the *DX* after the *486*—something about a *bus line*, a way for data to travel around. Most importantly, Sue learned that the number variations mattered because they were factors in determining the computer's capacity and speed.

Many buyers do select their personal computer systems merely on the basis of a sales pitch and price range. Those people could argue, with some success, that they do not need to know all the computer buzzwords any more than they need to know the technical details of their television sets or sound systems. They know that they do not have to understand a computer's innards to put it to work.

But there are rewards for those who want to dig a little deeper, learn a little more. Although this chapter is not designed to help you purchase a computer (see the "Buyer's Guide" for that), it does provide some background information and gives you the foundation on which future computer knowledge can be built.

The Central Processing Unit

The human element in computing is involved with data input and information output, but the controlling activities of the computer lie in between. The **central processing unit (CPU)** is a highly complex, extensive set of electrical circuits. It executes the stored program instructions that accept the input, process the data, and produce the output. As Figure 3-1 shows, it consists of two parts:

- The control unit
- The arithmetic/logic unit

Let us consider each of these components of the central processing unit.

The Control Unit

The **control unit** contains circuitry that uses electrical signals to direct and coordinate the entire computer system in carrying out, or executing,

Figure 3-1 The central processing unit.
The two parts of the CPU are the control unit and the arithmetic/logic unit. Memory holds data and instructions temporarily at the time the program is being executed. The CPU interacts closely with memory, referring to it for both instructions and data.

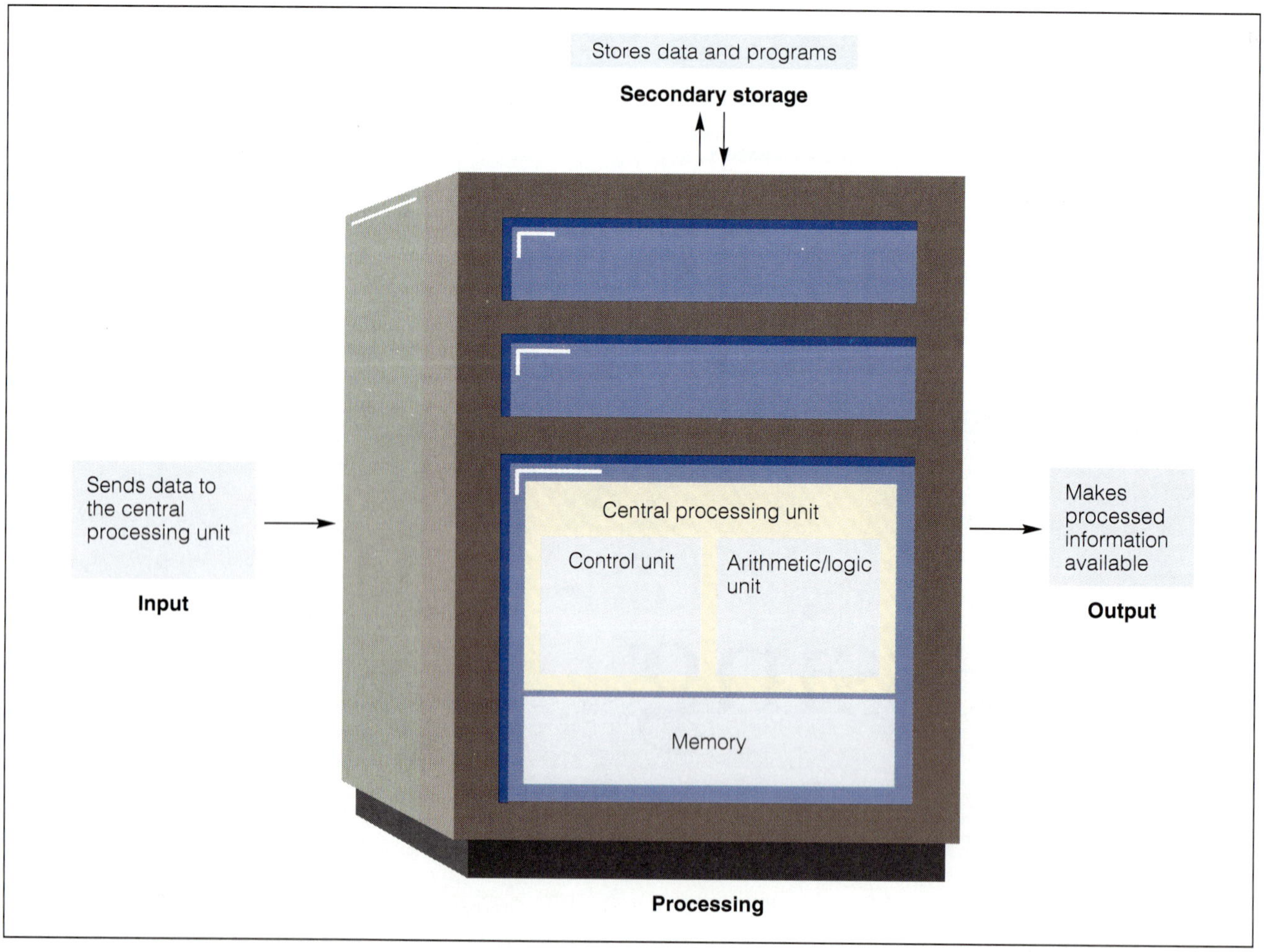

stored program instructions. Like an orchestra leader, the control unit does not execute the instructions itself; rather, it directs other parts of the system to do so. The control unit must communicate with both the arithmetic/logic unit and memory.

The Arithmetic/Logic Unit

The **arithmetic/logic unit (ALU)** contains the electronic circuitry that executes all **arithmetic operations,** such as addition and multiplication, and **logical operations,** which are usually comparing operations. The arithmetic/logic unit is able to compare numbers, letters, or special characters and take alternative courses of action. Comparing operations can determine whether one value is equal to, less than, or greater than another. This is a very important capability. It is by comparing that a computer is able to tell, for instance, whether an airplane has any unfilled seats, whether charge-card customers have exceeded their credit limits, or whether one candidate for Congress has more votes than another.

Registers: Temporary Storage Areas

As the control unit and the arithmetic/logic unit do their work, they use registers. **Registers** are temporary storage areas for instructions or data. Registers are associated with the CPU, not memory. They can operate very rapidly to accept, hold, and transfer instructions or data used in performing arithmetic or logical comparisons—all under the direction of the control unit of the CPU. In other words, they are temporary storage areas that assist transfers and arithmetic/logical operations.

Many machines assign special roles to certain types of registers, including

- An **accumulator,** which collects the results of computations.
- A **storage register,** which temporarily holds data taken from or about to be sent to memory.
- An **address register,** which tells where a given instruction or piece of data is stored in memory. Each storage location in memory is identified by an **address,** just as each apartment in an apartment building is identified by an address.
- A **general-purpose register,** which is used for several functions—for example, arithmetic and addressing purposes.

Consider registers in the context of the operation of the entire machine. Registers hold data *immediately* related to the operation being executed. Memory is used to store data that will be used in the *near future*. In contrast, secondary storage holds data that may be needed *later* in the same program execution or perhaps at some more remote time in the future. To compare the uses of registers, memory, and secondary storage, consider a payroll program as the computer calculates the salary of an employee. As the multiplication of hours worked by rate of pay of an employee is about to take place, these two figures are ready in their respective registers. Other data related to the salary calculation—overtime hours, bonuses, deductions, and so forth—is waiting nearby in memory. The data for other employees is available in secondary storage. As the computer continues executing the payroll program, the data for

Personal Computers In Action

A Computer in Your Pocket

When most people think of personal computers "in action," they picture someone sitting at a keyboard. What if your personal computer—or possibly one of your personal computers—were the size of your wallet? In fact, what if that tiny personal computer had everything in it that your wallet now carries, and also information that used to be maintained on your calendar or notebook?

Think about the contents of your wallet. Most of the items there are for some sort of identification: driver's license, credit cards, office entry key cards, perhaps a membership card for a health organization. Your pocket personal computer could contain all your authentication credentials, which could be displayed on a small flat screen. Furthermore, the computer could store important dates, meetings, and your daily schedule. It could even include pictures of the kids, whose smiling faces would beam from the screen on command.

This is part of the vision of the future put forth by Bill Gates, the energetic chairman of Microsoft Corporation, the world's largest software company. Noting that computers have made once-common items such as typewriters, ledger books, ticker tape, and adding machines pretty much obsolete, Gates thinks that the ordinary wallet will someday be added to that list.

the next employee is brought from secondary storage into memory and eventually into the registers as the calculations for that employee are ready to begin.

 Memory

Memory is also referred to as **primary storage, primary memory, main storage, internal storage,** and **main memory**—all these terms are used interchangeably. Memory (also called *random access memory*, or RAM, as noted in the previous chapter) is the part of the computer that holds data and instructions for processing. Although closely associated with the central processing unit, memory is technically separate from it. (However, specific items such as watches or microwave ovens may combine the CPU and memory on a single chip.) Memory is used only temporarily. That is, it holds your program and data only as long as your program is in operation. For this reason memory is often called the computer's scratch pad.

For the following reasons it is not feasible to keep your data in memory when your program is not running:

- Most types of memory store data only while the computer is turned on—the data disappears when the machine is turned off.
- If you share a computer (in a mainframe environment, for example), other people will be using the computer and need the memory space.

COMPUTING TRENDS

Don't Even Bother to Slow Down

Anyone who spends a few minutes of each day handing over change at a toll booth, or perhaps gingerly tossing coins out the car window into a toll container, will be pleased to learn about the trend toward automated toll collection. The concept is ingeniously simple and a solid example of how computers can help to iron out the wrinkles in everyday living.

Here's how it works. As a regular toll user, you buy a chip-imbedded tag and place it on your car's windshield. The tag has your identification and the amount of money in your prepaid toll account. As the car approaches the toll road, the tag exchanges radio signals with the highway's computers, which charge a toll against the prepaid account. Surveillance cameras record the license numbers of cars without proper tags. Fare beaters may be nabbed by the police on the spot or fined by mail.

These systems are in the works in half a dozen states. In addition to saving time for motorists, other benefits include increased safety at toll plazas and possibly, due to lower expenses, reduced tolls in the future.

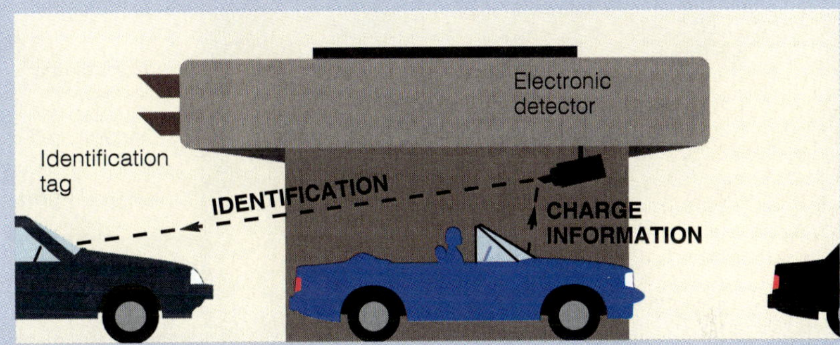

- The computer may not have enough room in memory to hold your processed data.

Therefore, data and programs are kept in secondary storage, usually on disk, when not in use.

Data and instructions from an input device are put into memory by the control unit. Data is then sent from memory to the registers, where an arithmetic operation or logical operation is performed by the arithmetic/logic unit. After being processed the information is returned to memory, where it is held until it is ready to be incorporated into other calculations or released to an output unit.

How the CPU Executes Program Instructions

Let us examine the way the central processing unit, in association with memory, executes a computer program. We will be looking at how just one instruction in the program is executed. In fact, most computers today can execute only one instruction at a time.

Before an instruction can be executed, program instructions and data must be placed into memory from an input device or a secondary storage device. In the payroll example the program instructions tell the computer the formula for computing a salary. (Keep in mind that a user would not need to know anything about the program itself, only how to give it input.)

As Figure 3-2 shows, the central processing unit then performs the following four steps for each instruction:

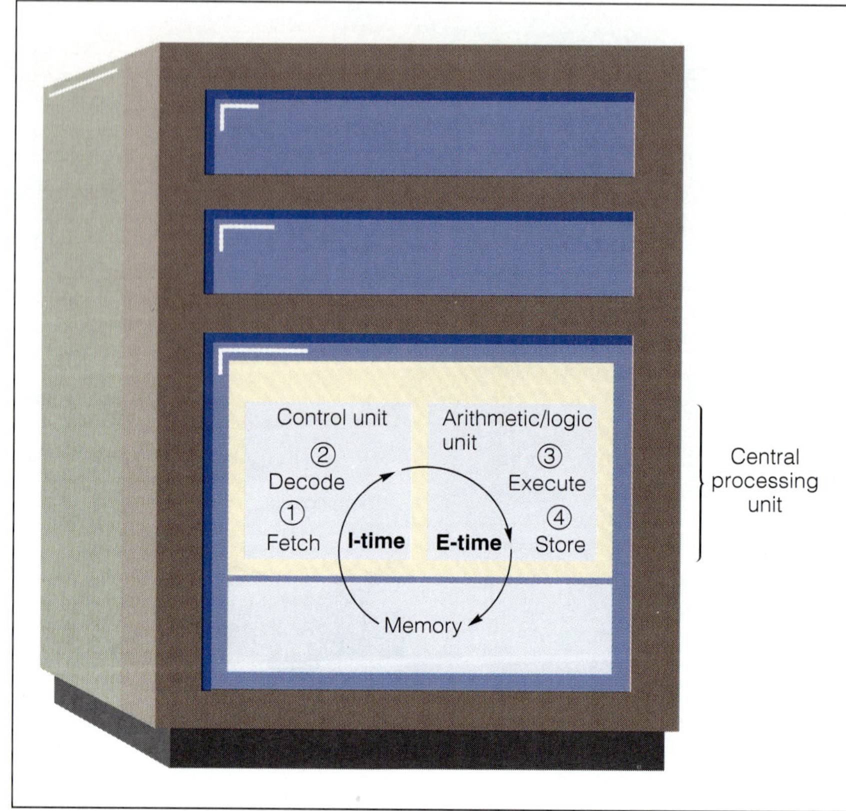

Figure 3-2 The machine cycle. Program instructions and data are brought into memory from an external device, either an input device or secondary storage. The machine cycle executes instructions one at a time.

1. The control unit "fetches" (gets) the instruction from memory.
2. The control unit decodes the instruction (decides what it means) and gives instructions for necessary data to be moved from memory to the arithmetic/logic unit. These first two steps are called instruction time, or **I-time.**
3. The arithmetic/logic unit executes arithmetic and logic instructions. That is, the ALU is given control and performs the actual operation on the data.
4. The result of this operation is stored in memory or in a temporary location, a register. Steps 3 and 4 are called execution time, or **E-time.**

After the appropriate instructions are executed, the control unit directs memory to release the results to an output device or a secondary storage device. The combination of I-time and E-time is called the **machine cycle.**

 Data Representation: On/Off

We think of computers as complex mechanisms, but the fact is that these machines basically know only two things: on and off. This on/off, yes/no, two-state system is called a **binary system.** Using the two states, which can be represented by electricity turned on or off, the computer can construct sophisticated ways of representing data.

Let us look at one way the two states can be used to represent data. Whereas the decimal number system has a base of 10 (with the digits 0, 1, 2, 3, 4, 5, 6, 7, 8, and 9), the binary system has a base of 2. This means it contains only two digits, 0 and 1, which correspond to the two states off and on. Physically, a 1 means an electrical circuit is on, whereas a 0 means the circuit is off.

Bits, Bytes, and Words

Each 0 or 1 in the binary system is called a **bit** (for *bi*nary digi*t*). The bit is the basic unit for representing data in computer memory. Since there are more numbers, letters, and special characters (such as $ and ?) than there are digits in the binary system, combinations of bits are used to represent them. Bits are put together in a group called a **byte.** Each byte, usually 8 bits, represents one character of data—a letter, a digit, or a special character. The process of coding groups of bits into bytes will be discussed shortly.

A computer **word,** typically the size of a register, is defined as the number of bits that constitute a common unit of data, as defined by the computer system. The length of a word varies by computer. Generally, the larger the word, the more powerful the computer. There was a time when word size alone could classify a computer. Common word lengths are 8 bits (for very early personal computers), 16 bits (for traditional minicomputers and some personal computers), 32 bits (for full-size mainframe computers, some minicomputers, and some personal computers), and 64 bits (traditionally for supercomputers). A recent microprocessor, Intel's Pentium, intended for both personal computers and larger machines, is a 64-bit chip. As you can see, the old stereotypes no longer fit very well. Note that an 8-bit machine can handle only one byte (character) at a time, whereas a 64-bit machine can handle 8 bytes at a time, making its processing speed eight times faster.

Computer manufacturers express the capacity of memory in terms of the number of bytes it can hold. The number of bytes is expressed as **kilobytes,** 2 to the 10th power (2^{10}), or 1024 bytes. *Kilobyte* is abbreviated **KB,** or simply **K.** Thus, the memory of a 640K computer can store 640 × 1024, or 655,360 bytes of data. Memory capacity is most often expressed in terms of a **megabyte** (1024 × 1024), abbreviated **MB.** One megabyte is roughly one million bytes. Some large computers express memory in terms of **gigabytes** (abbreviated **GB**)—billions of bytes.

Coding Schemes

As we said, a byte—a collection of bits—represents a character of data. But just what particular set of bits is equivalent to which character? In theory we could each make up our own definitions, declaring certain bit patterns to represent certain characters. Needless to say, this would be about as practical as each person speaking his or her own special language. Since we need to communicate with the computer and with each other, it is appropriate that we use a common scheme for data representation. That is, there must be agreement on which groups of bits represent which characters.

The code called **ASCII** (pronounced "AS-key"), which stands for American Standard Code for Information Interchange, uses 7 bits for

A Member of the Family: PENTIUM

The Intel Corporation has provided personal computer makers with several generations of microprocessor chips. The first was a standard-setter: the 8088 chip used by the first IBM PC (introduced in 1981) and its many imitators. The next member of the family, the 80186 chip, was merely a transitional chip, soon replaced by the 80286 chip, which powered the IBM PC AT and, again, a slew of clones.

Intel moved to increase power and flexibility with the introduction of the 80386 chip, first brought to the market in the Compaq 386. The 80386 chip let users run several programs at once, a capability formerly reserved for minicomputers and mainframes. Close on the heels of the 80386 chip was the 80486 (known as the 486), a chip whose speed and power made it popular through the early 1990s.

The next chip, trotted out in 1993, was expected to be christened the 80586. However, citing proprietary problems, Intel called it Pentium, based on the Latin root word meaning five. The amazing Pentium chip is twice as fast as the fastest 486 chip. But the most stunning news is its word size: 64 bits. Pentium's biggest contribution, however, may be that it can be used not only in personal computers but also in mid-size and mainframe computers, offering the possibility of using the same software on all these machines.

Character	ASCII–8
A	0100 0001
B	0100 0010
C	0100 0011
D	0100 0100
E	0100 0101
F	0100 0110
G	0100 0111
H	0100 1000
I	0100 1001
J	0100 1010
K	0100 1011
L	0100 1100
M	0100 1101
N	0100 1110
O	0100 1111
P	0101 0000
Q	0101 0001
R	0101 0010
S	0101 0011
T	0101 0100
U	0101 0101
V	0101 0110
W	0101 0111
X	0101 1000
Y	0101 1001
Z	0101 1010
0	0011 0000
1	0011 0001
2	0011 0010
3	0011 0011
4	0011 0100
5	0011 0101
6	0011 0110
7	0011 0111
8	0011 1000
9	0011 1001

(a)

Letter	ASCII–8
K	0100 1011
I	0100 1001
L	0100 1100
O	0100 1111
B	0100 0010
Y	0101 1001
T	0101 0100
E	0100 0101

(b)

Figure 3-3 The ASCII code.
(a) Shown are the ASCII-8 binary representations for letters and digits. This is not the complete code; there are many characters missing, such as lowercase letters and punctuation marks. The binary representation is in two columns to improve readability. (b) ASCII-8 representation for the word *KILOBYTE.*

each character. Since there are exactly 128 unique combinations of 7 bits, this 7-bit code can represent only characters. A more common version is ASCII-8, also called extended ASCII, which uses 8 bits per character and can represent 256 different characters. For example, the letter *A* is represented by 01000001. The ASCII representation has been adopted as a standard by the U.S. government and is found in a variety of computers, particularly minicomputers and microcomputers. Figure 3-3 shows part of the ASCII-8 code.

Personal Computer Chips Revisited

In Chapter 2 we gave you an overview of the microprocessor chip, and RAM and ROM memory chips. Here we will study them in more detail.

A Closer Look at Microprocessors

Over the years the architecture of microprocessors has become somewhat standardized. Microprocessors usually include these key components: a control unit and an arithmetic/logic unit (the CPU), registers, and a clock. (Clocks are often on a separate chip in personal computers.) Notably missing is memory, which usually comes on its own chips.

Three decades of extraordinary advances in technology have packed increasingly greater power onto increasingly smaller chips (Figure 3-4). Engineers can now imprint as much circuitry on a single chip as filled room-size computers in the early days of data processing.

Memory Components

Earlier in the chapter we talked about memory and how it interfaces with the central processing unit. Now we will examine the memory components. Historically, memory components have evolved from primitive vacuum tubes to today's modern semiconductors.

Semiconductor Storage

Most modern computers use **semiconductor storage,** which is made up of thousands of very small circuits—pathways for electric currents—on a silicon chip. Semiconductor storage has several advantages: reliability, compactness, low cost, and lower power usage. Since semiconductor memory can be mass-produced economically, the cost of memory has been considerably reduced. Chip prices have fallen and risen and fallen again, based on a variety of economic and political factors, but they remain a bargain. Semiconductor storage has one major disadvantage: It is **volatile.** That is, semiconductor storage requires continuous electric current to represent data. If the current is interrupted, the data is lost.

A chip is described as **monolithic** because the circuits on a single chip compose an inseparable unit of storage. Each circuit etched on a chip can be in one of two states: either conducting an electric current or not—on or off. The two states can be used to represent the binary digits 1 and 0. As we noted earlier, these digits can be combined to represent characters, thus making the memory chip a storage bin for data and instructions.

(a) (b)

Figure 3-4 Microprocessor chips.
(a) The tiny size of a microprocessor. (b) This is Intel's Pentium processor, which accommodates a 64-bit word. Although the circuitry is complex, the entire chip is smaller than your thumbnail.

Your Computerized Car

Does your car have a computer in it? Are you sure? Unless you are driving an old clunker, it is likely that your car has several, possibly dozens, of computers. Of course we are not talking about full cabinet housing or keyboard or monitor, just a series of microprocessor chips that run most everything. The following is a list of the functions that are computer-run on the Lincoln Continental: fuel injection, ignition timing, transmission shifting, suspension system, disc anti-lock braking system, power steering, wheel speed, and, finally, an air bag. Although the Lincoln is an expensive car, the list is fairly typical of microchips in modern cars.

RAM and ROM

RAM keeps the instructions and data for whatever programs you happen to be using at the moment. The data can be accessed in an easy and speedy manner. RAM is usually volatile; as previously noted, this means that its contents are lost once the power is shut off. RAM can be erased or written over at will by the computer software. ROM contains programs and data that are permanently recorded into this type of memory at the factory; they can be read and used, but they cannot be changed by the user. For example, a personal computer probably has a program for calculating square roots in ROM. ROM is nonvolatile—its contents do not disappear when the power is turned off.

The more RAM in your computer, the larger the programs you can run. In recent years the amount of RAM storage in a personal computer has increased dramatically. An early personal computer, for example, was advertised with "a full 4K RAM." Now an astonishing 8MB RAM is common. More memory has become a necessity because sophisticated personal computer software requires significant amounts of memory. You can augment your personal computer's RAM by buying extra memory chips to install in your memory board or by purchasing a **single in-line memory module (SIMM),** a board that contains memory chips. The SIMM board plugs into the computer's main circuit board, which is more convenient than attaching individual chips. In general, the more memory your computer has, the more (and bigger) tasks the computer can do.

Most personal computer memory is dynamic RAM, or **DRAM.** DRAM chips are periodically regenerated, allowing the chips to retain the stored data. Furthermore, DRAM chips offer size and cost advantages.

With specialized tools called **ROM burners,** the instructions within some ROM chips can be changed. These chips are known as **programmable read-only memory (PROM) chips.** There are other variations on ROM chips, depending on the methods used to alter them. The business of programming and altering ROM chips is the province of the computer engineer.

Speed and Power

The characteristic of speed is universally associated with computers. Power is a derivative of speed, as well as other factors such as memory size. What makes a computer fast? Or, more to the point, what makes one computer faster than another? Several factors are involved, including microprocessor speed, bus line size, and the availability of cache. A user who is concerned about speed will want to address all of them.

Computer Processing Speeds

Although all computers are fast, there is a wide diversity of computer speeds. The execution of an instruction on a very slow computer may be measured in less than a **millisecond,** which is one-thousandth of a second. Most computers can execute an instruction measured in **microseconds,** one-millionth of a second. Some modern computers have reached the **nanosecond** range—one-billionth of a second. Still to be broken is the **picosecond** barrier—one-trillionth of a second.

Microprocessor speeds are usually expressed in **megahertz (MHz),** millions of machine cycles per second. Thus, a personal computer listed at 25MHz can handle 25 million machine cycles per second. A top-speed personal computer will be more than twice as fast.

Bus Lines

As is so often the case, the computer term *bus* is borrowed from its common meaning—a mode of transportation. A **bus line** is an electrical path that internally transports data from one place to another within the computer system. The amount of data that can be carried at one time is called the bus width. The greater the width, the more data can be carried at a time. Microprocessors are sometimes obscurely affixed with notations that indicate their bus size. For example, a 486DX chip has a bus width of 32 bits, whereas a 486SX chip uses a 32-bit bus within the processor, but only a 16-bit bus between the processor and memory. A buyer who cares about speed would prefer the DX chip, which carries exactly twice as much data, and therefore is twice as fast, as the SX chip.

Cache

A **cache** (pronounced "cash") is a relatively small amount of very fast memory designed for the specific purpose of speeding up the internal transfer of data and software instructions. Think of cache as a selective memory: The data and instructions stored in cache are those that are most recently and/or most frequently used. Data or instructions, when first requested by the microprocessor, must be retrieved from main memory, which delivers them at a relatively slow pace compared to the microprocessor's capabilities. As they are retrieved, those same data/instructions are stored in cache. The next time the microprocessor needs data or instructions, it looks first in cache; if the needed items can be found there, they can be transferred at a rate that far exceeds a trip from main memory. Of course, cache is not big enough to hold everything, so the wanted data or instructions may not be there. But there is a good chance that frequently used items will be in cache. That is, since the most frequently used data and instructions are kept in a handy place, the net result is an improvement in processing speed.

Just how much cache speeds performance depends on a number of factors, including the size of the cache, the speed of the memory chips in the cache, and the software being run. Caching has become such a vital technique that some of the newer microprocessors have cache built into the processor's design. Intel's 486 chip has an 8-kilobyte cache, and the new Pentium processor has dual 8-kilobyte caches, one for data and one for software.

Flash Memory

We have stated that memory is volatile—that it disappears when the power is turned off—hence the need for secondary storage to keep data on a more permanent basis. A long-standing speed problem has been the rate of accessing data from a secondary storage device such as the hard disk, a rate significantly slower than internal computer speeds. It seemed unimaginable that data might someday be stored on nonvolatile memory chips—actual nonvolatile RAM—close at hand. A breakthrough has emerged in the form of nonvolatile **flash memory.** Flash chips are currently being used in cellular phones and cockpit flight recorders, and they are replacing disks in some hand-held computers.

Flash memory is not without problems. The market for these chips has been held up partially because they wear out rather quickly compared to RAM chips. But the main delay is the prohibitive cost of building manufacturing facilities to make flash chips. Although flash memory is not yet commonplace, it seems likely that it will become a mainstream component. Since data and instructions will be ever-closer to the microprocessor, conversion to flash memory chips would have a pivotal impact on a computer's processing speed.

Parallel Processing

The ultimate speed solution is **parallel processing,** a method of using several processors at the same time. Consider the description of computer processing you have seen so far in this chapter: The processor gets an instruction from memory, acts on it, returns processed data to memory, and then repeats the process. This is conventional serial processing.

The problem with the conventional computer is that the single electronic pathway, the bus line, acts like a bottleneck. The computer has a one-track mind because it is restricted to handling one piece of data at a time. For many applications, such as simulating the air flow around an entire airplane in flight, this is an exceedingly inefficient procedure. A better solution? Many processors, each with its own memory unit, working at the same time: parallel processing.

A number of parallel processors are being built and sold commercially. However, do not look for parallel processing in personal computers just yet. Thus far, this technology is limited to larger computers.

▼ ▼ ▼

Doggie Chips

You are in Alaska, bundled up in your parka, monitoring a checkpoint on the annual 1000-mile Iditarod dog sled race. Here they come. But wait. Are those the same dogs that started the race? Let's check the computer.

The computer? Yes, the dogs are individually identifiable, even as they speed by, because each dog wears its own microchip. Organizers of the race use a hypodermic needle to (painlessly) inject a microchip the size of a grain of rice into the fatty folds just under each dog's skin. Then, at certain checkpoints, the dogs are computer scanned to make sure they are the same animals who started the race, thus preventing illegal substitutions. In the prior system, officials spray-painted markings on the dogs for identification. The microchip system has proved to be more effective and harmless to the dogs.

The central processing unit, remaining unseen, continues to be an amazing workhorse, whether it labors inside a mammoth computer or within a tiny machine like a wristwatch. Users, however, invoke the power of the central processing unit by various computer input methods and reap the rewards from computer output. Input and output are the subjects of the next chapter.

Chapter **Review**

Summary and Key Terms

- The **central processing unit (CPU)** executes program instructions. It consists of a control unit and an arithmetic/logic unit.
- The **control unit** of the CPU coordinates the computer's execution of the program instructions by communicating with the arithmetic/logic unit—the part of the system that actually executes the program—and with memory.
- The **arithmetic/logic unit (ALU)** contains circuitry that executes **arithmetic operations** and **logical operations.** Logical operations are comparisons that determine if one value is equal to, less than, or greater than another.
- **Registers** are temporary storage areas associated with the CPU that quickly accept, hold, and transfer instructions or data. An **accumulator** is a register that collects the results of computations. A **storage register** temporarily holds data taken from memory or about to be sent to memory. An **address register** tells where instructions and data are stored in memory. Each storage location in memory is identified by an **address.** A **general-purpose register** can be used in several ways, such as for arithmetic operations or addressing.
- **Memory** is closely associated with the CPU but not part of it. Memory temporarily holds data and instructions before and after they are processed by the arithmetic/logic unit. Memory is also known as **primary storage, primary memory, main storage, internal storage,** and **main memory.**
- The central processing unit follows four main steps when executing an instruction: It (1) fetches (gets) the instruction from memory, (2) decodes the instruction and directs the transfer of data from memory to the arithmetic/logic unit, (3) directs the ALU to perform the actual operation on the data, and (4) sends the result of the operation to memory or a register. The first two steps are called **I-time** (instruction time), and the last two steps are called **E-time** (execution time). A **machine cycle** is the combination of I-time and E-time.
- Since a computer can only recognize whether electricity is on or off, data is represented by an off/on **binary system.** In a binary system two digits, 0 and 1, correspond to the two states off and on. Combinations of 0s and 1s can represent numbers, digits, or special characters.
- Each 0 or 1 in the binary system is called a **bit** (*bi*nary digi*t*). A group of bits is called a **byte.** Each byte can represent one character of data, such as a letter, digit, or special character. A computer **word** is defined as the number of bits that constitute a common unit of data, as defined by the computer system. Common word lengths are 8, 16, 32, and 64 bits. Memory capacity is expressed in **kilobytes** (**KB** or **K**), which are equal to 1024 bytes, and **megabytes (MB),** which are millions of bytes. A **gigabyte** (**GB**) is a billion bytes.
- A common coding scheme for representing characters is **ASCII** (American Standard Code for Information Interchange), which uses 7-bit characters. A variation of the code, called ASCII-8, uses 8 bits per character.
- **Semiconductor storage,** thousands of very small circuits on a silicon chip, is **volatile.** A chip is described as **monolithic** because the circuits on a single chip compose an inseparable unit of storage.

- RAM keeps the instructions and data for whatever programs you happen to be using at the moment. RAM is usually volatile. ROM contains programs and data that are permanently recorded into this type of memory at the factory; they can be read and used, but they cannot be changed by the user. ROM is nonvolatile.
- A **single in-line memory module (SIMM)** is a plug-in board that contains memory chips.
- Dynamic RAM (**DRAM**) chips are periodically regenerated, allowing the chips to retain the stored data.
- The instructions within some ROM chips can be changed using **ROM burners**; these chips are known as **programmable read-only memory (PROM) chips.**
- Computer instruction speeds fall in various ranges, from a **millisecond,** which is one-thousandth of a second; to a **microsecond,** one-millionth of a second; to a **nanosecond,** one-billionth of a second. Still to be achieved is the **picosecond** range—one-trillionth of a second.
- Microprocessor speeds are usually expressed in **megahertz (MHz),** millions of machine cycles per second.
- A **bus line** is an electrical path that transports data from one place to another internally within the computer system. The amount of data that can be carried at one time is called the bus width.
- A **cache** is a relatively small amount of very fast memory that stores data and instructions that are used frequently, resulting in an improved processing speed.
- The emerging technology of **flash memory** will provide memory chips that are nonvolatile.
- **Parallel processing** uses several processors in the same computer at the same time.

Student Personal Study Guide

True/False

T F 1. The control unit consists of the CPU and the ALU.
T F 2. Semiconductor storage is nonvolatile.
T F 3. A kilobyte (KB) is 1024 bytes.
T F 4. Primary storage is part of the central processing unit.
T F 5. A microsecond is briefer than a millisecond.
T F 6. Logical operations are comparing operations.
T F 7. A word represents one character of data.
T F 8. PROM chips are RAM chips.
T F 9. Parallel processing uses several processors at the same time.
T F 10. A SIMM is a type of register.

Multiple Choice

1. The electrical path that transports data:
   a. RAM c. bus line
   b. megahertz d. microprocessor
2. Fast memory that stores frequently used instructions and data:
   a. cache c. PROM
   b. ALU d. address register
3. Which is *not* another name for memory?
   a. register c. primary storage
   b. main memory d. internal storage

4. The combination of I-time and E-time:
   a. machine time
   b. machine cycle
   c. binary time
   d. megabyte
5. The American standard code for representing characters with bits:
   a. binary digits
   b. ASCII
   c. semiconductor storage
   d. cache
6. Which is *not* used to express memory capacity?
   a. DB
   b. MB
   c. GB
   d. KB
7. A plug-in board of memory chips:
   a. MB
   b. cache
   c. SIMM
   d. PROM
8. Fetch and decode instruction:
   a. CPU
   b. E-time
   c. accumulator register
   d. I-time
9. One-millionth of a second:
   a. millisecond
   b. picosecond
   c. nanosecond
   d. microsecond
10. Which is *not* a type of register?
    a. storage
    b. general purpose
    c. monolithic
    d. address

Fill-In

1. The combination of I-time and E-time: ____________________.
2. The two binary digits are ____________________.
3. Approximately a billion bytes: ____________________.
4. Emerging nonvolatile RAM: ____________________.
5. Combination of control unit and ALU: ____________________.
6. SIMM stands for ____________________.
7. Using several processors in the same computer at the same time: ________________.
8. A chip, whose circuits are on an inseparable unit, is said to be ________________.
9. Program instructions are executed by the ____________________.
10. An internal electrical path: ____________________.

Answers

True/False: 1. F, 2. F, 3. T, 4. F, 5. T, 6. T, 7. F, 8. F, 9. T, 10. F
Multiple choice: 1. c, 2. a , 3. a , 4. b, 5. b, 6. a, 7. c, 8. d, 9. d, 10.c
Fill-In: 1. machine cycle, 2. 0 and 1, 3. gigabyte, 4. flash memory, 5. central processing unit (CPU), 6. single in-line memory module, 7. parallel processing , 8. monolithic , 9. central processing unit (CPU), 10. bus line

Chapter Overview

Just how are input and output related in a computer system? How do you "get into" a computer system? More formally, how do you provide your own input in a way that the computer can accept? If you can figure that much out, how do you get something back from the computer? Finally, what might the output from the computer be, considering what you gave it as input? There are many possible answers to these questions, but Paul Yen's experience is fairly typical.

Input and

CHAPTER 4

Output

The User Connection

Paul did not have computers in mind as he thumbed through the catalog for Lands' End, a mail-order firm in Wisconsin that offers quality classic dress and sports clothing. Paul wanted to order a turtleneck shirt. He decided on a shirt and a leather belt, and he wrote these items on the order form. Paul's action, whether he knew it or not, started the computer action rolling.

The items on the order form became the input data to the computer system. In this example, input is the data related to the customer order—customer name, address, and (possibly) charge-card number—and data about each item—catalog number, quantity, description, and price. If this input data is handwritten on an order form, it is keyed into the system as soon as it arrives in the mail; if the order is received on the company's toll- free phone line, the Lands' End operator keys the data as the customer speaks the order. This data is placed on customer and order files to be used with files containing inventory and other related data.

The computer can process this data into a variety of outputs, as shown in Box 4-1. Some outputs are for individual customers, and some show information combined from several orders: warehouse orders, shipping labels (to send the shirt and belt), back-order notices, inventory reports, supply reorder reports, charge-card reports, demographic reports (showing which merchandise sells best where), and so forth. To keep the whole process going, Lands' End also computer-prints Paul's name and address on the next catalog.

How Users See Input and Output

The central processing unit is the unseen part of a computer system, and users are only dimly aware of its activity. But users are very much aware—and in control—of the input data given to the computer. They submit data to the computer to get processed data (information), which is the output. Output is what makes the computer useful to human beings.

Sometimes the output is an instant reaction to the input. For example:

- Zebra-striped bar codes on supermarket items provide input that permits instant retrieval of output, price, and item name, right at the checkout counter.
- You use a joystick—a kind of hand-controlled lever—to input data to guide the little airplane, rabbit, or whatever on the screen. The output is the movement of the on-screen object according to your wishes.
- A bank teller queries the computer through the small terminal at the teller window by inputting a customer's account number; the teller immediately receives output in the form of the customer's account balance on that same screen.
- A forklift operator speaks to a computer directly through a microphone. Words like *left*, *right*, and *lift* are the actual input data. The

Box 4-1 Lands' End.
At this mail-order house, customer order data is input, processed, and used to produce a variety of outputs.

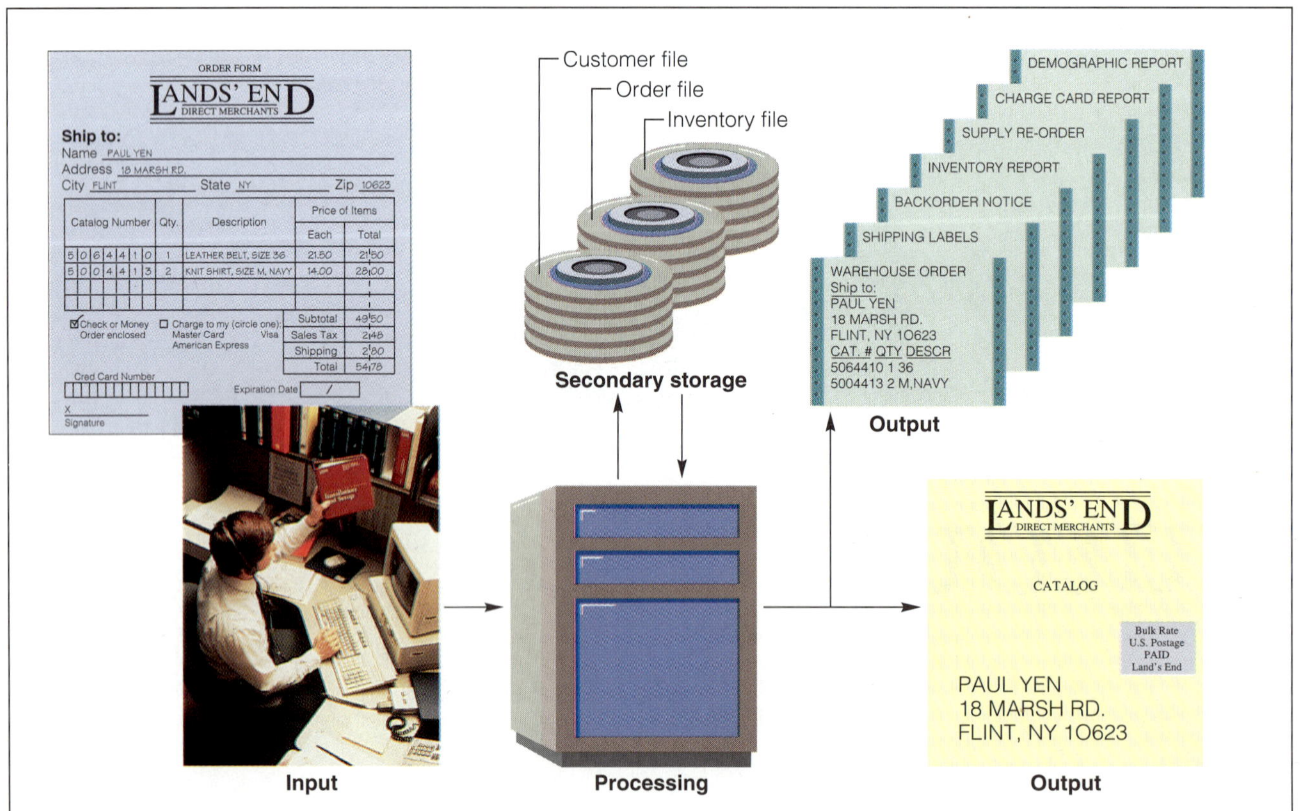

output is the computer's instant response, which causes the forklift to operate as requested.

- In an innovative restaurant, input is your finger touching the listing of the item of your choice on a computer screen. The output is the order that appears immediately on the kitchen screen, where employees get to work on your Chili Hamburger Deluxe.

Input and output are sometimes separated by time, distance, or both. Some examples are:

- Factory workers input data by using their plastic employee cards to punch in on a time clock as they go from task to task. The outputs, produced biweekly, are their paychecks and management reports that summarize hours per project and other information.
- Data from the checks we write is used as input to the bank's computer and eventually is processed to prepare a monthly bank statement.
- Charge-card transactions in a retail store provide input data that is processed at month's end to produce customer bills.
- Water-sample data is determined at lake and river sites, keyed in at the environmental agency office, and used to produce reports that show patterns of water quality.

The examples in this section have shown the diversity of computer applications, but in all cases the litany is the same: input–processing–output.

Input: How You Get Data Into The Computer

Some input data can go directly to the computer for processing, such as reading bar codes, touching a computer screen, or even speaking to the computer. On the other hand, some input data must go through a great deal of intermediate handling, such as when it is handwritten on a **source document** (jargon for the original written data) and then translated to a medium that a machine can read, such as magnetic disk. In either case the task is to gather facts to be processed by the computer—sometimes called *raw data*—and convert them into some form the computer can understand.

Various input devices are used to gather data for processing by the computer. Generally, the trend in input devices is toward equipment that is easy to use, fast, and accurate.

Keyboard Entry

The most common input device is the keyboard. A computer keyboard is usually similar to a typewriter, with the traditional QWERTY layout of letter and digit keys, and additional numerical pad and function keys (Figure 4-1a). The keyboard may be part of a personal computer or part of a terminal connected to a computer somewhere else. Not all keyboards are traditional. A fast-food franchise like McDonald's, for example, uses keyboards with keys that represent items, such as large fries or a Big Mac (Figure 4-1b).

Everyday Input and Output

One way or another, delivering input to a computer is a common activity in our daily lives. Input activities in which you may have engaged could include items on the following list.

- Inserting your credit card (with data encoded on the magnetic strip) into a bank's automated teller machine (ATM)
- Buying an item whose price tag was scanned with a wand reader
- Filling out an application for a magazine subscription
- Purchasing groceries whose bar codes were scanned
- Filling out registration forms
- Recording test answers by using a pencil on an optical-mark recognition sheet

Many other activities require us to provide input to a computer. Over time, we may supply input in these circumstances: seeking credit, paying taxes, applying for a job, entering a contest, paying bills, entering the armed services, signing a petition, going to the doctor, joining an organization, applying for a scholarship, seeking government assistance, giving charitable donations, ordering products through the mail, and on and on.

This data is supplied willingly, and most people give little thought to the route it will travel. Almost all the data will end up in computer files, to reside there indefinitely.

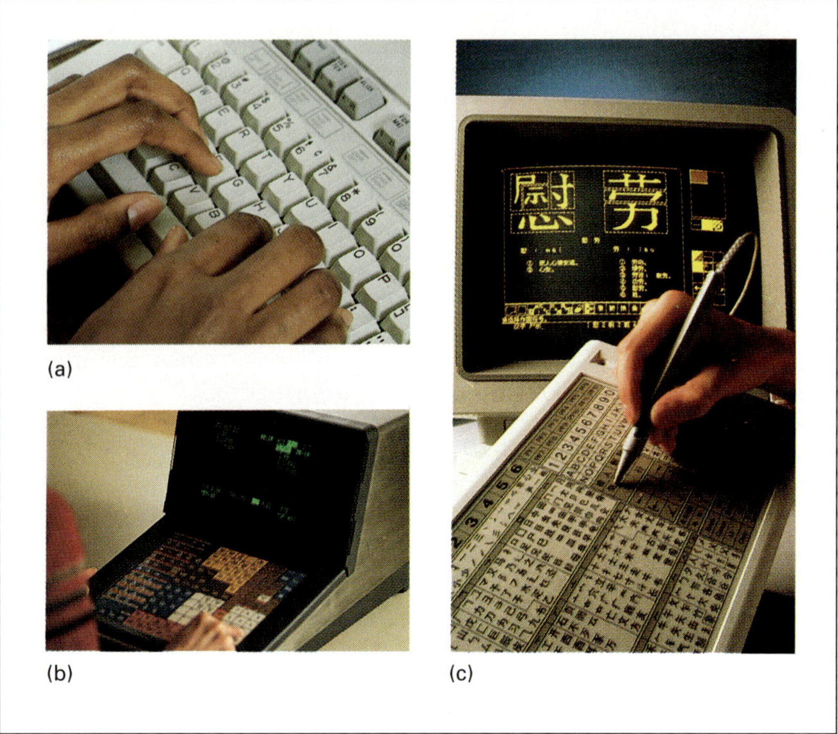

Figure 4-1 Keyboards.
(a) A traditional computer keyboard. (b) Workers at McDonald's press a key for each item ordered. The amount of the order is totaled by the computer system, then displayed on a small screen so the customer can see the amount owed. (c) Chinese characters are significantly more complicated than the letters and digits found on a standard keyboard. To enter Chinese characters into the computer system, a person uses a stylus on this special keyboard to select the character wanted. A graphics interpretation of the character can be displayed on the computer screen.

Mouse

A **mouse,** popularized by the Macintosh computer, is a computer input device that actually looks a little bit like a mouse (Figure 4-2). The mouse, which has a ball on its underside, is rolled on a flat surface, usually the desk on which your computer sits. The rolling movement that results when you push the mouse causes the related output, which is the corresponding movement on the screen. Moving the mouse allows you to reposition the **pointer,** or **cursor**—an indicator on the screen that shows where the next interaction with the computer will take place. The cursor is often flashing or blinking on and off, so it is easy to see. The cursor can also be moved by pressing various keyboard keys. In addition, you can communicate with the computer by pressing the button on top of the mouse. Many users turn to the mouse as a quick substitute for some functions of the keyboard.

Trackball

The mouse works fine until you find yourself without a flat surface on which to roll it. That is often the case for travelers using laptop computers. If you try to roll a mouse on a tiny airline tray, you will probably be digging an elbow into your neighbor. And, of course, an airport concourse or car offers no flat surface at all. The **trackball** is sort of an upside-down mouse. That is, the ball that usually rolls along a flat surface is facing up and is manipulated by hand. As with a mouse, movement of the ball causes a corresponding movement of the cursor on the screen. Trackballs are often built into laptop computers (Figure 4-3).

Figure 4-2 Mouse.
(a) As the ball on the underside of the mouse moves over a smooth surface such as a desktop, the pointer on the screen makes a corresponding movement. (b) The mouse is designed to fit smoothly under the hand. (c) Once the pointer is in position, a user can select an option from a list of choices, such as those shown here, by pressing the button on the mouse.

Source Data Automation: Collecting Data Where It Starts

The key to productive data entry is clear: Cut down the number of intermediate steps required between the data input and data processing. The best way to do this is by **source data automation**—by using special equipment to collect data at the source and send it directly to the computer. Source data automation is an enticing alternative to keyboarding input, because it eliminates the intermediate keying function; therefore, source data automation reduces both costs and opportunities for human-introduced mistakes. Since data about a transaction is collected when

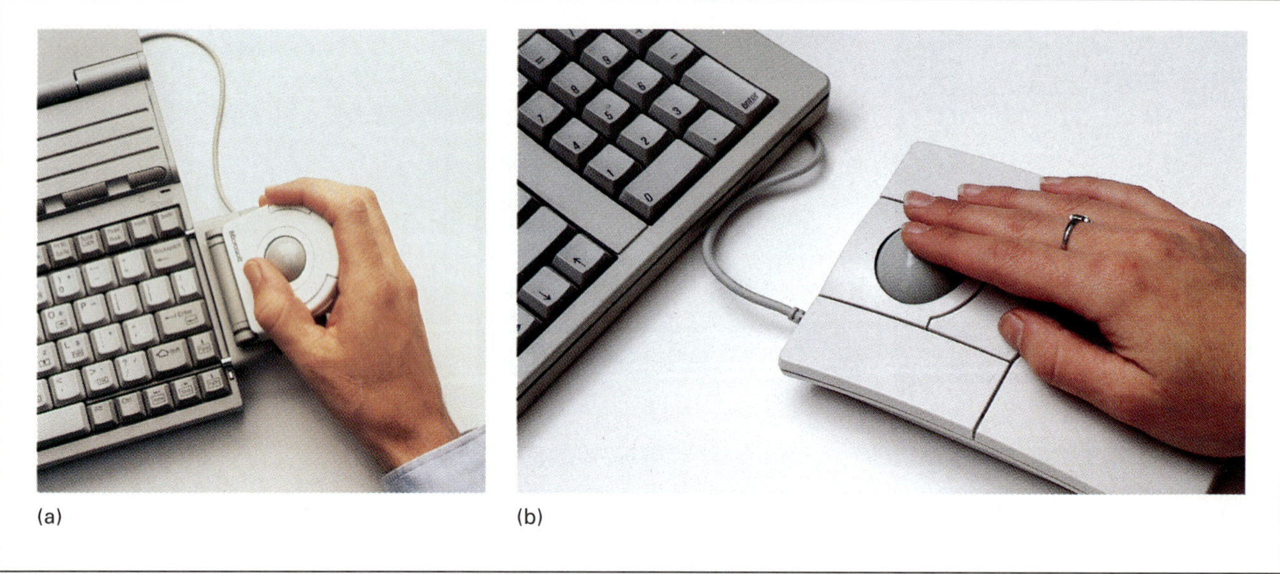

(a) (b)

Figure 4-3 Trackball.
The rotation of the ball causes a corresponding movement of the cursor on the screen. (a) Trackballs are often used with laptop computers because there may be no handy surface on which to roll a mouse. (b) Some users prefer trackballs even with their desktop computers.

and where the transaction takes place, source data automation also improves the speed of the input operation.

For convenience we will divide the discussion of source data automation into four areas: magnetic-ink character recognition, optical recognition, data collection devices, and voice input. Let us consider each of these in turn.

Magnetic-Ink Character Recognition

Magnetic-ink character recognition (MICR) is a method of machine-reading characters made of magnetized particles. The most familiar example of magnetic characters is the array of numbers on the bottom of your personal check. Figure 4-4 shows what these numbers represent.

The MICR process is, in fact, used mainly by banks for processing checks. Checks are read by a machine called a **MICR reader/sorter,** which sorts them into different compartments and sends electronic signals—read from the magnetic ink on the check—to the computer.

Optical Recognition

Optical recognition systems read numbers, letters, special characters, and marks. An electronic scanning device converts the data into electrical signals and sends the signals to the computer for processing. Various optical recognition devices can read these types of input:

- Optical marks
- Optical characters
- Handwritten characters
- Bar codes

The first type of system, **optical-mark recognition (OMR),** is sometimes called mark sensing because a machine senses marks on a piece of paper. As a student, you may immediately recognize this approach as a technique used to score certain tests. Using a pencil, you make a mark in a specified box or space that corresponds to your answer. The answer sheet is then graded by a device that uses a light beam to detect the marks

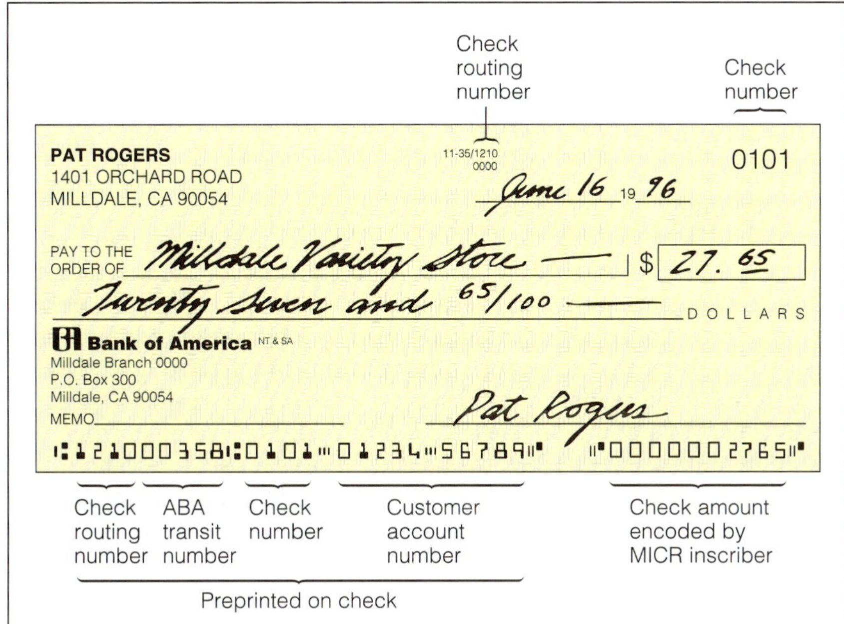

Figure 4-4 The symbols on your check. Magnetic-ink numbers and symbols run along the bottom of a check. The symbols on the left are preprinted; the MICR characters in the lower-right corner of a cashed check are entered by hand by the bank that receives it. Note that these latter numbers should correspond to the amount of the check.

and convert them to electrical signals, which are sent to the computer for processing.

Optical-character recognition (OCR) devices also use a light source to read special characters and convert them into electrical signals to be sent to the computer. The characters—letters, numbers, and symbols—can be read by both humans and machines. They are often found on sales tags in department stores or imprinted on credit-card slips in gas stations after the sale has been written up. A standard typeface for optical characters, called **OCR-A,** has been established by the American National Standards Institute (Figure 4-5).

The hand-held **wand reader** is a popular input device for reading OCR-A. In retail stores the wand reader is connected to a **point-of-sale (POS) terminal.** This terminal is like a cash register in many ways, but it performs many more functions. When a clerk passes the wand reader over the price tag, both the price and the merchandise number are entered into the computer system. Given the merchandise number, the computer can retrieve a description of the item from a file. This description is displayed on the screen of the POS terminal along with the price. (Some systems, by the way, input only the merchandise number and retrieve both price and description.) A small printer produces a customer receipt that also shows both the item description and the price. The computer calculates the subtotal, the sales tax, and the total. This information is displayed on the screen and printed on the receipt.

The raw purchase data becomes valuable information when summarized by the computer system. This information can be used by a business's accounting department to keep track of how much money is taken in each day, by buyers to determine what merchandise should be reordered and by the marketing department to analyze the effectiveness of its ad campaigns. Thus, capturing data at the time of the sale provides many benefits beyond giving the customer a computerized receipt along with the purchase.

Machines that can read **handwritten characters** are yet another means of reducing the number of intermediate steps between capturing

Figure 4-5 OCR-A typeface. This is a standard font for optical-character recognition systems.

data and processing it. In many instances it is preferable to write the data and immediately have it available for processing rather than having it keyed in later by data entry operators. However, not just any kind of handwritten scrawl will do; appropriate size, completeness, and legibility of the handwriting contribute to readability (Figure 4-6). The post office makes extensive use of these machines to sort mail by zip code.

Each product on your store shelf has its own unique number, which is part of the **Universal Product Code (UPC).** This code number, representing the manufacturer and the individual product, is depicted on the product's label by a pattern of vertical marks, or bars, called **bar codes.** These zebra stripes can be sensed and read by a **bar code reader,** a photoelectric scanner that reads the code by means of reflected light (lasers). As with the wand reader in retail stores, the bar code reader in grocery stores is part of a point-of-sale (POS) terminal. For example, when you buy an item in a supermarket, the checker moves it past the scanner that reads the bar code (Figure 4-7a). The bar code merely identifies the product to the store's computer; the code does not contain the price, which may vary. The price is stored in a file that is accessed by a computer. (Obviously, it is easier to change the price once it is in the computer than to restamp the price repeatedly on each item.) The computer automatically tells the POS terminal what the price is, and a printer prints the item description and price on a paper tape for the customer.

Although bar codes were once found primarily in the supermarket, they have a variety of other interesting applications. Bar coding has been described as an inexpensive and remarkably reliable way to get data into a computer. It is no wonder that virtually every industry has found a niche for bar codes. In Brisbane, Australia, as well as in other countries, bar codes help the Red Cross manage its blood bank inventory (Figure 4-7b). Also, Federal Express attributes a large part of the corporation's success to the bar-coding system they use to track thousands of packages every day. As each package wends its way through the transportation system, its unique bar code is read at each point, and the bar code number is fed to a central computer. An employee can use a computer terminal to check the location of a given shipment at any time; the sender can request a status report on a package and receive a response within 30 minutes.

Data Collection Devices

Another direct source of data entry is a **data collection device,** which may be in a warehouse or factory or wherever an activity generates data. Using such a device eliminates intermediate steps that endanger accu-

Figure 4-6 Handwritten characters. Legibility is important in making handwritten characters readable by optical recognition.

	Good	Bad
1. Make your letters big	TAPLEY	TAPLEY
2. Use simple shapes	25370	25370
3. Use block printing	STAN	STAN
4. Connect lines	B5T	135T
5. Close loops	9068	9068
6. Do not link characters	LOOP	LOOP

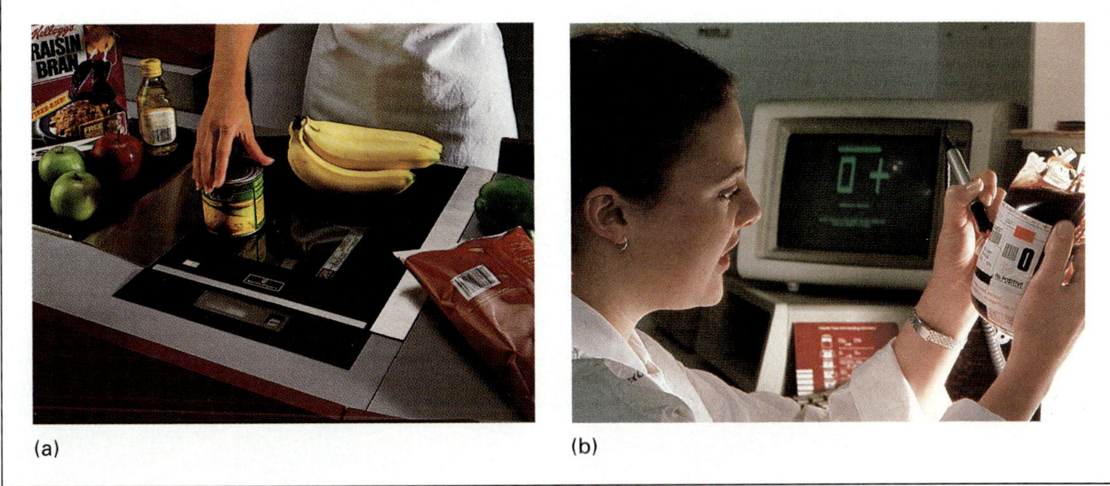

(a) (b)

Figure 4-7 Bar codes.
(a) This photoelectric bar code scanner, often seen at supermarket checkout counters, reads the product's zebra-striped bar code. The bar code identifies the product to the store's computer, which retrieves price information. The price is then automatically rung up on the POS terminal. (b) The Australian Red Cross combines personal computers and hand-held bar code readers to verify blood type labels.

racy. A factory employee who uses a plastic card to punch job data directly into a time clock is using a data collection device.

Data collection devices must be sturdy, trouble-free, and easy to use, because they are often in dusty, humid, or hot or cold locations. They are used by people such as warehouse workers, packers, forklift operators, and other nonclerical employees. Examples of remote data collection devices are machines for taking inventory, reading shipping labels, and recording job costs.

Voice Input

Have you talked to your computer recently? Has it talked to you? Both feats are possible with current technology, even though there are still some limitations. We will examine both "speakers"—you and the computer. Since we are discussing input here, we will begin with you, as you talk to your computer. What method of input could be more direct than speaking?

Voice input is the process of presenting input data to the computer through the spoken word. Voice input can be about twice as fast as keyed input entered by a skilled typist. A **speech recognition device** accepts the spoken word through a microphone and converts it into digital code that can be understood by the computer. This process has a great many uses, quite apart from its being an aid to those who hate to type. In fact, voice input has created new uses for computers (Figure 4-8). Typical users are those with "busy hands," hands that are too dirty for the keyboard, or hands that must remain cleaner than using a keyboard would permit. Among current uses are

- Controlling inventory in an auto junkyard
- Reporting analyses of pathology slides that are under a microscope

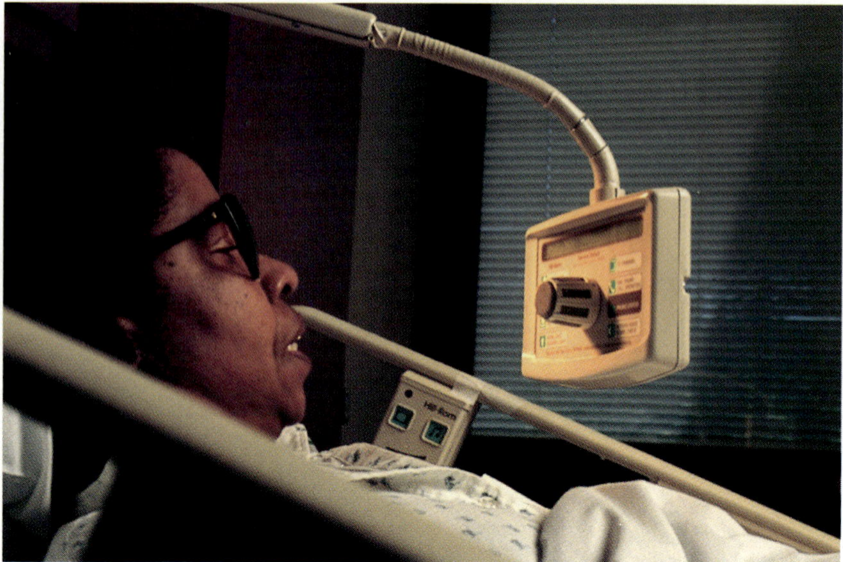

Figure 4-8. Voice input.
This hospital patient is giving voice commands to her computerized bed, which responds to a list of commands. Since not all patients need to use voice commands, the voice capability modules can be moved from one bed to another.

- Making phone calls from a car
- Calculating a correct anesthetic dosage for a patient in surgery
- Performing nonflight control jobs such as changing radio frequencies in airplane cockpits
- Asking for stock quotations over the phone
- Sorting packages
- Inspecting items moving along a factory assembly line
- Acting on commands from physically challenged users
- Commanding a car to start the motor, lock the doors, or turn on the windshield wipers

In a **speaker-dependent** system, the speech recognition device "learns" the voice of the user, who speaks isolated words repeatedly. The voiced words the system "knows" are then recognizable in the future. The worker sorting packages, for instance, can speak digits representing zip codes. The factory inspector can voice the simple words good or bad, yes or no. A biologist can tell a microscope to scan up, down, right, and left.

Speaker-independent systems, which can recognize commands from any speaker, are much more challenging to the computer industry. Experts have tagged speech recognition as one of the most difficult things for a computer to do, partly because human speech varies so much in accent, tone, and clarity. Someday machines that recognize speech will be commonplace. People will routinely talk to their computers, toys, TV sets, refrigerators, ovens, automobiles, and door locks. And no one will stare at them when they do.

Output: How Information Comes Back To You

As we have already seen, output can take many forms, such as screen output, paper printouts, and voice. Other forms of output include overhead transparencies, 35mm slides, and microfilm. Even within the same orga-

COMPUTING TRENDS

Computers in the Courtroom

Computers are not strangers to the courtroom. They have long been used by judges and their clerks for a variety of purposes, including monitoring dockets and checking defendant records. Now, in a giant leap forward, computers have gone beyond clerical functions.

In fact, attorneys are now using computers to re-create the crime scene, based on the recollection of eyewitnesses and crime scene data. It is conservatively estimated that such simulations save many hours of testimony, thus sparing the jury and helping to unclog the overcrowded courts. However, some experts worry that such high-tech representations of evidence may sway jurors by lending an aura of factuality.

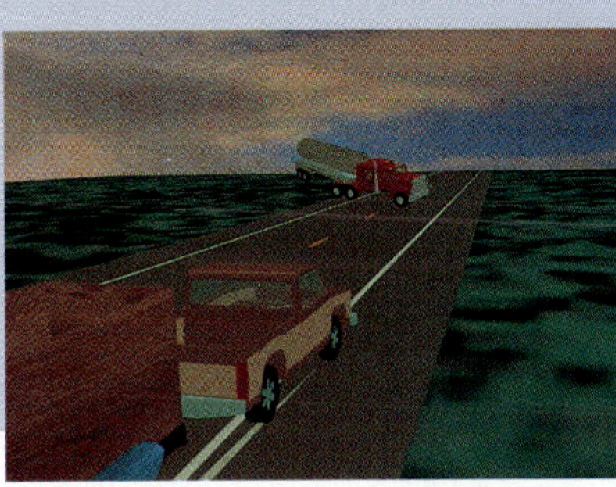

nization, there can be different kinds of output. You can see this the next time you go to a travel agency that uses a computer system. If you ask for airline flights to, for example, Toronto, Calgary, and Vancouver, the travel agent will probably make a few queries to the system and receive output on a screen: information about the availability of various flights. After the reservations have been confirmed, the agent can ask for printed output in three forms: the tickets, the traveler's itinerary, and the invoice. In addition, for management purposes the agency may periodically receive printed reports and charts, such as monthly summaries of sales figures or pie charts of regional costs.

Computer Screen Technology

A user's first interaction with a computer screen may be the screen response to the user's input. When data is entered, it appears on the screen. Furthermore, the computer response to that data—the output—also appears on the screen. Computer screens come in many varieties, but the most common kind is the **cathode ray tube (CRT).** Most CRT screens use a technology called **raster-scan technology.** The backing of the screen display has a phosphorous coating that will glow whenever it is hit by a beam of electrons. As the user, you tell the computer what image you want on the screen by typing, say, the letter *M*, and the computer sends the appropriate image to be beamed on the screen. This is essentially the same process used to produce television images.

A computer display screen that can be used for graphics is divided into dots that are called addressable because they can be *addressed* individually by the graphics software. Each dot can be illuminated individually on the screen. Each dot is potentially a *pic*ture *el*ement, or **pixel**. The **resolution** of the screen— its clarity—is directly related to the number of pixels on the screen: The more pixels, the higher the resolution.

There have been several color screen standards, relating paricularly to resolution. The first color display was **CGA** (color graphics adaptor), which had low resolution by today's standards: 320 by 200 pixels. This was followed by the sharper **EGA** (enhanced graphics adaptor), featuring

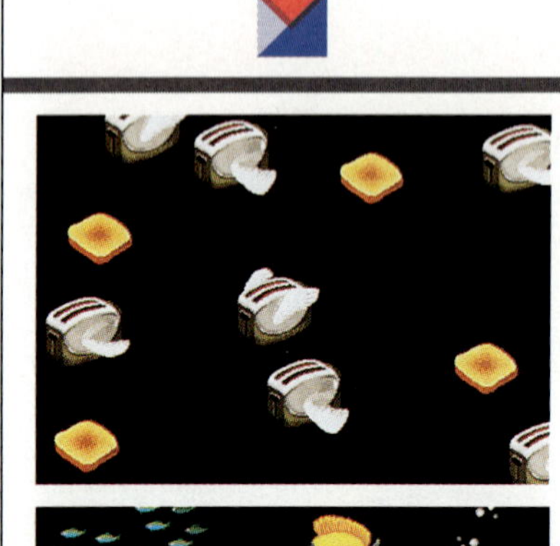

Flying Toasters

The computer industry has come up with an entertaining solution to a pesky problem. The problem is the possibility of screen burnout. Users often leave their computers unattended for periods of time to answer the phone, attend a meeting, or for any number of other reasons. While they are gone the static image that remains on the screen can "burn" into the screen, leaving a permanent faint shadow in the background whenever the monitor is turned on.

An early solution was screen saver software that caused the screen to go blank after a given period of non-use, perhaps a few minutes. When the user returned, the screen was easily revived to its prior display by the touch of any key.

Recent screen saver software is more fanciful, sending a variety of images coursing across the screen. The best-selling After Dark software allows you to choose from moving images of flying toasters, cityscapes, geometric shapes, aquariums, rain storms, spotlights, stained glass windows, and much more. Many people enjoy the novelty of bright images on their home or office computer screens.

640 by 350 pixels. Today, **VGA** (video graphics array), with 640 by 480 pixels, is a common standard. **SVGA** (super VGA) offers 800 by 600 pixels or 1024 by 768 pixels, the ultimate in clarity.

Types of Screens

Color monitors that display text and graphics in color are in common use today (Figure 4-9a). Some screens are **monochrome,** meaning only one color appears on a dark background. A common monochrome screen display is green text on a dark background, but amber characters are also available and are thought to be easier on the eyes (Figure 4-9b). Another type of screen is the **liquid crystal display (LCD),** a flat display often seen on watches and calculators. LCD screens are used on laptop computers (Figure 4-9c). These screens are usually smaller and lighter than CRTs, and the quality—both color and contrast—suffers somewhat. Screen size can vary from large screens that can show two facing pages to small screens on some point-of-sale terminals, which are just large enough to display the item name and price.

Terminals

A screen may be the monitor of a self-contained personal computer, or it may be part of a terminal that is one of many terminals attached to a large computer. A **terminal** consists of an input device, an output device, and a communications link to the main computer. Most commonly, a terminal has a keyboard for an input device and a screen for an output device, although there are many variations on this theme.

Printers

A **printer** is a device that produces printed paper output—known in the trade as **hard copy** because it is tangible and permanent (unlike **soft copy,** which is displayed on a screen). Some printers produce only letters and numbers, but most can also produce graphics.

Letters and numbers are formed by a printer either as solid characters or as dot-matrix characters. **Dot-matrix printers** create characters in the same way that individual lights in a pattern spell out words on a basketball scoreboard. A dot-matrix printer constructs a character by activating a matrix of pins that produce the shape of the character. Figure 4-10 shows how this works. A traditional matrix is 5×7—that is, five dots wide and seven dots high. These printers are sometimes called nine-pin printers, because they have two extra vertical dots for descenders on the lowercase letters *g*, *j*, *p*, and *y*. The 24-pin dot-matrix printer, which uses a series of overlapping dots, dominates the dot-matrix market. The more dots, the better the quality of the character produced. Some dot-matrix printers can produce color images.

There are two ways of printing an image on paper: the impact method and the nonimpact method. Let us take a closer look at the difference.

Impact Printers

The term *impact* refers to the fact that an **impact printer** uses some sort of physical contact with the paper to produce an image, physically striking paper, ribbon, and print hammer together. The impact may be produced by a print hammer character, like that of a typewriter key striking

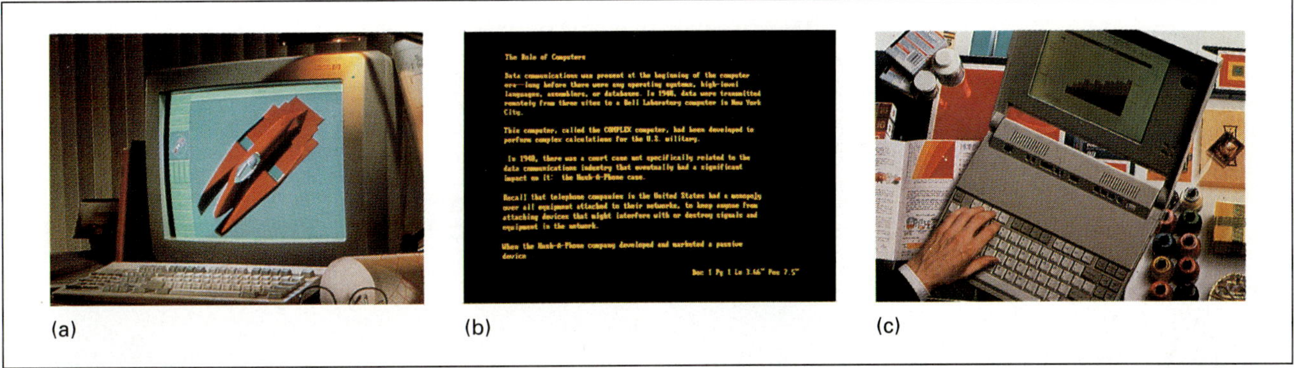

Figure 4-9 A variety of screens.
(a) This high-resolution brilliance is available only on a color graphics display. (b) An amber screen. (c) Laptop computers use liquid crystal display (LCD) technology for their small, lightweight screens.

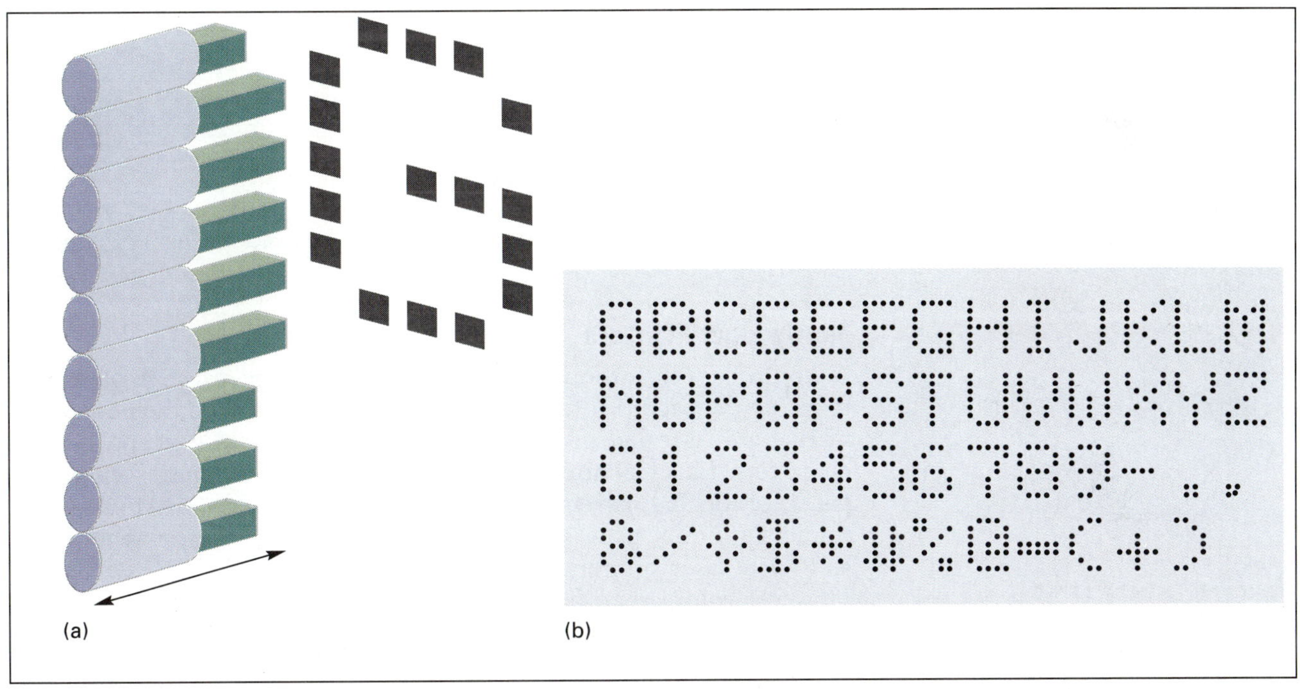

Figure 4-10 Forming dot-matrix characters.
(a) This art shows the letter *G* being printed as a 5×7 dot-matrix character. The moving matrix head has nine vertical pins, which move in and out as necessary to form each letter. (b) Letters, numbers, and special characters formed as 5×7 dot-matrix characters. Although not shown in this figure, dot-matrix printers can print lowercase letters too. The two lowest pins are used for the parts of the lowercase letters *g*, *j*, *p*, and *y* that go below the line.

a ribbon against the paper, or by a print hammer hitting paper and ribbon against a character. A dot-matrix printer is one example of an impact printer. High-quality impact printers print only one character at a time. However, users who are more concerned about high volume than high quality usually use line printers, impact printers that print an entire line at a time.

(a)

(b)

Figure 4-11 Printers.
(a) The high-quality print of the Hewlett-Packard LaserJet printers make them best-sellers. (b) Ink-jet printers are noted for high-quality graphics output.

Nonimpact Printers

A **nonimpact printer** places an image on a page without physically touching the page. The major technologies competing in the nonimpact market are laser and ink-jet. Both use the dot-matrix concept to form characters. **Laser printers** use a light beam to help transfer images to paper, producing extremely high-quality results (Figure 4-11a). Laser printers print one page at a time. Initially very expensive, low-end black-and-white laser printers can now be purchased for well under $1000. However, color laser printers remain very expensive.

There are many advantages to nonimpact printers, but there are two major reasons for their growing popularity: They are faster and quieter. Other advantages of nonimpact printers over conventional mechanical printers are their ability to change typefaces automatically and their ability to produce high-quality graphics.

The rush to laser printers has been influenced by the trend toward desktop publishing—using a personal computer, a laser printer, and special software to make professional-looking publications, such as newsletters. We will examine desktop publishing in Chapter 12.

Ink-jet printers, by spraying ink from multiple jet nozzles, can print in several different colors of ink to produce excellent graphics (Figure 4-11b). As good as they are, color printers are not perfect. The color you see on your computer screen is not necessarily the color you will see on the printed output. Nor is it likely to be the color you would see on a four-color offset printing press. Nevertheless, with low-end printers now

Personal Computers In Action

Computer As Cadaver

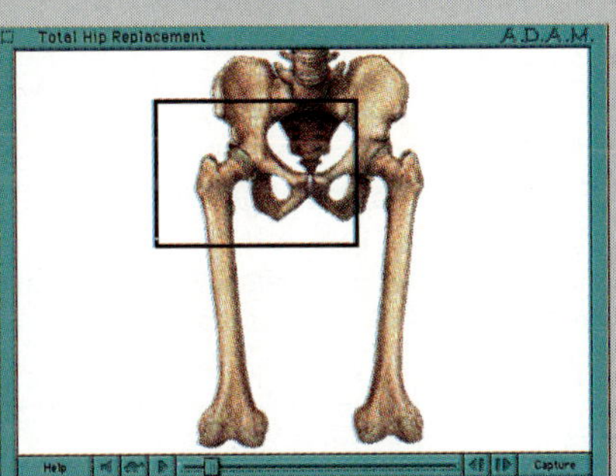

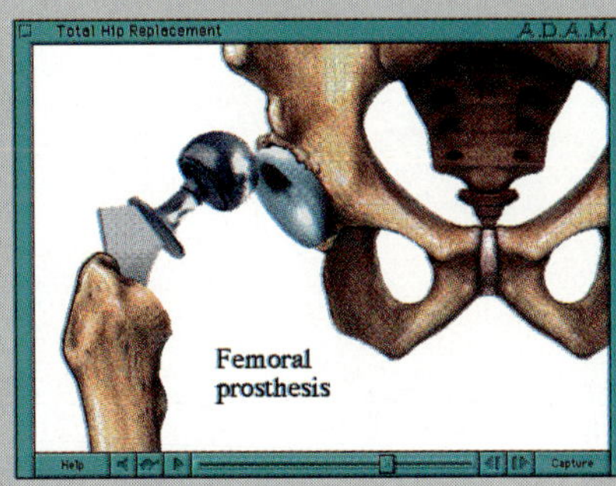

Many of us have heard the stories of medical students and their laboratory cadavers, often given affectionate nicknames. We have an appreciation for what medical students must do to learn about human anatomy; some people go even further and will their bodies to science. But this is one science tradition that may be coming to a close. In just a few years, it is predicted, medical students will be using software on their personal computers for most of their training, using cadavers only occasionally.

The screens shown here, illustrating hip replacement, are generated by a software package called ADAM, which lets students use a mouse to click away layers from skin to bone. A student can zoom in on specific tendons, muscles, and tissues, rotating the images to obtain different perspectives.

Medical personnel can look forward to having software that can be updated with the latest medical technology and can focus on a particular specialty such as cardiology or pediatrics. The direction of the future seems clear: Just as architects and engineers use computers to simulate the real world, so will medical students—and even doctors—take voyages through the body.

under $1000, they may be a bargain for users who want their own color output capability.

Printers are discussed further in the "Buyer's Guide."

Voice Output

We have already examined voice input, a technology that still challenges the industry. **Speech synthesis**—the process of enabling machines to talk to people—is much easier than speech recognition.

"The door is ajar," your car says to you in a human-like voice. But this is not a real human voice; it is the product of a **voice synthesizer** (also called a **voice-output device** or **audio-response unit**), which produces sounds understandable as speech to humans.

Voice output has become common in such places as airline and bus terminals, banks, and brokerage houses. It is typically used when an inquiry is followed by a short reply (such as a bank balance or flight time). Many businesses have found other creative uses for voice output as it applies to the telephone. Automatic telephone voices ("Hello, this is a computer speaking . . . ") take surveys, inform customers that catalog orders are ready to pick up, and remind consumers that they have not paid their bills. Voice output is also used extensively in school administration to call families of students to remind them of such things as PTA meetings, Open Houses, and children's absences.

Music Output

Personal computer users have occasionally sent primitive musical messages, feeble tones that wheezed from the tiny internal speaker. Many users remain at this level, but a significant change is in progress.

Professional musicians lead the way, using special sound chips that simulate different instruments. A sound card, installed internally in the computer, and attached speakers complete the output environment. Now the computer can produce the sound of an orchestra or a rock band. Those of us who simply enjoy music can have a full sight/sound

Figure 4-12 Computer graphics.
The world can look just a bit different when computer graphics enter the picture. (a,b, and d) These images were generated entirely on the computer by graphics artists. (c) This image is a wily combination of computer graphics and digitized photographs.

(a)

(b)

(c)

(d)

experience using multimedia, which we will explore in more detail in the next chapter, and also in a separate multimedia gallery.

Computer Graphics

Computer output in the form of graphics has come into its own in a major—and sometimes spectacular—way. Many readers of this book have seen the application of graphics to video games. Just about everyone has seen TV commercials or movies that use computer-produced animated graphics. Computer graphics can also be found in education, computer art, science, sports, and more (Figure 4-12). But perhaps their most prevalent use today is in business.

Business Graphics

It might seem wasteful to display in color graphics what could more inexpensively be shown to managers as numbers in standard computer printouts. However, colorful graphics, maps, and charts can help managers compare data more easily, spot trends, and make decisions more quickly. Also, the use of color helps people get the picture, literally. Finally, although color graphs and charts have been used in business for years—usually to make presentations to higher management or outside clients—the computer allows them to be rendered quickly, before information becomes outdated. One user refers to business graphics as "computer-assisted insight."

Video Graphics

Unfettered by reality, **video graphics** can be as creative as an animated cartoon (Figure 4-13). Although they operate on the same principle as a moving picture or cartoon—one frame at a time in quick succession—**video graphics** are produced by computers. Video graphics have made their biggest splash on television, but many people do not realize they are watching computers at work. The next time you watch television, skip the trip to the kitchen and pay special attention to the commercials. Unless there is a live human in the advertisement, there is a good chance that the moving objects you see, such as floating cars and bobbing electric razors, are computer output. Another fertile ground for video graphics is each television network's logo and theme. Accompanied by music and swooshing sounds, the network symbol spins and cavorts and turns itself inside out, all with the finesse that only a computer could supply.

Video graphics do not have to be commercial in nature. Some video artists produce beauty for its own sake. In science, video graphics have helped produce moving models, such as a model of DNA molecules whose atoms, represented by gleaming spheres, twist and fold.

Figure 4-13 Video graphics. These screens are from a computer-animated series featuring a walking clock—time marches on.

Computer-Aided Design/Computer-Aided Manufacturing

For more than a decade, computer graphics have also been part and parcel of a field known by the abbreviation **CAD/CAM**—short for **computer-aided design/computer-aided manufacturing.** In this area computers are used to create two- and three-dimensional pictures of

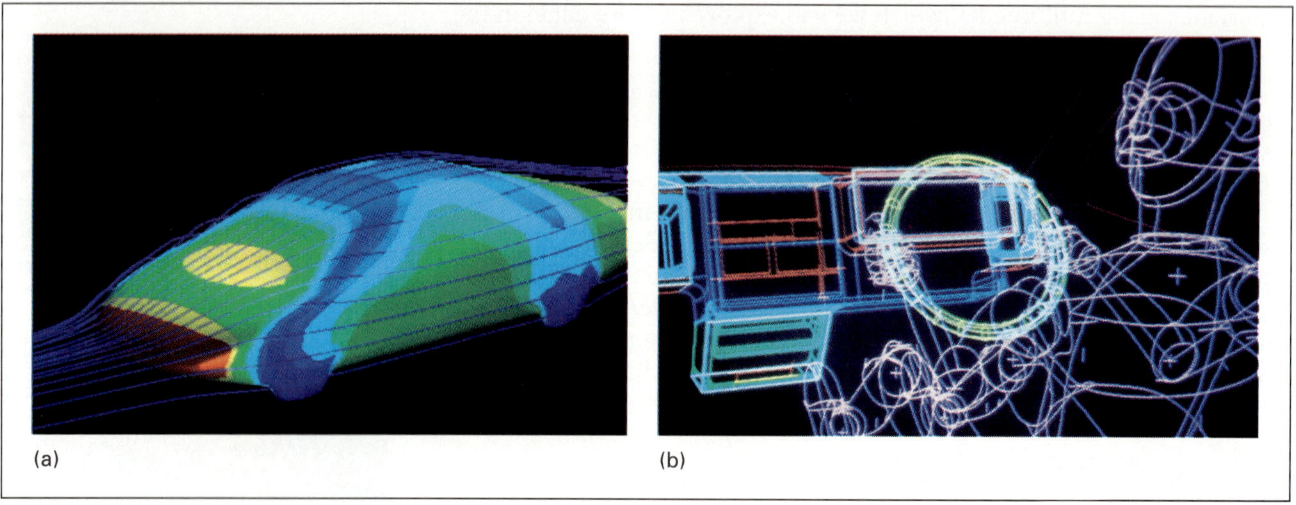

Figure 4-14 CAD/CAM.
With computer-aided design/computer-aided manufacturing (CAD/CAM), the computer can keep track of all details, maintain designs of parts in memory, and combine parts electronically as required. (a) A computer-aided design wireframe used to study design possibilities. (b) Engineers also use graphics to test designs relative to the customer who will use the car.

everything from hand tools to tractors. CAD/CAM provides a bridge between design (planning what a product will be) and manufacturing (actually making the planned product). As a manager at Chrysler said, "Many companies have design data and manufacturing data and the two are never the same. At Chrysler we have only one set of data that everyone dips into." For an example of their efforts, see Figure 4-14.

Graphics Input Devices

There are many ways to produce and interact with screen graphics. We have already described the mouse; the following are some other common devices that allow the user to interact with screen graphics.

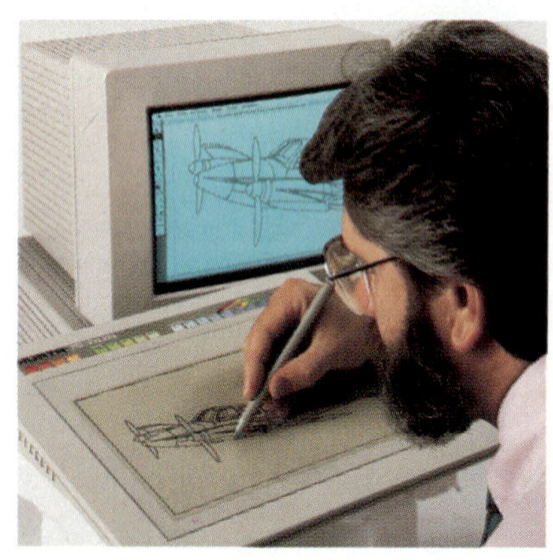

Figure 4-15 Digitizer.
This engineer is using a digitizing tablet to input his drawing to the computer.

Digitizer

An image, whether a drawing or a photo, can be scanned by a device called a digitizer, which converts the image into digital data that the computer can accept and represent on the screen. However, a digitizing tablet lets you create your own images (Figure 4-15). This device has a special stylus that can be used to draw or trace images, which are then converted to digital data that can be processed by the computer.

Light Pen

For direct interaction with your computer screen, the light pen is ideal. It is versatile enough to modify screen graphics or make a menu selection—that is, to choose from a list of activity choices on the screen. A **light pen** has a light-sensitive cell at one end. When the light pen is placed against the screen, it closes a photoelectric circuit that pinpoints the spot the pen is touching. This tells the computer where to enter or modify pictures or data on the screen.

Joystick

Another well-known graphics input device is the **joystick,** dear to the hearts of video game fans. This device allows fingertip control of figures on a CRT screen.

Touch Screen

If you disdain pens and sticks and mice, perhaps you would prefer the direct human touch, your finger. **Touch screens** accept input data by letting you point at the screen to select your choice (Figure 4-16). Sensors on the edges of the screen pinpoint the touch location and cause a corresponding response on the screen. Touch screens are widely used in public places, such as hospitals and airports to give directions, and tourist attractions such as Epcot Center to involve the user in demonstrations. Touch screens are even used for bridal registries in large department stores.

Figure 4-16 Touch screen.
A pointing finger interrupts light beams emitted from the edges of the screen. The computer translates the interruption into a point on the screen.

Scanner

"You are about to witness something amazing." This sentence is part of a demonstration of a hand-held **scanner.** The demonstration *is* rather amazing. As you watch the scanner being moved over written text and pictures, the same text and pictures appear on the screen of the attached computer and are stored in a disk file. Scanners come in both hand-held and desktop models (Figure 4-17). Although all scanners can scan images, they vary in their ability to scan text. Some files created by scanning can be used like any other file; that is, they can be edited, printed, and so forth.

Who would use such a device? Anyone who prefers scanning to typing. For example, teachers can scan text in books or magazines for use in class-

Figure 4-17 Scanners.
(a) With a desktop scanner, the picture is laid face down on the scanner, which looks somewhat like a small copy machine. Once an image is scanned into the computer, it can be altered and combined with text to produce documents complete with illustrations. (b) As this hand-held scanner is moved over a picture, the image appears on the computer screen.

(a)

(b)

Figure 4-18 Plotter.
Designers of circuit boards, street maps, schematic diagrams, and similar applications can work in fine detail on a computer screen, and then print the results on a plotter.

room exercises. Lawyers can scan contracts. In addition, a variety of users may wish to scan art or photographs to be manipulated by the computer.

Graphics Output Devices

Just as there are many different ways to input graphics to the computer, there also are many different ways to output graphics. Graphics are most commonly output on a screen or printed paper, as previously discussed. Another popular graphics output device is the **plotter,** which can draw hard-copy graphics output in the form of maps, bar charts, engineering drawings, and even two- or three-dimensional illustrations (Figure 4-18). A plotter often comes with a set of four pens in four different colors. Most plotters also offer shading features.

New forms of computer input and output are developed regularly, with an array of benefits for human use. The effectiveness of the new forms, however, depends on two components that we have not yet discussed: storage and software. We will study the first of these in the next chapter.

Chapter **Review**

Summary and Key Terms

- The keyboard is a common input device for personal computer users, as well as for those who use computer terminals to enter data from **source documents.**
- A **cursor** is an indicator on a screen that shows where the next interaction with the computer will take place.
- A **mouse** is an input device whose movement on a flat surface causes corresponding movement of the **pointer,** or **cursor,** on the screen.
- The **trackball** is sort of an upside-down mouse, in that the ball that usually rolls along a flat surface is facing up and is manipulated by hand, causing corresponding movement of the cursor on the screen.
- **Source data automation,** the use of special equipment to collect data and send it directly to the computer, is a more efficient method of data entry than keyboarding. Four means of source data automation are magnetic-ink character recognition, optical recognition, data collection devices, and voice input.
- **Magnetic-ink character recognition (MICR)** readers read characters made of magnetized particles, such as the preprinted characters on a personal check.
- **Optical recognition** systems convert optical marks, optical characters, handwritten characters, and bar codes into electrical signals sent to the computer. **Optical-mark recognition (OMR)** devices use a light beam to recognize marks on paper. **Optical-character recognition (OCR)** devices use a light beam to read special characters, such as those on price tags. These characters are often in a standard typeface called **OCR-A.** A commonly used OCR device is the hand-held **wand reader,** which is often connected to a **point-of-sale (POS) terminal** in a retail store. Some optical scanners can read precise **handwritten characters.** A **bar code reader** is a stationary photoelectric scanner used to input a **bar code,** the pattern of vertical marks representing the **Universal Product Code (UPC)** that identifies a product.
- **Data collection devices** allow direct, accurate data entry. **Voice input** processes data to the computer through the spoken word. **Speech recognition devices** convert spoken words into a digital code for the computer. In a **speaker-dependent** system, the speech recognition device "learns" the voice of the user; **speaker-independent** systems can recognize commands from any speaker.
- Some computer screens are **monochrome**—the characters appear in one color on a black background. Color screens display color text and graphics. The most common type of screen is the **cathode ray tube (CRT).** Using **raster-scan technology,** a screen image is formed by beaming electrons on a phosphorous-backed screen, causing it to glow.
- Each screen dot is potentially a *pic*ture *el*ement, or **pixel**. The more pixels, the higher the screen's **resolution,** or clarity.
- Color screen standards include **CGA** (color graphics adaptor) with 320 by 200 pixels, **EGA** (enhanced graphics adaptor) with 640 by 350 pixels, the common **VGA** (video graphics array) with 640 by 480 pixels, and **SVGA** (super VGA) with 800 by 600 pixels or 1024 by 768 pixels.
- Some screens are **monochrome**, meaning that only one color appears on a dark background. Another type is the **liquid crystal display (LCD),** a flat screen found on portable computers.

- A screen may be the monitor of a self-contained personal computer, or it may be part of a **terminal,** an input-output device linked to a main computer.
- **Printers** produce **hard copy,** or printed paper output. (**Soft copy** is displayed on a screen.) Some printers produce solid characters; **dot-matrix printers,** however, construct characters by producing closely spaced dots.
- Printers can be classified as being either **impact printers,** which form characters by physically striking the paper, or **nonimpact printers,** which use a noncontact printing method. Nonimpact printers, which include **laser** and **ink-jet printers,** are faster and quieter than impact printers.
- Computer **speech synthesis** has been accomplished through **voice synthesizers** (also called **voice-output devices** or **audio-response units**).
- **Video graphics** are computer-produced pictures.
- In **computer-aided design/computer-aided manufacturing (CAD/CAM)**, computers are used to create two- and three-dimensional pictures of manufactured products such as hand tools and vehicles.
- Common graphics input devices include the mouse, **light pen, digitizer, digitizing tablet, joystick, touch screen, and scanner**.
- Graphics output devices include screens, printers, and **plotters**.

Student Personal Study Guide

True/False

T F 1. A trackball is particularly appropriate for a laptop computer.
T F 2. Screen output is called soft copy.
T F 3. The 24-pin is the most popular dot-matrix printer.
T F 4. An ink-jet printer prints color output that exactly matches the screen colors.
T F 5. A pointer and cursor are the same thing.
T F 6. LCD stands for liquid crystal display.
T F 7. Bar code scanning is an optical recognition system.
T F 8. The cursor shows where the next computer interaction will take place.
T F 9. Laser printers use a light beam to transfer images to paper.
T F 10. Speaker-dependent systems can recognize the voice of any speaker.

Multiple Choice

1. A screen with one color on a black background:
   a. OCR-A   c. UPC
   b. dot matrix   d. monochrome
2. A printer that forms characters by physically striking the paper:
   a. laser   c. ink-jet
   b. nonimpact   d. impact
3. Which is *not* a graphics input device?
   a. plotter   c. light pen
   b. scanner   d. digitizer
4. The most common type of monitor:
   a. CRT   c. OMR
   b. UPC   d. LCD
5. Which is *not* a type of optical recognition?
   a. OMR   c. OCR
   b. CAD/CAM   d. UPC

6. MICR is used primarily in:
   a. retail — c. hospitals
   b. banking — d. testing
7. A "cash register" terminal in retail store:
   a. POS — c. bar code
   b. UPC — d. wand
8. The flat screen usually found on laptop computers:
   a. UPC — c. POS
   b. LCD — d. CRT
9. A voice synthesizer is also called:
   a. CAD/CAM — c. audio-response unit
   b. raster-scan unit — d. video unit
10. A graphics output device:
   a. plotter — c. light pen
   b. trackball — d. digitizer

Fill-In

1. A one-color screen is called : ____________________.
2. The technology to create a screen image: ____________________.
3. The use of special equipment to collect data at the source: ____________________.
4. The method used mainly by banks for processing checks: ____________________.
5. Screen output is called: ____________________.
6. Printed computer output is called: ____________________.
7. This device converts a graphic image to digital data: ____________________.
8. UPC stands for: ____________________.
9. CAD/CAM stands for: ____________________.
10. Computer-produced animated pictures: ____________________.

Answers

True/False: 1. T, 2. T, 3. T, 4. F, 5. T, 6. T, 7. T, 8. T, 9. T, 10. F
Multiple choice: 1. d, 2. d , 3. a , 4. a, 5. b, 6. b, 7. a, 8. b, 9. c, 10. a
Fill-In: 1. monochrome, 2. raster-scan technology, 3. source data automation, 4. MICR, 5. soft copy, 6. hard copy, 7. scanner, 8. Universal Product Code, 9. computer-aided design/computer-aided manufacturing, 10. video graphics

Storage

Chapter Overview

Barbara McCormick, CEO for a sporting goods manufacturer, bought a personal computer for her office. She had seen what several of her colleagues were able to do with their computers and was intrigued. She knew that if computing was good for everyone else in the company, it would probably be good for her, too. Barbara was, of course, a little concerned about starting out and making all the right equipment choices.

Barbara took time to investigate personal computers. She wanted a machine that had growth potential. Working with a professional from the information systems department, Barbara decided on a midpriced model with ample speed and memory, a color monitor, and a laser printer.

Barbara hesitated about the storage, however. The information systems consultant convinced her that having both a diskette drive and a hard drive was a necessity. (As we will see, this arrangement is timesaving and convenient.) But Barbara had some misgivings about the capacity of the hard disk. Could she ever really use the 250-megabyte disk the consultant recommended? How could she possibly come up with 250 *million* characters of data? The consultant pointed out that Barbara would be storing software as well as data on her hard disk. Barbara finally chose a 100-megabyte disk, which seemed more than adequate to her at the time.

Barbara's hard disk *was* adequate for its original purposes—storing a few software packages plus her own data—notes, letters, outlines, documents, speeches, and position papers. However, Barbara soon began branching out in other directions, using various types of software. She tracked names and phone numbers, analyzed financial data, and produced business graphics. She began using her computer to file ideas that could be accessed instantaneously. All her new software and data used disk space, and Barbara eventually found that her hard disk was getting crowded.

To prevent a possible dilemma, computer professionals usually advise computer buyers to estimate disk needs generously and then double the estimate. However, estimating future needs is rarely easy. In particular, people tend to think only in terms of what data they might generate, not realizing that ever-emerging and attractive software packages will take up considerable disk space. Many users, therefore, make later adjustments. In this chapter we will examine several storage options, including the type of hard disk Barbara originally chose.

Devices

Electronic Filing Cabinets

Take Me Off Your Mailing List!

Tired of getting junk mail? Concerned about the impact of all that paper on the environment? You can write to the Direct Marketing Association, an organization that assists customers who do not want advertising mail. The address is:

P.O. Box 3861
11 West 42nd Street
New York, NY 10163-3861

The association will send your name to hundreds of mail-order houses and other institutions, requesting that you not be sent advertising mail. By the way, most people receive junk mail under several names—Maureen Allaire receives mail addressed to Maureen G. Allaire or M. G. Allaire, for example—so be sure to include each name. Keep in mind that this request only prevents your name from being sold, traded, or given away to be added to *new* lists. If you have done business with a firm, you will have to write to that firm individually to stop its mailings.

The DMA updates its files quarterly; once you make a request it may take several months before you notice any results. Eventually, your junk mail should be cut by more than half.

Why Secondary Storage?

Whether considering your own personal computer storage or the broader needs of a corporation or government agency, the choices can be complicated. Picture, if you can, how many filing-cabinet drawers would be required to hold the millions of files of, say, criminal records kept by the U.S. Justice Department or employee records kept by General Motors. The rooms to hold the filing cabinets would have to be enormous. Computer storage, which allows the storage of many records in extremely compressed form and provides quick access to them, is unquestionably one of the computer's most valuable assets.

Secondary storage is needed for two reasons. First, primary storage—memory—is limited in size, whereas secondary storage media can store as much information as necessary. Also, memory can be used only temporarily; data disappears from memory when you turn most computers off. You need secondary storage to store indefinitely the data you have used or the information you have derived from processing.

Suppose, for example, you spend a long afternoon at the computer as part of your assignment as a management trainee. You have created and reworked a special report for the vice president of marketing to take on an upcoming sales trip. The report needs only another couple of hours of polishing, which you can do the next morning. It would be out of the question to begin again from scratch. Thus you need secondary storage, or **auxiliary storage,** to save your work so that you can retrieve it at a later time and carry on where you left off.

Personal computer users know that they need secondary storage as a place to keep the files they create. Files can include letters, memos, reports, and even complex output such as financial calculations or graphics. Writing files onto a personal computer output medium, usually a disk, is a relatively simple matter. A user needs only to learn the output commands associated with the software being used; the software package takes care of the details.

Working with business systems, whether on large or small computers, is often more complex. To begin with, business systems are usually concerned with records—possibly data about products, customers, or employees. A user who needs to plan computer output must understand how data is organized and processed and know the type of storage medium that will hold the data.

We begin by considering how data is organized and how it is processed. From there we will move on to different types of storage media, first for large computers and then for personal computers.

Data: Getting Organized

We have already described data representation in terms of bits and bytes in Chapter 3. Recall that a byte represents a character of data and that a series of bits represents a byte in the computer. We now consider how to organize data in convenient groupings. To be processed by the computer, data—represented by characters—is often organized into fields, records, files, and sometimes databases (Figure 5-1). Here is a brief description of each of these elements:

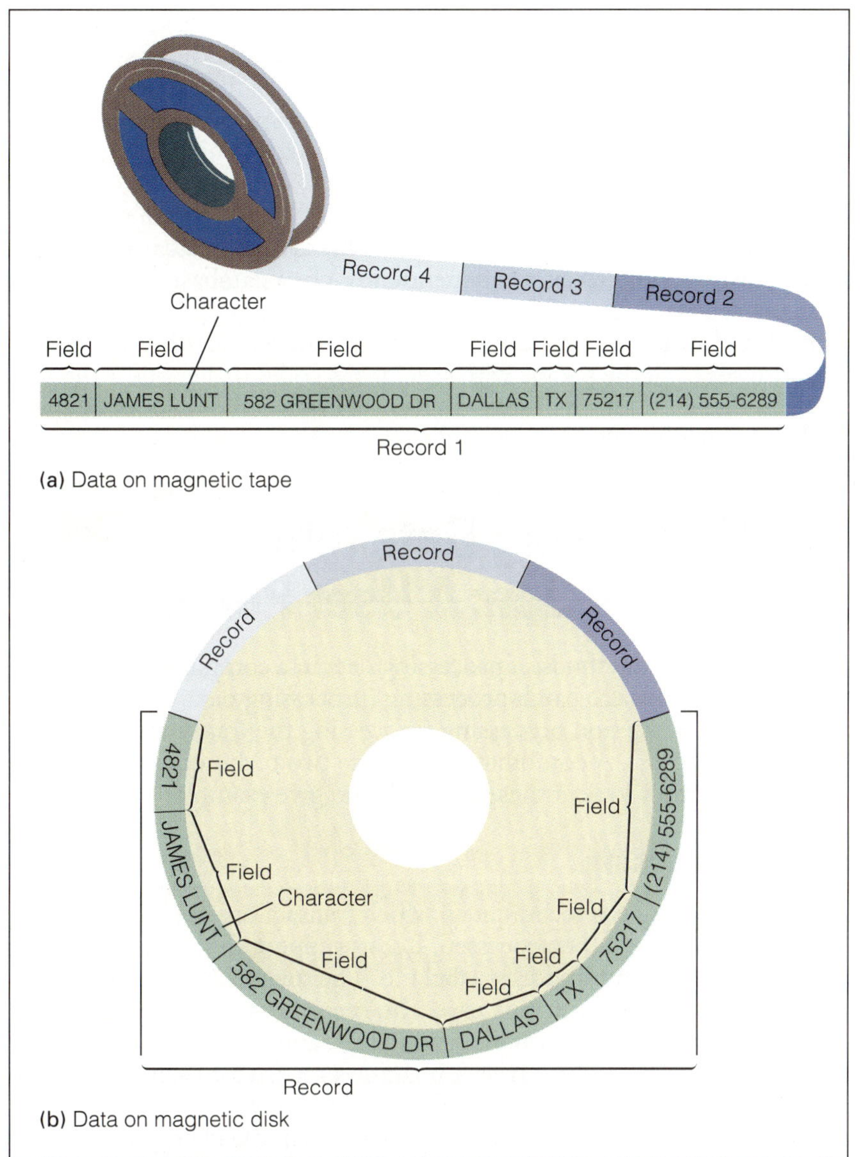

Figure 5-1 How data is organized.
Data, represented by characters, is organized into fields, records, and files. A file is a collection of related records.

- A **character** is a letter, digit, or special character (such as $, ?, or *). One or more related characters constitute a field.
- A **field** contains a set of related characters. For example, suppose a health club is making address labels for a mailing. For each person it has fields for membership number, name, street address, city, state, zip code, and phone number.
- A **record** is a collection of related fields. Thus, on the health club list, one person's membership number, name, address, city, state, zip code, and phone number constitute a record. (The fields are considered related because they are for the same person.)

- One kind of **file** is a collection of related records. All the member records for the health club compose a membership file. Note, however, that not all files are collections of records; a file can also contain, for example, a letter, an essay, a graphic, or a spreadsheet. But in the following section regarding processing, the files being discussed are collections of records.
- A **database** may be a collection of records or a collection of interrelated files stored together. (However, a file is not necessarily part of a database; many files exist independently.) In a database, specific data items can be retrieved for various applications. For instance, if the health club is opening a new outlet, it can extract the names and addresses of all the people with specific zip codes that are near the new club. The club can then send a special announcement about opening day to those people.

Processing Data Into Information: A User Perspective

There are several methods of processing data in a computer system. The two main methods are batch processing (processing data transactions in groups) and transaction processing (processing the transactions one at a time as they occur). A combination of these two techniques may also be used. We will now look at these methods and give examples of their use.

Batch Processing

Batch processing is a technique in which transactions are collected into groups, or batches, to be processed. Let us suppose that we are going to update the health club's address label file. The **master file,** a semipermanent set of records, is, in this case, the records of all members of the health club, including their names, addresses, and so forth.

To use an ordinary comparison, imagine a record for each member on a separate sheet of paper, and the file of collected records—the sheets of paper—in a file drawer. If we wanted to make simple changes manually, we could simply add a new sheet for a new member, scratch out an old phone number and pencil in the new number on the sheet for an existing member, or perhaps remove a sheet altogether for a member who is resigning from the health club. This method of updating a file drawer is cumbersome and time-consuming for a large file. Computerized batch processing takes a different approach to accomplish the same task more efficiently. All changes to be made to the master file are compiled on a separate **transaction file.** Such changes can be of the following types:

- *Additions* are transactions to create new master records for new members. If Beth Andrews is joining the club, a transaction containing the fields for Ms. Andrews—including her membership number, name, address, and so forth—will be prepared to add the new membership record to the file.
- *Revisions* are transactions to change fields, such as street addresses or phone numbers, on the master records. For example, if Jim Lawler changes his address and phone number, a transaction is prepared to reflect these changes on his record in the master file.

- *Deletions* are transactions with instructions to remove master records of people who have resigned from the health club. For example, if Thuy Tran resigns from the club, a transaction is prepared to remove her record from the file.

At regular intervals, perhaps monthly, the master file is **updated** with the changes called for on the separate transaction file, which has been sorted in order by a key field such as a social security number. The result is a new, up-to-date master file. The new file in this example has a new record for Beth Andrews, has a changed record for Jim Lawler, and no longer has a record for Thuy Tran.

An advantage of batch processing is that it is usually less expensive than other types of processing because it is more efficient: A group of records is processed at the same time. A disadvantage of batch processing is that it is not immediate. Anyone who wants to know the exact status—customers or business users—has to wait. It does not matter that you want to know what the gasoline bill for your car is now; you have to wait until the end of the month, when all your credit-card gas purchases are processed together with those of other customers. Batch processing cannot give you a quick response to your question.

Transaction Processing

Transaction processing is a technique of processing transactions one at a time in random order—that is, in any order they occur. Since transactions are processed at the time the transaction occurs, the files are always up-to-date.Transaction processing is handy for anyone who needs an immediate update or feedback from the computer, such as a contractor who needs to check a supplier's rates, an airline clerk making a reservation, or a retailer who wants to confirm product inventory. Transaction processing has become a staple in all kinds of service industries in which speedy service is a must.

Transaction processing is real-time processing. **Real-time processing** can obtain data from the computer system in time to affect the activity at hand. In other words, a transaction is processed fast enough for the results to come back and be acted upon immediately. For example, a teller at a bank (or you at an automatic teller machine) can find out immediately what your bank balance is. You can then decide how much money you can afford to withdraw. For processing to be real-time, it must also be **online**—that is, the user's terminal must be directly connected to the computer to which the data files are available.

The great leap forward that transaction processing represents was made possible by the development of magnetic disk as a means of storing data. With magnetic tape it is not efficient to go directly to the particular record you are looking for; the tape might have to be advanced several feet first. However, with disk you can go directly to one particular record. The development of magnetic disk meant that data processing is more likely to be **interactive,** as is possible with the personal computer. The user can communicate directly with the computer, maintaining a dialogue back and forth. The direct access to data on disk dramatically increased the use of interactive computing.

There are several advantages to transaction processing. The first is that you do not need to wait. For instance, a department store salesclerk using a POS terminal can key in a customer's charge-card number and a code that asks the computer "Is this charge card acceptable?" and get an immediate reply. Immediacy is a distinct benefit, since everyone expects fast service these days. Second, the process permits continual updating of a customer's record. Thus the salesclerk not only can verify your credit but also can record the sale in the computer, and you will eventually be billed through the computerized billing process.

Figure 5-2 provides an example of transaction processing, in which a patient submits a prescription.

Batch and Transaction Processing: Complementary

Numerous computer systems combine the best features of both of these methods of processing. A bank, for instance, may record your withdrawal transaction during the day at the teller window whenever you demand your cash. However, the deposit that you leave in an envelope in an

Figure 5-2 How transaction processing works.
The purposes of this hospital-clinic pharmacy system are to verify that a patient's prescription is safe, produce a prescription label for the medication bottle, and update the patient's medical records. Since there is a possibility of patients having the same name, the file is organized by unique patient numbers rather than by names. Here Ryan Johnson, patient number 32689, brings his prescription to the pharmacist. (1) Through a terminal the pharmacist queries the computer system whether the ampicillin prescribed is apt to conflict with any other medication the patient is taking. (2) The computer screen verifies that 32689 is Ryan Johnson and displays the message "No conflict." The computer then updates Johnson's file so other physicians can see later that ampicillin was prescribed for him. (3) A printer attached to the computer system prints a prescription label that the pharmacist can place on the ampicillin bottle. All this is done while the patient is waiting.

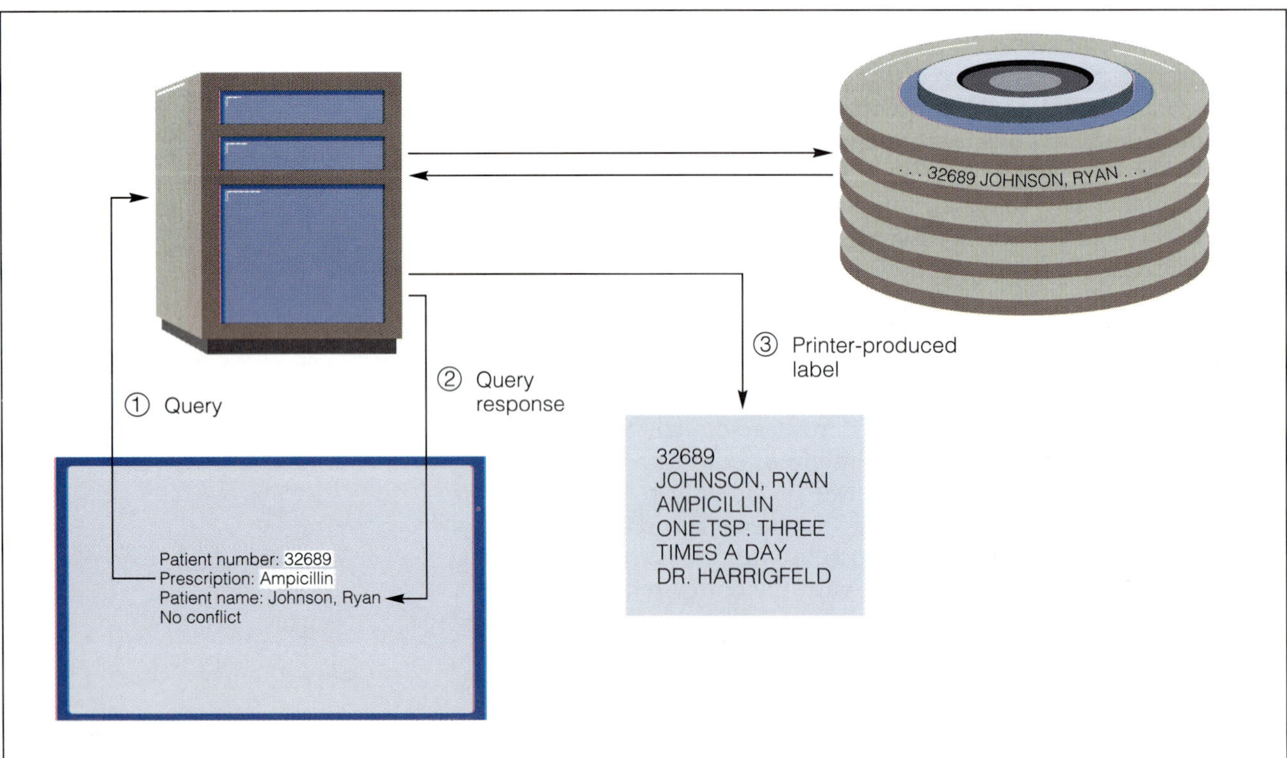

"instant" deposit drop may be recorded during the night by means of batch processing.

Another common example of both batch and transaction processing is in retail sales. Using POS terminals, inventory data is captured as sales are made; this data is processed later in batches to produce inventory reports.

Figure 5-3 Magnetic tape.
Magnetic tape on 10½-inch-diameter reels has been the workhorse of data processing for years. However, a smaller tape cartridge has been introduced that can hold 20 percent more data in 75 percent less space.

Storage Media

As we have mentioned, two primary media for storing data are magnetic tape and magnetic disk. Since these media have been the staples of the computer industry for three decades, we will begin with them.

Magnetic Tape Storage

Magnetic tape looks like the plastic Mylar tape used in home tape recorders. Large computer systems typically use tape that is ½ inch wide and wound on a 10½-inch-diameter reel (Figure 5-3). Personal computers use tape only to back up disk files, that is, for emergency use if any harm comes to the disk files. Tape has an iron-oxide coating that can be magnetized. Data is stored as extremely small magnetized spots, which can then be read by a tape unit into the computer's main storage.

Figure 5-4a shows a **magnetic tape unit** that is part of a large computer system. The purpose of the unit is to write and to read—that is, to record data on and retrieve data from—magnetic tape. This is done by a

Figure 5-4 Magnetic tape units.
Tapes are always covered—in this case, by glass doors—to protect them from outside dust and dirt. (a) Magnetic tape on reels runs on these tape drives. (b) This diagram highlights the read/write head and the erase head found in magnetic tape units.

(a)

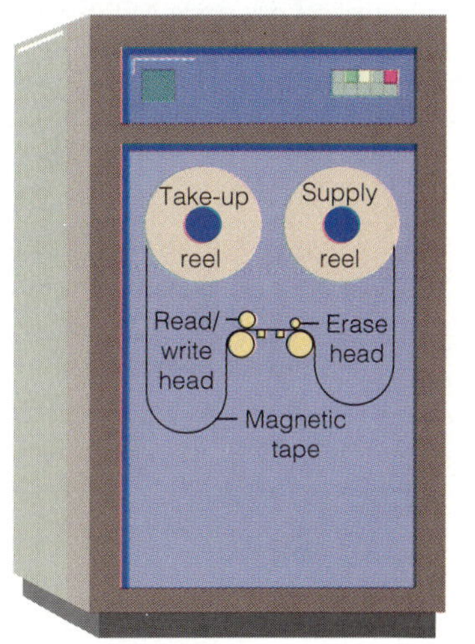

(b)

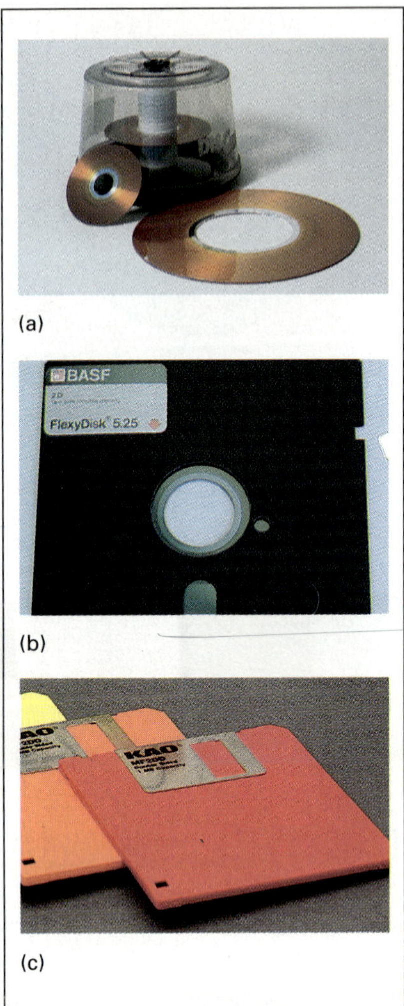

Figure 5-5 Magnetic disks.
(a) Hard magnetic disks come in a variety of sizes, as shown by these three individual disks. Disk packs can vary in the number of disks they contain. (b) This 5¼-inch diskette is in a square protective thin plastic jacket. (c) This 3½-inch diskette is protected by a firm plastic exterior cover.

read/write head (Figure 5-4b). Reading is done by an electromagnet that senses the magnetized areas on the tape and converts them into electrical impulses, which are sent to the processor. The reverse process is called writing. Before the machine writes on the tape, the **erase head** erases any previously recorded data, permitting the write head to write over the top of the erased data.

Records are stored on tape sequentially—in order by some identifier such as a social security number.

Magnetic Disk Storage

Magnetic disk storage is another common form of secondary storage. A **hard magnetic disk,** or **hard disk,** is a metal platter coated with magnetic oxide that looks something like a large brown compact disk. Hard disks come in a variety of sizes: 14, 5¼, and 3½ inches are typical diameters. Several disks of the same size can be assembled together to form a **disk pack** (Figure 5-5a). A disk pack looks like a stack of stereo records, except that daylight can be seen between the disks. There are different types of disk packs, with the number of platters varying by model. Each disk has a top and bottom surface on which to record data.

Another form of magnetic disk storage is the **diskette,** which is a round piece of plastic coated with magnetic oxide (Figure 5-5b, c). Both diskettes and hard disks are used with personal computers. We will discuss secondary storage for personal computers later in this chapter, but keep in mind that the principles of disk storage discussed here also apply to disk storage for personal computers.

How Data Is Stored on a Magnetic Disk

As Figure 5-6 shows, the surface of each disk has tracks on it. Data is recorded as magnetic spots on the tracks. The number of tracks per surface varies with the particular type of disk. A track on a disk is a closed circle, so any point on a particular track is always the same distance from the center. All tracks on one disk are concentric; that is, they are circles with the same center.

A magnetic disk drive is a **direct access storage device (DASD).** With such a random access device, you can go directly to the record you want. With tape storage, on the other hand, you must read all preceding records in the file until you come to the desired record. Records can be stored either sequentially or randomly (in whatever order the records occur) on a direct access storage device.

The Disk Drive

A **disk drive** is a device that allows data to be read from a disk or written on a disk. A diskette is inserted into a disk drive that is part of a personal computer. A disk pack, on the other hand, is mounted on a disk drive that is a separate unit connected to a large, shared computer. Some disks are permanently mounted inside a disk drive. Generally, these are used in personal computers or in cases where several users are sharing data. A typical example is a disk with files containing flight information that is used by several airline reservations agents.

The mechanism for reading or writing data on a disk is an **access arm** (Figure 5-7a). The access arm acts somewhat like the arm on a record

The screen photo that opens this gallery is taken from a multimedia offering called *From Alice to Ocean,* which beautifully chronicles a young woman's journey, with her camels, across the Australian outback.

Multimedia

The New Sight and Sound

The Multimedia Story

Multimedia is different. For example, have you ever thought that you could see a film clip from *Gone with the Wind* on your computer screen? One could argue that such treats are already available on videocassette, but the computer version provides an added dimension for this and other movies: reviews by critics, photographs of movie stars, lists of Academy Awards, and much more.

Although an "ordinary" personal computer is certainly adequate for most personal and business uses, a computer equipped for multimedia offers a greater variety of information. Multimedia software typically presents information with text, illustrations, photos, narration, music, animation, and film clips.

A multimedia computer looks much like an ordinary personal computer on the surface. The main difference that can be seen is the speakers on either side.

How Is This Possible?

The key to multimedia is the high-volume capacity of optical disks. One CD-ROM disk can hold approximately 500 times as much data as an ordinary data diskette. This capacity accommodates the kinds of data that take up huge amounts of storage space, such as photographs, film clips, and music.

From a hardware standpoint, a multimedia computer must be equipped with a CD-ROM drive to read the disks. Also needed are a sound card (installed internally) and speakers, which normally rest on either side of the computer. Special software accompanies the drive and sound card.

To Buy or Not To Buy

Should your next computer be a multimedia personal computer? Absolutely. There is no doubt that multimedia applications will be the standard very shortly. Furthermore, if you get multimedia components pre-installed, it is the computer maker's job to see that everything works together properly.

But suppose you already own a personal computer and do not plan to get a new one any time soon. Should you upgrade your current computer with a multimedia kit? This is a tougher question. A multimedia kit usually includes a CD-ROM drive, a sound card, speakers, required software, and several application diskettes. Installing the required hardware and software is not usually an easy task. Unless you are fairly skilled, you should make sure you have support from a vendor or some other source before you begin this task. Once a multimedia system is set up, you can take advantage of the growing list of multimedia software packages.

The Coming Deluge

If you take a moment to peruse the racks of multimedia software in your local store, you can see that most of the current offerings come under the categories of entertainment or education — or possibly both. You can study *and hear* works by Stravinsky or Schubert. You can explore the planets or the ocean bottom through film clips and narrations by experts. You can be "elected" to Congress, after which you tour the Capitol, decorate your office, hire staff, and vote on issues. You can study the Japanese language, seeing the symbols and hearing the intonation. You can buy reference books, magazines, children's books, and entire novels.

But this is just the beginning. Businesses are already moving to this high-capacity environment for street atlases, national phone directories, and sales catalogs. Coming offerings will include every kind of standard business application — all tricked out with fancy animation, photos, and sound. Educators will be able to draw upon the new sight and sound for everything from human anatomy to time travel. And just imagine the library of the future, consisting of not only the printed word but also photos, film, animation, and sound recordings — all flowing from the computer.

These scenes are from a multimedia package that provides a narrated tour of the London Gallery of Art. The scene above, by Titian, depicts the ancient myth of *Bacchus and Ariadne*. The scene below, by Renoir, is called *Boating on the Seine*.

People who wish to upgrade their existing computers can buy a multimedia kit, which typically contains a CD-ROM drive, a sound card, speakers, and several diskettes.

1

A2

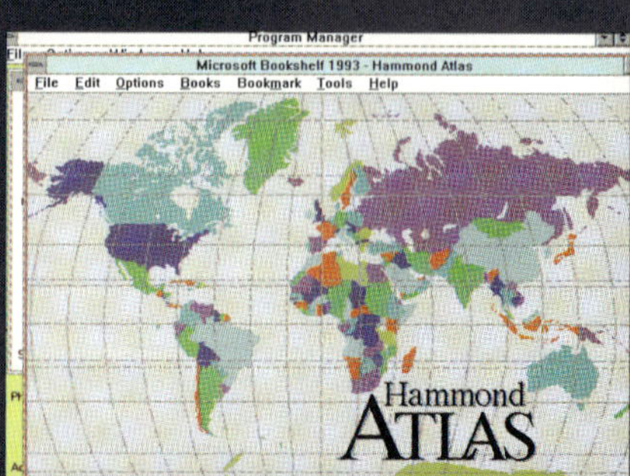

3

The pictures on the following pages are taken from screens presented by various multimedia packages. The photos must be shown in limited sizes to retain their clarity. However, this means that there is room for more screen shots.

1. The Microsoft Bookshelf software opens with this screen shot of actual volumes. Click on any book to access the information within. **2.** In the Bookshelf version of *Bartlett's Familiar Quotations,* a user can, by clicking a microphone icon, hear the words from John F. Kennedy's inaugural speech actually spoken by Kennedy. **3.** This world map is one of many in the Hammond Atlas that is part of Bookshelf.

The software called *Beyond Planet Earth* provides a complete tour of all the planets. Shown here are **4,** Jupiter's atmosphere and **5,** the phenomenon known as Jupiter's great red spot.

6. *Just Grandma and Me* is one of the Living Books series, in which youngsters of all ages can interact with and even change the story. **7.** In this deceptively simple scene, a click of the mouse on any object provokes action. A click on the tree, for example, prompts a chipmunk to poke its head out of a hole in the tree and chatter.

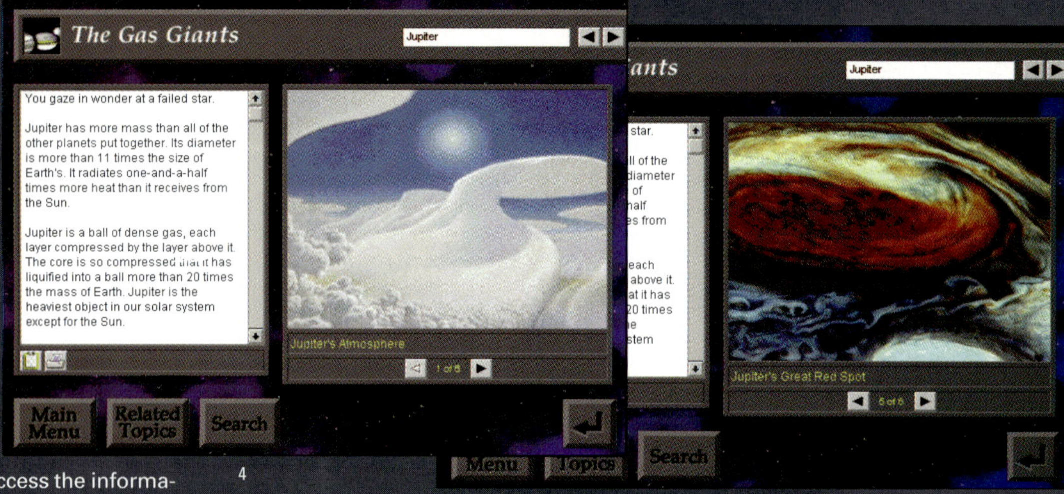

4 5

6 7

8

9

10

11

12

13

A multimedia package that tours the London Gallery of Art offers commentary on hundreds of paintings. Shown here are **8.** Seurat's *Bathers at Asnieres;* **9,** a vase of flowers by Gauguin; **10,** Degas' *Ballet Dancers;* **11,** Van Gogh's painting of a chair; **12,** Picasso's *Child with a Dove;* and **13,** *The Beach at Trouville,* by Monet.

The wonderful Dinosaurs offering shows dinosaurs of every size and shape, complete with ominous dinosaur snorting. Shown here are **14,** a Jurassic era scene, **15,** a stegosaurus eating, and **16,** a baryonyx fishing.

14

15

16

All multimedia packages offer several methods of exploring the information offered, including a menu of some sort. Here, **17** shows a menu that greets users of a package called *In the Company of Whales.* To the accompaniment of whale singing and much splashing, a user is presented with a variety of shots, including **18,** whales in shallow water and **19,** a killer whale breaching the water.

17

18

19

20

21

22

23

Several comprehensive musical packages are offered through multimedia, including Franz Schubert's *Trout Quintet.* Although the emphasis is on listening, the package incudes many offerings, including **20,** a portrait of Schubert, **21,** a picture of a manuscript with his glasses, and **22,** a "trout game," an audio matching game.

23. In this unusual multimedia package, the first track contains exhaustive information on the life and music of jazz great Louis Armstrong, including film clips of contemporaries, such as Dave Brubeck, narrating portions of that history. The remaining tracks, to be played on an audio CD system, contain performances by Armstrong.

24

25

A very tuneful package indeed, the screens from the package *Musical Instruments* exhort users to click icons to play an instrument in a variety of ways. **24.** Here, the French horn can be ripped (played rapidly) or hand stopped (moving hand to change pitch). Clicking on any word gives a closeup, **25,** such as this valve tube.

26

27

28

The comprehensive *Twain's World* package includes Mark Twain's novels, speeches, and personal letters. The media used are narration, period music, illustrations, photos, animation, and even a film clip of Twain himself in 1909. **26.** Mark Twain, shown in his later years. These illustrations accompany two of Twain's novels, **27,** *The Adventures of Huckleberry Finn* and **28,** *The Prince and the Pauper.*

29

30

31

32

33

34

The package called *Cinemania* provides users with everything they want to know about movies and movie stars. This package specializes in film clips of action scenes from movies as diverse as *Amadeus* and *Star Wars,* and even has Gene Kelly performing *"Singing in the Rain."* Photos are available of any star, including **29,** Denzel Washington, **30,** Julia Roberts, and **31,** James Dean. **32.** This screen, for *A Few Good Men,* shows a photo scene and, to the left, a menu of choices. Similar screens are shown here for **33,** *Sleepless in Seattle* and **34,** *Beauty and the Beast.*

35. This browse screen is one of several menu presentations for *Microsoft Encarta,* a multimedia encyclopedia that features photos, illustrations, narration, and animation. **36.** Screens typically present a photo accompanied by text, as shown here for the image orthicon tube. Other screen photos of interest, clockwise from the top, are **37,** integral calculus; **38,** a dry cell battery; **39,** a marmoset; **40,** altocumulus clouds; **41,** the *Mississippi Queen* paddleboat; **42,** Mount Rushmore; **43,** The University of Virginia; **44,** the international flag alphabet; and **45,** pilot Amelia Earhart.

COMPUTING TRENDS

Bride, Groom, Computer

A wedding really needs only a few essential ingredients: a bride, a groom, someone to marry them, and witnesses. So, how is it that wedding plans take weeks or months of frantic activity, with everyone desperately hoping that everything will go as planned? Those who have participated know about the complications, from invitations to caterers to photographers.

A new software offering called The Wedding Planner takes on all these activities and smooths the way. The software guides you in compiling and maintaining lists of invitations, RSVPs, gifts, and thank you notes—all on your own computer's storage. Furthermore, the software helps manage your budget, keeping a running tally of expenditures. The calendar feature guides you prior to the wedding, giving detailed planning instructions sometimes months in advance. When it comes to the wedding day, specific times are listed, as well as a list of reminders and such homey tips as "allow more time than you would expect for taking a posed photograph." It is almost like having a wedding consultant at your service, day or night. Interested? The phone number is 1-800-265-5555.

player, although its read/write heads do not actually touch the surface of the disk (Figure 5-7b). A disk pack has a series of access arms that slip in between the disks in the pack (Figure 5-7c). Two read/write heads are on each arm, one facing up for the surface above it, one facing down for the surface below it. However, only one read/write head can operate at any one time.

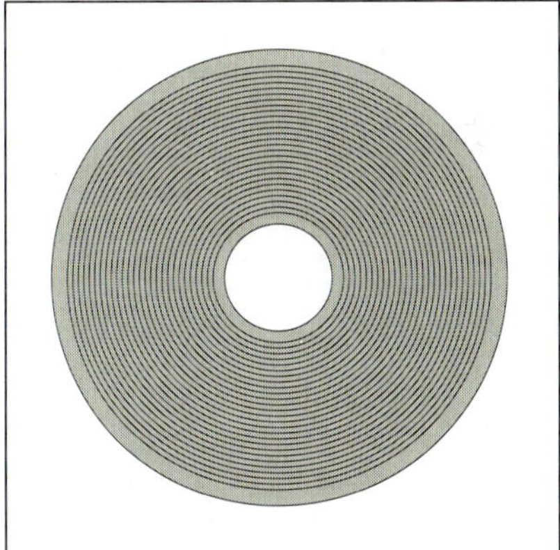

Figure 5-6 Surface of a disk.
Note that each track is a closed circle, unlike the tracks on a stereo record. This drawing is only to illustrate the location of the tracks; you cannot actually see tracks on the disk surface.

Winchester Disks

In some disk drives the access arms can be retracted, and then the disk pack can be removed from the drive. In other cases the disks, access arms, and read/write heads are combined in a **sealed module** called a **Winchester disk.** Winchester disk assemblies are put together in clean rooms so even microscopic dust particles do not get on disk surfaces. Many Winchester disks are built in, but some are removable in the sense that the entire module can be lifted from the drive. The removed module remains sealed and contains the disks and access arms.

Winchester disks were originally 14 inches in diameter, but now smaller versions are available. Hard disks on personal computers—5¼ and 3½-inch disks—always employ Winchester technology. Until 1980 the most common type of high-speed storage consisted of removable disk packs. Since then that technology has been supplanted by Winchester disks; today around 85 percent of all disk storage units sold are of the fixed Winchester variety. The principal reason is that, compared to removable disk packs, Winchester disks cost about half as much and go twice as long between failures. This increased reliability results because operators do not handle the Winchester disk at all and because the sealed module keeps the disks free from contamination.

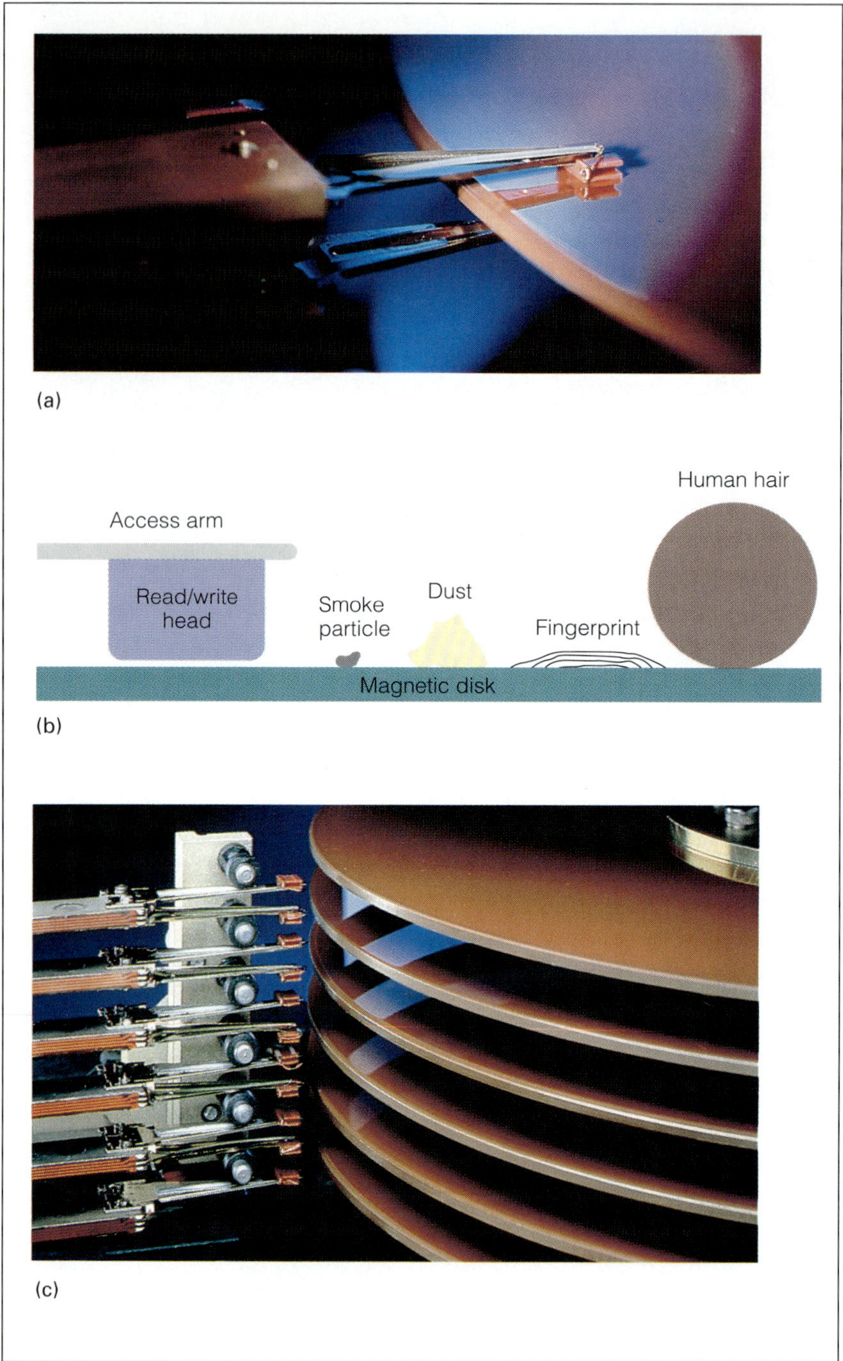

Figure 5-7 Read/write heads and access arms.
(a) This photo shows a read/write head on the end of an access arm poised over a hard disk. (b) When in operation the read/write head comes very close to the disk surface. In fact, particles as small as smoke, dust, fingerprints, and a hair loom large when they are on a disk. If the read/write head crashes into a particle like one of these, data is destroyed and the disk damaged. You can see why it is important to keep disks and disk drives clean. (c) Note that there are two read/write heads on each access arm. Each arm slips between two disks in the pack. The access arms move simultaneously, but only one read/write head operates at any one time.

MACINTOSH

Making Your Disk Space Count

Sooner or later it happens to almost everyone. No matter how inexhaustible we imagined our hard disks to be, the day arrives when we run out of storage space. The primary reason for this is that storage devices are getting less expensive: Every year you can get more megabytes per dollar when you buy a hard disk. So the 20-MB disk that seemed so boundless in capacity a few years ago is now considered minimal as users are opting for larger hard disks when they purchase their computers.

The increasing demand for disk space is likely to continue as storage prices decline. If you want your computer to be the powerful machine it was intended to be, you need to pay attention to your disk's capacity.

One way of increasing your storage potential is to invest in a compression utility program. SuperDoubler, developed by Symantec Corporation, will compress files to as little as half their size. When the files need to be accessed, SuperDoubler decompresses them back into their normal format. SuperDoubler's enormous popularity is largely due to its ability to compress your files "in the background," so that you never have to go through the steps of compressing and decompressing them. SuperDoubler can nearly double your available disk space, and the process is invisible to you, the user. The only problem with this option is that the activities of compression and decompression require some of your processor's time and can slow the performance of your machine a little.

As an alternative you should consider investing in a larger disk. If you already have an internal hard drive in your Mac and you don't want to replace it, look into an external drive, which resides in a case of its own and sits next to or under your Mac. If you anticipate that your storage needs will continue to grow, you might consider buying a removable hard drive, for which you can purchase indefinitely many 40MB or 80MB disks that pop in and out of the drive, just like 3½-inch disks. If you work heavily with sounds, images, or desktop publications, a removable drive can be of great value to you. A further advantage of a removable drive is that it facilitates easy porting of huge amounts of data to other machines that have the same kind of drive.

A removable hard drive can increase the capacity of your system's memory indefinitely with disks that have 40MB or 80MB of memory.

If you do buy a new hard disk, be sure to invest in plenty of extra capacity. The trend of programs and data files getting larger is one that's likely to continue, so planning now will ensure you have enough disk space to last years. A few years ago, a 40-MB hard drive was considered huge; now, many users are buying machines with 80MB, 170MB, 240MB, or even larger drives.

Comparison of Disk and Tape Storage

As you can see, disk storage has many advantages over tape storage. There are those in the industry who wonder why tape is still around at all. Disk does indeed seem the very model of an effective storage medium for the following reasons:

- Disk has high data-volume capacity and allows very fast access.
- Disk is reliable; barring a catastrophe, the data you put there will still be there when you want to retrieve it.
- Disk files permit direct access to read or write any given record. This is the biggest advantage and is basic to real-time systems, such as those providing instant credit checks and airline reservations.

However, tape storage has its own unique advantages. Tape is portable: A reel of tape can be carried or mailed. It is relatively inexpensive: A 2400-foot reel of tape costs less than $15. (Compare this with a full-size disk pack, which costs $300 or more.)

The chief use of magnetic tape today is as a backup medium for disk files. Although a hard disk is an extremely reliable device, the drive is subject to electromechanical failure. With any method of data storage, a **backup system**—a method of storing data in more than one place to protect it from damage or loss—is vital. Backup copies of disk files are made regularly on tape as insurance against disk failure and accidental file deletions. This topic is an important one and will be addressed more fully as a security measure in Chapter 10.

Personal Computer Storage

The market for data storage devices is being profoundly affected by the surge in popularity of personal computers. Storage media are available in two basic forms: diskettes and hard disk; most personal computers today come with both. Let us consider each of these in turn.

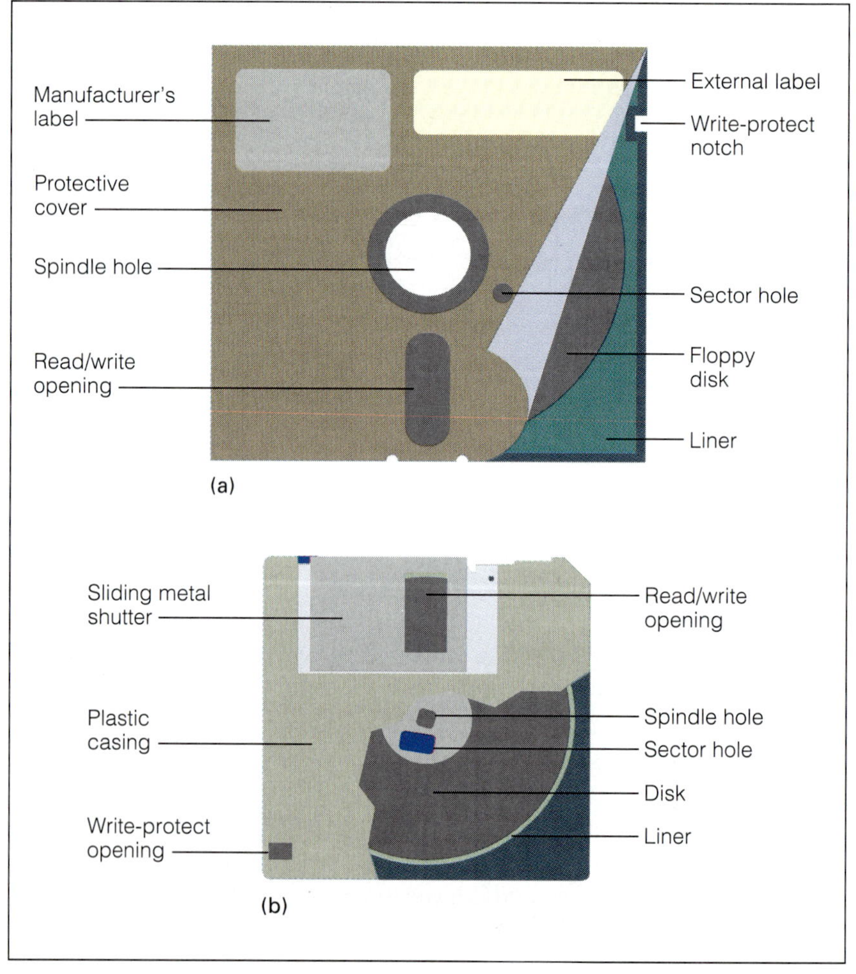

Figure 5-8 Diskettes.
(a) Cutaway view of a 5¼-inch diskette. (b) Cutaway view of a 3½ -inch diskette.

Diskettes

Diskettes, sometimes called *floppy disks,* are popular among personal computer users. Diskettes are transferable from one computer to another, provided the density, or capacity, of the borrowed disk does not exceed what the disk drive can handle. Also, diskette drives are relatively inexpensive. The 5¼-inch diskette was popular in the 1980s; however, the newer 3½-inch diskette, which can hold more data, is supplanting the 5¼-inch diskette (Figure 5-8). As a side note, some users prefer to buy a system with both 3½- and 5¼-inch diskette drives, so that their computers can accept data prepared by a computer with either size diskette drive.

The smaller disk is easier to store, and it fits handily into a shirt pocket or purse. Its hard plastic jacket provides better protection for the diskette than does the thin jacket of the larger disk. The higher capacity of the 3½-inch diskette lets users store many files on a disk, so users do not have to shuffle so many disks around. Finally, since the 3½-inch disk drive is small, manufacturers can make their computers smaller, so they take up less desk space.

In a shared computer system, such as computers in a college lab or in an office, users keep their data files on their own diskettes, which can be kept separately from the shared system.

Hard Disks

Personal computer hard disks are 5¼-inch or 3½-inch Winchester disks in sealed modules (Figure 5-9a). The cost of hard disks has come down substantially: A hard disk with a capacity of hundreds of megabytes of

Figure 5-9 Hard disks.
Innards of a 3½-inch hard disk with the access arm visible.

Figure 5-10 Optical disk.

storage now costs only a few hundred dollars or less, down from several thousand dollars just a few years ago. Winchester disks are extremely reliable because they are sealed against contamination from outside air or human hands.

Hard disks can save you time as well as space. Just the way the hard disk speeds up your computing can make it worthwhile, even if you do not need all the storage hard disk provides. Accessing files on hard disk is significantly faster than on diskettes—up to about 20 times faster. Furthermore, users find that accessing files from a hard disk is more convenient than handling diskettes.Unlike a diskette, however, most hard disk units cannot be transported from one computer to another. For that reason most hard disk systems include at least one diskette drive to provide users with software and data portability.

Optical Storage

Would you like to have an encyclopedia at your fingertips? Such a demand can now be met thanks to the technology that is now upon us: the **optical disk** (Figure 5-10). The explosive growth in storage needs compelled the computer industry to provide high-capacity storage devices that are a demand tailor-made for the optical disk. The contents of a typical encyclopedia fit nicely on a single optical disk.

Optical Disk Technology

Optical storage works like this. A laser beam hits a layer of metallic material spread over the surface of the disk. When data is written to the disk, heat from the laser produces tiny spots on the disk's surface. To read the data, the laser scans the disk and a lens picks up different light reflections from the various spots.

Optical storage technology is categorized according to its read/write capability. Data is recorded on **read-only media** by the manufacturer and can be read from but not written to by the user (you can read it, but you cannot change it). This technology is sometimes referred to as **optical read-only memory (OROM).** Obviously, you could not use an OROM disk to store your files, but manufacturers could use it to supply software. A current multiple-application, or integrated, package—a product that provides software for word processing, spreadsheets, graphics, and a database—sometimes takes as many as a dozen diskettes; the contents could fit easily on one OROM disk.

Write once, read many (WORM) media may be written to once. When the WORM disk is filled, it becomes read-only media. A WORM disk is nonerasable. For applications demanding secure storage of original versions of valuable documents, such as wills or other legal papers, the primary advantage of nonerasability is clear: Once they are recorded, no one can erase or modify them.

CD-ROM: A New Best-Seller

A popular variation on optical technology is **compact disk read-only memory (CD-ROM).** CD-ROM has a major advantage over other

Personal Computers In Action

How to Handle Diskettes

Do not lock your diskette in the trunk of your car on a hot day, leave it on the dashboard in the sun, or stick it to the door of your refrigerator with a magnet. Avoid smoking cigarettes around your computer, since smoke particles caught under the read/write head can scratch the disk surface.

These are only a few of the rules for taking care of diskettes. The main forces hostile to diskettes are dust, magnetic fields, liquids, vapors, and temperature extremes. Although 3½-inch diskettes in their sturdy plastic jackets are not especially fragile, be careful not to bend the metal clips lest a disk gets stuck in the disk drive.

1. Do not touch the disk surface. It is easily contaminated, which causes errors. 
2. Do not use alcohol, thinners, or freon to clean the disk. 
   Alcohol Thinner Freon
3. Do not use magnets or magnetized objects near the disk. Data can be lost from a disk exposed to a magnetic field. 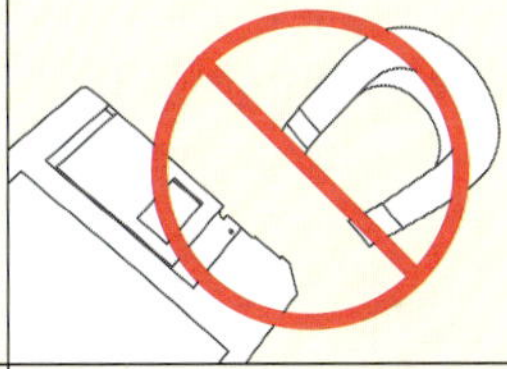
4. Do not bend or fold the disk. 
5. Do not place heavy objects on the disk. 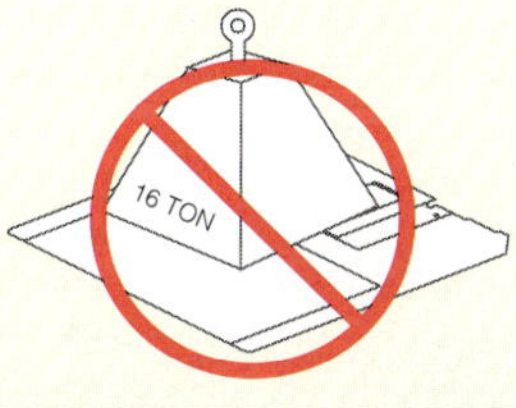
   16 TON
6. Do not use rubber bands or paper clips on the disk. 
7. Do not use erasers on the disk. 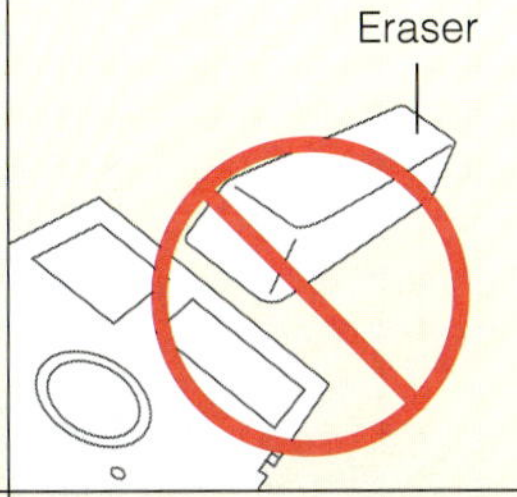
   Eraser
8. Do not expose the disk to excessive heat or sunlight. 
9. Do not use labels in layers. 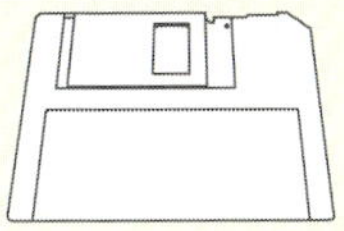
10. Write on the index label with felt-tip pen only, before you put the label on the disk. 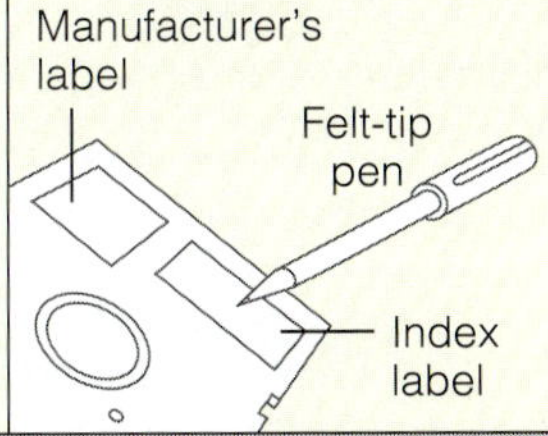
    Manufacturer's label
    Felt-tip pen
    Index label
11. Insert carefully, by grasping upper edge of disk and placing it into the disk drive. 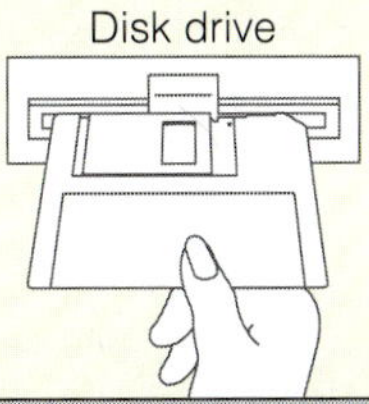
    Disk drive
12. Keep 5 1/4" disk in its protective envelope when not in use.
    Floppy disk
    Envelope

Curling Up with a Good Computer

The computer industry has for years touted reading books from a screen as one of the futuristic advantages of having a computer. However, people seem to prefer sitting in their own comfortable chair and turning paper pages.

Finally, along comes an offering that is so exciting on-screen that it surpasses the paper-only version. A CD-ROM package called From Alice to Ocean includes a well-written, glossy adventure book, lavish color photos, and two digital disks. This material chronicles a six-month trek across Australia's outback by a woman accompanied by four camels and a dog. The beautifully done CD-ROM disks, complete with pictures and text, make the product surpass what the book could have achieved alone.

optical disk designs: The disk format is identical to that of *audio* compact disks, so the same dust-free manufacturing plants that are now stamping out digital versions of Mozart or Pearl Jam or Reba McEntire can easily convert to producing anything from software to the aforementioned encyclopedia. Since manufacturing CD-ROM disks is simply a matter of pressing out copies from a master disk, it is much more economical than traditional magnetic storage, which makes copies byte by byte. Furthermore, CD-ROM storage is gargantuan—up to 660 megabytes per disk, the equivalent of over 400 3½-inch diskettes.

The popularity of CD-ROM disks is a relatively recent phenomenon. Early uses in the late 1980s focused on reference materials: dictionaries, thesauruses, encyclopedias, and atlases. The key advantage was speed: It is faster and easier to type a key word or two and let the computer look up the subject matter, rather than shuffling through weighty volumes. Early users were mostly businesses who were burdened with massive amounts of information. As interest in CD-ROMs increased, manufacturers expanded the variety of applications, leaning more to the consumer market (Figure 5-11). Of particular interest to college students is Monarch Notes, which provides a computerized set of crib notes for studying literary classics.

The CD-ROM market is being driven by two factors: the flood of enticing new offerings and the falling prices of both the disks and the disk drives. Keep in mind that a CD-ROM disk cannot be used in your magnetic disk drive; you must have a CD-ROM drive installed on your computer. If you have a CD-ROM drive, you could be on your way to one of the computer industry's great adventures: multimedia.

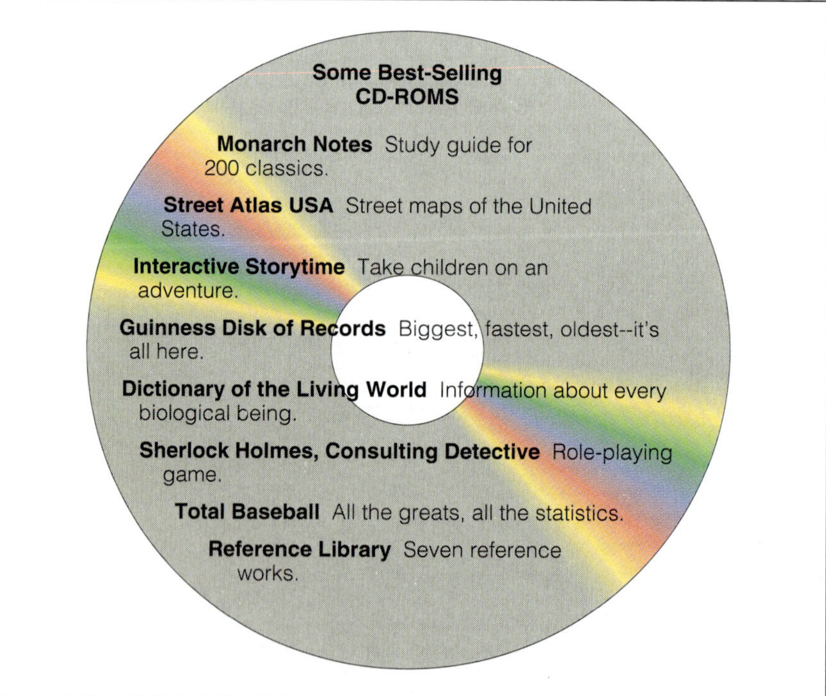

Figure 5-11 Popular CD-ROM software.

Multimedia: The Computer As Centerpiece

Photography, video, music, recorded voice—all these media have something to offer. Now, thanks to the high capacity of CD-ROM disks, these media can be offered on your computer. **Multimedia** is the term used to describe the hardware and software combination that provides access to all these media. Multimedia software typically presents information with text, illustrations, photos, narration, music, animation, and film clips. In addition to a CD-ROM drive, you will need a sound card (installed internally), a set of inexpensive speakers, and the required software to

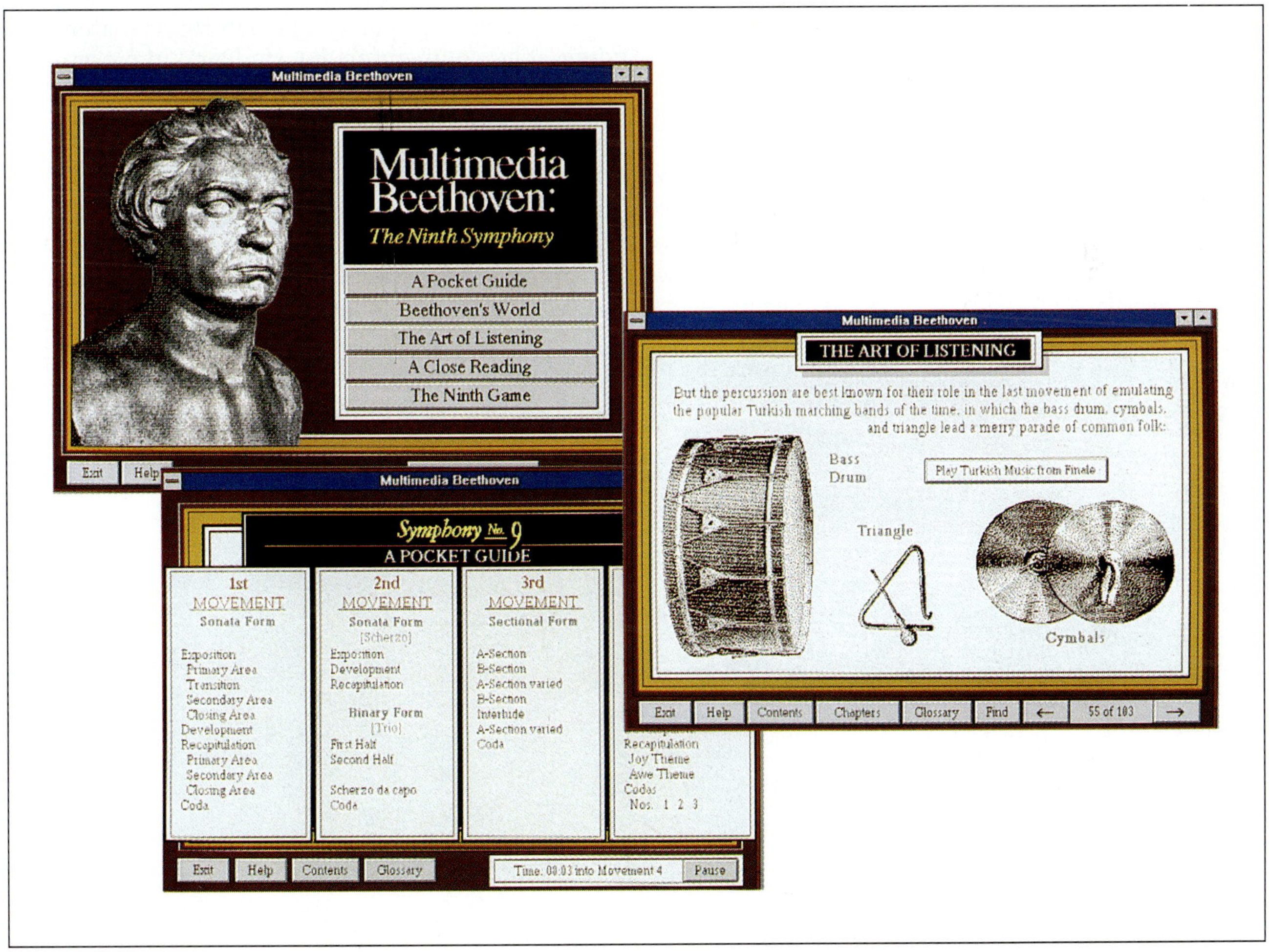

Figure 5-12 Multimedia application.
This educational approach makes learning a pleasure. The name of the application is Multimedia Beethoven: The Ninth Symphony. It contains an overview of the most famous symphony ever written, along with a biography of the composer that places the work in historical context. As the Vienna Philharmonic plays the symphony, the screen text provides a running commentary from which even a sophisticated musician can learn. A user can also highlight passages and have the program repeat a line. The disk also includes a game that doubles as a test of knowledge.

take advantage of multimedia offerings. (Be sure to examine the multimedia gallery, which describes multimedia in more detail and presents several examples of colorful multimedia offerings.)

A good example of a multimedia program is Sherlock Holmes,Consulting Detective. The program begins with a blast of Victorian-sounding music and an animation sequence showing a book opening. The title page offers three different murder mysteries from which to choose. Pick one, and Sherlock Holmes and Dr. Watson appear in a digitized video clip of an old movie. The video plays right on the computer screen, almost like a television movie. The object of the game is to solve the mystery with as few clues as possible. This kind of application illustrates the somewhat fanciful claim that CD-ROM technology may eventually allow the computer industry and Hollywood to merge (Figure 5-12).

Multimedia is making swift inroads into educational settings, where students can switch from the late President John F. Kennedy's inauguration speech to footage of Martin Luther King's civil rights marches to the first moon landing. The competition for students' interests is so lively and intense today that schools want to get every edge they can in attracting and holding it. Multimedia may be one component of success.

What is the future of storage? Whatever the technology, it seems likely that we will be seeing greater storage capacities in the future. Such capabilities have awesome implications—think of the huge data files for law, medicine, science, education, and government.

To have access to all that data from any location we need data communications, the topic of the next chapter.

Chapter **Review**

Summary and Key Terms

- **Secondary storage,** or **auxiliary storage,** is necessary because primary storage, or memory, can be used only temporarily.
- To be processed by a computer, data represented by characters is organized into fields, records, files, and sometimes databases. A **character** is a letter, digit, or special character (such as $). A **field** is a set of related characters, a **record** is a collection of related fields, a **file** may be a collection of related records, and a **database** is a collection of interrelated files.
- The two main methods of large-scale data processing are **batch processing** (processing data transactions in groups) and **transaction processing** (processing data transactions one at a time).
- Batch processing involves a **master file,** which contains semipermanent data, and a **transaction file,** which contains additions, deletions, and changes to be made to **update** the master file. An advantage of batch processing is the cost savings resulting from processing records in groups; the main disadvantage is the delay of receiving output.
- In transaction processing, the transactions are processed in the order they occur. This is **real-time processing** because the results of the transaction are available quickly enough to affect the activity at hand. Real-time processing requires having the user's terminal **online**—directly connected to the computer. The development of disk storage permitted **interactive** processing—a computer/user dialogue—by providing users with easier access to data.
- **Magnetic tape** is a plastic storage medium coated with iron oxide. A **magnetic tape unit** records and retrieves data by using a **read/write head,** an electromagnet that can convert magnetized areas into electrical impulses (to read) or reverse the process (to write). Before the machine writes, the **erase head** erases any previously recorded data.
- A **hard magnetic disk,** or **hard disk,** is a metal platter coated with magnetic oxide. Several disks can be assembled in a **disk pack.** A **diskette** is a round piece of plastic coated with magnetic oxide.
- The surface of a magnetic disk has tracks on which data is recorded as magnetic spots.
- A disk storage device is a **direct access storage device (DASD)** because the read/write head can directly locate a record on it.
- A **disk drive** rapidly rotates a disk or disk pack as an **access arm** moves a read/write head that detects the magnetized data.
- A **Winchester disk** combines disks, access arms, and read/write heads in a **sealed module**.
- Advantages of disk storage are that it provides high-volume data capacity and allows users to find and update records immediately. Tape storage can be used only for batch processing, but it is portable and less expensive than disk storage.
- A **backup system**—a method of storing data in more than one place to protect it from damage or loss—is vital. Backup copies of disk files are made regularly on tape as insurance against disk failure.
- Diskettes and hard disks are the most common storage media for personal computers. Diskettes are available in 5¼-inch and 3½-inch sizes. A hard disk is more expensive than a diskette and usually cannot be moved from computer to computer, but it does provide more storage and faster processing than using diskettes.

- In **optical disk** technology, a laser beam enters data by producing tiny spots on the optical disk's metallic surface. Data is read by having the laser scan the disk surface while a lens picks up different light reflections from the spots.
- Optical storage technology is categorized according to its read/write capability. The manufacturer records on **read-only media** through a technology sometimes called **optical read-only memory (OROM)**; the user can read the recorded media but cannot change it. **Write once, read many (WORM)** media can be written to once; then the disk becomes read-only. **Compact disk read-only memory (CD-ROM)** disks have the same format as audio compact disks.
- **Multimedia** is the term used to describe the hardware and software combination that can present information with text, illustrations, photos, narration, music, animation, and film clips.

Student Personal Study Guide

True/False

T F 1. Real-time processing gives results fast enough to affect the computer user's next action.
T F 2. Processing data by groups of transactions is called batch processing.
T F 3. A transaction file contains records to update the master file.
T F 4. The quickest way to back up a hard disk is to use diskettes.
T F 5. Another name for magnetic tape is DASD.
T F 6. Transaction processing systems are usually real-time systems.
T F 7. A drawback of magnetic tape storage is that it is very expensive.
T F 8. An optical disk can never be erased.
T F 9. A field is a set of related records.
T F 10. Auxiliary storage can be used only temporarily.

Multiple Choice

1. The kind of processing in which data is processed as it occurs:
   a. batch c. transaction
   b. field d. master
2. A direct access storage device:
   a. optical tape c. magnetic tape
   b. erase head d. DASD
3. Another name for secondary storage:
   a. auxiliary c. memory
   b. drive d. master file
4. Semipermanent data:
   a. transaction file c. batches
   b. master file d. erase head
5. A set of related characters:
   a. database c. field
   b. file d. record
6. Write once, read many:
   a. backup c. WORM
   b. OROM d. magnetic tape
7. Several disks assembled together:
   a. database c. disk pack
   b. optical disk d. diskette

8. Disk, access arms, and read/write heads in a sealed module:
   a. hard drive c. Winchester disk
   b. diskette d. optical disk
9. A group of related fields comprises a:
   a. database c. record
   b. file d. field
10. Processing data in groups:
   a. master c. transaction
   b. field d. batch

Fill-In

1. The two most common media for secondary storage are: ________________ and ________________.
2. A technique for processing transactions in any order they occur: ________________.
3. DASD stands for: ________________.
4. User/computer dialogue: ________________.
5. Optical storage technology is categorized according to this ability: ________________.
6. CD-ROM stands for: ________________.
7. The technology supporting a sealed disk module: ________________.
8. Records that can add, delete, or revise master file records are called: ________________.
9. Data is usually backed up on what media: ________________.
10. The storage technology that uses a laser beam: ________________.

Answers

True/False: 1. T, 2. T, 3. T, 4. F, 5. F, 6. T, 7. F, 8. F, 9. F, 10. F
Multiple choice: 1. c, 2. d , 3. a , 4. b, 5. c, 6. c, 7. c, 8. c, 9. c, 10. d
Fill-In: 1. magnetic tape and magnetic disk, 2. transaction processing, 3. direct access storage device, 4. interactive, 5. read/write, 6. compact disk read-only memory, 7. Winchester, 8. transactions, 9. tape, 10. optical disk

Chapter Overview

At age 43, Lucas Eiffert was laid off from his job as a midlevel marketing manager for a toy manufacturer. Even as he sent out résumés and sought out his old contacts, he knew that the whole industry was paring middle management and that his chances of finding something in his current field were slim. Lucas decided to augment one of his job-related skills, computers.

Lucas had no formal computer training except a brief word processing course. He had picked up desktop publishing and a smattering of computer graphics on the job. Even so, he was still very much a user, not a computer professional. Lucas figured out how to survive for a year while both going to school and working part time. He went to his local community college and took the basic courses in programming. He eventually took courses in systems analysis and design, database management, and—the one that captured his interest—data communications. Data communications, he discovered, was basically a marriage of computers and communications links such as the telephone.

As Lucas learned the technical end of data communications, he could see how the technology applied to situations at the toy company. He remembered, for example, the limited number of quality printers and the inconvenience of using someone else's printer. He realized that, using a data communications network in which machines and resources such as printers are hooked together, users could easily share printers. He also recalled the confusion over data duplication and who had what in which disk file; again, a network would let users establish one file for one purpose and give all users access to the same file. Lucas also remembered trying to reach people to set up a meeting; leaving messages by computer was the obvious solution. Finally, he recalled his boss complaining about the expenses of trips to meet with branch managers to plan marketing campaigns. Lucas now knew that, through data communications technology, these meetings could be done by computer, with everyone staying at home.

Lucas served an internship with a networking consultant company. He helped install the hardware and software for several office networks. To continue his job search in his new field, Lucas revamped his résumé and told *everyone* that he was job hunting.

Through an unexpected source (his mail carrier) Lucas found a job with a kitchen products sales company that was about to install a data communications network. Lucas' dual backgrounds in marketing and data communications made a favorable impression. He was hired as an assistant to the personal computer manager, and the two of them soon began planning a data communications network for the office.

All this happened in 1990–1991. Lucas now owns his own data communications consulting company.

Communications

Computer Connections

Sit Back and Relax with Your Laptop

Business travelers used to look forward to flights as a way to get away from the office and maybe catch up on a novel. No more. Now they tote their laptops along and feel guilty if they do not get some work done on the trip.

The airlines are both helping and hindering the effort. On one hand airlines have announced plans to have computers aboard, with the screen imbedded on the back of the seat in front of you. Just bring along your own diskettes and get to work. They even plan to include an air-to-ground system for data communications so you can exchange data with the office. Ah, but there lies the problem.

The problem is that the airlines have some realistic fears about communications from any kind of device interfering with the airplane's navigational systems. At this writing, most airlines prohibit the use of any portable device during takeoff and landing. Back to that novel.

Data Communications Now

Merging communications and computers can help you get full value from each technology. Possible benefits include access to services like computer banking and computer shopping and to other workers in a computer network. People who use computer communications technology are just as casual about linking up with a computer in another state or country as they are about using the telephone. The technology that makes it possible is called data communications.

Data communications systems—computer systems that transmit data over communications lines such as public telephone lines or private network cables—have been gradually evolving since the mid-1960s. When computers were still a novelty, users placed everything—all processing, hardware, software, and storage—in one central location, a scheme now called **centralized data processing.** Centralization, however, proved inconvenient. The next logical step was **teleprocessing**—connecting users to a central computer via telephone lines and terminals right in their own offices.

The most innovative scheme, however, is **distributed data processing (DDP),** which is similar to teleprocessing but accommodates both remote *access* and also remote *processing*. Processing and files are dispersed among several remote locations and can be handled by local computers—usually mini- or microcomputers—all hooked up to the central host computer and sometimes to each other as well. A typical application of a distributed data processing system is a business or organization with many locations, branch offices, or retail outlets.

The whole picture of distributed data processing has changed dramatically with the advent of networks of personal computers. A **network** is a computer system that uses communications equipment to connect two or more computers and their resources, such as printers and hard disks. DDP systems are networks. We will examine networking in more detail in later sections of the chapter.

The Complete Communications System: How It All Fits Together

Suppose you work at a sporting goods store. You learn the first day that the store has a computer that is part of a network. The network is connected to the warehouse and to other stores so that you can exchange inventory and other information. What components are in place to help you do your job?

The basic configuration—how the components are put together—is straightforward, but the choices for each component vary, and the technology is ever changing. Assume that you have some data—a message—to transmit from one place to another. The basic hardware components of a data communications system to transmit that message are (1) the sending device, (2) a communications link, and (3) the receiving device. In the sporting goods store, you might want to send a message to the warehouse to inquire about a particular skateboard, an item you need for a customer. In this case the sending device is your terminal or personal computer at the store, the communications link is the phone line, and the receiving machine is the computer at the warehouse. As you will see later, there are many other possible configurations.

There is another often-needed component in this basic configuration, as you can see in Figure 6-1. This component is a modem, which may be needed to convert computer data to signals that can be carried by the communications channel and vice versa.

Let us see how these components work together, beginning with how data is transmitted.

Sending Your Data: Data Transmission

If you want to communicate with other computers, you must overcome a significant obstacle: the inherent incompatibility of computers with some communications links. A terminal or computer produces digital signals, and most communications travel along telephone lines, which were built for voice transmission and require analog signals. We will look at these two types of transmissions and then consider modems, which translate between them.

Types of Transmission: Digital and Analog

Digital transmission sends data as distinct pulses, either on or off, and thus can accept computer-generated data directly. However, most communications media—such as telephone lines, coaxial cables, and microwave circuits—are not digital. For most users transmitting via one of these common means is more practical than establishing a means of digital transmission. Furthermore, the common communications media have a common characteristic: They all use analog transmission.

Figure 6-1 Communications system components.
Data originating from (1) a sending device is (2) converted by a modem to data that can be carried over (3) a link and (4) reconverted by a modem at the receiving end before (5) being sent to the receiving computer. Although we show external modems here for the purpose of illustration, most modems are inside the computer's housing.

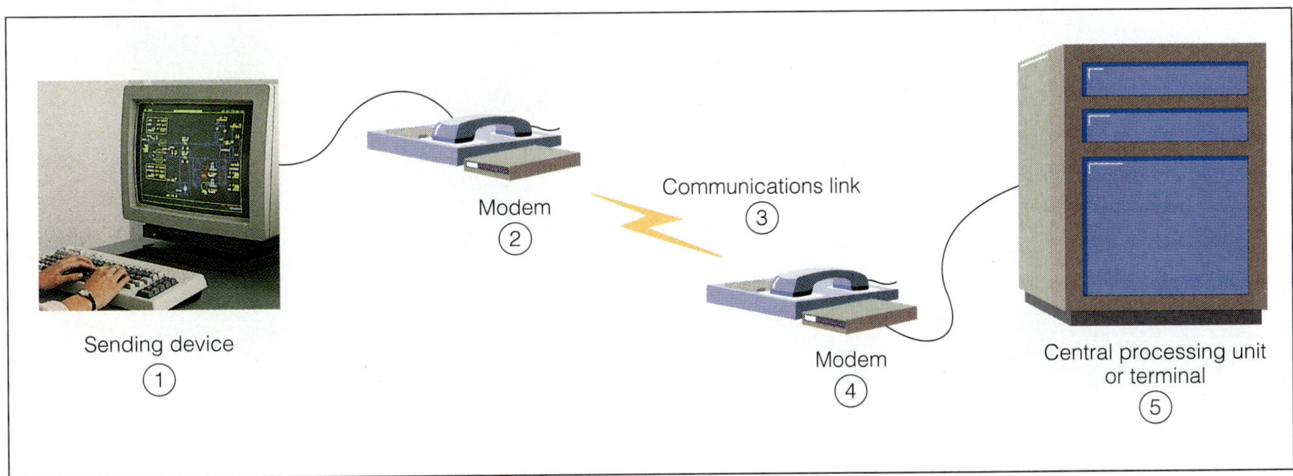

Analog transmission uses a continuous electrical signal in the form of a wave. A digital signal must be converted to analog before it can be sent over analog lines. Conversion from digital to analog signals is called **modulation,** and the reverse process—reconstructing the original digital message at the other end of the transmission—is called **demodulation.** So we see that the marriage of computers to communications is not a perfect one. Instead of just "joining hands," a third party may be needed in between to make signal conversions. This extra device is called a modem.

Making the Switch: Modems

A **modem** is a device that converts a digital signal to an analog signal and vice versa (Figure 6-2a). *Modem* is short for *mo*dulator/*dem*odulator. Once a modem is attached to your computer, all you have to do is send the data; the modem will take care of the translation automatically.

Figure 6-2 Modems.
(a) Modems convert, or modulate, digital data signals to analog signals for traveling over communications links; then they reverse the process, or demodulate, at the other end. (b) This external modem rests under the telephone that hooks the computer to the outside world. (c) This internal modem slips into an expansion slot inside the computer. The phone cord plugs into a jack, accessible through the back of the computer.

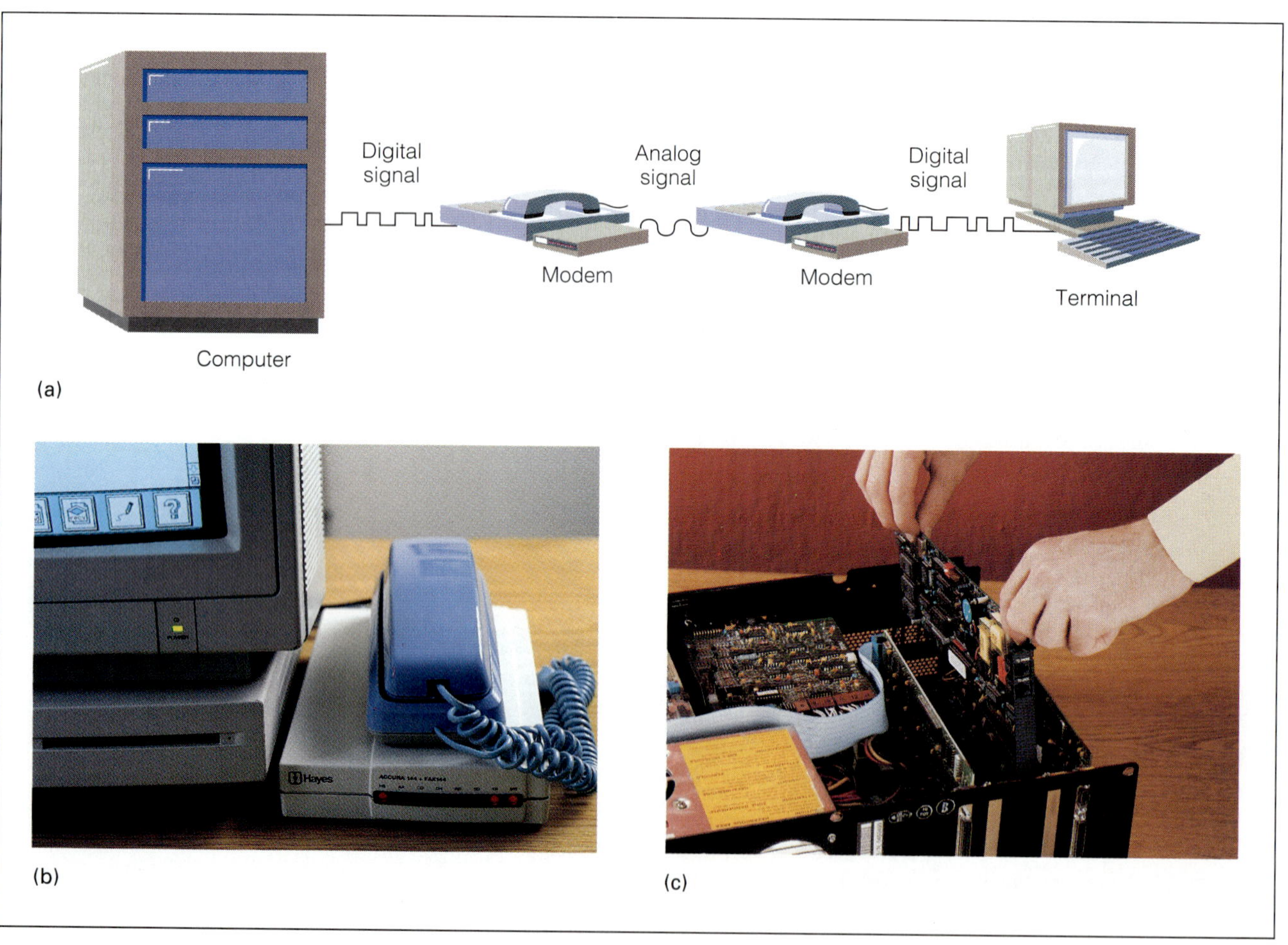

Most modems today are **direct-connect modems,** directly connected to telephone lines by means of telephone jacks. Although some users still use **external modems,** which are placed outside computers (Figure 6-2b), most personal computer users prefer **internal modems,** which can be inserted inside computers (Figure 6-2c).

A modem's speed of transmission is an important consideration. In general, modem users use normal telephone lines to connect their computers and pay telephone charges based on the time they are connected. Thus there is a strong incentive to transmit as quickly as possible. Although some modems still operate at slower speeds, common transmission speeds today are 2400 bits per second (bps) and 9600 bps. At 2400 bps, a modem can transmit a 20-page single-spaced report in five minutes; the same report can be transmitted at 9600 bps in just over one minute. The fastest modem on the market today can transmit data at an amazing 14,400 bps, sending that same report in less than one minute.

Now that we have discussed translating the data and the rates at which it can be sent, let us turn to the media that transmit it.

Carrying Your Data: Communications Links

What communications link will you choose to send your data? A communications **link** is the physical medium used for transmission. If your computer is at home, you will doubtless hook up to another computer through the telephone system. Large organizations, on the other hand, have more choices and must consider the cost factor. The cost for linking machines can be substantial (as much as one-third of the data processing budget), so it is worthwhile to examine the communications options.

Among the most common communications media are **wire pairs,** also known as **twisted pairs** (Figure 6-3a). Wire pairs are wires twisted together to form a cable, which is then insulated. Wire pairs are inexpensive and frequently used to transmit information over short distances, such as in a phone system within a metropolitan area.

Known for contributing to high-quality transmission, **coaxial cables** are insulated wires within a shield enclosure (Figure 6-3b). These cables can be laid underground or undersea, and they can transmit data at rates much higher than telephone lines. Coaxial cables have been the mainstay of cable television.

Traditionally, most phone lines have transmitted data electrically over wires made of metal, usually copper. These wires must be protected from water and other corrosive substances. **Fiber optics** technology was developed by Bell Laboratories to solve these and other problems (Figure 6-3c). Instead of using electricity to send data, fiber optics uses light. The cables are made of glass fibers, thinner than a human hair, that guide light beams for miles. Fiber optics can transmit data faster than some technologies, yet the materials are lighter and less expensive than wire cables.

Also popular is **microwave transmission** (Figure 6-4a), which uses line-of-sight transmission of data signals through the atmosphere. Since these signals cannot bend around the curvature of the earth, relay stations—usually antennas in high places such as the tops of mountains,

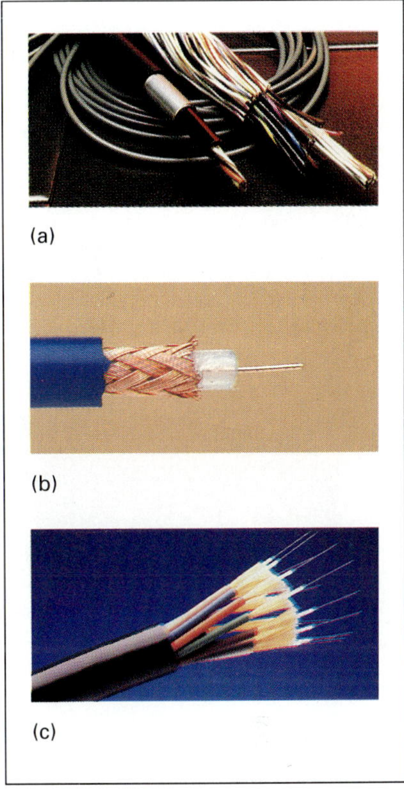

Figure 6-3 Communications links. (a) Wire pairs are twisted together to form a cable, which is then insulated. (b) A coaxial cable. (c) Fiber optics are hair-like glass fibers that carry voice, television, and data signals.

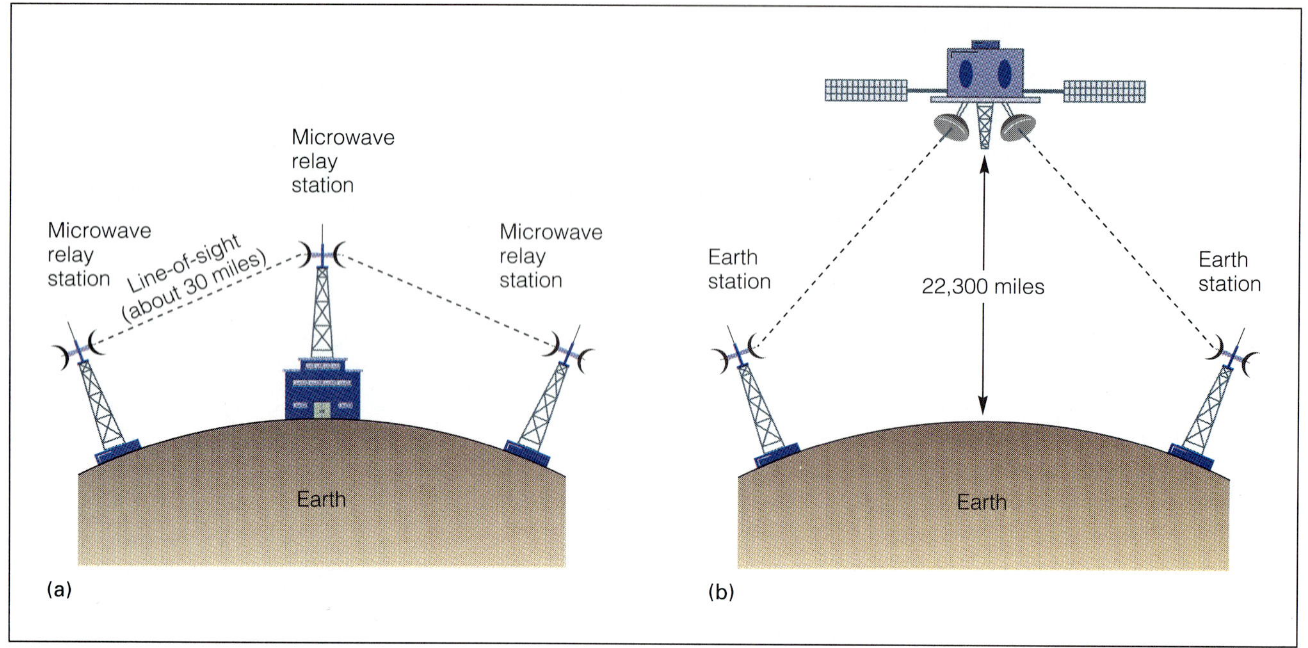

Figure 6-4 Microwave transmission.
(a) To relay microwave signals, dish-shaped antennas are placed atop buildings, towers, and mountains. Microwave signals can follow only a line-of-sight path, so stations must relay this signal at regular intervals to avoid interference from the earth's curvature. (b) A satellite acts as a relay station and can transmit data signals from one earth station to another. A signal is sent from an earth station to the relay satellite in the sky, which changes the signal frequency before transmitting it to the next earth station.

towers, and buildings—are positioned at points approximately 30 miles apart to continue the transmission. Microwave transmission offers speed, cost-effectiveness, and ease of implementation.

Communications satellites are very far away: 22,300 miles above the earth. The basic components of **satellite transmission** are the earth stations that send and receive signals and the satellite component, which is called a transponder. The **transponder** receives the transmission from earth, changes the signal, and retransmits the data to a receiving earth station (Figure 6-4b). This entire process takes less than a second.

Hooking Up to the Big Computer: Wide Area Networks

As noted earlier, computers that are connected so they can communicate among themselves form a network. Two important kinds of networks are wide area networks and local area networks. Wide area networks send data over long distances. Most of these networks use the telephone system, although some companies have implemented their own microwave and satellite networks. Local area networks allow communication among computers linked together in one building or in buildings that are close together. Let us first consider wide area networks.

Teleconferencing

An office automation development with great promise is **teleconferencing,** a method of using technology to bring people and ideas together despite geographic barriers. The technology has been available for years, but the acceptance of it is quite recent.

There are several varieties of teleconferencing. The simplest, **computer conferencing,** is a method of sending, receiving, and storing typed messages within a network of users. Computer conferences can be used to coordinate complex projects over great distances and for extended periods. Participants can communicate at the same time or in different time frames, at the users' convenience.

A computer conferencing system is a single software package designed to organize communication. The conferencing software runs on a network's host computer, be it a micro, mini, or mainframe. In addition to access to the host computer and the conferencing software, each participant needs a personal computer or terminal, a telephone, a modem, and communications network software. Computer conferencing is a many-to-many arrangement; everyone is able to "talk" to everyone else via computer. Messages may be sent to a specified individual or set of individuals or broadcast to all receivers. Recipients are automatically notified of incoming messages.

Would you like your picture broadcast live across the miles for meetings? Add cameras and audio to computer conferencing, and you have another form of teleconferencing called **videoconferencing** (Figure 6-7). The technology varies, but the pieces normally put in place are a large (possibly wall-size) screen, cameras, and a computer system to record communication among participants.

Although this setup is expensive to rent and even more expensive to own, the costs seem trivial when compared to time and travel expenses for in-person meetings.

Figure 6-7 A videoconferencing system.
Geographically distant groups can hold a meeting with the help of videoconferencing. The people shown on the screen are participants in another locale.

The Revolution Comes Full Cycle

Could it be that we are back where we started? The original idea behind the personal computer was that it was, indeed, *personal*. You were on your own: your computer, your data, your business. Individual users had truly broken away from the large computers that were located elsewhere and used for heavy-duty computer tasks.

Personal computer pioneers smile at that notion now. Personal computer users, whether at home or in the office, are busily connecting their computers to everything in sight. In fact, the very power of a personal computer is coming to be defined in terms of what it is connected to. And what about those big computers, the ones personal computer users left behind? Users now gleefully connect to the big computer to access massive databases, to route messages, and much more.

Users once were willing to isolate themselves on personal computers rather than be an insignificant cog in the large computer system. Now, with networking, they have the best of both worlds.

Figure 6-8 Faxing it.
This facsimile machine can send text and graphics long distance via the telephone in the background.

Facsimile Technology

To save the money and even the time associated with overnight mail service, you can use computers and data communications technology to transmit drawings and documents from one location to another. **Facsimile technology,** operating something like a copy machine connected to a telephone, uses computer technology to send graphics, charts, text, and even signatures almost anywhere in the world. The drawing, or whatever, is placed in the facsimile machine at one end (as shown in Figure 6-8), where it is digitized. Those digits are transmitted across the miles and then reassembled at the other end into the original picture. All this takes only minutes, or less. Facsimile is not only faster than overnight letter services, it is less expensive too. Facsimile is abbreviated **fax,** as in "I sent a fax" and "I faxed the report to the Chicago office." Faxing has become common in many businesses and some home offices.

A variation on the fax machine is the **fax board,** which fits inside a personal computer, thus facilitating transmission of computer-generated text and graphics. (If the document to be sent is on paper, it must be scanned by a scanner and stored in the computer first.) Incoming faxes are stored on the computer's hard disk; later they can be reviewed on screen and, if desired, printed. Another option is a **fax-modem board,** which, as its name indicates, performs the functions of both fax machine and modem.

Electronic Fund Transfers: Instant Banking

You may already be handling some financial transactions electronically instead of using checks. In **electronic fund transfers (EFTs),** people pay for goods and services by having funds transferred from various checking and savings accounts electronically, using computer technology. One of the most visible manifestations of EFT is the ATM—the automated teller machine.

Incidentally, many millions of social security checks have been disbursed by the government directly into the recipients' checking accounts via EFT rather than by mail. Unlike those sent via U.S. mail, such payments are unlikely to be lost. Moreover, EFT payments are traceable—again unlike the ordinary mail. A more recent trend is electronic transfer of salaries from businesses to employees' bank accounts. No more extra trips to the bank on payday. In addition, many people elect to have the bank pay their recurring bills, such as monthly mortgage payments, by electronically debiting their account and forwarding the money to the creditor.

Carrying this one step further, many people use their personal computers to pay all their bills, that is, to transfer funds from their bank accounts to the accounts of their creditors. A record of these transactions is included on the billpayer's monthly bank statement.

Bulletin Boards

Person-to-person data communications is one of the more exhilarating ways of using your personal computer, and its popularity is increasing at breakneck speed. A **bulletin board system (BBS)** uses data communications to link personal computers to provide public access to messages.

Electronic bulletin boards are somewhat like the bulletin boards you see in student lounges or employee lunchrooms. Somebody leaves a message, perhaps selling something, but the person who picks up the message does not have to know the person who left it. To get access to a bulletin board on someone else's computer, all you really have to know is that bulletin board's phone number. You can use any kind of computer, but you need a modem so you can communicate over the phone lines. Users find bulletin boards helpful in all the ways that people can help each other with advice or companionship. In particular, people with questions about their computers can get all sorts of free advice. You just leave the question and come back to pick up the answers. Anyone who has a personal computer can set up a bulletin board: It takes a computer, a phone line, a couple of disk drives, and free or inexpensive software.

Commercial Communications Services

We have talked about specific services, but some companies offer a wide range of services. Users can connect their personal computers to commercial, consumer-oriented communications systems via telephone lines. These services—known as **information utilities**—are widely used by both home and business customers. Three popular information utilities are CompuServe Information Service, Prodigy, and America Online (Figure 6-9). In each case you must take a few minutes to install the system software on your personal computer. Then, for a fee, the world opens up to you via computer.

These three utilities each offer myriad services, including news, weather, shopping, games, educational materials, electronic mail, forums, and financial information. Generally speaking, *CompuServe* is of greatest value to sophisticated users and computer professionals, offering program packages, text editors, a software exchange, and a number of programming languages. *Prodigy* is newer and much more user friendly, mainly because of its splashy graphics screens. Prodigy is also family-oriented, offering services such as meal-planning advice and children's educational games. *America Online*, the newest of these three, offers a superior, easy-to-use graphical environment, with mouse-controlled icons and overlayed screen windows. Macintosh or Windows users are familiar with this type of environment.

Charges for these services vary. Most charge a nominal sum for the initial setup software. The services offer some sort of ongoing package deal, usually a monthly fee that includes all basic services and a certain amount of connection time, with extra charges for extra time. People who live in populated areas can connect to the service at no extra charge through a local phone number. However, be warned: People in remote areas may have to access the service through a long distance phone number, a disadvantage that can generate a shocking phone bill.

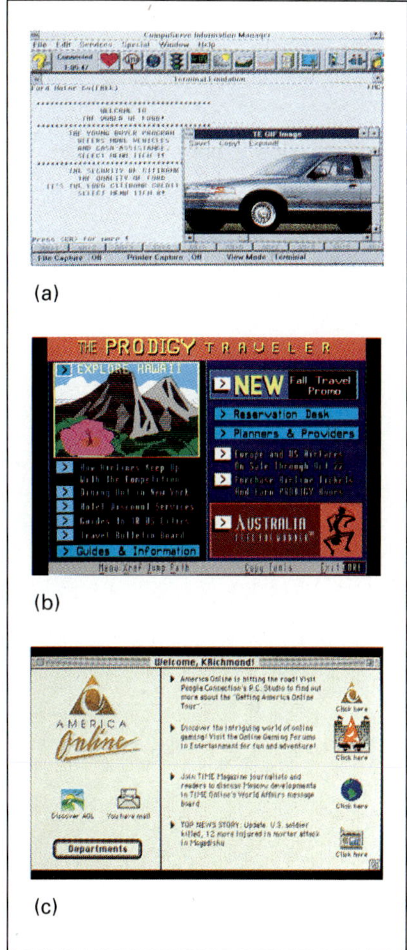

Figure 6-9 Information utilities. (a) CompuServe. (b) Prodigy. (c) America Online.

Internet

Internet is the largest and most far-flung network system of them all, with more than 20 million users worldwide. Surprisingly, Internet is not really a network at all, but a loosely organized collection of networks. In fact, no one owns Internet and it is run by volunteers. It has no central headquarters, no centrally offered services, and no online index to tell you what information is available. Originally developed by, and still subsidized by the United States government, Internet now connects libraries, college campuses, research labs, and businesses.

The great attraction of Internet for these users is that, once they have paid the sign-up fees, there are no extra charges. Therefore, and this is the key drawing card, electronic mail is free, regardless of the amount of use. In contrast, individuals using Internet must pay ongoing monthly fees. Internet is available to individuals through third-party vendors, such as Delphi or America Online. Alternatively, individuals can install personal computer software and be billed at an hourly rate for access to Internet.

Experts predict exponential growth for Internet in the next few years.

Computer Commuting

A logical outcome of computer networks is **telecommuting**, the substitution of data communications and computers for the commute to work (Figure 6-10). Many in the work force are information workers; if they do not need frequent face-to-face contact to do their jobs, they are candidates for using telecommuting to work at home. Although the number of telecommuters is still small, it is growing. In 1989, 3 million people telecommuted; by 1994 that number had risen to almost 8 million.

Although the original idea was that people would work at home all the time, telecommuting has evolved into a part-time activity. That is, most telecommuters stay home two or three days a week and come into the

Figure 6-10
This telecommuter is wearing a headset to talk to and listen to customers. Her hands are free to input data during the conversation.

Personal Computers In Action

Living Online

Millions of people spend a part of each day online, connected to their favorite network, probably an information utility. Here are some of the things they can do with their connected computers:

Make travel plans. Andy Crowley travels several times a month for his business. He signs onto CompuServe and looks over flights going his way on the American Airlines EAASY SABRE reservation system. He makes his choices, charges them to his credit card, and picks up his tickets at the airport. Andy likes the convenience, but he also likes the chance to comparison-shop routes and prices and get the best deal.

Pay bills. Using Prodigy, Mary Deininger has listed and filed the names and addresses of all her creditors. Once a month she takes a stack of bills, hooks up to Prodigy, and keys in dollar amounts next to the appropriate creditors. Prodigy transfers the money to the creditors' computer systems. For Mary's dentist, Prodigy generates and mails a check. For Mary it is no checks, no envelopes, and no stamps.

Check a bulletin board. Somewhere there is a bulletin board that exactly matches your interests. Here are some samples of existing boards, from the mundane to the bizarre: genealogy, careers, automotive, collecting bottles or baseball cards or teddy bears, peace, astronomy, ecology, beer, atheists. And, lastly, yes it really exists (on Internet), there is a bulletin board devoted to Spam, a canned hamlike product.

Stay in touch. Networking is especially valuable to those in outlying locations. Jackson Qunit, who lives in a remote Alaskan village, relies on Internet to send and receive messages. He notes that it is like having pen pals, except that there is an instant response. Others find friends or even romance. People get acquainted on screen, eventually meet, and—sometimes—marry.

Follow your investments. Most services offer stock quotes and even quotes for your particular portfolio. But Roger Vaughn went a step further on America Online. He entered his individual stocks by price and quantity. Now, whenever he calls up his portfolio, the screen shows one line for each stock: original price, quantity, current price, and profit or loss. On the top of the screen is the total value of the portfolio and the total profit or loss to date.

Do research. Biochemist Barbara Aragona makes extensive use, through Internet, of NSFnet, the heavily used National Science Foundation network that is a key information exchange for scientists. Journalist Dorothy Moore finds the reference library on CompuServe both convenient and useful, especially the listings for business demographics, census data, consumer reports, and government publications.

Shop. Many people do a substantial amount of shopping at the hundreds of stores in the electronic shopping malls. Some find it particularly convenient to select and buy gifts, which the stores will gift wrap and send. Some people even use their computers to check out new cars.

A cross-section of popular shop stops: Lands' End, Books on Tape, Gimmee Jimmy's Cookies, J. C. Penney, Metropolitan Museum of Art, Brooks Brothers, Coca-Cola Catalog, Florida Fruit Shipper, Spiegel, The Flower Shop, Musicworks, and the Contact Lens Replacement Center.

Hang out. Although most people who sign onto one of America Online's "lobbies" are individuals, Jody and Marty Czyzowicz enjoy this activity as a couple. When they click the People Connection icon on the screen, America Online assigns them to a lobby with other people (23 maximum) who will join in the "conversation" that appears on-screen. On one fairly typical evening, these topics were tossed around: the federal budget, a current movie, joining the Marines, Microsoft's multimedia encyclopedia, gays, and the weather. The last item was actually the most interesting, since participants are from all over the country.

Figure 6-11
In perhaps the ultimate in telecommuting, this column writer shows up in the office only once a week for a staff meeting.

office the other days. Time in the office permits the needed personal communication with fellow workers and also provides a sense of participation and continuity.

The near future in data communications is not difficult to see. The demand for services is just beginning to swell. Electronic mail already pervades the office, the campus, and the home. Expect instant access to all manner of databases from a variety of convenient locations. Prepare to become blasé about services made available through data communications in your own home, office, and everywhere you go.

Chapter Review

Summary and Key Terms

- **Data communications systems** are computer systems that transmit data over communications lines such as public telephone lines or private network cables.
- **Centralized data processing** places all processing, hardware, software, and storage in one central location. In **teleprocessing** systems, terminals at various locations are connected by communications lines to the central computer, which does the processing.
- Businesses with many locations or offices often use **distributed data processing (DDP),** which allows both remote access and remote processing. Processing can be done by both the central computer and the other computers that are hooked up to it.
- A **network** is a computer system that uses communications equipment to connect two or more computers and their resources.
- The components of the simplest data communications system are a sending device, a communications link, and a receiving device.
- **Digital transmission** sends data as distinct on or off pulses. **Analog transmission** uses a continuous electrical signal.
- Computers produce digital signals, but most types of communications equipment use analog signals. Therefore, transmission of computer data involves altering the signal. Digital signals are converted to analog signals by **modulation. Demodulation** is the reverse process; both processes are performed by a device called a **modem.**
- Most modems today are **direct-connect modems,** directly connected to the telephone line by means of a telephone jack. An **external modem** is outside the computer; an **internal modem** can be inserted inside the computer.
- A communications **link** is the physical medium used for transmission. Common communications links include **wire pairs** (also called **twisted pairs**), **coaxial cables, microwave transmission, satellite transmission,** and **fiber optics.** In satellite transmission a **transponder** receives and retransmits the signal.
- A **wide area network (WAN)** is a network of geographically distant computers and terminals. The computer to which the terminal is attached is called the **host** computer. A personal computer can access these larger computers only if it uses special software called **emulation software** to imitate, or emulate, a terminal. Special software allows **downloading** files—retrieving files from the host computer—or **uploading** files—sending files from a personal computer to the host computer.
- A **local area network (LAN)** is a collection of personal computers that share hardware, software, and information. Personal computers attached to a LAN are referred to as **workstations.** All the devices—personal computers and other hardware—attached to the LAN are called **nodes** on the LAN. The physical layout of a local area network is called its **topology.** A **star network** has a central computer that is responsible for managing the LAN; it is to this central computer—sometimes called a **server**—that the shared disks and printers are usually attached. A **ring network** links all nodes together in a circular manner. Since only one node can send data at a time, a system called **token passing** controls the sender; the node possessing the token can send a message. A **bus network** assigns a portion of network management to each computer but preserves the system if one node fails.
- A **peer-to-peer network** physically cables computers one to another and grapevines messages to the recipient.

- **Office automation** is the use of technology to help achieve the goals of the office. **Electronic mail (e-mail)** and **voice mail** allow workers to transmit messages to the computer files of other workers. **Teleconferencing** includes **computer conferencing**—in which typed messages are shared among many users—and **videoconferencing**—computer conferencing combined with cameras and screens. **Facsimile (fax) technology** can transmit graphics, charts, and signatures. **Fax boards** can be inserted inside computers. A **fax-modem board** performs the functions of both a fax machine and a modem. In **electronic fund transfers (EFTs),** people pay for goods and services by having funds transferred from various checking and savings accounts electronically, using computer technology.
- A **bulletin board system (BBS)** uses data communications systems to link personal computers to provide public-access message systems.
- *CompuServe*, *Prodigy*, and *America Online* are three major commercial communications services, or **information utilities.**
- *Internet* is a loosely organized collection of networks whose key drawing card is free electronic mail.
- **Telecommuting** is the substitution of communications and computers for the commute to work.

Student Personal Study Guide

True/False

T F 1. Teleprocessing allows a user to query a central computer a thousand miles away.
T F 2. Analog transmission sends distinct on/off pulses.
T F 3. A modem can be used for either modulation or demodulation.
T F 4. Microwave uses line-of-sight transmission.
T F 5. Fiber optics is a cheaper form of communications link than wire pairs.
T F 6. The majority of LANs use a ring structure.
T F 7. E-mail and voice mail are identical technologies.
T F 8. A ring network has no central host computer.
T F 9. Fax boards can be inserted into computers.
T F 10. Telecommute is a type of network structure.

Multiple Choice

1. Distinct on/off pulse transmission:
   a. analog c. server
   b. bit pattern d. digital
2. The topology in which each network computer does some network management:
   a. ring c. star
   b. any topology d. bus
3. A personal computer attached to a network:
   a. node c. token
   b. WAN d. bus
4. Which is *not* an information utility?
   a. Prodigy c. CompuServe
   b. Ethernet d. America Online
5. All processing, hardware, and software in one location:
   a. network processing c. teleprocessing
   b. centralized processing d. DDP

6. Which is *not* a type of communication link?
   a. coaxial cables c. microwave transmission
   b. fiber optics d. modem
7. Computers plus cameras plus screens:
   a. videoconferencing c. facsimile
   b. BBS d. star network
8. Analog to digital conversion:
   a. modulation c. LAN
   b. fax d. demodulation
9. System that combines computers and communications:
   a. topology c. centralized processing
   b. data communications d. network interface
10. Transferring funds via computer:
   a. EFT c. WAN
   b. BBS d. LAN

Fill-In

1. The kind of signal most telephone lines require: ________________.
2. Converts a digital signal to an analog signal or vice versa: ________________.
3. Prodigy and CompuServe are examples of: ________________.
4. The general term for the use of technology in the office: ________________.
5. The collection of networks subsidized by the government: ________________.
6. Process of converting analog signals to digital: ________________.
7. The physical medium used for transmission is called: ________________.
8. Networks that share resources in a limited geographical location: ________________.
9. A satellite device to receive and transmit the signal: ________________.
10. BBS stands for: ________________.

Answers

True/False: 1. T, 2. F, 3. T, 4. T, 5. T, 6. F, 7. F, 8. T, 9. T, 10. F
Multiple choice: 1.d, 2. d , 3. a , 4. b, 5. b, 6. d, 7. a, 8. d, 9. b, 10. a
Fill-In: 1. analog, 2. modem, 3. information utilities, 4. office automation, 5. Internet, 6. demodulation, 7. communications link, 8. local area network, 9. transponder, 10. bulletin board system

Interview: Computers at the Bottom of the Ocean

Judith Connor, who works for the Monterey Bay Aquarium Research Institute — usually called MBARI — talks about computer application to ocean sciences.

Tell us a little about the institute first.

MBARI was started in 1987 by David Packard, one of the founders of Hewlett-Packard, and continues to be privately funded. He was really excited about the idea of bringing technology to ocean sciences. MBARI's primary focus is research, although we have a secondary mission of education.

Can you give me an overview of the educational activities at MBARI?

Very generally, we're set up to let the public peek over the shoulders of scientists at work. We have a ship in Monterey Bay that controls a robotic submarine, officially called a remotely operated vehicle, or ROV. The robot, which is about the size of a car, is manipulated from the ship by joysticks. The robot's camera takes video images of the sea life, which are sent by cable back to the ship.

Microwave technology brings the video images from the robot to the aquarium where they are instantly shown on a screen to a public audience. There is only a 3-second delay, so the audience really gets the feeling of looking under water with the scientist.

The physical data that the robot is sensing, such as temperature, salinity, and oxygen, also is sent back to land and later stored on the mainframe. This information is of interest to scientists; we keep extensive database files.

How deep can the robot go down?

The robot itself is capable of withstanding pressures down to 6000 feet, but the cable that connects the robot with the mother ship is only 4000 feet long. Also, they leave a lot of give in the cable. So the deepest they've worked so far with this robot is 3300 feet.

How do you fit into the picture here?

My official title is senior research associate, but I am really a marine biologist. My undergraduate work was in botany and chemistry, but for my first job I ended up living on a boat for three years in the Caribbean doing field research. I came back thinking that this is what I want to do with my life, so I went to

Exploring

PART

3

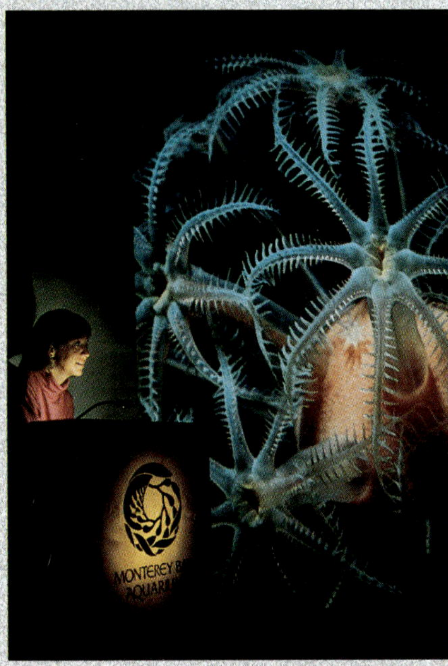

graduate school in marine biology.

How did you pick up a computer background?
When I went for my Ph.D. at U.C. Berkeley, the computer science department gave any student who wanted it $300 worth of time on the mainframe computer. Nobody was using it. I used up my $300 and they gave me more, so I wrote my dissertation using the mainframe. I had a newborn baby at the time, so I rented a computer and a modem, wrote at home and sent my work to the mainframe. That was my introduction to computers.

How do you keep records from the images that come in from the robot?
We get about 10 video tapes every day that the robot goes out. We want to pare that down to the good stuff, and that's another place the computer comes in. I can put a tape in the VCR and then give the computer a file of time codes. For each time code the computer will automatically steal five image frames and lay them down on a laser disk. Later, instead of spending hours pouring over half-hour tapes to get to individual frames that are interesting, you can put in an hour-long laser disk and zip through it. You can put a disk in the machine and zoom—you're on the ocean bottom, and you can see the animals.

Are you connected to a network?
All our personal computers are tied into a network. We use the network for e-mail and tend not to use the telephone. Our real purpose is to focus on research. Phones are an interruption, whereas e-mail can wait. I can check my e-mail when I want to, but sometimes I just wait and do all the messages at the end of the day. And, of course, we hook into Internet, so we have access to colleagues anywhere in the world.

You can put a disk in the machine and zoom—you're on the ocean bottom, and you can see the animals.

And they to you. Is this information—all these videos and lasers—can they access them from you through Internet?
Not yet, but maybe down the road. But we definitely connect. For example, I have a colleague in Florida who sent me e-mail this morning to ask about our krill sightings, because he is monitoring an animal that might be feeding on krill. So I can go into the database and generate a file of information that I can e-mail to him the same day.

Any final thoughts?
There's an ethic now that's very strong in scientists that we have a responsibility to give good information to help the decision makers make good decisions. We want to be thoughtful advocates of the environment.

Software

Programming

Chapter Overview

Bill Stanhope, trained as a programmer, was hired by a large midwestern auto insurance company. He was well-qualified technically and had some understanding of the process of programming. His management considered the programming process so important that they regularly sent their programmers, Bill among them, for further training.

So Bill had the programming process re-enforced. The first lesson was always the same: Be sure you understand the client's problem before you start solving it. That amused Bill because he knew very well that eager programmers, himself included, are tempted to start writing programs prematurely. The next step in the programming process is to come up with a solution; only then does actual programming begin. Then, once a program is written, it must be tested thoroughly. Finally, and perhaps most important, the programmer must document the program on an ongoing basis, that is, keep records about it.

CHAPTER 7

Even though Bill was fully indoctrinated on the programming process, he found that he and others in his organization did not always follow it. In particular, in the rush toward deadlines, Bill never quite kept his documentation up-to-date. Eventually, Bill became a supervisor in charge of the claims department. He wanted to do well by both his programmers and his clients, the company's claims adjusters. His programmers were trained in the programming process, but with the ever-mounting pressure of deadlines, Bill did not pay much attention to the formalities. This neglect, as it turned out, cost him dearly. Deadlines drifted, budgets swelled, and clients became irritable.

It all came to a head in a client meeting. Client Sam Mehter made a request for a small change to a program. Bill responded that it would take a long time because the programmer who wrote that program had left the company and no one else understood the program very well. He did not say so, but Bill could have added that the reason no one could understand it was that the program was never documented properly. Sam then attacked the budget overrun, to which Bill replied that mounting expenses were directly related to Sam's constant requests for changes. At this, Sam exploded. Bill and his programmers, he said, had not taken the time to understand what the client needed. He, Sam, was forced to make changes because nothing had been properly understood in the first place. Bill ruefully remembered all the lessons in the programming process and, after some soul searching, realized he had permitted the programmers to forge ahead without a proper understanding of the problem and without proper documentation.

Bill had some serious fence-mending to do with his client, but, more importantly, he realized he was going to have to change the ways he enforced the programming process. In this chapter, as we take a look at programming, we will examine the programming process and why it is so important.

and Languages

A Glimpse of What Programmers Do

Programmers in the Scheme of Things

What kind of people become programmers? What training do they need? What companies do they work for? And, finally, do they like being programmers?

People who become programmers are usually people with logical minds—often, but not always, the same ones who are good at math and who like to solve puzzles. Programmers need some credentials, most often a two- or four-year degree in computer information systems or computer science. Jobs vary by organization and region, but it is fair to say that many programmers work for medium-size to large business organizations such as banks, insurance companies, and retailers. The programmers who write software for personal computers often have a degree in computer science.

As for whether they like being programmers, surveys of programmers consistently report a high level of job satisfaction. There are several reasons for this contentment. One is the challenge—most jobs in the computer industry are not routine. Another is security—established computer professionals can usually find work. Finally, the work pays well—you will probably not be rich, but you should be comfortable.

Why Programming?

You may already have used commercial software to solve problems or perform certain tasks. But perhaps now you are ready to learn something about how software is written. As we noted earlier, a **program** is a set of step-by-step instructions that directs the computer to do the tasks you want it to do and produce the results you want. This chapter introduces you to the programming process and what programmers do.

What Programmers Do

Suppose you manage an urban entertainment complex that features movies and various live performances. You need to schedule a year in advance, considering the availability of performers, the time of year, and the need to present a balanced selection. Several factors vary with the type of act and must be considered in the early planning stages, including local props, special lighting effects, union extras, work permits, and so forth. The set of tasks is complex and difficult to coordinate. You need to enlist the aid of a computer because you have work that requires computer power.

The easiest way to get the computer's help is to use an existing commercial software package—a package you can buy off the shelf or from a vendor. Using existing software is also the fastest and least expensive way if the software fits your needs. Commercial scheduling software could solve some of your scheduling problems. But, after consulting with a computer professional, it seems clear that most of your problems are too complicated and too company-specific for commercial software. You need a customized program and someone to write it: a **programmer.**

In general, the programmer's job is to convert a problem solution, such as a scheme for handling the entertainment-complex problems just described, into instructions for the computer. That is, the programmer prepares the instructions of a computer program and runs, tests, and corrects the program. The programmer also documents the way the program works. These activities are all done for the purpose of helping a user fill a need—to manage a business, pay employees, bill customers, admit students to college, and so forth. Programmers help the user develop new programs to solve problems, weed out errors in existing programs, or make changes to programs as a result of new requirements (such as a change in a payroll program to make automatic union dues deductions).

A programmer typically interacts with a variety of people. For example, if a program is part of a system of several programs, the programmer probably coordinates with a systems analyst (see Chapter 9) and other programmers to make sure that the programs operate well together.

Let us turn now from programmers to programming.

The Programming Process

Developing a program requires five steps:

1. Defining the problem
2. Planning the solution

3. Coding the program
4. Testing the program
5. Documenting the program

Let us discuss each of these in turn.

Defining the Problem

Suppose you are a programmer. Users consult with you because they need your services. You meet with users from a client organization to analyze a problem, or you meet with a systems analyst who outlines a project. Eventually, you produce a written agreement that, among other things, specifies the kind of input, processing, and output required. This is not a simple process. It is closely related to the process of systems analysis, which we will discuss in Chapter 9.

Planning the Solution

People spend a lot of time solving problems, often by just talking them over with a friend. But a programmer using a computer to solve a client's problem must use a methodical approach. A solution can be thought of as an ordered set of activities that will convert the given input into the desired output. This is often the most complex part of the entire programming process.

There are many approaches to planning solutions, most of them beyond the scope of this book. Although this chapter is not intended to make you a programmer, we will present two common ways of planning the solution to a programming problem: drawing a flowchart and writing pseudocode. Essentially, a **flowchart** is a symbolic diagram of an orderly step-by-step solution to a problem. It is a map of what your program is going to do and how it is going to do it. **Pseudocode** is an English-like language that you can use to state your solution with more precision than you can in plain English but with less precision than is required when using a formal programming language. We will discuss flowcharts and pseudocode in greater detail later in this chapter.

Coding the Program

As the programmer, your next step is to code the program; you need to express your solution in a language the computer understands—a programming language. You can translate the logic from the flowchart or pseudocode to a programming language. There are many programming languages: BASIC, COBOL, Pascal, FORTRAN, and C are common examples. These languages operate grammatically, somewhat like a simple version of the English language, but they are much more precise. To get your program to work, you have to follow exactly the rules, or **syntax**, of the language you are using. Of course, using the language correctly is no guarantee that your program will work, any more than speaking grammatically correct English means you will actually communicate. The point is that correct use of the language is the required first step. The program must also correctly and logically express the solution. Your coded program must be keyed, often at a terminal, in a form the computer can understand. We will discuss programming languages in more detail later in the chapter.

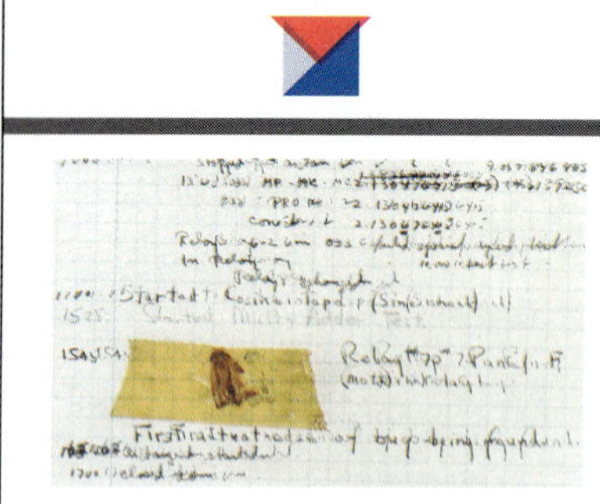

Tell Us About the Bugs

Computer literacy books are bursting with bits and bytes, disks and chips, and lessons on writing programs in BASIC. All this is to provide quick enlightenment for the computer illiterate. But the average newcomer to computing has not been told about the bugs.

It is a bit of a surprise, then, to find that the software you are using does not always work quite right. Or perhaps the programmer who is doing some work for you cannot seem to get the program to work correctly. Both problems are bugs—errors that were introduced unintentionally into a program when it was written. The term *bug* comes from an experience in the early days of computing. One summer day in 1945, the Mark I computer came to a halt. Working to find the problem, computer personnel actually found a moth inside the computer (see photo). They removed the offending bug, and the computer was fine. From that day forward any mysterious problem was said to be a bug.

Testing the Program

Some experts support the notion that a well-designed program can be written correctly the first time. However, the imperfections of the world are still with us, so most programmers get used to the idea that there will be a few errors in the early versions of their programs.

After coding and keying the program, you test it to find the mistakes. Many programmers use these phases: desk-checking, translating, and debugging.

Desk-Checking

In **desk-checking,** you simply sit down and mentally trace, or check, the logic and the syntax of the individual instructions of the program to ensure that the program is error-free and workable. This phase, similar to proofreading, may uncover several errors and possibly save several computer runs. In businesses that account for every second of computer time, this phase is especially important.

Translating

A **translator** is a program that converts your program into language the computer can understand. A by-product of the process is that the translator tells you if you have improperly used the programming language in some way. Such mistakes in programming-language usage are called **syntax errors.** The translator produces descriptive error messages. For instance, if in FORTRAN you mistakenly type N=2*(I+J))—which has two closing parentheses instead of one—you will get a message something like "UNMATCHED PARENTHESES." Programs are most commonly translated by still other software—a compiler or an interpreter. A **compiler** translates your entire program at one time, giving you all the syntax error messages—called **diagnostics**—at once. The compiler usually places these diagnostics in context in a **source program listing,** which is a list of the program, as written by the programmer, that can be used to make any corrections necessary to the program. An **interpreter,** often used for the BASIC language, translates your program one line at a time.

As shown in Figure 7-1, the original program, called a **source module,** is translated to an **object module,** to which prewritten programs may be added during the **link/load phase** to create a load module. The **load module** can then be executed by the computer.

Debugging

A term used extensively in programming, **debugging** is detecting, locating, and correcting bugs (mistakes) by running the program. These bugs are **logic errors,** such as telling a computer to repeat an operation but not telling it how to stop repeating. In this phase you run the program against test data that you devise. You must plan the test data carefully to make sure you test every part of the program.

Documenting the Program

Documentation is a written detailed description of the programming cycle and specific facts about the program. Documenting is an ongoing

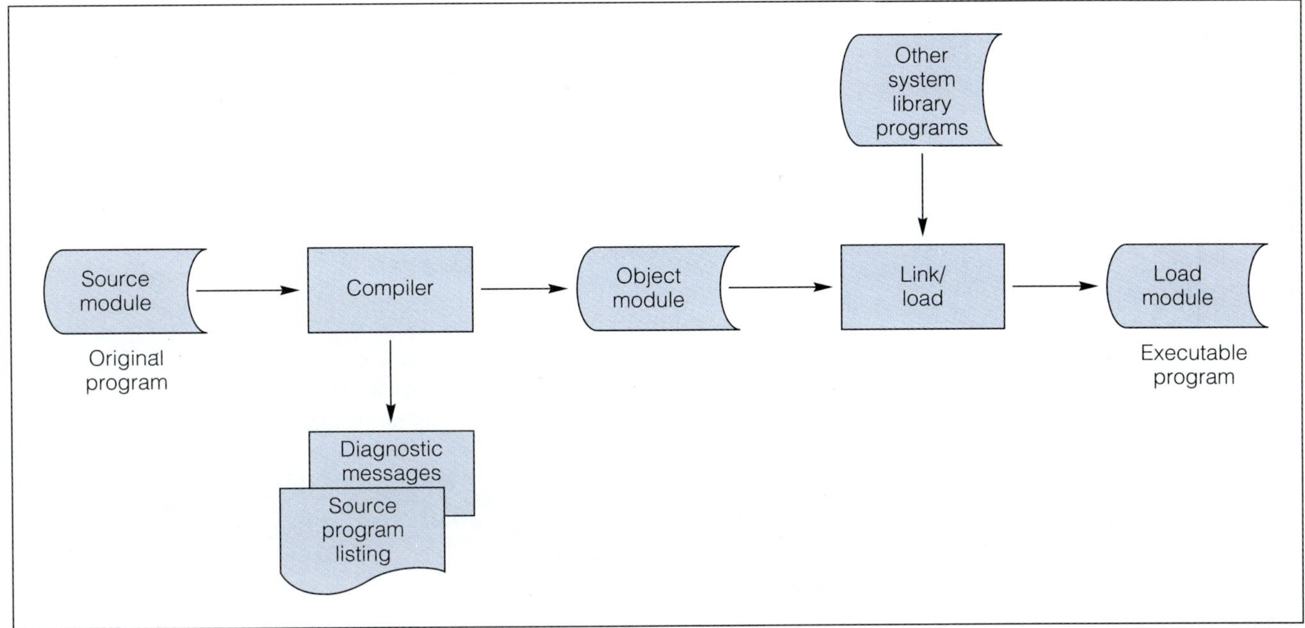

Figure 7-1 Preparing your program for execution.
Your original program, the source module, is translated by the compiler into an object module, which represents the program in machine language that the computer can understand. The compiler may produce diagnostic messages, indicating syntax errors. A listing of the source program may also be output from the compiler. After the program successfully compiles, the object module is linked in the link/load phase with system library programs as needed, and the result is a load module, or executable program.

process needed to supplement human memory and to help organize program planning. Also, documentation is critical to communication with others who have an interest in the program. Typical program documentation materials include the origin and nature of the problem, a brief narrative description of the program, logic tools such as flowcharts and pseudocode, data descriptions, program listings, and testing results. Comments embedded in the program itself are also considered an essential part of documentation.

In a broader sense, program documentation could be part of the documentation for an entire system.

Planning the Solution: A Closer Look at Flowcharts and Pseudocode

We have described the five steps of the programming process in a general way. We noted that the first step, defining the problem, is related to the larger arena of systems analysis and design. The last three steps—coding, testing, and documenting the program—are done in the context of a particular programming language.

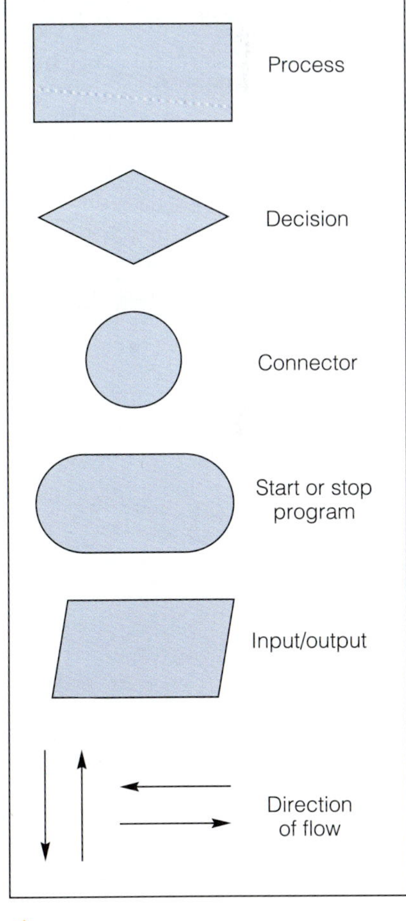

Figure 7-2 ANSI flowchart symbols.

COMPUTING TRENDS

Can I Afford the Premiums?

A most unwelcome trend, but a trend nonetheless, is liability insurance for programmers. Look at it this way. Does the software you use really work? Are you sure? Did the programmer who wrote it absolutely, positively guarantee that it would never have a glitch that would ruin your work? Some jobs have little room for error or second guessing; the job must be done right the first time. An air traffic controller has such a job; for example, directing a plane to the wrong altitude could have fatal consequences. Programmers, on the other hand, have many opportunities to ponder, to test, to rethink. Given those opportunities, it seems reasonable to hope that the completed software will have a high degree of reliability. In fact, some people think that a programmer should indeed be able to absolutely, positively guarantee that the software works as it is supposed to.

However, reliability has not been the hallmark of computer software. There are several reasons for this. One is the inherent complexity of most software. The most vexing is that, despite heroic efforts by the programmer or programmers, the nature of the desired software often changes as it is developed, causing time and budget crunches. Finally, as in every field, there are some incompetent people writing computer programs.

Although software may be less than perfect when first tested, programmers usually work out the kinks until it is acceptable. Sometimes, however, unreliable software is inadvertently released to an organization or to the public. This is why some clients are now suing programmers, and why some programmers are taking out insurance.

In this section we will study the second step, planning the solution. This discussion will help you understand how program logic is developed. The following sections offer an introduction to flowcharting and pseudocode.

Some standard flowchart symbols have been established and are accepted by most programmers. These symbols, shown in Figure 7-2, are called ANSI flowchart symbols. (**ANSI** stands for American National Standards Institute.) The most common symbols a programmer uses represent process, decision, connector, start/stop, input/output, and direction of flow.

Pseudocode is easy to maintain. Since pseudocode is just words, you can keep it on a computer file and change it easily, using text editing or word processing. Although pseudocode is not a visual tool, it is nevertheless an effective vehicle for stating and following program logic. For these reasons, flowcharts have fallen out of favor among professionals and pseudocode has become popular. But flowcharting is still useful for beginners and in complex programming situations, so we include it here.

Example: Preparing a Letter

Figure 7-3 shows how you might diagram the steps of preparing a letter for mailing. There is usually more than one correct way to design a flowchart; this becomes obvious with more complicated examples.

The rectangular **process boxes** indicate actions to be taken: "Address envelope," "Fold letter," "Place letter in envelope." Sometimes the order in which actions appear is important, sometimes not. In this case the letter must be folded before it can be placed in the envelope.

The diamond-shaped box ("Have stamp?") is a **decision box.** The decision box asks a question that requires a yes or no answer. It has two **paths,** or **branches:** One path represents the response yes, the other no. Note that the decision box is the only box that allows a choice; no other box has more than one exit. Whether you do have a stamp or do not, you take a path that comes back to a circle that puts you on a path to the end. The circle is called a **connector** because it connects the paths. Notice that the flowchart begins and ends with oval **start/stop** symbols.

This example suggests how you can take almost any activity and diagram it in flowchart form—assuming, that is, that you can always express your decisions as choices between yes and no, or something equally specific, such as true or false. Now let us use flowcharting for an example related to computer programming.

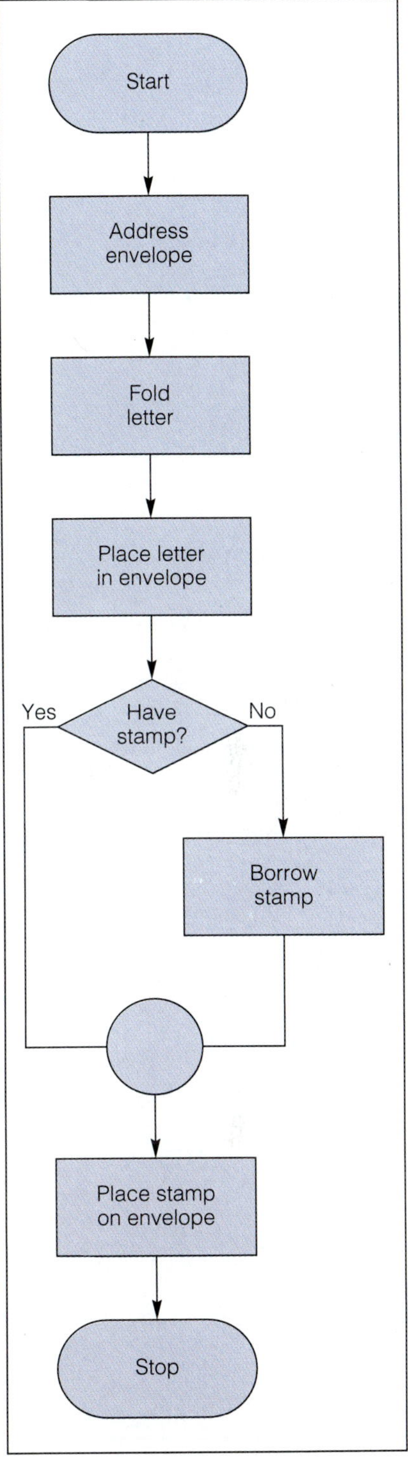

Figure 7-3 A simple flowchart.
This flowchart shows how to prepare a letter for mailing.

Example: Summing Numbers from 1 through 100

Figure 7-4 shows how you might flowchart a program to find the sum of all numbers from 1 through 100. You should observe several things about this flowchart.

First, the program uses two locations in the computer's memory as storage locations, or places to keep intermediate results. In one location is a counter, which might be like a car odometer: Every time a mile passes, the quantity 1 is added to the counter. In the other location is a sum—that is, a running total of the numbers counted. The sum location will eventually contain the sum of all numbers from 1 through 100: 1+2+3+4+5+. . . +100.

Second, note that you must initialize the counter and the sum. When you **initialize,** you set the starting values of certain storage locations, called **variables,** usually as program execution begins. For this example the sum is initialized to 0 and the counter to 1.

Third, note the looping. You add the quantity stored in the counter to the sum, add a 1 to the counter, and then come to the decision diamond, which asks if the counter is greater than 100. If the answer is no, the computer loops back around and repeats the process. The decision box contains a **compare operation;** the computer compares two numbers and performs alternative operations based on the comparison. If the result of the comparison is yes, the computer produces the sum as output, as indicated by the print instruction. Notice that the parallelogram-shaped symbol is used for printing the sum because it represents an output process.

A **loop** is the heart of computer programming. The beauty of the loop, which may be defined as instructions causing the repetition of actions under certain conditions, is that you, as the programmer, have to describe certain actions only once rather than describing them repeat-

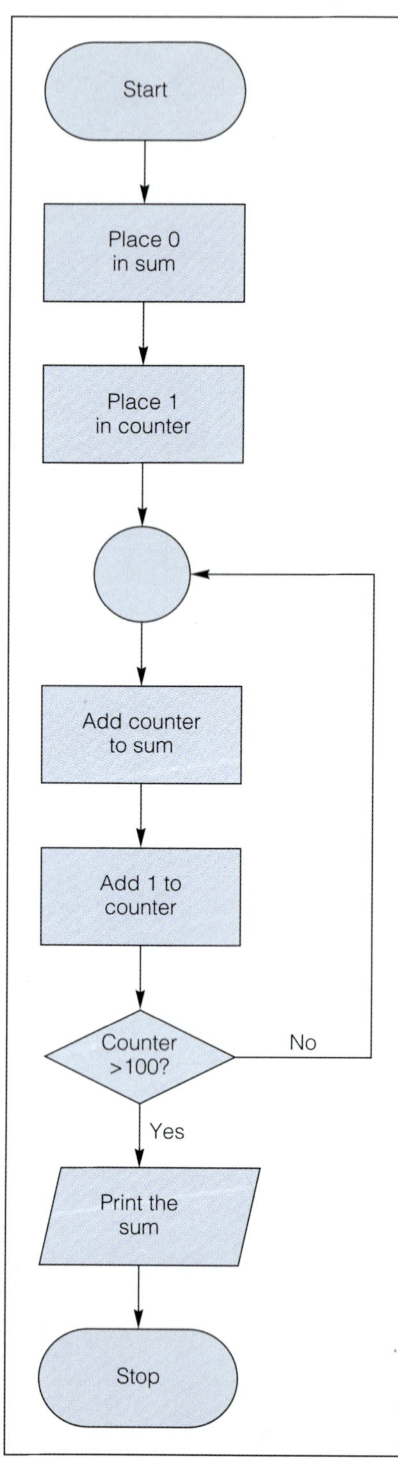

Figure 7-4 Loop example.
This flowchart uses a loop to find the sum of numbers from 1 through 100.

edly. One trip around the loop is called an **iteration.** Once the programmer has established the loop pattern and the conditions for concluding (exiting from) the loop, the computer begins looping and exits as it has been instructed to do. The flowchart can be modified easily to sum the numbers from 1 to 1000, from 500 to 700, or any other variation.

Example: Student Grades

Now let us see how a flowchart or pseudocode is translated into a program. Figure 7-5 shows a flowchart, pseudocode, and program designed to compute student grades. You could enter this program directly into your computer. The computer would deliver back to you, on the monitor or in printout form, the output shown in Figure 7-5d.

The problem is to compute the student grades (ranging from 0 through 100) for six students, and, second, to count the number of students whose computed scores are lower than 60. The grade points are based on student performance on two tests, a midterm exam and a final exam. These scores have been weighted in a certain way.

The program is written in the programming language called BASIC. There are several dialects of the BASIC language, but for this example we have chosen a version called Microsoft QBASIC.

In Figure 7-5c, the numbers in the far left of each line are called statement numbers. REM stands for remark statement. REM statements are used to document the program, providing a brief description of what the program is supposed to do and a list of all variable names—symbolic names of locations in memory. The PRINT statement tells the computer what message or data to print out, the READ statement reads the data to be processed, and the DATA statements list the data to be read by the computer. The IF statement executes a certain statement (here adding 1 to the count) if the condition is found to be true. The WHILE and WEND statements are used to form a loop: The lines between WHILE and WEND will be executed repeatedly while the condition on the WHILE line (in this case NUM <> -9999) holds true, and then control will transfer to the line following the WEND. In this example, when NUM equals -9999, as it will once the last line of data is read (from program line 480), then control will pass out of the loop to line 390.

BASIC is similar to English in many ways, so you can probably follow the program in a general way, even with no knowledge of BASIC. The following section introduces other programming languages.

Programming Languages

What language will a programmer use to communicate with the computer? Surely not the English language, which—like any human language—can be loose and ambiguous and full of slang, variations, and complexities. A programming language is needed. A **programming language**—a set of rules that provides a way of telling the computer what operations to perform—is anything but loose and ambiguous.

A programming language, the key to communicating with the computer, has certain definite characteristics. It has a limited vocabulary. Each "word" in it has precise meaning. Even though a programming language has limitations, it can still be used in a step-by-step fashion to solve complex problems. There is not, however, just one programming language; there are many.

As we will see, the languages in use today tend to meet specific needs, such as programming for scientific or business applications. Before we turn to the discussion of specific languages, however, we need to discuss levels of language.

Levels of Language

Programming languages are said to be low level or high level, depending on whether they are close to the language the computer itself uses (0s and 1s—low level) or to the language people use (more English-like—high level). We will consider five levels of programming language. They are numbered 1 through 5 to correspond to what are called the generations of programming languages. Each generation has improved on the ease of use and capabilities of its predecessors. The five generations of languages are

1. Machine language
2. Assembly languages
3. High-level languages
4. Very high-level languages
5. Natural languages

Figure 7-6 is a time line for language generations. Let us look at each of these categories.

Old and Difficult: Machine Language and Assembly Languages

Humans do not like to deal in numbers alone; we prefer letters and words. But numbers are what machine language is. This lowest level of language, **machine language,** represents information as 1s and 0s—binary digits corresponding to the on and off electrical states in the computer. Each type of computer has its own machine language.

In the early days of computing, programmers had rudimentary systems for combining numbers to represent instructions such as add or compare. Primitive by today's standards, the programs were not at all convenient for people to read and use. The computer industry moved to develop assembly languages.

Today **assembly languages** are considered very low level—that is, they are inconvenient compared to more recent languages, although they have the advantage of executing quickly. At the time they were developed, however, they were considered a great leap forward. Rather than using simply 1s and 0s, assembly languages use abbreviations or mnemonic codes as substitutes for machine language: A for Add, C for Compare, MP for Multiply, and so on.

The programmer who uses an assembly language requires a software translator, called an **assembler program,** to convert his or her assembly language program into machine language. A translator is needed because machine language is the only language the computer can actually exe-

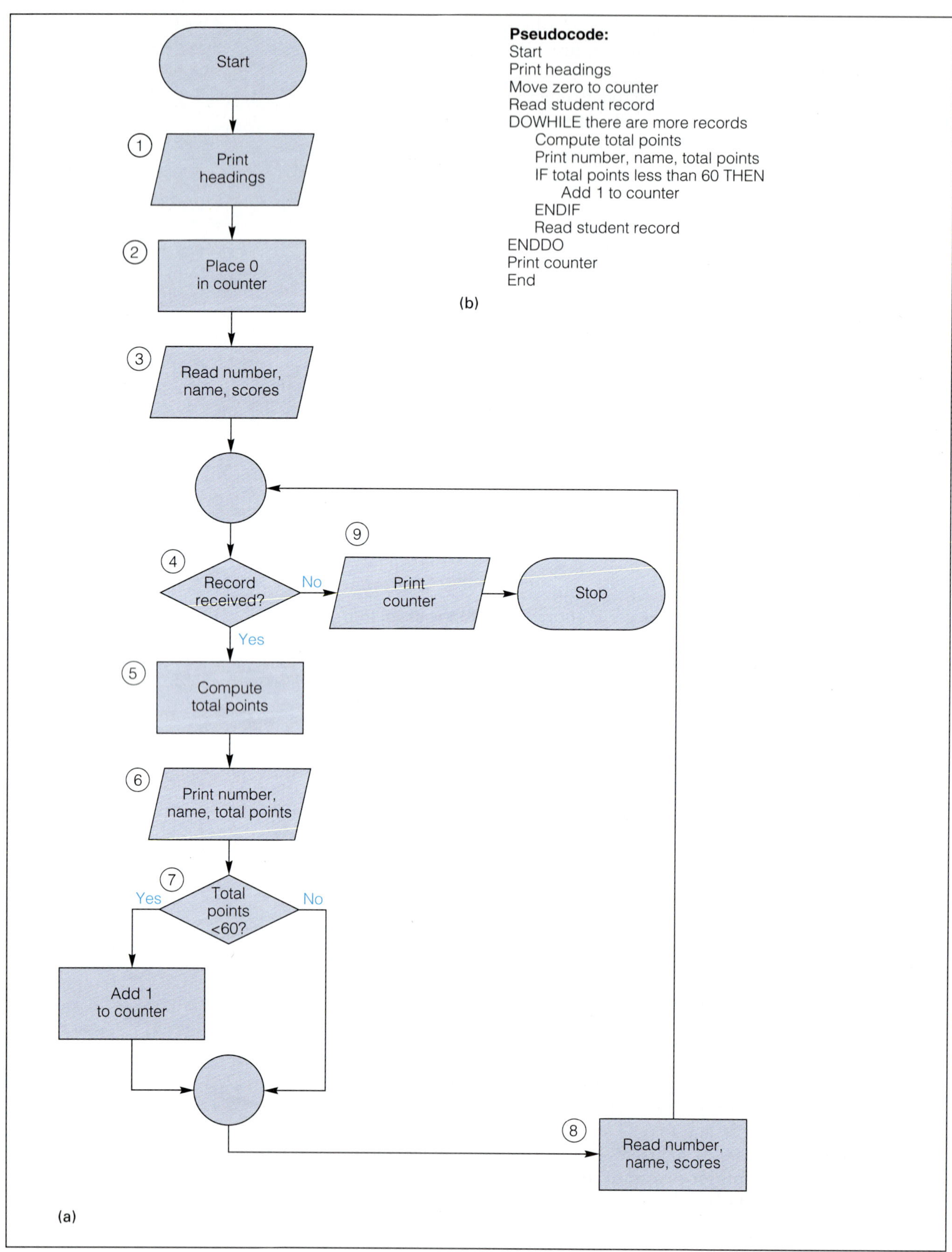

Pseudocode:

```
Start
Print headings
Move zero to counter
Read student record
DOWHILE there are more records
    Compute total points
    Print number, name, total points
    IF total points less than 60 THEN
        Add 1 to counter
    ENDIF
    Read student record
ENDDO
Print counter
End
```

(b)

```
10    REM PROGRAM TO COMPUTE STUDENT POINTS
20    REM
30    REM THIS PROGRAM READS, FOR EACH STUDENT,
40    REM   STUDENT NUMBER, STUDENT NAME, AND
50    REM   4 TEST SCORES. THE SCORES ARE TO
60    REM   BE WEIGHTED AS FOLLOWS:
70    REM
80    REM     TEST 1: 20 PERCENT
90    REM     TEST 2: 20 PERCENT
100   REM     MIDTERM: 25 PERCENT
110   REM     FINAL: 35 PERCENT
120   REM
130   REM VARIABLE NAMES USED:
140   REM
150   REM   COUNT    COUNT OF STUDENTS SCORING LESS THAN 60
160   REM   NUM      STUDENT NUMBER
170   REM   NAM$     STUDENT NAME
180   REM   TEST1    SCORE FOR TEST 1
190   REM   TEST2    SCORE FOR TEST 2
200   REM   TEST3    SCORE FOR MIDTERM
210   REM   TEST4    SCORE FOR FINAL
220   REM   TOTAL    TOTAL STUDENT POINTS
230   REM
240   PRINT
250   PRINT "    STUDENT GRADE REPORT"
260   PRINT
270   PRINT "STUDENT","STUDENT","TOTAL"
280   PRINT "NUMBER","NAME","POINTS"
290   PRINT
300   PRINT
310   LET COUNT = 0
320   READ NUM,NAM$,TEST1,TEST2,TEST3,TEST4
330   WHILE NUM <> -9999
340   LET TOTAL = TEST1 + .2 * TEST2 + .25 * TEST3 + .35 * TEST4
350   PRINT NUM,NAM$,TOTAL
360   IF TOTAL < 60 THEN COUNT = COUNT+1
370   READ NUM,NAM$,TEST1,TEST2,TEST3,TEST4
380   WEND
390   PRINT
400   PRINT "NUMBER OF STUDENTS WITH POINTS < 60:";COUNT
410   STOP
420   DATA 2164,ALLEN SCHWAB,60,64,73,78
430   DATA 2644,MARTIN CHAN,80,78,85,90
440   DATA 3171,CHRISTY BURNER,91,95,90,88
450   DATA 5725,CRAIG BARNES,61,41,70,53
460   DATA 6994,RAOUL GARCIA,95 96,90,92
470   DATA 7001,KAY MITCHELL,55,60,58,55
480   DATA -9999,XXX,0,0,0,0
490   END
```

(c)

```
              STUDENT GRADE REPORT

STUDENT         STUDENT               TOTAL
NUMBER          NAME                  POINTS


2164            ALLEN SCHWAB          70.4
2644            MARTIN CHAN           84.4
3171            CHRISTY BURNER        90.5
5725            CRAIG BARNES          56.5
6994            RAOUL GARCIA          92.9
7001            KAY MITCHELL          56.8

   NUMBER OF STUDENTS WITH POINTS <60:2
```

(d)

Figure 7-5 Student grades.
The (a) flowchart and (b) pseudocode for (c) the program that produces (d) a student grade report.

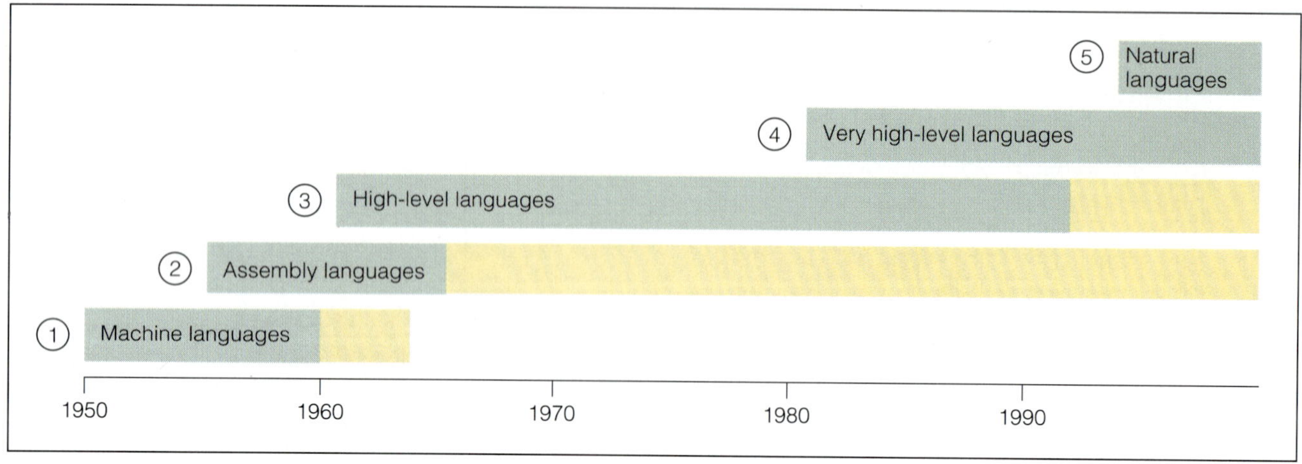

Figure 7-6 Language generations on a time line.
The darker shading indicates the period of greater use by applications programmers; the lighter shading indicates the time during which a generation faded from popular use.

cute. A programmer need not worry about the translating aspect; the translation is taken care of by the computer system.

Although assembly languages represent a step forward, they still have the disadvantage of requiring the programmer to describe in excruciating detail every small step involved in the program.

Readable: High-Level Languages

The first widespread use of **high-level languages** in the early 1960s transformed programming into something quite different from what it had been. The harried programmer working on the nitty-gritty details of assembly language codes became a programmer who, by using a better language, had more time to spend solving the client's problems. Programs in high-level languages were written in an English-like manner, thus making them more convenient to use and to debug.

Of course, a translator was needed to translate the symbolic statements of a high-level language into computer-executable machine language; this translator is usually a compiler.

More Like English: Very High-Level Languages

Languages called **very high-level languages** are often known by their generation number. That is, they are called **fourth-generation languages** or, more simply, **4GLs.** But if the name is easy, the definition is not. There is no consensus about what constitutes a fourth-generation language.

One characteristic of 4GLs is they are somewhat nonprocedural. A **procedural language** tells the computer *how* a task is done: add this, compare that, do this if something is true, and so forth—a very specific step-by-step process. The first three generations of languages are all procedural. In a **nonprocedural language,** the concept changes. Users define only *what* they want the computer to do; the user does not provide the details of just how it is to be done. Obviously, it is a lot easier and faster to just say what you want rather than explain how to get it. This leads us to the issue of productivity, a key characteristic of fourth-generation languages.

Consider this task: Produce a report showing the total units sold for each product, by customer, in each month and year, and with a subtotal for each customer. In addition, each new customer must start on a new page. The 4GL request looks something like this:

```
TABLE FILE SALES
SUM UNITS BY MONTH BY CUSTOMER BY PRODUCT
ON CUSTOMER SUBTOTAL PAGE BREAK
END
```

Even though some training is required to do even this much, you can see that it is pretty simple. The third-generation language COBOL, however, would typically require hundreds of statements to fulfill the same request. If we define productivity as producing equivalent results in less time, then fourth-generation languages clearly increase productivity.

Weird Programs Wanted

Lots of programmers idle away hours on their own time to come up with a fantastic program—something new and different. Some of them even come up with programs that could be called weird—amusing to them but with not much potential for sales. But change is in the wind. They may not get rich from their weird programs, but at least they can enter them in a contest.

According to the officials for the Weird Software contest, all you need are programming skills and a vivid imagination. The competition is held annually in conjunction with the San Diego Computer Fair. Prizes are cash, T-shirts, and books. Hint: One winner was a screen-saver software that displayed bungee-jumping cows.

Everyday Speech: Natural Languages

The word *natural* has become almost as popular in computing circles as it has in the supermarket. But fifth-generation languages are, as you may guess, even harder to define than fourth-generation languages. Those in the fifth generation are most often called **natural languages** because of their resemblance to the "natural" spoken English language. Instead of being forced to key correct commands and data names in correct order, a manager (programmers are not needed) tells the computer what to do by keying in his or her own words. Figure 7-7 illustrates a natural language.

A manager can say the same thing any number of ways. For example, "Get me tennis racket sales for January" works just as well as "I want Jan-

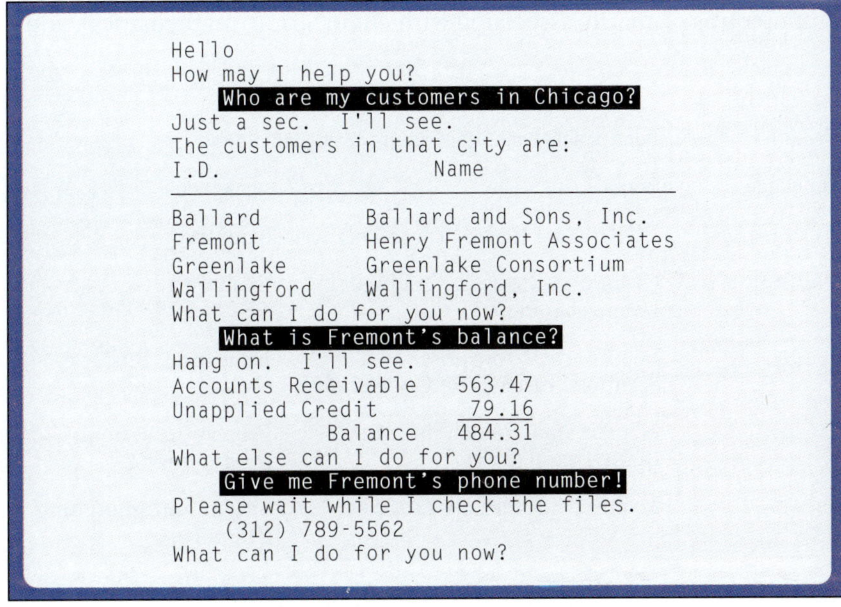

Figure 7-7 A natural language. This package, called Cash Management System, uses a language that is so "natural" that some might think it is a little too cute, as in "Just a sec."

uary tennis racket revenues." Such a request may contain misspelled words, lack articles and verbs, and even use slang. The natural language translates human instructions—bad grammar, slang, and all—into code the computer understands. If it is not sure what the user has in mind, it politely asks for further explanation.

Some Popular Languages

How does a programmer choose the language in which to write a program? Perhaps a particular language is the standard at the programmer's place of business. Perhaps the manager decrees that everyone on a project will use a certain language.

A sensible approach is to pick the language that is most suitable for the particular program application. The following sections on individual languages provide an overview of the languages in common use. We describe these languages: FORTRAN, COBOL, BASIC, Pascal, and C—all third-generation languages in common use today. Special features of each language are noted, including the types of applications for which they are often used. Table 7-1 summarizes the languages and their applications.

To accompany our discussion of particular languages, we will show a program and its output to give you a sense of what each language looks like. Since we are performing the same task in each program, finding the average of three numbers, you can see some of the differences and similarities among the languages. We do not expect you to understand each line of these programs; they are here merely as illustrations. Figure 7-8 provides a flowchart and pseudocode for the task of averaging numbers.

FORTRAN: The First High-Level Language

Developed by IBM and introduced in 1954, **FORTRAN**, which stands for FORmula TRANslator, was the first high-level language. FORTRAN is a scientifically oriented language; in the early days use of the computer was primarily associated with engineering, mathematical, and

Table 7-1 Applications of some important programming languages.

Language	Origin	Application
FORTRAN	FORmula TRANslator (1954)	Scientific
COBOL	COmmon Business-Oriented Language (1959)	Business
BASIC	Beginner's All-purpose Symbolic Instruction Code (1965)	Education, Business
Pascal	Named after French inventor Blaise Pascal (1971)	Education, systems programming
C	Invented at Bell Labs (1972)	Systems programming, general use

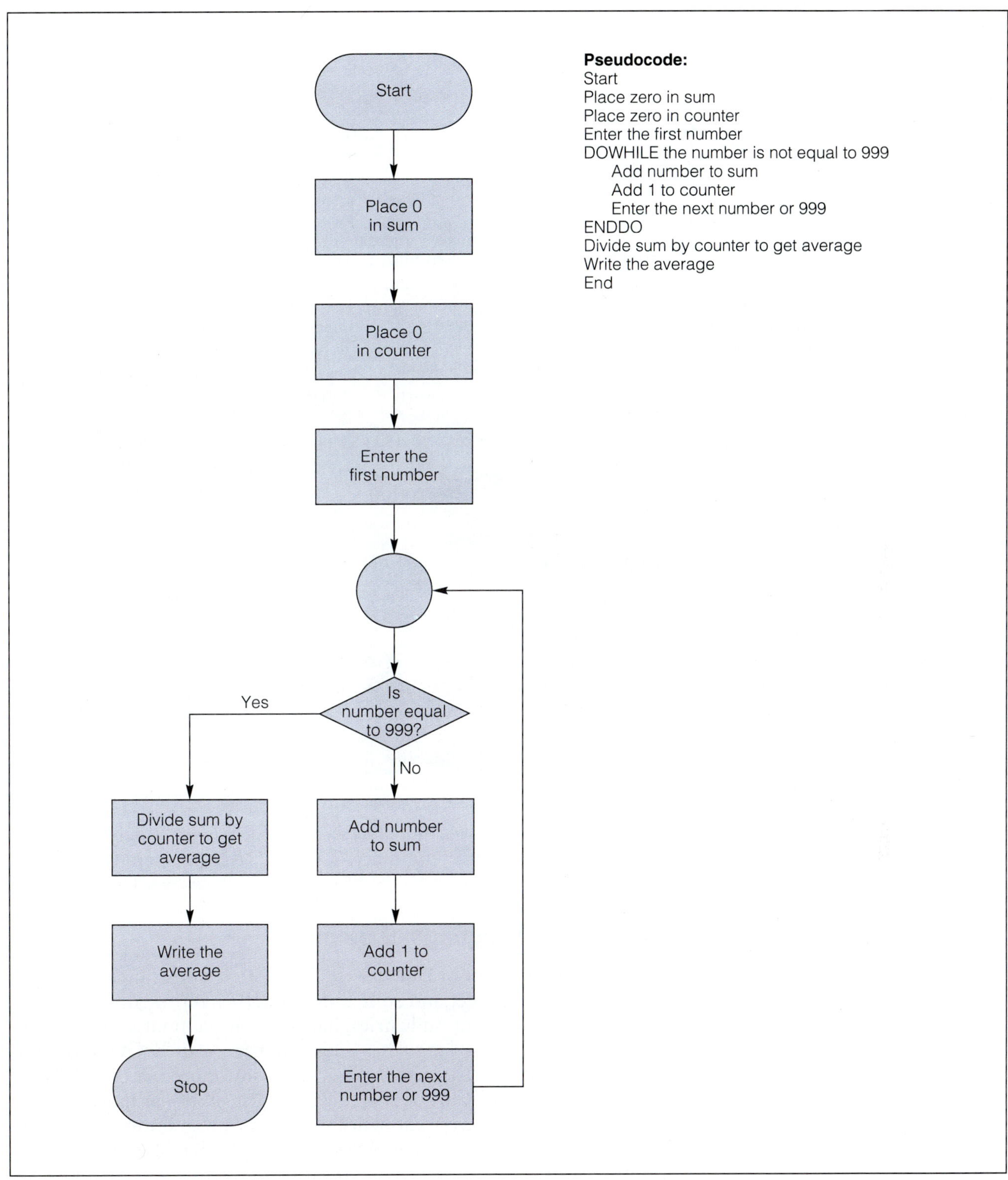

Figure 7-8 Flowchart and pseudocode for averaging numbers.
This flowchart and matching pseudocode show the logic for a program to let a user enter numbers through the keyboard; the program then averages the numbers. Any number of numbers can be entered, one at a time; the signal that all data has been entered is 999. The logic to enter the numbers forms a loop: entering the number, adding it to the sum, and adding 1 to the counter. When 999 is keyed, the loop is exited. The average is then computed and displayed on the screen. This logic is used for the programs, in various languages, that follow in Figures 7-9 through 7-12.

Personal Computers In Action

Home Sweet Home

Maybe programmers should work at home. The idea is not new, but new factors are affecting the decision to work at home or in the office. The first factor is the freedom derived from the personal computer, and the second is the newly acknowledged influence of environment on productivity.

First the personal computer. Many programmers in the office still work on terminals that interact with a large mainframe computer. The response time from the mainframe is either uniformly awful or so unpredictable that it becomes difficult to plan work effectively. In contrast, a single-user personal computer provides relatively instant and uniform response times for most programming tasks. A programmer working with a personal computer at home can sit right down and get to business.

Now, what about the environment? Recent studies have shown that a programmer's physical work environment influences his or her productivity more profoundly than managers had suspected. Although programming productivity has long been known to vary dramatically from one individual to another, these variances have usually been attributed to differences in experience and ability. But studies suggest something quite different. When groups of people in different environments are compared, productivity is improved by such environmental factors as desk size, noise levels, and privacy.

The direction seems clear. Get a personal computer for home use, place it on a large desk in a quiet room, and lock yourself in. Your productivity should soar. Well, it is hardly that simple, but the findings are worthy of consideration by all who want to work at home.

scientific research tasks. FORTRAN is still the most widely used language in the scientific community. A FORTRAN program is shown in Figure 7-9.

COBOL: The Language of Business

The U.S. Department of Defense was interested in creating a standardized business language, and so it called together representatives from government and various industries, including the computer industry, to come up with such a language. This language, called **COBOL,** for COmmon Business-Oriented Language, was introduced in 1959. The principal feature of COBOL is that it is English-like—far more so than FORTRAN. Even if you know nothing about programming, you can still read a COBOL program and have some understanding of its general purpose. COBOL is also renowned for being **machine independent;** that is, a program written in COBOL can be run on different computers. A COBOL program is shown in Figure 7-10.

BASIC: For Beginners and Others

We have already shown **BASIC**—Beginner's All-purpose Symbolic Instruction Code—earlier in the chapter (Figure 7-5c). Developed at

```
C       FORTRAN PROGRAM
C       AVERAGING INTEGERS ENTERED THROUGH THE KEYBOARD
        WRITE (6,10)
        SUM = 0
        COUNTER = 0
        WRITE (6,60)
        READ (5,40) NUMBER
    1   IF (NUMBER .EQ. 999) GOTO 2
        SUM = SUM + NUMBER
        COUNTER = COUNTER + 1
        WRITE (6,70)
        READ (5,40) NUMBER
        GO TO 1
    2   AVERAGE = SUM / COUNTER
        WRITE (6,80) AVERAGE
   10   FORMAT (1X, 'THIS PROGRAM WILL FIND THE AVERAGE OF ',
       'INTEGERS YOU ENTER ',/1X, 'THROUGH THE ',
        'KEYBOARD. TYPE 999 TO INDICATE END OF DATA.',/)
   40 * FORMAT (13)
   60 * FORMAT (1X, 'PLEASE ENTER A NUMBER ')
   70   FORMAT (1X, 'PLEASE ENTER THE NEXT NUMBER ')
   80   FORMAT (1X, 'THE AVERAGE OF THE NUMBERS IS ',F6.2)
        STOP
        END
```

(a)

```
THIS PROGRAM WILL FIND THE AVERAGE OF INTEGERS YOU ENTER
THROUGH THE KEYBOARD.  TYPE 999 TO INDICATE END OF DATA.
PLEASE ENTER A NUMBER    6
PLEASE ENTER THE NEXT NUMBER      4
PLEASE ENTER THE NEXT NUMBER     11
PLEASE ENTER THE NEXT NUMBER    999
THE AVERAGE OF THE NUMBERS IS      7.00
```

(b)

Figure 7-9 A FORTRAN program and sample output for averaging numbers. This program is interactive, prompting the user to supply data. (a) The first two lines are comments, as they are in the other programs in this chapter. The WRITE statements send output to the screen in the format matching the number in the WRITE parentheses. The READ statements accept data from the user and place it in location NUMBER, where it can be added to the accumulated SUM. The IF statement checks for number 999 and, when it is received, diverts the program logic to statement 2, where the average is computed. The average is then displayed. (b) This screen display shows the interaction between program and user.

Dartmouth College by John Kemeny and Thomas Kurtz in 1965, BASIC was originally intended for use by students in an academic environment. In the late 1960s it became widely used in universities and colleges. The use of BASIC has extended to all kinds of users, especially those using personal computers. The primary advantage of BASIC is one that may be of interest to many readers of this book: BASIC is relatively easy to learn, even for a person who has never programmed before. There are different versions of BASIC; two popular commercial forms are Quick BASIC and Microsoft BASIC.

Figure 7-10 A COBOL program and sample output for averaging numbers.
The purpose of this program and its results are the same as those of the FORTRAN program in Figure 7-9, but the look of the COBOL program is very different. (a) Note the four divisions. In particular, note that the logic in the procedure division uses a series of PERFORM statements, diverting logic flow to other places in the program. After a section has been performed, logic flow returns to the statement after the one that called the PERFORM. DISPLAY writes to the screen, and ACCEPT takes the user input. (b) This screen display shows the interaction between program and user.

```
************************************************************
IDENTIFICATION DIVISION.
************************************************************
PROGRAM-ID.  AVERAGE.
* COBOL PROGRAM
* AVERAGING INTEGERS ENTERED THROUGH THE KEYBOARD.
************************************************************
ENVIRONMENT DIVISION.
************************************************************
CONFIGURATION SECTION.
SOURCE-COMPUTER.          H-P 3000.
OBJECT-COMPUTER.          H-P 3000.
************************************************************
DATA DIVISION.
************************************************************
FILE SECTION.
WORKING-STORAGE SECTION.
01 AVERAGE      PIC ---9.99.
01 COUNTER      PIC 9(02)       VALUE ZERO.
01 NUMBER-ITEM  PIC S9(03).
01 SUM-ITEM     PIC S9(06)      VALUE ZERO.
01 BLANK-LINE   PIC X(80)       VALUE SPACES.
************************************************************
PROCEDURE DIVISION.
************************************************************
100-CONTROL-ROUTINE.
    PERFORM 200-DISPLAY-INSTRUCTIONS.
    PERFORM 300-INITIALIZATION-ROUTINE.
    PERFORM 400-ENTER-AND-ADD
             UNTIL NUMBER-ITEM = 999.
    PERFORM 500-CALCULATE-AVERAGE.
    PERFORM 600-DISPLAY-RESULTS.
    STOP RUN.
200-DISPLAY-INSTRUCTIONS.
    DISPLAY
      "THIS PROGRAM WILL FIND THE AVERAGE OF INTEGERS YOU ENTER".
    DISPLAY
      "THROUGH THE KEYBOARD. TYPE 999 TO INDICATE END OF DATA.".
    DISPLAY BLANK-LINE.
300-INITIALIZATION-ROUTINE.
    DISPLAY "PLEASE ENTER A NUMBER".
    ACCEPT NUMBER-ITEM.
400-ENTER-AND-ADD
    ADD NUMBER-ITEM TO SUM-ITEM.
    ADD 1 TO COUNTER.
    DISPLAY "PLEASE ENTER THE NEXT NUMBER".
    ACCEPT NUMBER-ITEM.
500-CALCULATE-AVERAGE.
    DIVIDE SUM-ITEM BY COUNTER GIVING AVERAGE.
600-DISPLAY-RESULTS.
    DISPLAY "THE AVERAGE OF THE NUMBERS IS ",AVERAGE.
```

(a)

```
THIS PROGRAM WILL FIND THE AVERAGE OF
INTEGERS YOU ENTER THROUGH THE KEYBOARD.
TYPE 999 TO INDICATE END OF DATA.

PLEASE ENTER A NUMBER
6
PLEASE ENTER THE NEXT NUMBER
4
PLEASE ENTER THE NEXT NUMBER
11
PLEASE ENTER THE NEXT NUMBER
999
THE AVERAGE OF THE NUMBERS IS   7.00
```

(b)

Pascal: The Language of Simplicity

Named for Blaise Pascal, the 17th-century French mathematician, **Pascal** was developed as a teaching language by a Swiss computer scientist, Niklaus Wirth, and first became available in 1971. Since that time it has become quite popular, first in Europe and now in the United States, particularly in universities and colleges offering computer science programs.

The foremost feature of Pascal is that it is simpler than most other languages: It has fewer features and is less wordy than most. Because of its limited input/output capabilities, however, it is unlikely to have a serious impact on the business community in its present form. Figure 7-11 presents an example of a Pascal program.

C: A Sophisticated Language

C was invented by Dennis Ritchie at Bell Labs in 1972. Its unromantic name evolved from earlier versions called A and B. C lends itself to sophisticated programming as well as to more mundane programming tasks. Further, C produces code that approaches assembly language in efficiency while still offering high-level language features.

Although C is simple and elegant, it is not particularly simple to learn. C was originally developed for professional programmers, and, except for elementary tasks, requires a serious learning period. Figure 7-12 shows an example of a C program and sample output.

Object-Oriented Programming

Imagine having to write an inventory program for a large manufacturer. Using a conventional programming language, such as those described in the previous section, a programmer would have to write a line of program code for the tiniest detail of the system. Actually, this would probably take many programmers many months to write many thousands of lines of code. But what if the programmers could take a shortcut? What if they could use some code already written—and tested—for another program? In other words, what if they did not have to reinvent the wheel every time they sat down to write a new program? Many people in the computer industry have asked these questions.

In recent years a new approach to writing programs has emerged. **Object-oriented programming (OOP)** means building a new program from standardized, precoded modules (Figure 7-13). Those precoded modules, together with the data to be processed, are called **objects.** Each object performs a certain function and is self-contained. Steve Jobs, a founder of Apple Computer, likes to use a laundry example. He lists the normal procedures for doing laundry at the laundromat: sort clothes, load washer, select temperature, input quarters, add detergent, and so forth. If, for some reason, this same information should be needed repeatedly, it could be stored as an object, perhaps called CLEAN. When next needed, rather than start from scratch, the object CLEAN could be invoked.

Currently, the two most widely used languages that embody object-oriented programming are **Smalltalk** and **C++.** Proponents of Smalltalk

```
PROGRAM AVERAGE (INPUT, OUTPUT);
(* PASCAL PROGRAM *)
(* AVERAGING INTEGERS ENTERED THROUGH THE KEYBOARD *)
VAR
    COUNTER, NUMBER, SUM : INTEGER;
    AVERAGE : REAL;
BEGIN
WRITELN ('THIS PROGRAM WILL FIND THE AVERAGE OF INTEGERS YOU ENTER');
WRITELN ('THROUGH THE KEYBOARD. TYPE 999 TO INDICATE END OF DATA.');
WRITELN;
SUM := 0;
COUNTER := 0;
WRITELN ('PLEASE ENTER A NUMBER');
READ (NUMBER);
WHILE NUMBER <> 999 DO
    BEGIN
    SUM :=SUM + NUMBER;
    COUNTER := COUNTER + 1;
    WRITELN ('PLEASE ENTER THE NEXT NUMBER');
    READ (NUMBER);
    END;
AVERAGE := SUM / COUNTER;
WRITELN ('THE AVERAGE OF THE NUMBERS IS',AVERAGE :6:2);
END.
```

(a)

```
THIS PROGRAM WILL FIND THE AVERAGE OF INTEGERS YOU ENTER
THROUGH THE KEYBOARD. TYPE 999 TO INDICATE END OF DATA.

PLEASE ENTER A NUMBER
6
PLEASE ENTER THE NEXT NUMBER
4
PLEASE ENTER THE NEXT NUMBER
11
PLEASE ENTER THE NEXT NUMBER
999
THE AVERAGE OF THE NUMBERS IS   7.00
```

(b)

Figure 7-11 A Pascal program and sample output for averaging numbers.
(a) Comments are from (* to *). Each variable name must be declared. The symbol := assigns a value to the variable on the left; the symbol <> means not equal to. WRITELN by itself puts a blank line on the screen. (b) This screen display shows the interaction between program and user.

```
/* C PROGRAM */
/* AVERAGING INTEGERS ENTERED THROUGH THE KEYBOARD */
main()
{ float average;
  int counter = 0; number = 0; sum = 0;
printf("THIS PROGRAM WILL FIND THE AVERAGE OF INTEGERS YOU ENTER\n");
printf("THROUGH THE KEYBOARD. TYPE 999 TO INDICATE END OF DATA. \n\n");
printf("PLEASE ENTER A NUMBER");
scanf("%d",&number);
while (number != 999)
    {
      sum = sum + number;
      counter ++ ;
      printf("PLEASE ENTER THE NEXT NUMBER");
      scanf("%d",&number);
    }
  average = sum / counter;
  printf("THE AVERAGE OF THE NUMBERS IS ",AVERAGE);
}
```

(a)

```
THIS PROGRAM WILL FIND THE AVERAGE OF INTEGERS YOU ENTER
THROUGH THE KEYBOARD. TYPE 999 TO INDICATE END OF DATA.

PLEASE ENTER A NUMBER
6
PLEASE ENTER THE NEXT NUMBER
4
PLEASE ENTER THE NEXT NUMBER
11
PLEASE ENTER THE NEXT NUMBER
999
THE AVERAGE OF THE NUMBERS IS   7.00
```

(b)

Figure 7-12 A C program and sample output for averaging numbers.
(a) Comments are between /* and */. The command printf sends output to the screen, and the scanf command accepts data from the user. (b) This screen display shows the interaction between program and user.

say it is the only "pure" OOP language, but supporters of C++, chiefly programmers who develop commercial software products, see its extension from the C language as an advantage. Despite its popularity in theory and in the press, large-scale use of object-oriented programming is still far from common. Two reasons for hanging back are the decades-long entrenchment of COBOL programs and the rather steep learning curve to change the programming orientation of an entire organization.

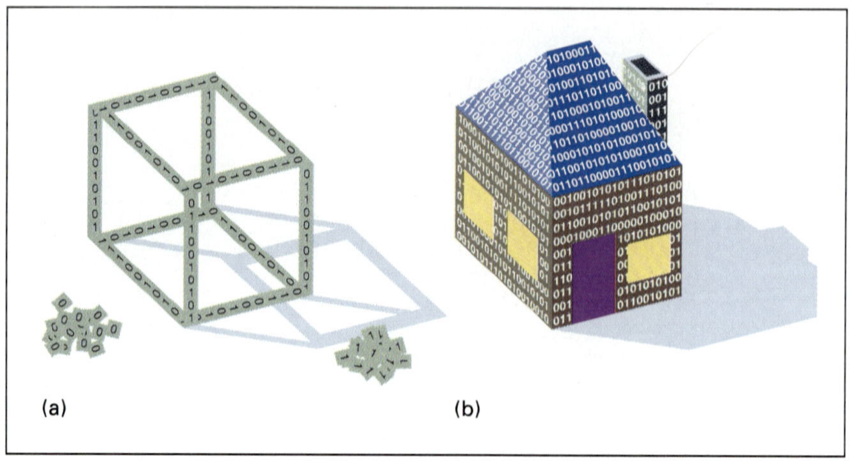

Figure 7-13 Object-oriented programming.
(a) In traditional programming, programmers typically divide up the task and write thousands of lines of program code from scratch. (b) In an object-oriented approach, a programmer searches a library of objects (precoded chunks of software) and incorporates those that are useful to the task.

But change is in the wind. Electronic Data Systems (EDS), a programming powerhouse, provides one stunning example. EDS ran a test to compare two programming teams, one OOP and one not, performing the same task. Guess which team used 10 person-months for the task and which used 152 person-months. These kinds of real-life illustrations tend to move, eventually, even the most recalcitrant organizations.

In this chapter we have glimpsed the planning and care required to write programs and looked at the direction of language development. We now turn to one special set of programs—the operating system.

Chapter **Review**

Summary and Key Terms

- A **programmer** converts solutions to the user's problems into a **program,** or instructions for the computer, by defining the problem, planning the solution, coding the program, testing the program, and documenting the program.
- Defining the problem means discussing it with the users to determine the necessary input, processing, and output.
- Planning can be done by using a **flowchart,** which is a pictorial representation of the step-by-step solution, and by using **pseudocode,** which is an English-like language.
- Coding the program means expressing the solution in a programming language.
- Testing the program consists of desk-checking, translating, and debugging. The rules of a programming language are referred to as its **syntax. Desk-checking** is a mental checking or proofreading of the program before it is run.
- In translating, a **translator** program converts the program into language the computer can understand and in the process detects programming-language errors, which are called **syntax errors.** Two types of translators are a **compiler,** which translates the entire program at one time and gives all the error messages **(diagnostics)** at once, and an **interpreter,** which translates the program one line at a time. The compiler also produces a **source program listing.** The original program, called a **source module,** is translated to an **object module,** to which prewritten programs may be added during the **link/load phase** to create an executable **load module.**
- **Debugging** is running the program to detect, locate, and correct mistakes, called **logic errors.**
- **Documentation** is a detailed written description of the program and the test results.
- The standard symbols used in flowcharting are called **ANSI** (American National Standards Institute) symbols. The rectangular **process box** shows an action to be taken. The diamond-shaped **decision box**—with two **paths,** or **branches**—is the only symbol that allows a choice. The **connector** is a circle that connects paths. The oval **start/stop symbol** is used at the beginning and end of a flowchart.
- To **initialize** is to set the starting values of certain storage locations, or **variables,** before running a program.
- A **loop** is a set of instructions causing the repetition of actions under certain conditions. An **iteration** is one trip through the loop. The computer can recognize the conditions by performing a **compare operation.**
- Pseudocode allows a programmer to plan a program, without being concerned about the rules of a specific programming language.
- A **programming language** is a set of rules for instructing the computer what operations to perform.
- **Machine language,** the lowest-level programming language, represents information as 0s and 1s.
- **Assembly languages** use letters as abbreviations or mnemonic codes to replace the 0s and 1s of machine language. An **assembler program** translates assembly language into machine language.
- **High-level languages** consist of English-like words. A compiler translates high-level languages into machine language.

- **Very high-level languages,** also called fourth-generation languages or **4GLs,** are basically nonprocedural. A **nonprocedural language** only defines *what* the computer should do, without detailing the procedure. A **procedural language** tells the computer specifically *how* to do the task.
- Fifth-generation languages are often called **natural languages** because they resemble natural human language.
- The first high-level language, **FORTRAN** (FORmula TRANslator), is a scientifically oriented language.
- **COBOL** (COmmon Business-Oriented Language) is a standard programming language for business that is considered **machine independent** because a COBOL program can be run on different computers.
- When introduced, **BASIC** (Beginner's All-purpose Symbolic Instruction Code) was intended for instruction, but its uses now include business and personal-computer systems.
- **Pascal** is popular in college computer courses.
- **C** offers high-level language features while producing efficient code.
- **Object-oriented programming (OOP)** means building a new program from standardized, precoded modules. The precoded modules, together with the data to be processed, are called **objects.** Each object performs a certain function and is self-contained. Two popular object-oriented languages are **Smalltalk** and **C++**.

Student Personal Study Guide

True/False

T F 1. Process boxes in flowcharting have two exits called paths.
T F 2. Lower-level languages are closer to the language the computer uses than are higher-level languages.
T F 3. A flowchart is an example of pseudocode.
T F 4. Desk-checking is the first phase of testing a program.
T F 5. A translator is hardware that translates a program into language the computer can understand.
T F 6. The highest-level languages are called, simply, high-level languages.
T F 7. Debugging is the process of locating program errors.
T F 8. Expressing a problem solution in Pascal is an example of coding a program.
T F 9. An advantage of pseudocode is that it can be used both to plan and execute a program.
T F 10. A 4GL increases clarity but reduces productivity.

Multiple Choice

1. A scientific language:
   a. 4GL c. FORTRAN
   b. BASIC d. COBOL
2. A programming language often used to teach programming to beginners:
   a. C c. BASIC
   b. assembly language d. pseudocode
3. Which is not part of testing a program?
   a. debugging c. initializing
   b. desk-checking d. diagnostics

4. The highest level of programming languages:
   a. assembly c. high range
   b. natural d. machine
5. A popular business-oriented language:
   a. assembly c. Pascal
   b. COBOL d. FORTRAN
6. Mentally "proofreading" the program:
   a. desk-checking c. linking
   b. compiling d. translating
7. The standard used for flowchart symbols:
   a. key c. ANSI
   b. magnetic tape d. syntax
8. Which is *not* a type of flowchart box?
   a. syntax c. connector
   b. process d. decision
9. A detailed written description of the program and the test results:
   a. coding c. compiling
   b. link/loading d. documentation
10. Which is not output from the compiler:
    a. load module c. source program listing
    b. object module d. diagnostics

Fill-In

1. Translates high-level languages into machine language: ____________________.
2. Two common methods of planning the solution to a problem: ________________.
3. A language written by Niklaus Wirth: ____________________.
4. A language specifically designed to write systems software: ____________________.
5. The standard symbols used in flowcharting are called: ____________________.
6. A kind of language that states *what* needs to be done, not *how*: ________________.
7. Languages that resemble spoken languages are called: ____________________.
8. Type of language that builds programs from objects: ____________________.
9. The error messages a translator provides are: ____________________.
10. One trip through a loop: ____________________.

Answers

True/False: 1. F, 2. T, 3. F, 4. T, 5. F, 6. F, 7. T, 8. T, 9. F, 10. F
Multiple choice: 1. c, 2. c, 3. c , 4. b, 5. b, 6. a, 7. c, 8. a, 9. d, 10. a
Fill-In: 1. compiler, 2. flowcharting, pseudocode, 3. Pascal, 4. C, 5. ANSI symbols, 6. non-procedural, 7. natural, 8. object-oriented, 9. diagnostics, 10. iteration

Chapter Overview

When Felicia Lee was taking a night class in applications software at a community college four years ago, she did not have to worry much about the operating system—the necessary software in the background. The college personal computers were on a network that managed all the computers. As Felicia sat down to begin work, the computer screen showed a menu of numbered choices reflecting the software packages available: 1. WordPerfect, 2. Microsoft Word, 3. Lotus 1-2-3, and so forth. At the bottom of the screen, Felicia was instructed to type the number of her chosen selection; if she typed 1, for example, the system put her into WordPerfect. Felicia did have to learn operating system commands to prepare her own diskettes and save data on them so she could take her work with her, but she had little other contact with the operating system.

Operating

For her job as a supervisor in airport freight, Felicia needed to use word processing, spreadsheets, and database software packages on her IBM personal computer. But no one had set up a menu shortcut here, so, with a little advice from colleagues, she learned what she needed to know about the operating system called MS-DOS. She learned, among other things, to execute the software she needed to use and to take care of her data files—copying files from one disk to another and sometimes renaming or deleting them. She eventually felt fairly comfortable with her operating system knowledge.

Eighteen months later, Felicia was informed by the company personal computer manager that all personal computers were going to be switched to Microsoft Windows, a sort of overlay for the operating system. Despite assurances that the new system would be colorful and easy to use, Felicia was less than thrilled to be making another change. But she did not say so. She knew that being a computer user meant being willing to adjust to change. So Felicia learned to use a mouse and mastered icons, overlapping windows, pull-down menus, and other mysteries.

Approximately six months later, Felicia took a job at another airline freight company. Part of the reason she was hired was her response to the revelation that the new company used Macintosh computers, which, she knew, used another operating system altogether. Felicia said, "Oh, I have learned several systems. It shouldn't be any problem learning another." She was right, of course. In fact, she thought the Macintosh operating system was the easiest of them all.

Systems

The Underlying Software

Operating Systems: Powerful Software in the Background

An **operating system** is a set of programs that allows the computer to control and manage its own resources, such as the central processing unit, memory, and secondary storage. Figure 8-1 gives a conceptual picture of operating system software as an intermediary between the hardware and applications programs, such as word processing and database programs. Much of the work of an operating system is hidden from the user; many necessary tasks are performed behind the scenes. In other words, whether or not you are aware of it, using any software application requires that you invoke, or call into action, the operating system as well. As a user you must be able to interact with an operating system at some level, however rudimentary.

Operating systems for mainframe and other large computers are complex indeed, since they must keep track of several programs from several users all running in the same time frame. Although some personal computer operating systems—most often those found in business or learning environments—can support multiple programs, many are concerned only with a single user running a single program at a given time. This chapter focuses on the interaction between a user and a personal computer operating system.

Operating Systems for Personal Computers

If you peruse software offerings at a retail store, you will generally find the software grouped according to the computer, probably IBM or Macintosh, with which the software can be used. But the distinction is actu-

Figure 8-1 A conceptual diagram of an operating system.
On the outer rim, closest to the user, are applications programs—software that helps a user compute a payroll or play a game or calculate the trajectory of a rocket. The operating system is the set of programs between the applications programs and the hardware.

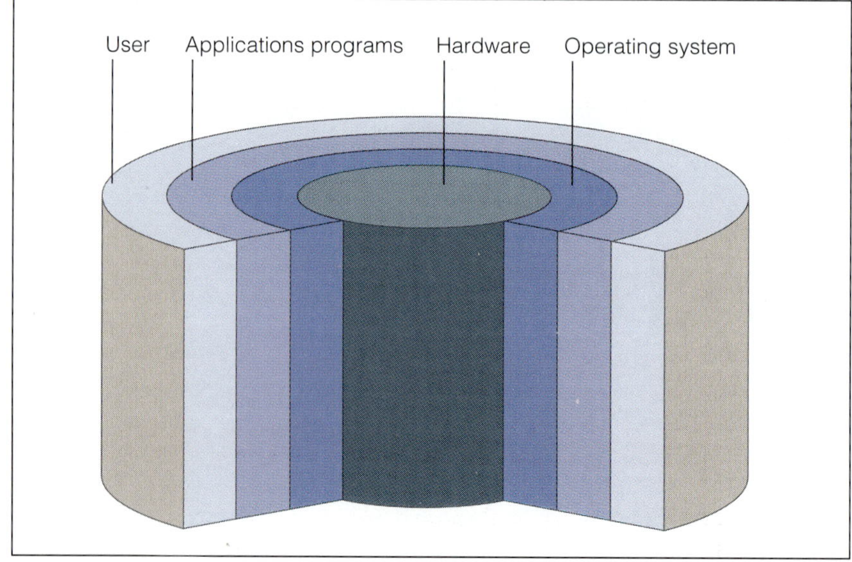

ally finer than the differences among computers: Applications programs—word processing, spreadsheets, games, or whatever—are really distinguished by the operating systems on which they can run.

Generally, an application program can run on just one operating system. Just as you cannot place a Nissan engine in a Ford truck, you cannot take a version of WordPerfect designed to run on an IBM machine and run it on an Apple Macintosh. IBM personal computers and others like them use Microsoft's operating system, called MS-DOS (for Microsoft Disk Operating System). Macintoshes use an entirely different operating system called System 7, which is produced by Apple. Most personal computers are limited to one of these two. The operating systems are different because the central processing units are different. Software makers must decide for which operating system to write a software package, although some make versions of their software for each operating system.

Users do not set out to buy operating systems; they want computers and the applications software to make them useful. Since the operating system determines what software is available for a given computer, many users observe the high volume of software available for MS-DOS machines and make their computer purchases accordingly. Others prefer the user-friendly style of the Macintosh operating system and choose Macs for that reason.

Although operating systems differ, many of their basic functions are similar. We will show some of the basic functions of operating systems by examining MS-DOS.

Getting Started with MS-DOS

Most users today have a computer with a hard disk drive. When the computer is turned on, the operating system will be loaded from the hard disk into the computer's memory, thus making it available for use. (Users without a hard disk drive must load the operating system from a diskette each time they use the computer.) The process of loading the operating system into memory is called bootstrapping, or **booting,** the system. The word *booting* is used because, figuratively speaking, the operating system pulls itself up by its own bootstraps. When the computer is switched on, a small program (in ROM—read-only memory) automatically pulls up the basic components of the operating system from the hard disk.

The net observable result of booting MS-DOS is that the characters C> (or possibly C:\>) appear on the screen. (Users without a hard drive will see A>). The C refers to the disk drive; the > is a **prompt,** a signal that the system is prompting you to do something. At that point you must give some instruction to the computer. Perhaps all you need to do is key certain letters to make the application software take the lead. But it could be more complicated than that because C> is actually a signal for direct communication between the user and the operating system.

Although the prompt is the only visible result of booting the system, MS-DOS also provides the basic software that coordinates the computer's hardware components and a set of programs that lets you perform the many computer system tasks you need to do. We will consider some of these tasks now.

Windows 95: The Latest and Greatest

As 50 million users can attest, the operating environment called Windows is an unqualified success. But even a popular software product can be improved. Here are some highlights of Windows 95:

User convenience. You can't miss it: the message "Click here to begin" bounces along the bottom, near the Start button in the lower left corner. From this launch, you can find a program or a file. And, by the way, all actions use only a single click of a mouse. Want to revise a memo? Just click its file name to retrieve it—the word processing program is automatically invoked too. As another example of convenience, long file names, up to 255 characters, are permitted.

Information center. Windows 95 puts all communications activities—e-mail, downloads, and so forth—in a single screen icon. Furthermore, Windows 95 includes software that makes it easier to configure computers for networks and the Internet.

Plug and play. Anyone who has added a new component—perhaps a modem or a sound card—to an existing computer knows that it may not work correctly right away. This is because the new component must be configured to the system, a process that may involve some tricky software and even hardware moves. Windows 95 supports plug and play, a concept that lets the computer configure itself when a new component is added. However, for plug and play to become a reality, hardware components must also feature the plug and play standard.

 Using MS-DOS

We will now refer to MS-DOS by its abbreviated name, DOS, pronounced to rhyme with *boss*. Recall that an operating system is actually a *set* of programs. To execute a given DOS program, a user must issue a **command,** a name that invokes a specific DOS program. Whole books have been written about DOS commands, but we will consider only the commands you need to use applications software. There are dozens of commands, but most people need just a few for ordinary activities. Here are some typical tasks you can do with DOS commands:

- Access files using DOS commands
- Prepare (format) new diskettes for use
- List the files on a disk
- Copy files from one disk to another
- Erase files from a disk

See the "Personal Computers in Action" box on page 167 for more details.

A Brief Disk Discussion

Since many DOS commands involve files on disk, we are particularly concerned about disk drives in this chapter.

Disk Drive Configuration

There are two kinds of disk drives associated with a personal computer: a diskette drive and a hard disk drive. A common configuration is a diskette drive as drive A and the hard drive as drive C. If you have a second diskette drive (perhaps one for 3½-inch diskettes and one for 5¼-inch diskettes), the second disk drive will be drive B. If you are lucky enough to have a CD-ROM drive, that will probably be drive D. Configurations vary, but the four most common are shown in Figure 8-2.

The Default Drive

Consider the DOS command DIR, which displays a list of files. How does DOS know which drive to look at when you type DIR? Just which set of files do you want? If you do not specify a particular drive, DOS will look at the default drive.

The **default drive,** also called the **current drive,** is the drive that the computer is currently using. Only one disk drive at a time can be the default drive. If you have a hard disk drive, then that drive—drive C—starts out as the current drive and usually stays as the current drive. DOS uses the prompt to remind you which drive is the current drive. If you see C> on the screen, then the current drive is C.

You can change the default to another drive if you wish. After the prompt, type the letter of the desired drive, followed by a colon, and then press Enter. Suppose, for example, that the default drive is currently drive C (as you can see from C> on the screen), but you want to access files on a diskette in drive A. To change the default drive to A, type A: (A followed by a colon) and then press Enter. (You can, by the way, type either an upper- or lowercase A—DOS recognizes both.) Now the screen should show A>.

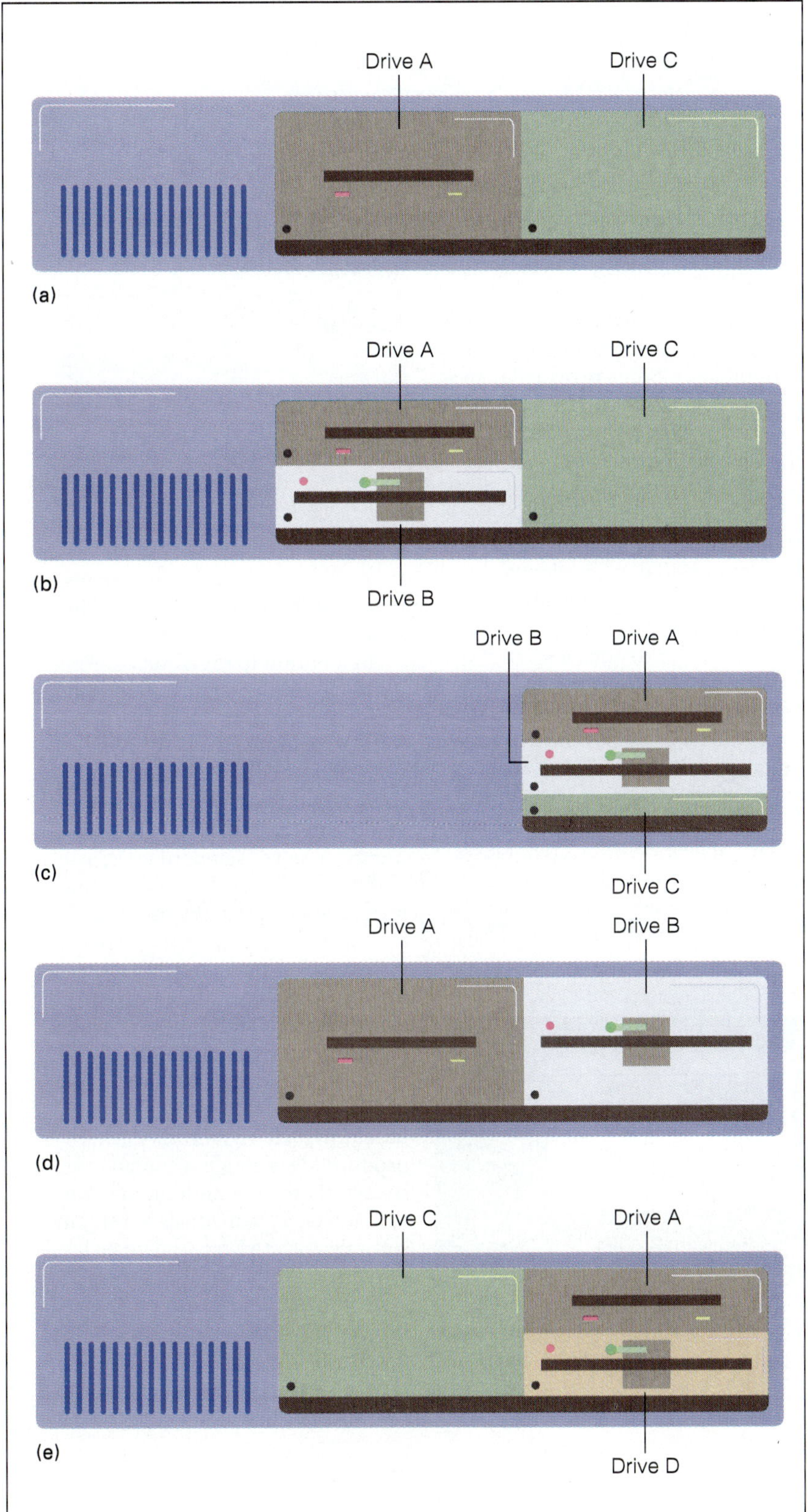

Figure 8-2 Disk drive configurations. As you use different computers, you may see several different types of disk drive combinations. The following are common. (a) Drive A for 3½-inch diskettes on the left, hard disk drive C on the right. (b) Drive A for 3½-inch diskettes on the top left; drive B for stacked 5¼-inch diskettes on the lower left; hard disk drive C on the right. (c) Drive A for 3½-inch diskettes on the top right; drive B for stacked 5¼-inch diskettes on the lower right; hard disk drive C may be on the bottom right or, in some cases, further back under the housing (in either case the indication that a drive is being used—that is, read or written—is the indicator light on the front panel, no matter where the actual drive is located). (d) On older systems without a hard disk drive, drive A for 3½-inch diskettes is on the left and drive B for stacked 5¼-inch diskettes is on the right. (e) Any of the first three may be complicated by the presence of a CD-ROM drive, which is usually drive D.

MACINTOSH

The Macintosh Applications Interface

Computers based on the DOS operating system are fundamentally different from Macintosh computers. The main difference has to do with the computer's hardware, especially the design of the processor. But the difference that most users notice first is the Macintosh's graphical user interface (GUI). While DOS-based programs have traditionally employed an interface that is textual (the user has to type in commands), the Mac's interface works by creating a graphical "world," displaying pictures of disks, folders, and even a trash can. Items in this world can be picked up, moved around, dropped, or discarded, using the same intuitive skills of grabbing and handling objects that we learn as children.

A typical GUI makes use of four basic elements: icons (pictures that symbolize items like files or disks); a pointer (a cursor moved around the screen using a mouse); windows (rectangular areas on the screen used to display information, easily moved or resized using the pointer); and pull-down menus (each of which offers a list of commands, which the user can choose from by using the pointer). These four elements together provide an interface that is surprisingly easy to learn. For instance, to copy a file from one disk to another, the user can simply "grab" the file's icon with the pointer and "drag" it onto the destination disk's icon. The Macintosh was the first example of this interface to succeed in the computer market, although its design had been created years earlier by researchers at XEROX's Palo Alto Research Center. And now Microsoft has provided a similar GUI for DOS-based machines called Microsoft Windows.

Another advantage to using the Mac is consistency. Before these interfaces became popular, every program had its own way of interacting with the user. Some provided menus, but you had to use special keystrokes to activate them. If you wanted to learn a new software package, you could count on having to learn a whole new set of keystrokes and commands. Apple was aware of this problem when they developed the first Macintosh and went about solving it in two ways.

First, they provided a set of programs called the Macintosh Toolbox, which is dedicated to providing standard windows, icons, menus, and pointers. The Toolbox is available for any application to make use of, so that when programmers are creating a new application, they do not have to trouble with the design of windows and menus: The details will be taken care of by the Toolbox. The payoff is that virtually every applica-

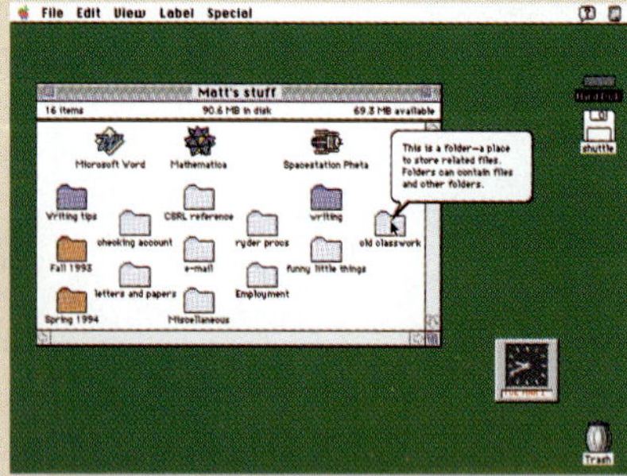

a) When Balloon Help is switched on, a user can get instant descriptions about any object in his environment by positioning the pointer over the object.

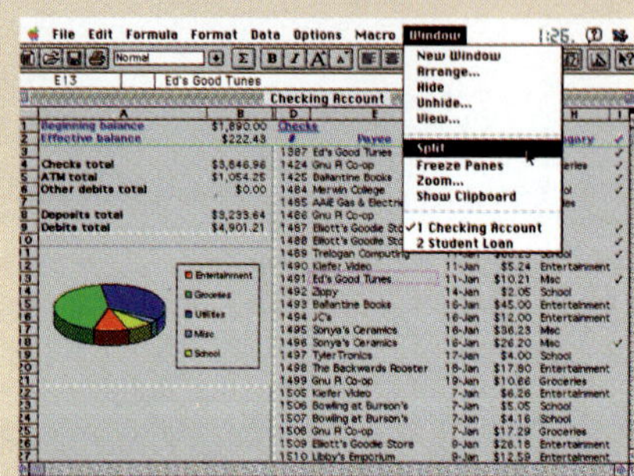

b) This spreadsheet document was created to balance a checkbook but has a look and feel similar to that of the Finder and other applications.

tion will have windows and menus that look and behave in exactly the same way.

In addition to the Toolbox, Apple put forth a set of standards to which applications should adhere. For instance, most Macintosh applications provide File and Edit menus, each of which contains standard commands for working with documents. A newer standard is the availability of Balloon Help. When this feature is activated, the user can get information on different components of an application simply by positioning the pointer over it; a cartoon-style balloon will then appear with a description of that element.

This consistency between applications gives the impression, quite falsely, that all Macintosh software is produced by a single manufacturer. In fact, there are hundreds of companies as well as individuals developing software for the Mac, and virtually all of them make a special effort to adhere to the Macintosh standard interface.

Personal Computers In Action

The MS-DOS Commands You Will Use Most

The instructions here assume you are using a computer with diskette drive A and hard disk drive C. Instructions for you to type are highlighted.

FORMAT (Prepare an unformatted diskette for use). Whether the data you are producing is a document, spreadsheet, database, or graph, you must have some place to keep it. Unless you are fortunate enough to have your own hard disk, the place to keep your data is on a diskette. However, a diskette fresh from the store may need to be formatted before it can be used, and that is the purpose of this command. Caution: *Never* format the hard disk in drive C; formatting destroys all data on a disk.

1. Insert the blank diskette in drive A.
2. `C:\>CD \DOS (Enter)` Change to the DOS directory.
3. `C:\DOS>FORMAT A: (Enter)` Type the command to format.
4. When asked, press Enter to confirm diskette present and also to skip volume label.

DIR (Directory). In no time at all, most computer users have lots of files on lots of disks; forgetting where these files are located is easy. DIR produces an on-screen list of file names. /P and /W add further options.

`C:\>DIR` Lists one line per file, with name, size in bytes, and date/time created.

`C:\>DIR /W` Lists file name only, in five columns across the screen.

`C:\>DIR /P` Lists one line per file, a page at a time; press any key to continue.

`C:\>DIR /W/P` Lists file name only, in five columns, a page at a time.

COPY (Make a copy of a file). One important reason to copy a file is to produce a backup copy. Another is to copy a data file generated on a community (school or office) hard disk to your own diskette. If we assume the file to be copied is on the current drive, in this case drive C, C need not be mentioned in the command. And, if you want the new file to have the same name in its new location, which is usually the case, you need not key it again on the new drive, in this case A.

`C:\>COPY MRKTDATA.SUM A:` Copies file MRKTDATA.SUM on drive C to drive A.

`C:\>COPY *.* A:` Copies all files in the directory to drive A.

DEL or ERASE (Delete a file). When your diskette gets cluttered with files you no longer want, it is time to clean house. Use DEL followed by the name of each file you want to delete.

RENAME (Give a file a new name). If you decide to change a file name, use the RENAME command, followed by the old name and then the new name. Assume that a file named MRKTDATA.SUM is on a diskette in drive A.

`A:\>RENAME MRKTDATA.SUM SSDATA.CHT` New name is SSDATA.CHT.

Other simple commands. These four commands can be invoked by simply keying the commands themselves, without the need for any additional information. **CHKDSK**, meaning check disk, causes a screen display of information about the status of the disk, including number of files, number of bytes used in files, and number of bytes available for use. **CLS** clears the screen. When you key **TIME** the proper time appears on the screen. If you wish, you may key a new time; this is convenient for switching back and forth between daylight savings time and standard time. **VER** will provide the

Types of Files

The three types of files you may use are (1) DOS system files, (2) applications software files, and (3) data files. DOS system files are the operating system programs. Applications software files are the software needed for an application, such as word processing. Data files hold data that is

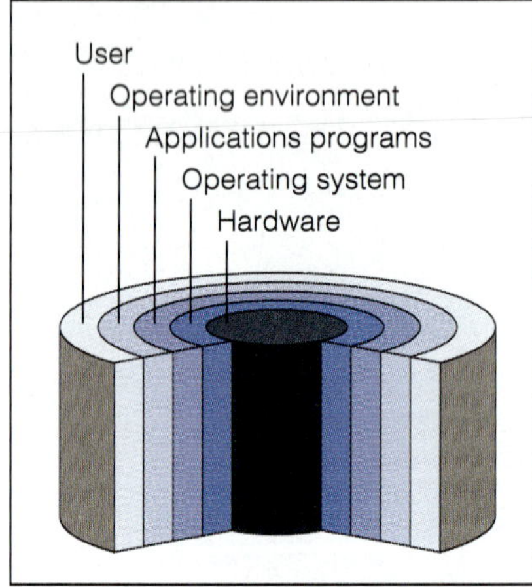

Figure 8-3 An operating environment. This illustration is identical to Figure 8-1, except that an operating environment layer has been added to shield the user from having to know commands of the operating system.

related to applications software, such as the memo or term paper you typed using word processing.

When are these files used? The DOS system files are used to start the computer system and, as you proceed, to provide services and control of software and files. Generally speaking, unless you invoke some command for a specific need, such as copying a file, you will not deal directly with the operating system files. If you do need to use the operating system files directly, you do so by issuing a command that invokes the program name. Application software files are invoked by you whenever you use that specific application, but again, you will probably have little direct interaction with the files themselves. Data files are used with applications software, either to supply input data or, more likely, to store the files you create.

Data files are different from DOS system and applications software files. To begin with, the DOS and applications software may belong to your school or company and may be used by several people. Input data files may also be files created by the school or company personnel. Output data files, on the other hand, usually contain data created by you and may be used only by you, especially in an academic environment. Once you place your school or personal data files on diskettes, then the files are in your exclusive control, to use, to destroy, or to take home with you.

When you first purchase a data diskette (disk) it contains no files—that is, the disk is empty. Although it is possible to purchase disks that are already formatted, traditionally disks come unformatted. To prepare an unformatted disk to receive the files you will create, you must use the FORMAT command. In contrast, DOS and applications software disks that you purchase already have been formatted, have files on them, and should not be formatted again.

When you use application software to create a data file, you must choose a name for the file. When there are several data files on the disk, you may want to see a list of all the file names. You may want to copy files from one data disk to another so you can have a backup copy. You may want to erase files you no longer need. To do these things, you need to know how to use the appropriate DOS commands, as shown in the "Personal Computers in Action" box.

Operating Environments

There is another, some say *better*, way to interact with the computer's operating system. Figure 8-3 tells the story: Another layer has been added to separate the operating system and the user. This layer is often called a **shell** because it forms a "coating" over the operating system. More formally, this layer is called an **operating environment** because it creates a new way of doing business and even presents a new screen appearance—one more palatable to many users than the C> prompt.

When using an operating environment, you see pictures and/or simply worded choices instead of C> or some other prompt. Instead of having to *know* some command to type, you have only to make a selection from the choices available on the screen. Apple's Macintosh paved the way for simple interfaces between users and the operating system, and

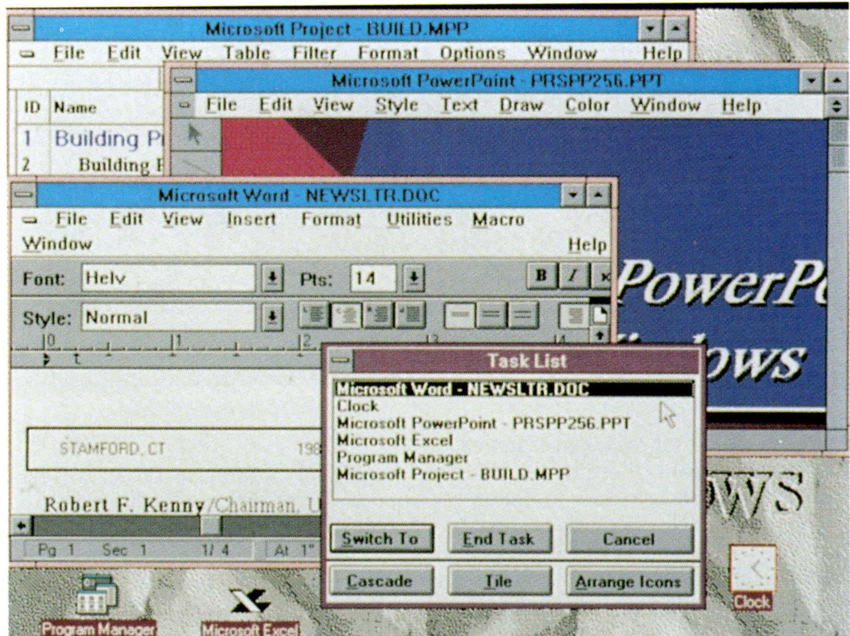

Figure 8-4 Microsoft Windows. The operating environment provided by Windows, a Microsoft product, can run several programs concurrently and let users follow their progress on screens divided into windows. Windows offers easy-to-use menu systems as well as user-friendly access to the operating system.

now Microsoft has captured the operating environment standard for DOS-based computers with Microsoft Windows.

Microsoft Windows: An Overview

Microsoft Windows—Windows for short—uses a colorful graphics interface that, among other things, eases access to the operating system (Figure 8-4). Although earlier versions of Windows were not especially successful, Windows 3.0, introduced in 1990 and followed by Windows 3.1 in 1992, received a warm welcome. The recent versions offer many improvements, including sophisticated screen graphics and faster operation. Almost immediately, many businesses large and small converted their personal computer systems to Windows. Now selling briskly, it is clear that Windows has become a new corporate standard. So, what is so special about Windows?

The feature that makes Windows so easy to use is a **graphical user interface** (**GUI**, pronounced "*goo*-ee"), in which users work more with on-screen pictures called **icons** and with **pull-down menus** rather than with keyed commands (Figure 8-5a). Furthermore, icons and menus encourage pointing and clicking with a mouse, an approach that can make computer use both faster and easier.

To enhance ease of use, Windows is usually set up so that the colorful Windows display is the first thing a user sees when the computer is turned on. The user points and clicks among a series of narrowing choices until arriving at the desired software.

Although the screen presentation and user interaction is the most visible evidence of a different kind of operating system, Windows offers changes that are even more fundamental. It is helpful at this point to make a comparison between Windows and traditional operating systems for large computers.

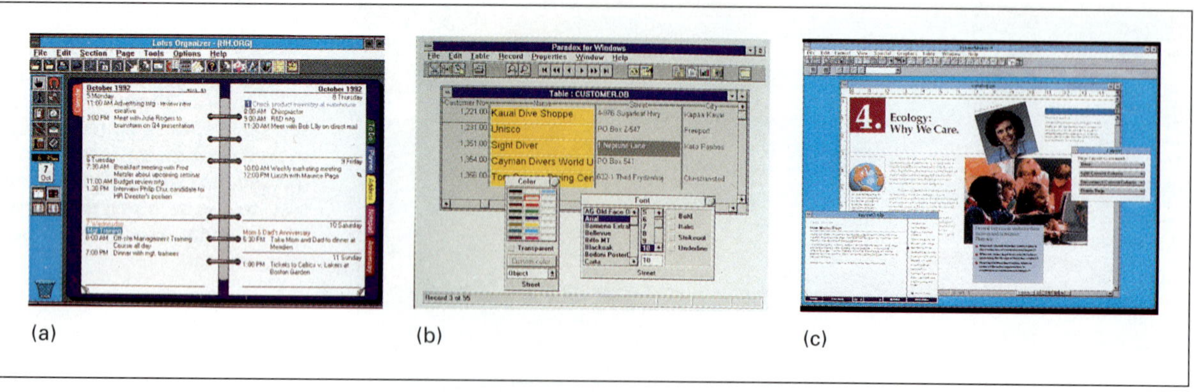

Figure 8-5 **Microsoft Windows in Action.**
These screens vividly illustrate the Windows graphical user interface (GUI). (a) This organizer program uses the concept of a notebook with tabs. Note also the icons to the left and top. Clicking a mouse on tabs or icons will cause corresponding action. (b) This database program screen demonstrates available color and fonts in different windows. (c) This desktop publishing software can pull together various elements from different windows.

Multiprogramming and Multitasking: Comparing Mainframe Operating Systems to Windows

Is the operating system action the same for big and small computers? The answer is yes—and no. Yes, if you are considering computer action from the perspective of the central processing unit (CPU). No, if you are taking the viewpoint of the user, who accesses the CPU and other computer resources via the operating system.

Large Computers

Considering the CPU for just a moment, recall how a computer executes instructions. The computer usually has a single processor that can do only one thing at a time, that is, one instruction at a time. Since there are invariably other tasks associated with running a program, such as reading from disk or printing, it would be wasteful if the CPU sat idle while these tasks were being accomplished. To maximize CPU use, the large computer's operating system includes a feature called **multiprogramming,** which permits the running of several programs in the same time frame, or **concurrently.** That is, multiprogramming permits several unrelated programs, probably from many different users, to compete for the processor. Remember that we are talking about large computers now—supercomputers, mainframes, and minicomputers.

Although programs are said to run concurrently, this does not mean that they run simultaneously. In fact, the programs take turns using the CPU. For example, one program could be using the CPU while another program prints a record. Amazingly, the operating systems keeps track of everything and makes sure that the programs do not get entangled with each other. From the point of view of the user, a program is executed by the computer just as if the computer and all its resources belong exclusively to that user. (In reality, sometimes a large computer is so overloaded that time delays make the shared nature of the machine more obvious.)

Personal Computers

Personal computers also have a CPU that handles just one instruction at a time. Until quite recently, computers using DOS were limited not only to one user at a time but also to one program at a time. If, for example, a user were using a word processing program to write a financial report and wanted to access some spreadsheet figures, he or she would have to perform a series of arcane steps: exit the word processing program, enter and exit the spreadsheet program, and then re-enter the word processing program to complete the report. This is wasteful in two ways: (1) The CPU is often idle because only one program is executing at a time, and (2) the user is required to move inconveniently from one program to another program.

The solution to this problem is a direct descendant of multiprogramming, an operating system approach called **multitasking.** The idea is the same as multiprogramming: Let several programs compete concurrently for the use of the CPU. In industry jargon, and for all practical purposes, we consider that these programs are running at the same time.

A key feature of Windows is its multitasking capability. From the user's perspective a window on the screen indicates each program currently in operation. Using the financial report example previously described, the user could access the spreadsheet program without closing down or leaving the word processing program. It is possible to run many programs at once in a multitasking environment. In fact, the name Windows refers to the fact that various software tools can be accessed and displayed on the screen in overlapping rectangles that look like windows. It is possible to use one application when you are right in the middle of another (Figure 8-5b).

Applications Software with Windows

Just what will Windows do for your favorite software application? Although you can tell Windows to access your existing software, you will not get the full benefits of Windows unless you use a software version especially designed for use with Windows. Anticipating the popularity of Windows, dozens of software manufacturers have been writing their programs for the Windows environment. Look around your local computer store and you will see an entire section reserved just for software written for Windows.

Reality Check

A Windows user needs a hard disk, and a color monitor is highly recommended. Two other serious considerations for Windows to run efficiently are speed and memory. Decent performance requires a computer with a speedy microprocessor, at least an 80386 and preferably an 80486 or Pentium. Also needed is at least 4 megabytes of memory, preferably 8MB. Many serious users, especially business users, already have such a system in place; those who do not should expect slow going with Windows.

Right This Way, Dummies

An online junkie we will call Helen was hooked up to her favorite information service and had selected an option in which several online users were in the same "room," with their keyed comments showing up on the screen. Helen saw the question "Are there any Windows experts here?" When no one answered right away, Helen keyed "Well, I'm a Windows dummy, if that helps. Try your question." Rather to her surprise, Helen was able to answer the question, something about preserving icon locations.

Helen was not computer illiterate; she had used computers extensively at home. When Windows came along, she picked up a couple of books to ease the transition, a quick reference guide and a book containing thousands of Windows "tips." Unfortunately, she found that neither book met her rather mundane needs; they tended to go into sophisticated aspects such as office networking and optimizing memory use.

Browsing in her computer store, Helen came across the book she needed. She was not embarrassed to report to the checkout counter with *Windows for Dummies.* It turned out to be very helpful, giving her more information on the basics of Windows.

COMPUTING TRENDS

Windows as Far as the Eye Can See

Anyone who has not figured out what the trend is for operating systems has missed the heavy press coverage of billionaire Bill Gates, the still-young founder of the Microsoft Corporation. Mr. Gates has graced the covers of *Time*, *Fortune*, and any other news magazine you could name (the photos here first appeared in *U.S News and Word Report*). Each time he is interviewed, Mr. Gates makes a pitch for his vision of the future, which features the operating system shell Microsoft Windows, or just Windows for short. (Incidentally, Microsoft was denied a patent on the word *windows*; the word was considered simply too common.)

Mr. Gates can let the numbers speak for themselves. Microsoft's operating system MS-DOS runs 90 percent of the world's personal computers. Windows, the operating environment software designed to run with MS-DOS, is selling one million copies a month.

An early spinoff product was Windows for Workgroups, a software/hardware package that lets users set up peer-to-peer networks with a Windows environment. But perhaps the greatest indicator of future direction is the product called Windows NT, a sophisticated operating system that will not only run on personal computers but will also power the newest and biggest mainframe computers. This is the first clear signal that environments for big and small computers will eventually merge.

▼▼▼

Do I really need to know all about the operating system? The answer to that question depends on how you expect to use a computer. If you use a computer primarily as a tool to complete a specific type of work, then you may have minimum interaction with an operating system. In that case, whether you are using a personal computer or a mainframe, you will learn to access the software of your choice very quickly.

But there are other ways to use a computer. In fact, there are far more options than we are able to present in this introductory chapter. Those who want or need to put the computer to its highest and best use will take direct command of the operating system, because doing so increases their effectiveness and flexibility with the computer. You can learn your way around the operating system of any computer through on-the-job training or manuals that accompany the software.

Chapter **Review**

Summary and Key Terms

- An **operating system** is a set of programs through which the computer manages its own resources, such as the CPU, memory, secondary storage devices, and input/output devices.
- Much of the work of an operating system is hidden from the user; many necessary tasks are performed behind the scenes.
- Operating systems for mainframe and other large computers must keep track of several programs from several users all running in the same time frame.
- Although some personal computer operating systems can support multiple programs, many are concerned only with a single user running a single program at a given time.
- In general, an application program can run on just one operating system.
- IBM personal computers and others like them use Microsoft's operating system, called MS-DOS, for Microsoft disk operating system. Macintoshes use an entirely different operating system, called System 7 and produced by Apple.
- Most personal computers are limited to either MS-DOS or System 7. The operating systems are different because the central processing units are different. Software makers must decide for which operating system to write a software package, although some make versions of their software for each operating system.
- Loading the operating system into memory is called **booting** the system.
- In the on-screen A> and C> prompts, the A and C refers to the disk drive. A **prompt** is a signal that the system is waiting for you to give a command to the computer.
- To execute a given DOS program, a user must issue a **command,** a name that invokes a specific DOS program. Typical tasks that can be performed with DOS commands are: access files, format new diskettes, list the files on a disk, copy files from one disk to another, and erase files from a disk.
- The **default drive,** also called the **current drive,** is the drive that the computer is currently using.
- Diskettes may hold DOS files, applications software files, or data files.
- Some operating systems provide pictures, worded choices, or both instead of giving a prompt. In effect, these pictures and choices form a user-friendly "coating," or **shell,** over the operating system. They create a comfortable **operating environment** for the user, who does not have to remember or look up the appropriate commands.
- A key shell product is Microsoft Windows 3.1, software with a colorful **graphical user interface (GUI).** Windows offers on-screen pictures called **icons** and **pull-down menus,** both of which encourage pointing and clicking with a mouse, an approach that can make computer use faster and easier.
- On mainframe operating systems, **multiprogramming** permits the running of several programs in the same time frame, or **concurrently.** That is, multiprogramming permits several unrelated programs, probably from many different users, to compete for the processor. From the point of view of the user, his or her program is executed by the computer just as if the computer and all its resources belonged exclusively to that user.
- Using Windows, **multitasking** lets several programs compete concurrently for the use of the CPU; for all practical purposes, these programs are considered to be running at the same time.

- The name Windows refers to the fact that various software tools can be accessed simultaneously and displayed on the screen in overlapping rectangles that look like windows.
- Although software makers are designing products especially for use with Windows, decent performance with Windows requires a fast computer and at least 4 megabytes of memory.

Student Personal Study Guide

True/False

T F 1. The key feature of Microsoft Windows is user–keyboard interaction.
T F 2. FORMAT is an example of a DOS command.
T F 3. C> on the screen means that C is the current drive.
T F 4. The default drive is the current drive.
T F 5. A multiprogramming environment runs programs concurrently.
T F 6. A GUI uses icons.
T F 7. Windows runs well on any computer.
T F 8. An operating system is not needed if a shell is used.
T F 9. The name Windows refers to circular drawings on the screen.
T F 10. Loading the operating system into memory is called booting.

Multiple Choice

1. A graphical interface:
   a. GUI c. C>
   b. boot d. prompt
2. The Windows capability for running more than one program at a time:
   a. multiprogramming c. pull-down menus
   b. interface d. multitasking
3. Load the operating system:
   a. default c. prompt
   b. boot d. command
4. The command to change default drive from C to A:
   a. FORMAT A: c. COPY *. A:
   b. A: d. RENAME C A
5. Which is *not* a resource managed by the operating system?
   a. memory c. printer
   b. interface d. CPU
6. Another name for current drive:
   a. default c. GUI
   b. command d. boot
7. A signal that the computer is waiting for command from the user:
   a. task c. prompt
   b. window d. command
8. Programs running in the same time frame:
   a. commands c. menus
   b. prompts d. concurrent operation
9. An operating environment:
   a. shell c. task
   b. boot d. command

10. A set of programs to manage the computer's resources:
    a. operating system
    b. disk
    c. diskette
    d. command

Fill-In

1. Waiting for a command, the computer displays a: ____________________.
2. If your computer has a hard drive, the initial default drive is: ____________________.
3. Another name for an operating environment: ____________________.
4. GUI stands for: ____________________.
5. Loading the operating system is called: ____________________.
6. Another name for the current drive: ____________________.
7. The DOS command to list files: ____________________.
8. The DOS command to get a disk ready to accept files: ____________________.
9. The DOS command to move a file to another disk: ____________________.
10. The DOS command to erase a file: ____________________.

Answers

True/False: 1. F, 2. T, 3. T, 4. T, 5. T, 6. T, 7. F, 8. F, 9. F, 10. T
Multiple choice: 1. a, 2. d , 3. b , 4. b, 5. b, 6. a, 7. c, 8. d, 9. a, 10. a
Fill-In: 1. prompt, 2. C, 3. shell, 4. graphical user interface, 5. booting, 6. default, 7. DIR, 8. FORMAT, 9. COPY, 10. DEL or ERASE

Interview: Real Estate by Computer

Mary Ferrari, a real estate agent, talks about using computers in the office and in the field.

It seems to me that the real estate industry is just beginning to exploit personal computers. How long have you been using a personal computer?
I have been using a personal computer about four years. My computing days began when I saw a flyer that advertised software for real estate agents that could be used to pull up every house listed in the area. The screen could show a picture of a house, as well as all pertinent details, such as number of bedrooms and price. And I thought, "Wow!"

So it was like an electronic multiple listing?
Yes, exactly. It piqued my interest because they were promoting the hardware—a laptop computer—and software as a package, and they offered financing in a way that any agent could afford. I went to the seminar and signed up. At the same time, I bought a desktop computer for home use.

The laptop, of course, is for portability. I take it with me on listing appointments and when I go out with buyers to show them houses. It has a modem, too. The office where I work today is fully computerized. I can dial into the multiple listing service at any time of the day or night, and load all the new listings and all of the current sales. The computer at home is the one I use for artwork and editing and the fancy charts we put out for our clients who are selling their homes.

I was impressed that you can personalize the client sheet. You can add your own name to it, so that the client can remember the agent's name.
That's part of the software. The computer really helps us get new business. Suppose someone calls up and says, "Gee, we're thinking about selling our house, and we want you to do a market analysis." I can go to the computer and in a matter of minutes have a personalized handout sheet for that client when we go to their house to discuss the listing. The sheet shows everything that is a similar property to theirs that has sold or is in escrow or is on the market. The software also lets me prepare a personalized cover sheet, which says something such as "This is a presentation exclusively for Mr. and Mrs. John Doe on March 29, 1995," and includes the agent's phone numbers. The customer is blown away by it because it's

Computers

Evolution of Personal Computer Use

The evolution of personal computers on the job seems to fall into three phases. Personal computers were first used in business by individual users to transform work tasks. The constantly retyped document, for example, became the quickly modified word-processed document. Similarly, the much-erased manual spreadsheet became the automatically recalculated electronic spreadsheet, and overflowing file drawers were transformed into automated databases. This individual productivity boost could be considered the first phase of on-the-job personal computer acceptance. Some organizations are still in phase 1.

Many more organizations have entered the second phase: They have gone beyond the individual and use personal computers to transform a working group or department. This department-oriented phase probably embraces a network and may also include personal computer access to mainframe computers. The second phase requires planning and structure.

The third phase in the evolution of personal computer use in business is the most dramatic, calling for the transformation of the entire business. Practically speaking, however, phase 3 is just an extension of the earlier phases: Each individual and each department uses computers to enhance the company as a whole. Few companies have fully entered phase 3.

This three-stage transformation—individual, department, and business—broadly describes the progress a company makes in blending computers into its business activities.

The Impact of Personal Computers

People who dismiss the impact of the personal computer sometimes say, "It's just another tool." But what a tool! In the decades to come, personal computers will continue to alter the business world radically, much as the automobile did. For more than 50 years, the automobile fueled the economy, spawning dozens of industries from oil companies to supermarkets. Other industries, such as real estate and restaurants, were transformed by the mobility the car provided. Personal computers will have a similar effect for two reasons: (1) Computers are now cost-effective at a level affordable to most businesses, and (2) few businesses without computers can provide the levels of service their computerized competitors provide.

Computers are changing the way individuals and organizations work. By providing timely access to data, computers let us spend less time checking and rechecking data and more time getting work done. In addition to increasing overall productivity, computers have had a fundamental impact on the way some people approach their jobs.

Who's Running the Information Revolution?

Before the widespread use of personal computers, anyone who needed computer services made a formal request to the computer professionals.

We begin this section with a brief look at those professionals and then move on to examine the diversified control of computing power.

The Information Systems Manager

An **information system (IS)** may be defined as a set of business procedures designed to provide information for an organization. Today the term *information system* usually means a system that includes at least one computer as a major component. Information serves no purpose unless it gets to its users in a timely way; the computer can act quickly to produce and distribute information.

An information system uses computer technology to solve problems for an entire organization, instead of attacking problems piecemeal. Although in some companies a complete information system is still only an idea, the scope of information systems is expanding rapidly.

The **information systems manager** runs the information systems department. For many years, this meant managing systems running on mainframe computers. The advent of personal computers has changed the role of the information systems manager significantly.

Breaking Away

In the early days of personal computers, users saw the personal computer as their ticket to independence from the computer professionals. Personal computers burst on the business scene in the early 1980s, with little warning and even less planning. People who saw the value of personal computers for their work were able to buy inexpensive computers out of existing budgets, so they did not have to ask anyone's permission. Some managers began to see that personal computers were providing workers with the computer power the information systems department was not. By mastering software for word processing, spreadsheets, and database access, many users were able to declare their freedom from the information systems department.

Soon, however, managers were faced with several problems. The first was incompatibility. The new computers came in an assortment of brands and models that did not mesh well. Software that worked on one machine did not necessarily work on another. In addition, users were not as independent of the information systems department as they had thought; they needed assistance in a variety of ways. In particular, they needed data from the information systems department, and they needed it in formats compatible with their personal computers. Finally, no one person was in charge of the headlong plunge into personal computers. Many organizations began to solve these management problems in the following ways:

- They addressed the compatibility problem by establishing hardware and software acquisition standards and policies.
- They solved the assistance problem by creating information centers that provided, among other things, in-house training.
- They eliminated the management problem by creating a new position, often called the personal computer manager.

In addition to these problems and their solutions, many companies today have impacted the personal computer scene further by downsiz-

COMPUTING TRENDS

Don't Leave Home Without It

Your computer, that is. Many workers attribute their success to plain hard work—and they want to be able to take their work with them wherever they go. The trend today is that taking work along means taking the computer along. Early laptop users were workers for whom travel was a key component: sales people, executives, insurance adjusters, and reporters. Now laptops have reached a much broader market and include just about anyone who wants to have computer access, whether in the office, at home, or on the road.

The Tools of Portability. The portable worker typically needs a laptop computer equipped with a lightweight nickel-hydrade battery and a recharger, a keyboard with a trackball, a screen, a hard disk drive with sufficient space to hold software and data, a diskette drive, and a modem. Some users may need color screens, which are available on some models. If you absolutely need hard copy on the road, consider a lightweight—about three pounds—printer. Another possibility is to use a fax modem and just fax output to a nearby plain-paper fax machine. In addition to standard software packaging, such as word processing, software made especially for computer-savvy travelers helps users to plan routes, pick hotels, and even prevent jet lag by giving you a timed regimen for eating, sleeping, and exposure to light.

Tips for traveling with a computer:

- ✓ Never check your laptop computer as baggage and do not carry it through metal detectors.
- ✓ Make sure your batteries are sufficiently charged so that you can boot the computer, to show airport authorities that it is not just an empty shell.
- ✓ Do not use your laptop during takeoff and landing.
- ✓ Since you may not be able to find an outlet near the desk in your hotel room, carry an extension cord.
- ✓ If you plan to use a modem, ask in advance for a hotel room with removable phone jacks.
- ✓ To avoid running out of battery time, carry an extra battery and, of course, a recharger.
- ✓ Save and back up data often.
- ✓ Copy your critical data to diskettes.

Free at last. Some say that computing portability goes beyond convenience, that a better word is *liberation*. Liberation from the confines of the office. Liberation from the 9-to-5 day with a commute on each end. Liberation from "telephone tag." Liberation from time-zone barriers. When you own a portable computer, you decide when and where you work. Workers can, for all practical purposes, stay in touch with the office and the action where and when they choose—24 hours a day, 7 days a week—from almost any location.

ing—moving applications from big to small computers—and by teaming personal computer users into workgroups.

Let us examine the issues of acquisition, the information center, the personal computer manager, downsizing, and workgroups, respectively.

Personal Computer Acquisition

In an office environment managers know they must control the acquisition and use of personal computers. Consider this example: A user's budget process may call for certain data that resides in the files of another worker's personal computer or perhaps output incorporating the figures produced by yet a third person. If the software and machines these workers use are different, accessing or outputting the data may become a major problem. Most companies avoid this problem by purchasing uniform hardware and software and, most probably, hook the computers together in a network so that data can be shared.

The Information Center

If personal computer users compared notes, they would probably find that their experiences are similar. The experience of budget analyst Manuella Lopez is typical. She convinced her boss to let her have her own personal computer so she could analyze financial data. She learned to use a popular spreadsheet program. She soon thought about branching out with other products. She wanted a statistics software package but was not sure which one was appropriate. She thought a modem for data communications would be useful and wanted to discuss the features of the various modems available on the market. Most of all, Manuella felt her productivity would increase significantly if she could access the data in the corporate data files.

The company **information center** is the solution to these kinds of needs. Although no two centers are alike, all information centers are devoted exclusively to giving users service. Best of all, user assistance is often immediate, with little or no red tape.

Information centers often offer the following services:

- **Software selection.** Information center staff members help users determine which software packages suit their needs.
- **Data access.** If appropriate, the staff helps users get data, in formats compatible with the users' own computers, from the large corporate computer systems.
- **Training.** Education is a principal reason for an information center's existence. Classes are usually small, frequent, and on a variety of topics (Figure 9-2).
- **Technical assistance.** Information center staff members are ready to assist in any way possible, short of actually doing the users' work for them. That help includes aiding in the selection and use of software, finding errors, helping submit formal requests to the information systems department, and so forth.

Figure 9-2 The information center. Classes are often held in the company information center to teach employees how to use company computers.

To be successful, the information center must be placed in an accessible location. The center should be equipped with personal computers and terminals, a stockpile of software packages, and perhaps a library. It should be staffed with people who have technical backgrounds but whose explanations feature plain words that the user can understand. Their mandate must be that the user comes first.

The Personal Computer Manager

The benefits of personal computers for individual users have been clear almost from the beginning: increased productivity, worker enthusiasm, and easier access to information. But once personal computers move beyond entry status, standard corporate accountability becomes a factor; large companies are spending millions of dollars on personal computers, and top-level managers want to know where all this money is going. Company auditors begin worrying about data security. The company legal department begins to worry about workers illegally copying software. Before long, everyone is involved, and it is clear that someone must be placed in charge of personal computer use. That person is the **personal computer manager,** also known as the **microcomputer manager.** In addition, if computers are networked, there may be a separate position called the **network manager.**

Four key areas need the attention of the personal computer manager:

- **Technology overload.** The personal computer manager must maintain a clear vision of company goals so that users are not overwhelmed by the massive and conflicting claims of aggressive vendors. Users engulfed by phrases like *network topologies* or *file gateways* or a jumble of acronyms can turn to the personal computer manager for guidance with their purchases.
- **Cost control.** Many people who work with personal computers believe the initial costs are paid back rapidly, and they think that should satisfy managers who hound them about expenses. But the real costs entail training, support, hardware and software extras, and communications networks—much more than just the cost of the computer itself. The personal computer manager's role includes monitoring *all* the expenses.
- **Data security and integrity.** Access to corporate data is a touchy issue. Many personal computer users find they want to download data from the corporate mainframe to their own machines, and this presents an array of problems. Are they entitled to the data? Will they manipulate the data in new ways and then present it as the official version? Will they expect the information systems department to take the data back after they have done who-knows-what with it? The answers to these perplexing questions are not always clear-cut, but at least the personal computer manager will be tuned in to the issues.
- **Computer junkies.** What about the employees feverish with the new power and freedom of the computer? Some users, unable to resist the allure of their machines, overuse them and neglect their other work. These user-abusers are often called "junkies" because their fascination with the computer seems like an addiction. Personal computer managers usually respond to this problem by working with managers to set guidelines for computer use.

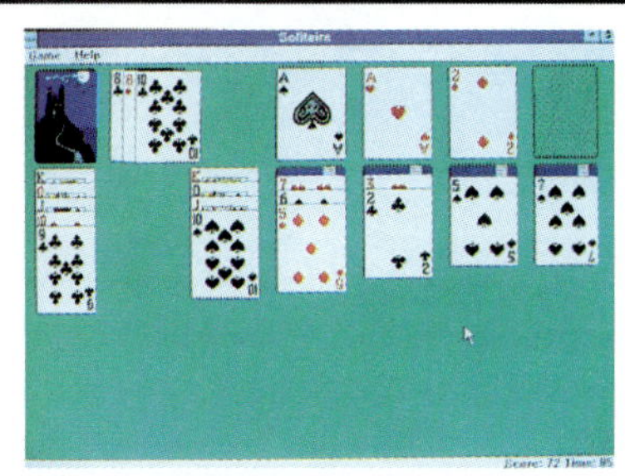

Honestly, Only on My Lunch Hour

Should you be playing solitaire on your personal computer at the office? Maybe. The game was included as an extra in Microsoft Windows™, partly to promote friendliness to home users. Rather to the surprise of its author, Wes Cherry, people have spent hours and hours playing the game at work. This was also a surprise, not an especially pleasant one, to the companies whose employees are using Windows.

Some managers have adopted the attitude that a little relaxation with a computer game relieves stress, but many more have reacted negatively, prohibiting employees from playing games at the office. Some have gone so far as to remove all games from the company's personal computers.

The person selected to be the personal computer manager is usually from the information systems area. Ideally, he or she has a broad technical background, understands both the potential and limitations of personal computers, and is well known to a diverse group of users. In small companies the personal computer manager may be a jack-of-all-trades, as long as the trade is computers. That is, in addition to the duties listed here, the personal computer manager may handle computer acquisitions and fill the functions normally assumed by information center personnel.

Downsizing

A new and interesting challenge facing established companies is **downsizing,** the process of shifting mainframe applications to a system of smaller computers, often a local area network (LAN) of personal computers. (*Downsizing* has also been used as a generic term to describe reducing a company's workforce; this is not the topic here.) Simply put, companies are dumping their big expensive computers in favor of smaller, less expensive computers. Downsizing has considerable allure because modern personal computers now have substantial power at a fraction of the cost of mainframes.

The downsizing craze began in earnest in the 1980s, but many larger corporations are only now taking the plunge. Switching to a smaller system ultimately has its rewards, but it is not a neat and tidy process. The snags generally fall into two categories: technical and political. Programmers find that they are lacking the same tools they once had on the larger systems. Security and file backup may be more difficult and time-consuming. Politically, entrenched information systems managers tend to fight the changes and cause delays that boost costs. But perhaps the biggest problem is knowing when to downsize, and when not to. For example, applications that use very large databases that must respond quickly to user requests need the resources provided by the mainframe.

Finally, consider the social aspects of downsizing. Until recently, despite the inroads made by personal computers, the power structure of computing was locked in on mainframes. Downsizing, more than any other personal computer phenomenon, has brought power to the people—*office* people.

Workgroups

First the hype: Using workgroups, worker productivity doubles and quality skyrockets. Employees communicate easily, and peace and harmony descend on the company. These statements are, of course, overblown rhetoric, but not so very far from the promises being made, and fulfilled, for workgroup computing. Loosely defined, **workgroup computing** refers to every aspect of a related group of workers (perhaps a department) using computer technology to meet a common goal.

A large factor in workgroup computing is **groupware**—software specifically designed to help groups work together. Groupware allows teams of workers on a network to swap information and collaborate on projects. For example, different users can access the same document and leave notes or suggestions for each other on the same computer file. Lotus Notes™ is the runaway application leader in this market (Figure 9-3), with Windows for Workgroups™ approaching the same task via a

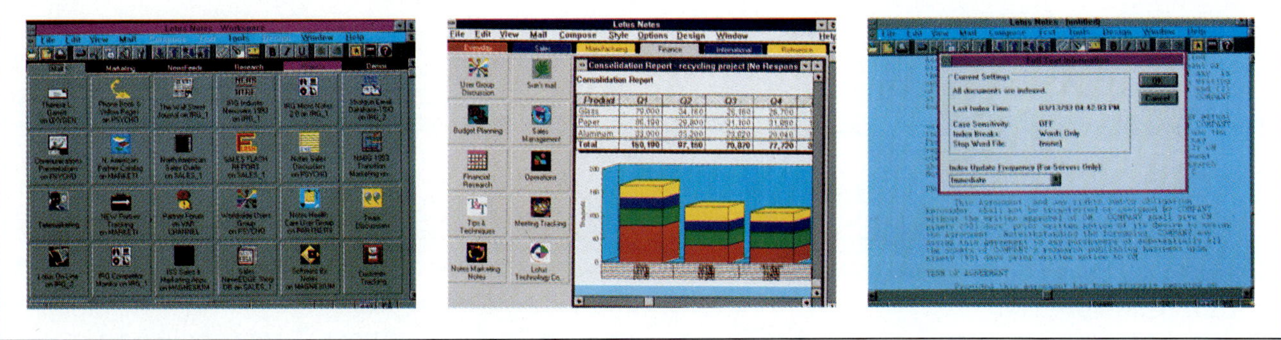

Figure 9-3 Lotus Notes.

variation on the operating system. Eventually, groupware will probably control most of the document-management tasks that users do on networks, from retrieving electronic news clippings to tracking customer service to engaging in user focus groups.

What about worker productivity? Recent surveys show that, despite anticipated setbacks, the return on investment in workgroup computing—hardware, software, and administrative costs—has been over 100 percent.

The Distribution of Power

As access to computers has been expanded, so has the power, both technical and political, that goes with it. Distribution of power has come in a variety of ways. For example, placing minicomputers in remote locations, such as branch offices, gave computer users better access and more control. But the biggest change was made by placing personal computers directly in the hands of users. Connecting personal computers in networks, downsizing, and adding workgroup software has further increased power at the user level.

In many companies the role of those in the information systems department is changing. They used to be caretakers of large computers; now they are becoming supporters of personal computers and their users. Their support is offered right in the user's environment. Some companies choose to spin off a new department, usually called something like user computing support, to focus on personal computer use. In effect, even the management style of the information systems manager is changing to meet the challenges of personal computers.

Systems

The original idea of personal computers emphasized the *personal* concept—one person, one computer, an island alone. Although this idea remains largely unchanged in the home environment, it has changed in a number of ways in business. Today, in companies large and small, personal computers may be linked in a network to each other and/or to a larger computer. As soon as a personal computer becomes part of a larger world in this way, it is part of a system. Furthermore, the personal computer user will deal with a person who plans systems—the systems analyst.

Personal Computers In Action

Art in the Numbers

All kinds of publications, from business to computers to sports, want to give their readers charts of numbers that provide information about their particular subjects. These days, numbers often are presented in the form of lively computer-produced graphics. Here are three different examples. The report card illustration, from *Registered Representative* magazine is used to portray "Grades" awarded to different investment firms. *PickWorld* magazine uses graphics to illustrate the relationship between the two operating systems PICK and DOS. *Runners' World* magazine uses cartoons to show information about lactate threshold, oxidative enzymes, and muscle glycogen.

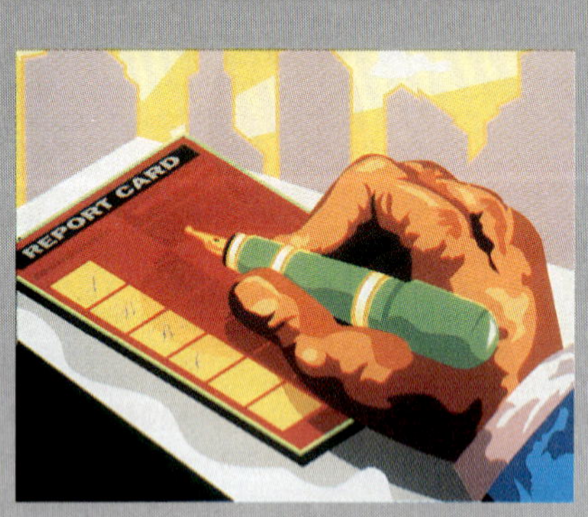

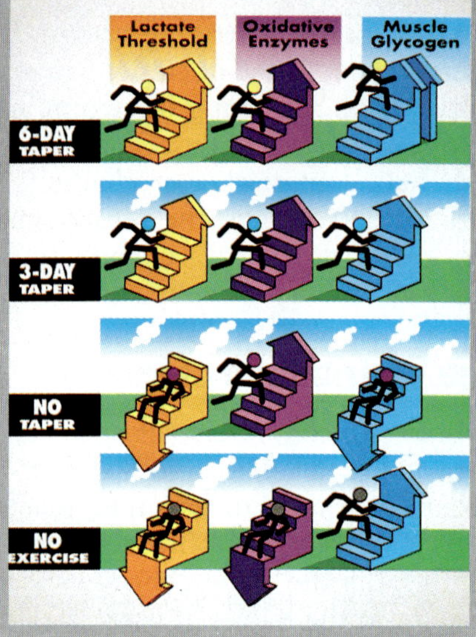

The System and the Systems Analyst

A **system** is an organized set of related components established to accomplish a certain task. There are natural systems, such as the cardiovascular system, but many systems have been planned and deliberately put into place by people. For example, the forms you fill out and the tests you take at the Department of Motor Vehicles compose a system to get your driver's license. A **computer system** is a system that has one or more computers as components.

A **systems analyst** analyzes existing systems and plans new, improved systems. **Systems analysis** is the process of studying an existing system to determine how it works and how effectively it meets user needs; **systems design** is the process of planning a new system.

Classic Systems-Development Life Cycle

For many years systems analysts have created a new system or revised an existing system by using the **systems-development life cycle (SDLC)** model, which consists of five phases (Figure 9-4):

1. Preliminary investigation—determining the problem
2. Analysis—understanding the existing system

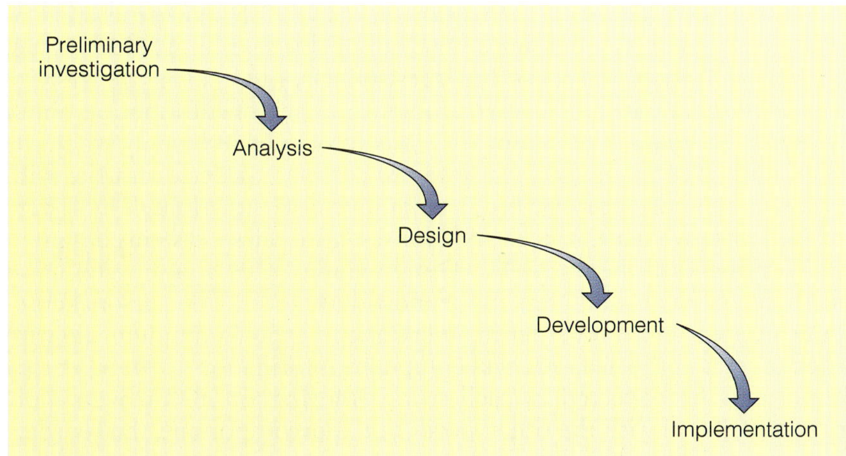

Figure 9-4 Systems development life cycle.

3. Design—planning the new system
4. Development—doing the work to bring the new system into being
5. Implementation—converting to the new system

The first two phases, preliminary investigation and systems analysis, lay the groundwork for improvements to a system. The analysis involves an investigation, which usually involves establishing relationships with the client for whom the analysis is being done and with the users of the system. The **client** is the person or organization retaining the analyst to have the work done. The **users** are the people who will have contact with the system, usually employees and customers. For instance, in a college registration system the client is the administration and the users are the school employees and the students. The system to be analyzed may be a manual system or an already-automated system. In either case computers will be components of the new system.

Systems design, the third phase, is the process of developing a plan for an improved system, based on the results of the systems analysis. Once the design of the new system is approved, it can be developed—a process that includes purchasing software or perhaps writing and testing custom software. During the implementation process, the old system is phased out and the new system phased in.

Although describing them is beyond the scope of this book, we must at least mention that, in addition to the classic life cycle noted here, there are many modern approaches, sometimes used in conjunction with the classic life cycle, that differ in approach and implementation.

Life Cycle Example

Consider this example. Systems analyst Walter Dinteman responded to a request from Pacific Sound Technology, a chain of stores carrying a broad selection of television sets, VCRs, and sound system components. The company manager, Amy Nguyan, was disturbed about inventory problems, which caused frequent stock shortages and increased customer dissatisfaction. Although the company had a minicomputer at the headquarters office, Ms. Nguyan envisioned a more sophisticated technology to track inventory.

Mr. Dinteman first did a preliminary investigation, talking to company employees and studying records. He and Ms. Nguyan agreed that the system warranted further study, so Mr. Dinteman proceeded to phase two. Analysis techniques vary, but in this case he studied written records and used interviews and questionnaires to analyze the system. His analysis uncovered several problems: a lack of information about inventory supplies; a tendency for stock to be reordered only when the shelf was empty; and, finally, no way to correlate order quantities with past sales records, future projections, or inventory situations. The system needed improvement, which called for the third phase, systems design.

Working with the users, Mr. Dinteman designed a new system that featured personal computers in the individual stores. The personal computers were hooked together in a network and could communicate with each other and the headquarters computer. Information about inventory could now be collected in each store. Information about oversupply could be shared with the other stores but, more important, the reordering process could begin before the shelves were empty.

Once the new design was approved, Mr. Dinteman was ready to move to the next phase, development. In this case he was able to procure commercial software packages that met the needs of the planned system. Finally, Mr. Dinteman, again working closely with the users over a period of several weeks, moved though the fifth phase, and the new system was implemented.

The Pacific Sound Technology example is greatly oversimplified, but it does demonstrate two important points: (1) The old system must be analyzed before a new system can be designed, and (2) users of the system must be involved in both analysis and design.

The User's Role

The systems analyst fills the role of **change agent.** That is, even though the initial idea may come from the boss, the analyst is the catalyst who overcomes the natural inertia and reluctance to change within an organization. The key to the analyst's success is involving the people of the client organization in the development of the new system. The common industry phrase is **user involvement,** and nothing could be more important to the success of a system. The finest system in the world will not suffice if users do not perceive it as useful.

If you are a user, it is to your advantage to work with the systems analyst to make the system what you want it to be. Keep in mind that you know the subject matter intimately because you work with it on a daily basis. The systems analyst knows the technical end but not how your business or department works. That is, the systems analyst depends heavily on the user to supply information and to help design a new system that meets user needs.

Someone once remarked, somewhat facetiously, that all top management—presidents, chief executive officers, and so forth—should be drawn from the ranks of computer specialists. After all, the argument went, computers pervade the entire company, and people who work with computer systems can bring broad experience to any job. Today, most presidents and CEOs still come from legal, financial, or marketing backgrounds. But as the computer industry and its professionals mature, that pattern could change.

Chapter Review

Summary and Key Terms

- Some businesses in which personal computers are used include retailing, finance, insurance, real estate, health care, education, government, legal services, sports, politics, publishing, transportation, manufacturing, agriculture, and construction.
- The evolution of personal computers seems to fall into three phases, involving the transformations of individuals, departments, and businesses.
- Personal computers are radically altering the business world for two reasons: (1) Computers are now cost-effective at a level affordable to most businesses, and (2) few businesses without computers can provide the levels of service their computerized competitors provide.
- An **information system (IS)** is a set of business systems, usually with at least one computer among its components, designed to provide information for decision making.
- The **information systems manager,** a person familiar with both computer technology and the organization's business, runs the information systems department.
- If the software and machines workers use are different, accessing or outputting data may become a problem. Most companies avoid this problem by purchasing uniform hardware and software in volume and, most probably, connecting the computers in a network.
- An **information center** typically offers employees classes on a variety of computer topics, advice on selecting software, help in getting data from corporate computer systems, and technical assistance on such matters as hardware purchases and requests to the information systems department.
- The main concerns of a **personal computer manager,** also known as a **microcomputer manager,** are (1) avoiding technology overload, (2) monitoring all the expenses connected with personal computers, (3) being aware of potential data security problems when users download data from the corporate mainframe to their own personal computers, and (4) setting guidelines for personal computer use to combat user-abusers.
- A person designated to run the network is called the **network manager.**
- **Downsizing** is the process of shifting mainframe applications to a system of smaller computers, often a local area network of personal computers.
- **Workgroup computing** refers to every aspect of a group of workers using computer technology to meet a common goal. **Groupware** refers to a kind of software that allows teams of workers on a network to swap information and collaborate on projects.
- As soon as a personal computer becomes part of a network, it is part of a **system**—an organized set of related components established to accomplish certain tasks. A **computer system** is a system that has one or more computers as components.
- A **systems analyst** studies existing systems and plans new, improved systems. **Systems analysis** is the process of studying existing systems to determine how they work and how they meet users' needs; **systems design** is the process of planning new systems.
- The **systems-development life cycle (SDLC)** model consists of five phases: (1) preliminary investigation—determining the problem, (2) analysis—understanding the existing system, (3) design—planning the new system, (4) development—doing the work to bring the new system into being, and (5) implementation—converting to the new system.

- The **client** is the person or organization contracting to have a system modified or created. The **users** are the people who will have contact with the system, usually employees and customers of the client organization. For instance, in a college registration system, the client is the administration and the users are the school employees and the students.
- The systems analyst fills the role of **change agent**—the catalyst who overcomes reluctance to change within an organization. The key to a system's success is **user involvement.**

Student Personal Study Guide

True/False

T F 1. A systems analyst's role is to design and then analyze systems.
T F 2. The information systems manager and the personal computer manager are usually the same person.
T F 3. In an organization, a client and a user could be the same person but usually are not.
T F 4. There are no security risks when applications are downsized.
T F 5. One function of an information center is to do users' work for them when they get overloaded.
T F 6. An information system usually has one or more computers as components.
T F 7. The SDLC has seven phases.
T F 8. In business, personal computers are usually found only in formal office environments.
T F 9. A systems analyst, sometimes called a change agent, overcomes an organization's reluctance to change.
T F 10. To be cooperative, a user should let the systems analyst decide how a new system should work.

Multiple Choice

1. The person who runs the computer network:
   a. systems analyst
   b. systems designer
   c. network manager
   d. information systems manager
2. Which is *not* a phase of the systems development life cycle?
   a. analysis
   b. information center
   c. implementation
   d. preliminary investigation
3. Software that allows network users to collaborate:
   a. groupware
   b. downsize
   c. SDLC
   d. workware
4. Which assistance, typically, is *not* a function of the information center?
   a. software selection
   b. implementation
   c. training
   d. hardware purchases
5. Shifting mainframe applications to smaller computers:
   a. designing
   b. downsizing
   c. implementing
   d. grouping
6. The analyst's role to overcome resistance to change:
   a. worker
   b. change agent
   c. downsizer
   d. designer
7. People who only have contact with a system:
   a. users
   b. client
   c. designer
   d. analyst

8. The final phase in the evolution of personal computers is the transformation of:
   a. individuals c. divisions
   b. businesses d. departments
9. Moving data from the corporate computer to a personal computer:
   a. grouping c. downsizing
   b. analyzing d. downloading
10. Workers collaborating on a project over a network:
   a. downsizing c. downloading
   b. workgroup computing d. designing

Fill-In

1. An organized set of components to accomplish a task: ___________________.
2. The entity retaining an analyst to create or modify a system : ___________________.
3. Number of phases in the classic SDLC: ___________________.
4. A set of business procedures, with computers as components: ___________________.
5. Computer abusers on the job are sometimes called: ___________________.
6. A person who analyzes and designs systems: ___________________.
7. The first phase of the systems development life cycle: ___________________.
8. Studying an existing system with an eye to improving it: ___________________.
9. The person who monitors expenses of company personal computers:

   ___________________.

10. Planning a new computer system: ___________________.

Answers

True/False: 1. F, 2. F, 3. T, 4. F, 5. F, 6. T, 7. F, 8. F, 9. T, 10. F
Multiple choice: 1. c, 2. b , 3. a , 4. b, 5.b, 6. b, 7. a, 8. b, 9. d, 10. b
Fill-In: 1. system, 2. client, 3. five, 4. information system, 5. computer junkies, 6. systems analyst, 7. preliminary investigation, 8. systems analysis, 9. personal computer manager, 10. systems design

Chapter Overview

Beth Daultry is the administrative assistant to the head of the Business Division at Southwind Community College. Her responsibilities include setting up meetings, coordinating classes and classrooms, assisting faculty and students, and supervising two secretaries. For these and other tasks, Beth uses word processing, spreadsheet, and scheduling software on her personal computer, producing dozens of files each week.

Security,

CHAPTER

Beth knew that she was responsible for the safety and well-being of her computer files. In fact, she had attended training seminars on this very subject. In particular, she learned that it is prudent to make extra copies of her files, so that her work will not be impaired if the original files on hard disk are accidentally destroyed. As a class assignment Beth wrote down all the reasons a person might neglect to back up files properly. Her list was as follows: (1) It takes too much time. (2) It is too boring, just nuisance work. (3) I have more pressing tasks. (4) I have used this computer for a year and nothing has gone wrong yet. But, somehow, knowing what she should do was not enough. On a sunny Thursday afternoon, Beth's hard disk drive crashed, and the files on her hard disk were destroyed. Subsequent inspection revealed that less than 40 percent of her files had been backed up—copied to another place.

Beth asked herself just one question: Why? Why, indeed! How could she have been so careless, so thoughtless? While Beth castigates herself, we can reflect on human nature. We tend to think that bad things happen to other people, not us. It is hard to perform consistently the chores that help us avoid the *possibilty* of something bad happening. Instead, we spend our time on other tasks and put our files at risk.

The good news is that users in a business setting today are likely to have procedures in place for regular file backup. The users most at risk are individuals who use computers in other environments, probably at home or at school. Although this chapter covers a variety of threats to computer systems, the most common by far is the loss of files due to improper backup techniques.

Privacy, and Ethics

Protecting Hardware, Software, and Data

Computer Crime

It was 5 o'clock in the morning, and 14-year-old Randy Miller was startled to see a man climbing through his bedroom window. "FBI," the man announced, "and that computer is mine." So ended the computer caper in San Diego, California, where 23 teenagers, ages 13 to 17, had used their home computers to invade systems as far away as Massachusetts. The teenagers were **hackers**—people who attempt to gain access to computer systems illegally, usually from a personal computer, via a data communications network.

The term *hacker* used to mean a person with significant computer expertise, but the term has taken on the more sinister meaning with the advent of computer miscreants, particularly teenagers. In the case of Randy Miller, he and his fellow hackers did not use the system to steal money or property. They did change system passwords, however, preventing legitimate access to the computer accounts. They also created fictitious accounts and destroyed or changed some data files. The FBI's entry through the window was calculated—they figured that, given even a moment's warning, the teenagers were clever enough to alert each other via computer.

This story—except for the name—is true. Hackers ply their craft for a variety of reasons: to show off for their peers, to harass people they do not like, to get computer services without paying, and sometimes to get information they can sell. However, hackers are only a small fraction of the security problem. The most serious losses are caused by electronic pickpockets who are usually a good deal older and not so harmless. Consider the following examples:

- A Denver brokerage clerk sat at his terminal and, with a few taps of the keys, transformed 1700 shares of his own stock worth $1.50 each to the same number of shares in another company worth ten times that much.
- A Seattle bank employee used her electronic funds transfer code to move certain bank funds to an account held by her boyfriend as a "joke"; both the money and the boyfriend disappeared.
- In an Oakland department store, a keyboard operator changed some delivery addresses to divert several thousands of dollars worth of store goods into the hands of accomplices.
- A stockbroker used the company's computer system to buy and sell cocaine.

These stories point out that computer crime is not always the flashy, front-page news about geniuses getting away with millions of dollars. Computer systems have been used to steal valuable information, software, phone service, and credit card numbers. These thieves pass along or sell their services and techniques to others—including organized crime.

The problems of computer crime have been aggravated in recent years by increased access to computers (Figure 10-1). More employees now have access to computers in their jobs. In fact, computer crime is often just white-collar crime with a new medium: Every time an employee is trained on the computer at work, he or she gains knowledge that could be used to harm the company.

Disgruntled or militant employee could
- Sabotage equipment or programs
- Hold data or programs hostage

Competitor could
- Sabotage operations
- Engage in espionage
- Steal data or programs
- Photograph records, documentation, or CRT screen displays

Data control worker could
- Insert data
- Delete data
- Bypass controls
- Sell information

Clerk/supervisor could
- Forge or falsify data
- Embezzle funds
- Engage in collusion with people inside or outside the company

System user could
- Sell data to competitors
- Obtain unauthorized information

Operator could
- Copy files
- Destroy files

User requesting reports could
- Sell information to competitors
- Receive unauthorized information

Engineer could
- Install "bugs"
- Sabotage system
- Access security information

Data conversion worker could
- Change codes
- Insert data
- Delete data

Programmer could
- Steal programs or data
- Embezzle via programming
- Bypass controls

Report distribution worker could
- Examine confidential reports
- Keep duplicates of reports

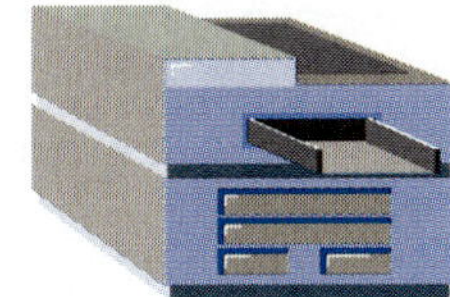

Trash collector could
- Sell reports or duplicates to competitors

Figure 10-1 The perils of increased access.
By letting your imagination run wild, you can visualize numerous ways in which people can compromise computer security. Computer-related crime would be far more rampant if all the people in these positions took advantage of their access to computers.

A Glossary of Computer Crime

Although the emphasis in this chapter is on preventing rather than committing crime, it is worthwhile being familiar with computer criminal terms and methods.

Data diddling: Changing data before or as it enters the system.

Data leakage: Obtaining copies of data from the system—without leaving a trace.

Logic bomb technique: Sabotaging a program by setting up a trigger that is activated by certain conditions—usually at a later date, perhaps after the perpetrator has left the company.

Piggybacking: Using another person's identification code or using that person's files before he or she has logged off.

Salami technique: Using a large financial system to embezzle small "slices" of money that may never be missed.

Scavenging: Searching trash cans for printouts and carbons containing not-for-distribution information.

Trapdoor technique: Leaving illicit instructions within a completed program; the instructions allow unauthorized, and undetected, entry.

Trojan horse: Tricking a user into running a destructive program by giving it the name of a trusted program.

Zapping: Bypassing all security systems with an illicitly acquired software package.

What motivates the computer criminal? The causes are as varied as the offenders; however, a few frequent motives have been identified. A computer criminal is often a disgruntled employee, possibly a long-time, loyal worker out for revenge after being passed over for a raise or promotion. In another scenario, an otherwise model employee may commit a crime while suffering from personal or family problems. Not all motives are emotionally based. Some people are simply attracted to the challenge of the crime. In contrast, it is the ease of the crime that tempts others. In many cases the criminal activity is unobtrusive; it fits right in with regular job duties. The risk of detection is often quite low. Computer criminals think they can get away with it, and some have.

Types and Methods of Computer Crime

Computer crime falls into three basic categories:

- Theft of computer time, either for personal use or with the intention of making a profit. Miscreants may, for example, perform computer tasks for outside clients; work on personal projects, such as a hobby club budget or newsletter; or even write software for personal profit.
- Theft, destruction, or manipulation of programs or data.
- Alteration of data stored in a computer file.

Though it is not our purpose to be a how-to book on computer crime, the margin note called "A Glossary of Computer Crime" mentions some criminal methods.

Discovery and Prosecution

Prosecuting the computer criminal is complicated by the fact that discovery is often difficult. Most computer crimes simply go undetected, and those that are detected are usually discovered by accident. Furthermore, an estimated 85 percent of the time, crimes that are detected are not reported to the authorities. By law, banks have to make a report when their computer systems have been compromised, but other businesses do not. Often they choose not to report because they are worried about their reputations and credibility in the community.

Even if a computer crime is detected, a prosecution is by no means assured. There are a number of reasons for this. First, some law enforcement agencies do not fully understand the complexities of computer-related fraud. Second, few attorneys are qualified to handle computer crime cases. Third, judges and juries are not educated in the ways of computers and may not understand the value of data to a company.

This situation is changing, however. In 1986 Congress passed the latest version of the **Computer Fraud and Abuse Act** to fight the problem on the national level. Furthermore, most states have passed some form of computer crime law.

Security: Keeping Everything Safe

As you can see from the previous section, the computer industry has been vulnerable in the matter of security. Computer security once meant the physical security of the computer itself—guarded and locked doors. However, locking up the computer by no means prevents access, as we have seen.

What is security? We can define it as follows: **Security** is a system of safeguards designed to protect a computer system and data from deliberate or accidental damage or access by unauthorized persons. That means safeguarding the system against such threats as burglary, vandalism, fire, natural disasters, theft of data for ransom, industrial espionage, and various forms of white-collar crime.

Who Goes There? Identification and Access

How does a computer system detect whether you are a person who should be allowed access to it? Various means have been devised to give access to authorized people without compromising the system. The means fall into four broad categories: what you have, what you know, what you do, and who you are.

- **What you have.** You may have a key or a badge or a plastic card to give you physical access to the computer room or a locked-up terminal. A credit card with a magnetized strip, for example, can give you access to a gas pump at your local station. Taking this a step further, some employees begin each business day by donning an **active badge,** a clip-on identification card with an embedded computer chip. The badge signals its wearer's location—legal or otherwise—by sending out infrared signals that are read by sensors sprinkled around the building. The active badge, which is becoming increasingly common, presents a challenging problem: balancing an employee's privacy against a corporation's desire for efficiency and control.
- **What you know.** Standard what-you-know items are a system password or an identification number for your bank cash machine. Cipher or combination locks on doors require that you know the correct combination of numbers
- **What you do.** Your signature is difficult but not impossible to copy. Signature-access systems are better suited to human interaction than machine interaction. That is, humans can check a signature on sight, a feat more difficult for a computer.
- **What you are.** Now it gets interesting. Some security systems use **biometrics,** the science of measuring individual body characteristics. Fingerprinting is old news, but handprint geometry and voice recognition are relatively new. Even newer is the concept of identification by the retina of the eye, which has a pattern that is harder to duplicate than a voiceprint (Figure 10-2).

Figure 10-2 Identification by retina. The eye can be a means of personal identification. A user first keys a unique identification code number. The security system then matches the person's unique retinal pattern to the individual's computer-stored retina pattern, for conclusive identification of authorized users.

Some systems use a combination of these four categories. For example, access to an automated teller machine requires both something you have—a plastic card—and something you know—a personal identification number (PIN).

When Disaster Strikes: What Do You Have to Lose?

In California a poem, a pansy, a bag of Mrs. Field's cookies, and the message "Please have a cookie and a nice day" were left at the Vandenberg Air Force Base computer installation—along with five demolished mainframe computers. Computer installations of any kind can be struck by

Some Gentle Advice on Security

Being a security expert is an unusual job because, once the planning is done, there is not a lot to do except wait for something bad to happen. Security experts are often consultants who move from company to company. Their advice usually includes long and detailed checklists: Do this, do that, and you will be OK. We cannot offer a long set of lists, but here is a brief subset that includes some of the most effective approaches.

- Beware of disgruntled employees. Ed Street was angry. Seething. How could they pass over him for a promotion again? Well, if they were not going to give him what he deserved, he would take it himself. . . . Ah, the tale is too common. Be forewarned.
- Sensitize employees to security issues. Most people are eager to help others. They must be taught that some kinds of help, such as assisting unauthorized users with passwords, are inappropriate.
- Call back all remote-access terminals. Don't call us, we'll call you. If, before your system accepts a call, it must check a list of phone numbers to ensure that the caller has valid access, you eliminate most intruders. In such an arrangement your computer has to call the user back for the user to gain remote access, and your computer will do so only if the user's number is valid.
- Keep personnel privileges up-to-date. Furthermore, we might add, make sure they are enforced properly. Some of the biggest heists have been pulled by people who *formerly* had legitimate access to secured areas. In many cases they can still get in because the guard has known them by sight for years.

natural or man-made disasters that can lead to security violations. What kinds of problems might this cause an organization?

Your first thoughts might be of the hardware—the computer and its related equipment. But loss of hardware is not a major problem in itself; the loss can be covered by insurance, and hardware can be replaced. The true problem with hardware loss is the diminished processing ability that exists while managers find a substitute facility and return the installation to its former state. Loss of software should not be a problem if the organization has heeded industry warnings, and used common sense, to make backup copies.

A more important problem is the loss of data. Imagine trying to reassemble lost or destroyed master files of customer records, accounts receivable, or design data for a new airplane. The costs would be staggering. We continue with an overview of disaster recovery and then consider software and data security, worms and viruses that may affect files, and the all-important backing up of files.

Disaster Recovery Plan

A **disaster recovery plan** is a method of restoring data processing operations if those operations are halted by major damage or destruction. Preparing for such a loss is somewhat like installing smoke alarms or wearing seat belts: You hope you will never need them. There are various approaches to disaster recovery planning. Some organizations revert temporarily to manual services, but life without the computer can be difficult indeed. Others arrange to buy time at a service bureau, but this may be inconvenient for companies in remote or rural areas. If a single act, such as a fire, destroys your computing facility, it is possible that a mutual aid pact will help you get back on your feet. In such a plan two or more companies agree to lend each other computing power if one of them has a problem. This would be of little help, however, if there were a regional disaster and many companies needed assistance.

Banks and other organizations whose survival depends on computers sometimes form a **consortium**—a joint venture to support a complete computer facility. Such a facility is completely available and routinely tested but used only in the event of a disaster.

Computer installations regularly practice emergency drills. At some unexpected moment a notice is given that "disaster has struck," and the computer professionals must run the critical systems at some other site.

Software Security

According to a recent court case, Meredith England, a programmer, stands accused of using her key card to slip into the office at 3 o'clock in the morning and take some disks home with her. The problem is that Ms. England had been recently fired and the disks she allegedly took contained proprietary software worth about $15 million. Although Ms. England says she was on the premises merely to clean out her desk, a legal search of her home produced the copied disks.

Who owns custom-made software? Is the owner the person who writes the program or the company for which the author wrote the program? The answer to this question is well established. If a programmer is in the employ of an organization, the program belongs to the organization, not the programmer. If the programmer does her own work on her

Personal Computers In Action

Your Own Security Checklist

With the subject of security fresh in your mind, now is a good time to consider a checklist for your own home computer and its software:

- Do not eat, drink, or smoke near the computer.
- Do not place the computer near open windows or doors.
- Do not subject the computer to extreme temperatures.
- Clean equipment regularly, following manufacturer's directions.
- Place a cable lock on the computer. In particular, cable-lock your laptop to any nearby immovable object.
- Use a surge protector, a device that prevents electrical problems from affecting data files. The computer is plugged into the surge protector, which is plugged into the outlet.
- Store disks properly in a locked container.
- Maintain backup copies of all files.
- Store copies of critical files off site.
- Scan a diskette for viruses before use.

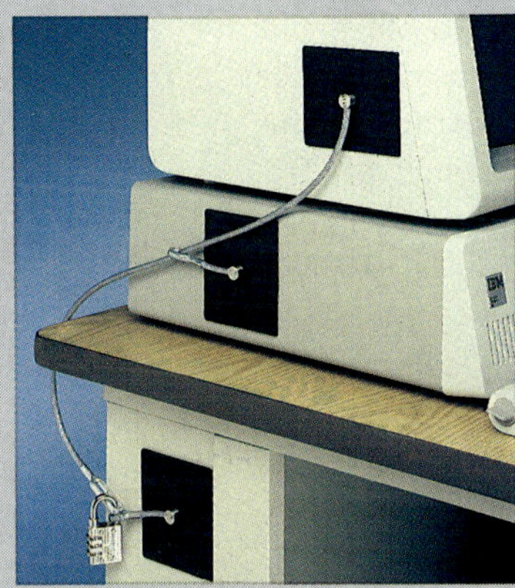

(a)

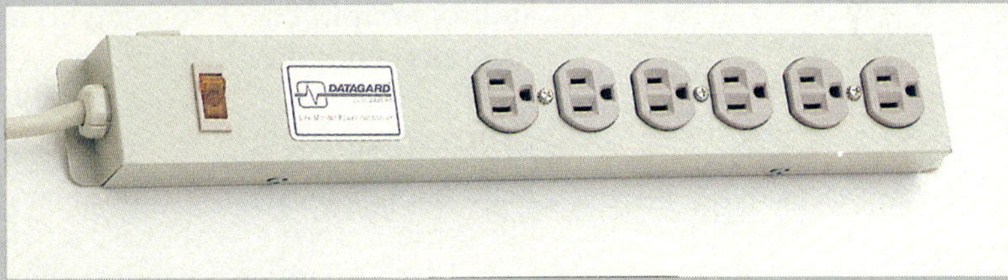

(b)

Security devices.
(a) Locking up your computer can help minimize theft. (b) A surge protector can protect your computer system and files from unpredictable electrical problems.

own computer on her own time, for no recompense, the program belongs to her.

Commercial software, especially software for personal computers, presents a different problem. Although specifically prohibited by law, software is copied as blatantly as music or video tapes. We will examine this issue more closely when we consider ethics later in the chapter.

Data Security

In addition to the possible loss of data, there are problems related to data safety. What steps can be taken to prevent theft or alteration of data? Several data protection techniques are in common use; these will not individually (or even collectively) guarantee security, but at least they make a good start.

Secured Waste

Discarded printouts, printer ribbons, and the like can be sources of information to unauthorized persons. This kind of waste can be made secure by the use of shredders or locked trash barrels.

Passwords

Passwords are the secret words or numbers that must be typed on the keyboard to gain access to a system or some part of a system. In some installations the passwords are changed so seldom that they become known to many people. Good data protection systems change passwords often and also compartmentalize information by passwords, so that only authorized persons can have access to certain data. Cracking passwords is the most prevalent method of illicit entry to computer systems. If you are able to choose your own password, do not name your password after your child or pet poodle. Recommended password creation techniques include using at least six characters, embedding at least one nonalphabetic character, and even mixing upper- and lowercase; for example, PIN*curve.

Internal Controls

Internal controls are controls that are planned as part of the computer system. One example is a transaction log—a file of all accesses or attempted accesses to certain data.

Auditor Checks

Most companies have auditors who go over the financial books. In the course of an audit, auditors with special training may also review computer programs and data. From a data security standpoint, for example, auditors might check to see who has accessed data during periods when that data is not usually used.

Cryptography

Data being sent over communications lines may be protected by scrambling the messages—that is, putting them in code that can be broken only by the person receiving the message. The process of scrambling messages is called **encryption.** The American National Standards Institute has endorsed a process called the **Data Encryption Standard (DES),** a standardized public key that senders and receivers can use to scramble and unscramble their messages. Although the DES code has been broken, companies still use it because the method makes it quite expensive to intercept coded messages, forcing interlopers to use methods of gathering data that carry a greater risk of detection.

Worms and Viruses

These rather unpleasant terms have entered the jargon of the computer industry to describe some of the insidious ways that computer systems and programs can be invaded. A **worm** is a program that transfers itself from computer to computer over a network and plants itself as a separate file on the target computer's disks. One newsworthy worm, originated by student Robert Morris at Cornell University, traveled the length and breadth of the land through an electronic mail network, shutting down thousands of computers. The worm was injected into the network and multiplied uncontrollably, clogging the memories of infected computers until they could no longer function.

A virus, as its name suggests, is contagious. That is, a **virus,** a set of illicit instructions, passes itself on to other programs with which it comes in contact. Viruses seem to show up when least expected. In one instance, a call came to the company's information center about 5:00 p.m.; the caller's computer was making a strange noise. With the exception of an occasional beep, computers performing routine business chores do not usually make noises. Soon calls came in from all over the company, all with "noisy" computers. One caller said that it might be a tune coming from the computer's small internal speaker. Finally, one caller recognized a tinny rendition of Yankee Doodle, confirmation that an old virus had struck once again. The Yankee Doodle virus, once attached to a system, is scheduled to go off at 5:00 p.m. every eight days. Viruses, once considered merely a nuisance, are costing American businesses collectively over $2 billion a year. Unfortunately, viruses are easily transmitted.

Transmitting a Virus

Consider this typical example. A programmer secretly inserts a few viral instructions into a game called Kriss-Kross, which she then offers free to others via a bulletin board. Any takers download the game to their own computers. Now, each time a user runs Kriss-Kross—that is, loads it into memory—the virus is loaded, too. The virus stays in memory, infecting any other program that is loaded. The virus now has spread to other programs, and the process can be repeated again and again. In fact, each newly infected program becomes a virus carrier. Although many viruses are transmitted just this way over bulletin boards, the most common method is by passing diskettes from computer to computer (Figure 10-3).

More insidious viruses attach to the operating system. One virus, called Cascade, causes random text letters to "drop" to a pile at the bottom of the screen (Figure 10-4). Viruses attached to the operating system itself have greater potential for mischief.

Figure 10-3 An example of a virus invasion.

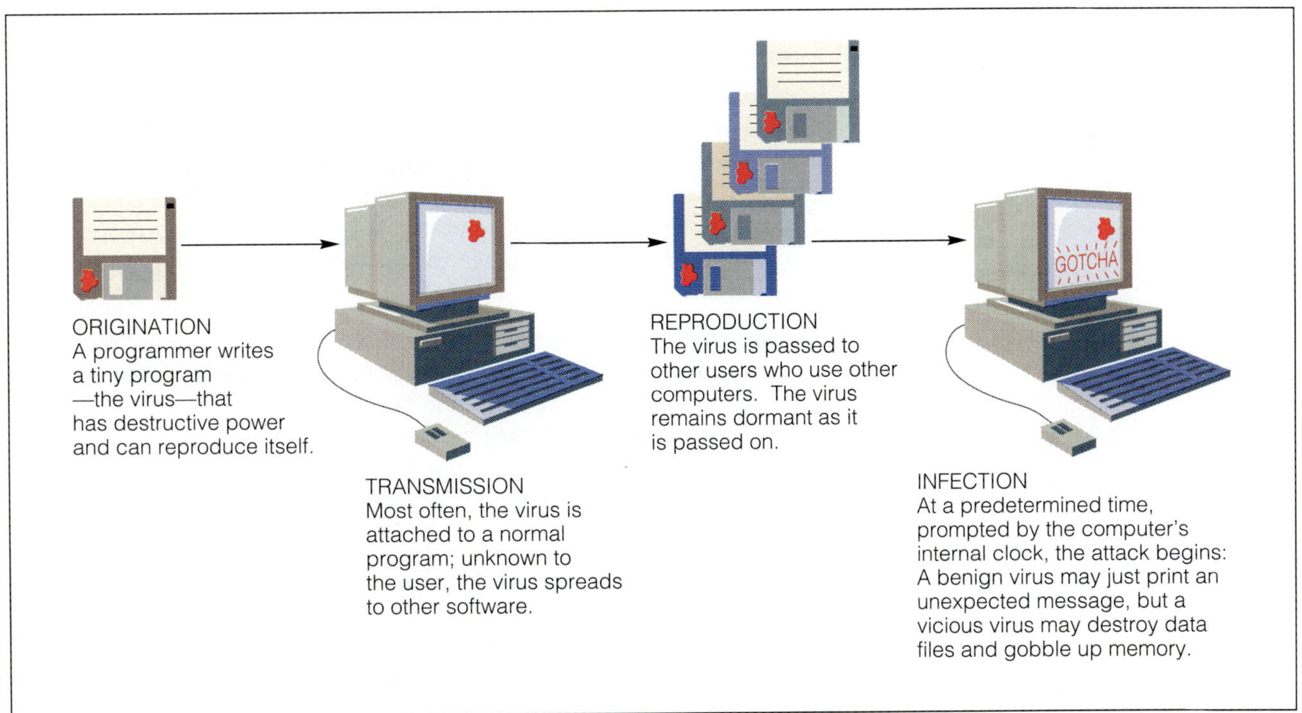

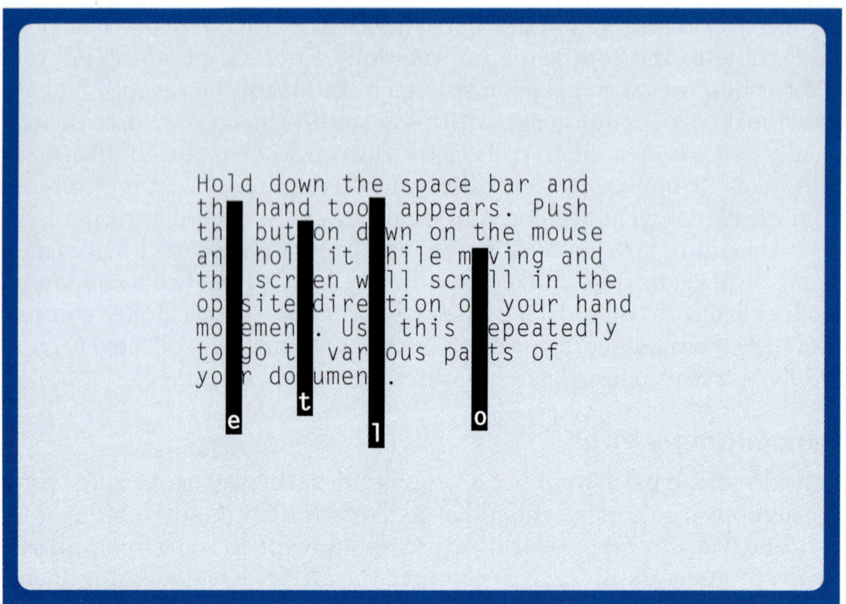

Figure 10-4 The Cascade virus. This virus attaches itself to the operating system itself and causes random letters in text to "drop" to a pile at the bottom of the screen display.

Damage from Viruses

The Yankee Doodle virus described earlier is relatively benign, as is the virus that simply displays a peace message. But many viruses do significant damage, often including destruction of files.

Most viruses remain dormant until triggered by some activity. For example, a virus called Jerusalem B activates itself every Friday the 13th and proceeds to erase any file you may try to load from your disk. Another virus includes instructions to add 1 to a counter each time the virus is copied to another disk. When the counter reaches 4, the virus erases all data files. But this is not the end of the destruction, of course; the three copied disks have also been infected.

Prevention

A word about prevention is in order. Although viruses are most commonly passed via diskettes, viruses use many other means to propagate—bulletin boards, local area networks, and electronic mail. If your personal computer has a disk drive, a modem, or a network connector, it is vulnerable. Furthermore, viruses are rampant on some college campuses and a source of considerable annoyance to students. Use these commonsense approaches to new files.

- Never install a program unless the diskette comes in a sealed package.
- Be especially wary of software that arrives unexpectedly from companies with whom you have not done business.
- Use virus-scanning software to check any file, no matter what the source, before loading it onto your hard disk.
- If your own diskette was used in another computer, scan it to see if it caught a virus.

Although there have been isolated instances of viruses in commercial software, viruses tend to show up on free software acquired from friends or through electronic bulletin board systems. Antivirus software can be installed to scan your hard disk every time you boot the computer or, if you prefer, at regularly scheduled intervals.

Prepare for the Worst: Back Up Your Files

During an impassioned speech, a computer expert said, "If you are not backing up your files regularly, you *deserve* to lose them." Strong words. One wonders why, with continuous admonishments and readily available procedures, some people still leave their precious files unprotected.

What Could Go Wrong?

A hard disk could physically malfunction, making your files inaccessible. This is not too likely, but it certainly does happen. It is even less likely that you lose your hard disk to fire or flood, but this is also possible. It is most likely that you will accidentally delete some files yourself. One fellow gave a command to delete all files with the file name extension BAK—there were four of them—but accidentally typed BAT instead, inadvertently wiping out 57 files. There is also the very real possibility of your files being infected with a virus. Experts estimate that average users experience a significant disk loss every year.

Ways to Back Up Files

Some people simply make another copy of their hard drive files on diskette. This is not too laborious if you do so as you go along. If you are at all vulnerable to viruses, you should back up all your files on a regular basis.

A better way is to back up all your files on a tape. Backing up to a tape drive is safer and faster. You can also use software that will automatically back up all your files at a certain time of day or on command. Sophisticated users place their files on a mirror hard disk, which simply makes a second copy of everything you put on the original disk; this approach, as you might expect, is expensive.

Keep backed up files in a cool, dry place off site. For those of you with a home computer, this may mean keeping copies of your important files at a friend's house.

Privacy: Keeping Personal Information Personal

Think about the forms you have willingly filled out: paperwork for loans or charge accounts; orders for merchandise through the mail; magazine subscription orders; applications for schools, jobs, and clubs; and so on. There may be some forms you filled out with less delight—for taxes, military draft registration, court petitions, insurance claims, or a stay in the hospital. Furthermore, consider all the checks you have written and the people who may have taken your name and address from them—retailers, fund-raisers, advertisers, petitioners, and others. We have only skimmed the possible sources of data, but we can say with certainty where all this data went: straight to computer files.

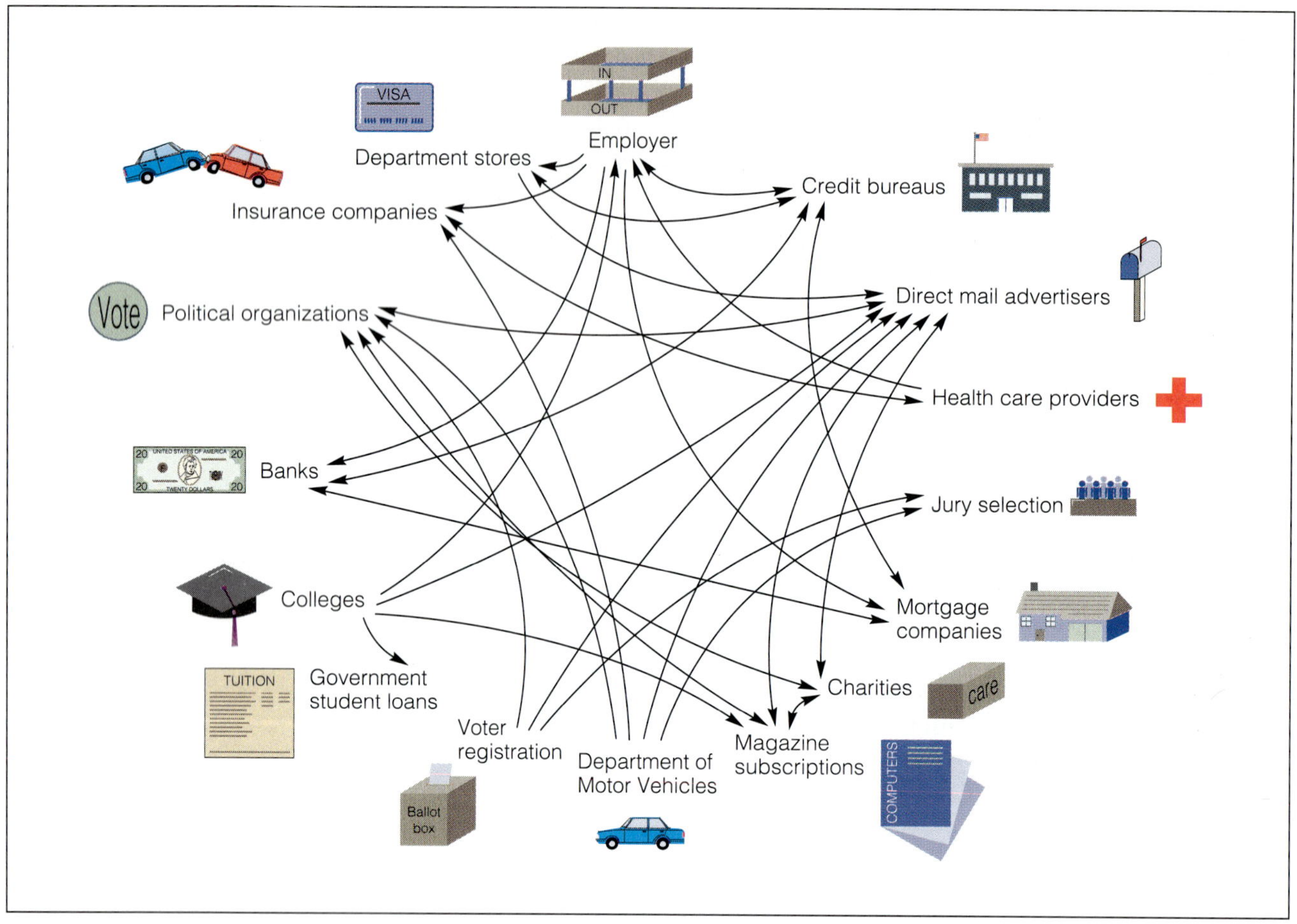

Figure 10-5 Potential paths of data.
When an organization acquires information about you, it is often shared with, or sold to, other organizations.

Where is that data now? Is it passed around? Who sees it? Will it ever be expunged? Or, to put it more bluntly, is anything private anymore? Much of the data is passed around, as anyone with a mailbox can attest. As for who sees your personal data, the answers are not comforting (Figure 10-5). Furthermore, about 20 states allow their motor vehicle departments to sell names and addresses, and sometimes even heights and weights, to anyone who pays a fee. Some states even sell computer tapes of their entire files to marketers, insurance companies, and other businesses.

There are matters you want to keep private. You have the right to do so. Although there is little you can do to stop data about you from circulating through computers, there are laws that give you access to some of it.

Significant legislation relating to privacy began with the **Fair Credit Reporting Act** in 1970. This law allows you to have access to and gives you the right to challenge the information in your credit records. In fact, this access must be given to you free of charge if you have been denied credit.

COMPUTING TRENDS

You Have No Privacy Whatever

No privacy on the company e-mail, that is. The company can snoop into messages you send or receive even if you think you erased it. But wait. A federal court recently has ruled that the Privacy Protection Act of 1980 applies to electronically stored information. So, just which way is this trend going?

Companies often failed to convey the message that e-mail, as a company conduit, is not private. Employees were often startled, after the fact, to discover that their messages had been invaded. Furthermore, some people specialize in extracting deleted messages for use as evidence in court. E-mail can be a dangerous time bomb in every corporation because litigators argue that, more than any other kind of written communication, e-mail reflects the real, unedited thoughts of the writer.

What to do? It is certainly degrading to have something you thought was private waved in front of you as evidence of malingering. As one computer expert put it, if nothing is private, just say so. Companies have begun doing exactly that. The company policy on e-mail is—or should be—expressed in a clear, written document.

How does the Privacy Protection Act fit into this? For now the courts have addressed only government trespassing, not internal company prying. The current trend is clear: You have no privacy on company e-mail. None whatever.

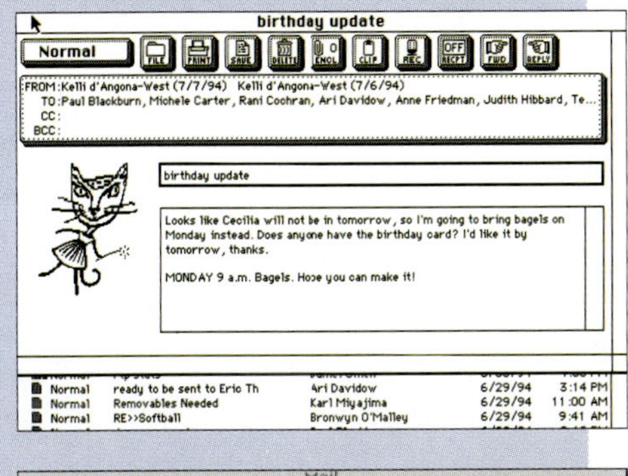

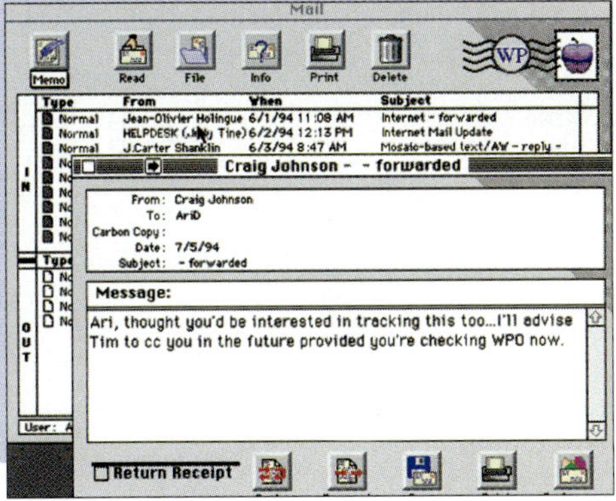

Businesses usually contribute financial information about their customers to a community credit bureau, which gives them the right to review a person's prior credit record with other companies. Before the Fair Credit Reporting Act, many people were turned down for credit, without explanation, because of inaccurate financial records about them. Now people may check their records to make sure they are accurate. The **Freedom of Information Act** was also passed in 1970. This landmark legislation allows ordinary citizens to have access to data about them that was gathered by federal agencies.

The most significant legislation protecting the privacy of individuals is the **Federal Privacy Act** of 1974. This act stipulates that there can be no secret personal files; individuals must be allowed to know what is stored in files about them, to know how the information is used, and to be able to correct it. The law applies not only to government agencies but also to private contractors dealing with government agencies. These organizations cannot obtain data willy-nilly for no specific purpose; they must justify obtaining it.

A more recent law is the **Video Privacy Protection Act** of 1988, which prevents retailers from disclosing a person's video rental records without a court order; privacy supporters want the same rule for medical and insurance files. Another step in that direction is the **Computer Matching and Privacy Protection Act** of 1988, which prevents the government from comparing certain records in an attempt to find a matchup. However, most comparisons are still unregulated. For example, the government routinely compares IRS records with draft registration records to catch those who have failed to register.

A Matter of Ethics

The fact that professional computer personnel have access to files has always presented the potential for problems. In theory, those with access could do something as simple as snooping into a friend's salary on a payroll file or as complex as selling military secrets to foreign countries. The problem has become more tangled as everyday people—not just computer professionals—have daily computer contact. They also have access to important files. As we noted earlier, data is the resource most difficult to replace, so increased access is the subject of much concern among security officers.

Where do you come in? As a student you could easily face ethical problems involving access and much more. Consider some of these examples. A nonstudent friend wants to borrow your password to get access to the school computer. Or you know of a student who has bypassed computer security and changed grades for himself and some friends. Perhaps a "computer jock" pal collects software and wants you to copy a software disk used in one of your classes.

The problems are not so different in the business world. You will recognize that, whether you are a computer professional or a user, you have a clear responsibility to your own organization and its customers to protect the security and privacy of their information. Any compromise of data, in particular, is considered a serious breach of ethics. Many corporations have formal statements stating as much and present them to employees individually for their signatures.

Copying Software

Let us move from general ethical principles to a very individual problem: copying software. Have you ever copied a friend's music CD or tape onto your own blank tape? Many people do so without much thought. It is also possible to photocopy a book. These acts are clearly illegal, although it is legal to copy a few pages of a book for educational purposes. There is much more fuss over individual illegal software copying than over copying music or books. Why is this? Well, to begin with, few of us are likely to undertake the laborious task of reproducing *War and Peace* on a copy machine. The other part of the issue is money. A pirated copy of a top-20 tape will set the recording company and the artist back about $10. On the other hand, pirated software may be valued at hundreds of dollars. The problem of stolen software has grown right along with the personal computer industry. Before we discuss industry solutions, we must distinguish among various kinds of software, based on its availability to the public.

OK If I Copy that Software?

Some software will not cost you a penny because it is free to all. Such software, considered in public domain, is sometimes called **freeware.** It is free because its generous maker, probably an individual at home or an educator, chooses to make it free. A variation on this theme is **shareware,** which may also be given away free. However, the shareware maker hopes for voluntary monetary compensation—that is, the author requests that, if you use it, you send a contribution. Some shareware is available only on a trial basis, in which a user must pay for the software after an evaluation period. Freeware and some shareware may be copied freely and given to other people. However, the software that people use most often, such as a word processing or spreadsheet package, is **licensed software**—software that costs money and may not be copied without permission from the manufacturer.

Making illegal copies of licensed software is called **software piracy.** It is considered stealing because software makers do not get the revenues to which they are entitled. Furthermore, if software developers are not properly compensated, they may not find it worthwhile to develop new software.

Don't Copy that Floppy

The Software Publishers Association has made mighty efforts to educate the public. Specifically, they would like people to stop making illegal copies of copyrighted software. The SPA made a video directed to young people, in which a rapper (accompanied by drums) intones the following:

Did I hear you right?
Did I hear you sayin'?
That you're gonna make a copy of a game without payin'?
You say I'll just make a copy for me and a friend.
Then he'll make one and she'll make one
and where will it end?

The verses continue, with the theme that if no one pays, eventually manufacturers will stop producing software.

Thinking of Copying? Think Again

Copying software is not always illegal; there are lots of legitimate reasons for copying. To begin with, after paying several hundred dollars for a piece of software, you will definitely want to make a backup copy in case of disk failure or accident. You will certainly want to copy the program onto a hard disk and use it, more conveniently, from there. Software publishers have no trouble with any of these types of copying. However, thousands of computer users copy software for another reason: to get the program without paying for it. And therein lies the problem. Pirated software costs the industry over $12 billion annually worldwide.

Software publishers first tried to solve the problem by placing on their software **copy protection**—a software or hardware roadblock that makes it difficult or impossible to make pirated copies. In effect, these devices punish the innocent with the guilty. There was vigorous opposition from software users, who argued that it was unfair to restrict paying customers just to outsmart a few thieves. Most software vendors have now dropped copy protection from their software, but they are still vigilant about illegal copies. Vendors have taken imaginative approaches to protecting their products and, at the same time, keeping customers happy. The most popular approach is site licensing.

Licensing Big Customers

An approach favored by some software makers is site licensing. Although there is no clear definition industrywide, in general a **site license** permits a customer to make multiple copies of a given piece of software. The customer needing all these copies is usually a corporation or a university, which can probably obtain a significant price discount for volume buying. The exact nature of the arrangement between the user and the software maker can vary considerably. Typically, however, a customer obtains the right to make a maximum number of copies of a product, agrees to keep track of who uses it, and takes responsibility for copying and distributing manuals to its own personnel.

Some software makers, however, oppose site licensing; they do not want to be bogged down in licensing negotiations. Industry leaders

Microsoft Corporation and the Lotus Development Corporation favor **concurrent licensing,** a system that charges a fee based on the number of users at a given time or perhaps at peak periods. Suppose, for example, that 20 users are on a network, but a maximum of 10 would be using Lotus at a given time. The company could pay for just 10 copies of the software. However, once 10 of the users are using the software at a given moment, an 11th potential user would be locked out.

Finally, the software industry persuaded Congress to amend the **Copyright Act** to raise software piracy from a misdemeanor to a felony. Under the 1992 law, a convicted pirate faces the possibility of up to five years' jail time and $250,000 in fines.

▼ ▼ ▼

The issues raised in this chapter are often the ones we think of after the fact, that is, when it is too late. The security and privacy factors are somewhat like insurance that we wish we did not have to buy. We buy insurance for our homes, cars, and lives because we know we dare not risk being without it. The computer industry also knows that it cannot risk being without safeguards for security and privacy. As a computer user, in whatever capacity, you can take comfort in the fact that the computer industry recognizes their importance.

Chapter **Review**

Summary and Key Terms

- A **hacker** is a person who gains access to computer systems illegally.
- Three basic categories of computer crime are (1) theft of computer time; (2) theft, destruction, or manipulation of programs or data; and (3) alteration of data stored in a computer file.
- In 1984 Congress passed the **Computer Fraud and Abuse Act,** which is supplemented by local laws in most of the states.
- **Security** is a system of safeguards designed to protect a computer system and data from deliberate or accidental damage or access by unauthorized persons.
- The means of giving access to authorized people are divided into four general categories: (1) what you have (a key, badge, or plastic card), (2) what you know (a system password or identification number), (3) what you do (signing your name), and (4) who you are (making use of **biometrics,** the science of measuring individual body characteristics such as fingerprints, voice, or retina). An **active badge,** with its embedded computer chip, signals its wearer's location by sending out infrared signals that are read by sensors sprinkled around the building.
- A **disaster recovery plan** is a method of restoring data processing operations if they are halted by major damage or destruction. Common approaches to disaster recovery include relying temporarily on manual services; buying time at a computer service bureau; making mutual assistance agreements with other companies; or forming a **consortium**—a joint venture with other organizations to support a complete computer facility.
- Common means of protecting data are securing waste, passwords, internal controls, auditor checks, and cryptography.
- Data sent over communications lines can be protected by **encryption**—the process of scrambling messages. The American National Standards Institute has endorsed a process called the **Data Encryption Standard (DES).**
- A **worm** is a program that transfers itself from computer to computer over a network, planting itself as a separate file on the target computer's disks. A **virus** is a set of illicit instructions that passes itself on to other programs with which it comes in contact.
- Files are subject to various types of losses and should be backed up on disk or tape.
- The security issue also extends to the use of information about individuals that is stored in the computer files of credit bureaus and government agencies. The **Fair Credit Reporting Act** allows individuals to check the accuracy of credit information about them. The **Freedom of Information Act** allows people access to data that federal agencies have gathered about them. The **Federal Privacy Act** allows individuals access to information about them that is held not only by government agencies but also by private contractors working for the government. Other recent laws supporting privacy are the **Video Privacy Protection Act,** which prohibits retailers from disclosing a customer's video rental records, and the **Computer Matching and Privacy Protection Act,** which regulates comparison of records held by different branches of government.
- Software in the public domain, called **freeware,** is free because its maker chooses to make it free. **Shareware** software is also free, but the maker hopes for voluntary monetary compensation. **Licensed software** costs money and may not be copied without

permission from the manufacturer. Making illegal copies of copyrighted software is called **software piracy.**

- **Copy protection** is a software or hardware roadblock that makes it difficult or impossible to make pirated copies of software.
- Many software publishers offer a **site license,** which permits a customer to make multiple copies of a given piece of software. **Concurrent licensing** allows a customer to use only a limited number of copies of a software product simultaneously.
- In 1992 Congress amended the **Copyright Act** to raise software piracy from a misdemeanor to a felony, with possible penalties of five years' jail time and $250,000 in fines.

Student Personal Study Guide

True/False

T F 1. One category of computer crime is alteration of stored data.
T F 2. Computer security is achieved by physically restricting access.
T F 3. The loss of hardware is the most serious potential security problem.
T F 4. A disaster recovery plan is a scheme to anticipate major software piracy.
T F 5. It is legitimate to make a copy of software for backup.
T F 6. Software piracy is a felony.
T F 7. Retailers are prohibited by law from disclosing a customer's video rentals.
T F 8. The American National Standards Institute has endorsed an encryption standard.
T F 9. Making a copy of a friend's software is generally considered acceptable.
T F 10. Approximately 90 percent of computer crimes are detected and prosecuted.

Multiple Choice

1. Software that may not be copied without permission:
   a. shareware c. licensed software
   b. encrypted software d. pirated software
2. Software that can be copied for voluntary compensation:
   a. shareware c. licensed software
   b. encrypted software d. pirated software
3. Illegal copies of copyrighted software:
   a. pirated software c. shareware
   b. licensed software d. video software
4. Measuring individual body characteristics:
   a. biometrics c. virus
   b. encryption d. active badge
5. Illegal program transferred over a network:
   a. backup c. encryption
   b. worm d. Trojan horse
6. Permission to make multiple copies of licensed software:
   a. site license c. encryption
   b. worm evader d. consortium
7. Gaining access to computer system illegally:
   a. key card c. hacking
   b. consorting d. biometrics
8. Illicit instructions copied from program to program:
   a. worm c. network
   b. encryption d. virus

9. Which is *not* a method of protecting data?
   a. auditor checks c. passwords
   b. cryptography d. worms
10. Which is *not* an approach to disaster recovery?
   a. manual services c. encryption
   b. buying computer time d. consortium

Fill-In

1. The most serious potential loss is loss of: ________________.
2. Computer system protection from damage or unauthorized access: ________________.
3. Unauthorized copying of software: ________________.
4. Legislation that allows people to check their credit rating: ________________.
5. Software in the public domain: ________________.
6. A permit to make multiple copies of software: ________________.
7. Legislation that allows access to data from federal agencies: ________________.
8. A joint venture for a computer facility: ________________.
9. A method of restoring computer facilities: ________________.
10. Scrambling messages over communications lines: ________________.

Answers

True/False: 1. T, 2. F, 3. F, 4. F, 5. T, 6. T, 7. T, 8. T, 9. F, 10. F
Multiple choice: 1. c, 2. a , 3. a , 4. a, 5. b, 6. a, 7. c, 8. d, 9. d, 10. c
Fill-In: 1. data, 2. security, 3. software piracy, 4. Fair Credit Reporting Act, 5. freeware, 6. site license, 7. Freedom of Information Act, 8. consortium , 9. disaster recovery plan , 10. encryption

Chapter Overview

Polina Troy worked as a credit consultant for Nordstrom, a chain of stores selling high-quality clothing. Polina had developed significant expertise over a period of years. Consider this example. A customer came to the store, selected a $300 coat, and handed her charge card to the sales clerk. However, the customer's credit limit was just $1000, and she had existing unpaid credit of $875. Should the customer be allowed to charge the coat anyway, or should the clerk adhere strictly to the credit limit? This ticklish question was turned over to Polina who, after quickly reviewing the customer's records, was able to grant the extra charge.

Computers on

CHAPTER

Although this seems like a system that works pretty well, Nordstrom recently converted the whole process to an expert system—a computer system in which the computer plays the role of expert. Why go to all that trouble and expense? Why not just stick with human experts? Well, there are problems with human experts. They are typically expensive, subject to biases and emotions, and they may even be inconsistent. Also, there have been occasions when experts have resigned or retired, leaving the company in a state of crisis. But the biggest problem is that the expertise of one individual is not readily available to multiple users at the same time. The computer, however, is ever present and just as available as the telephone.

When the new expert system was being developed at Nordstrom, computer specialists approached Polina to ask her how she made her decisions. Some experts cling to the notion that their decisions are based on instinct, some kind of gut reaction. Study always reveals, however, that their "instincts" are based on certain rules, possibly so embedded in their brains that the experts themselves are not even aware of them. Polina was able to articulate most of her procedures to the computer specialist. In the case of the customer buying the coat, the purchaser's records showed that she consistently paid her bill on time, that her average monthly balance was usually low, and that she had a good job. These insights, along with many other rules, became part of the new expert system.

What about Polina? Is she now out of a job? No. With the installation of the computerized system, her role as expert changed. She is now a consultant to the expert system, which needs constant updating and monitoring. Polina also has been assigned some management responsibilities and, generally, has a more interesting job than she had before.

the Cutting Edge

Artificial Intelligence, Expert Systems, Robotics, and Virtual Reality

Artificial Intelligence

Artificial intelligence (AI) is a field of study that explores how computers can be used for tasks that require the human characteristics of intelligence, imagination, and intuition. Computer scientists sometimes prefer a looser definition, calling AI the study of how to make computers do things that, at the present time, people can do better. The phrase "at the present time" is significant because artificial intelligence is an evolving science: As soon as a problem is solved, it is moved off the artificial intelligence agenda. A good example is the game of chess, once considered a mighty AI challenge. However, now that most computer chess programs can beat most human competitors, chess is no longer an object of study by AI scientists.

Today the term *artificial intelligence* is an umbrella expression that encompasses several subsets of interests (Figure 11-1):

- **Problem solving,** which covers a broad spectrum, from playing games to planning military strategy
- **Natural languages,** which involve a person—computer interface in unconstrained English language
- **Expert systems,** which present the computer as an expert on some particular topic
- **Robotics,** which endows computer-controlled machines with machine equivalents of vision, speech, and touch

Although considerable progress has been made in these sophisticated fields of study, success has not come easily. Before we examine current advances in these areas, let us pause to consider some moments in the development of artificial intelligence.

Early Mishaps

In the early days of artificial intelligence, scientists thought that the computer would experience something like an electronic childhood, in which it would gobble up the data in the world's libraries and then begin generating new wisdom. Few people talk like this today because the problem of simulating intelligence is far more complex than just stuffing facts into the computer. Facts are useless without the ability to interpret and learn from them.

One grand failure of artificial intelligence was the attempt to translate human languages via computer. Although scientists were able to pour vocabulary and rules of grammar into the machine, the literal word-for-word translations the machine produced were often ludicrous. In one infamous example, the computer was supposed to demonstrate its prowess by translating a phrase from English to Russian and then back to English. Despite the computer's best efforts, the phrase "The spirit is willing, but the flesh is weak" came back as "The vodka is good, but the meat is spoiled."

An unfortunate result of this widely published experiment was the ridicule of artificial intelligence scientists; they were considered dreamers who could not accept the limitations of a machine. Funding for AI research disappeared, plunging the artificial intelligence community into a slump from which it did not recover until expert systems emerged in

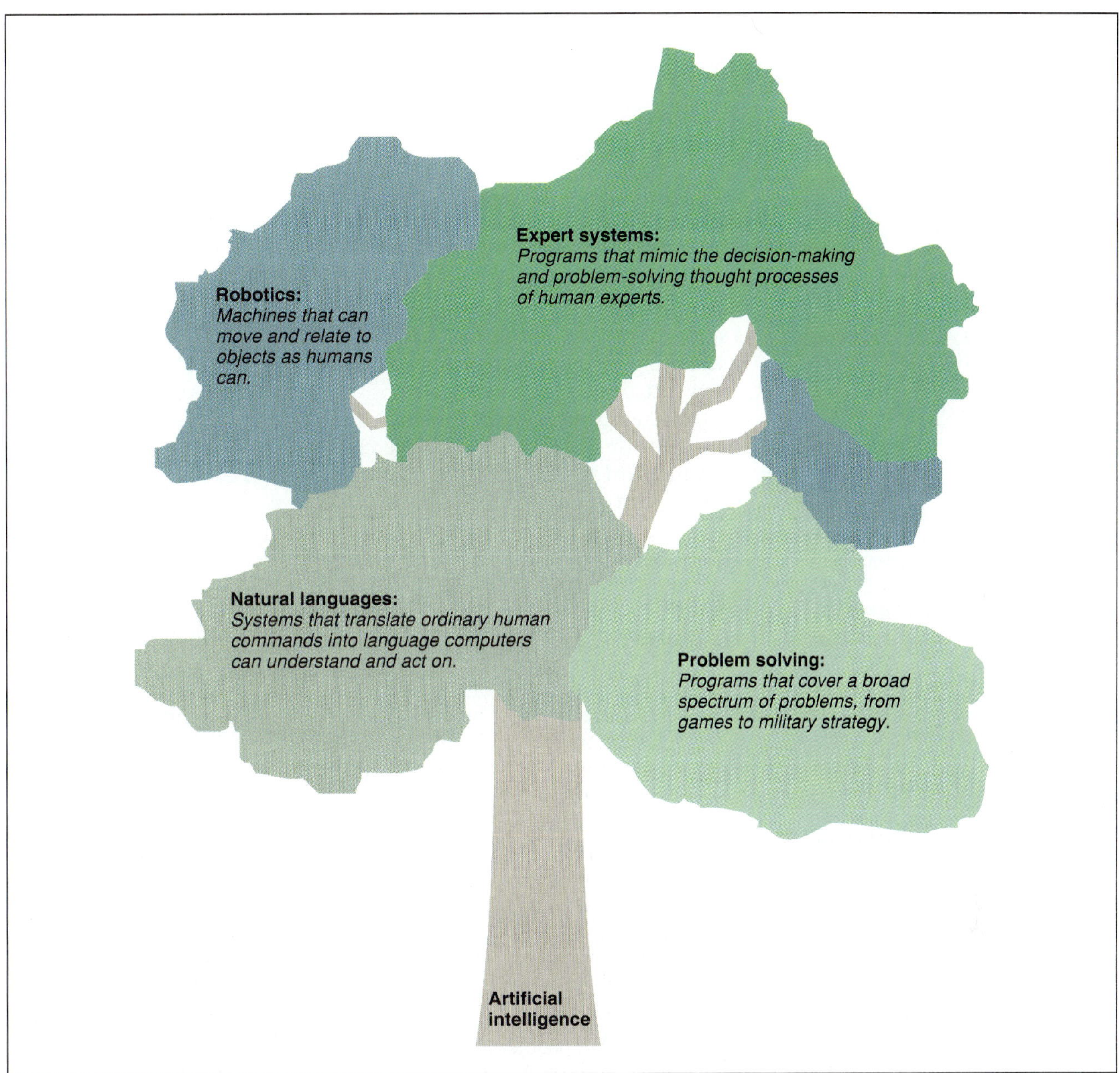

Figure 11-1 The artificial intelligence family tree.

the 1980s. Nevertheless, a hardy band of scientists continued to explore artificial intelligence, focusing on how computers learn.

How Computers Learn

The study of artificial intelligence is predicated on the computer's ability to learn and to improve performance based on past errors. One approach uses the two key elements called the knowledge base and the inference engine. A **knowledge base** is a set of facts and a corresponding set of rules about those facts. An **inference engine** accesses, selects, and inter-

Eliza

In the 1960s a computer scientist named Joseph Weizenbaum wrote a little program as an experiment in natural language. He named the program after Eliza Doolittle, the character in *My Fair Lady* who wanted to learn to speak proper English. The software allows the computer to act as a benign therapist who does not talk much but, instead, encourages the patient—the computer user—to talk.

The Eliza software has a storehouse of key phrases that the user's input triggers. For example, if a patient types "My mother never liked me," the software—cued by the word *mother*—can respond, "Tell me more about your family." If the patient's input does not contain a word the software can respond to directly, the computer responds neutrally with a phrase such as "I see" or "That's very interesting" or "Why do you think that?" If a patient gives yes or no answers, the computer may respond, "I prefer complete sentences." With party tricks like these, the program is able to move along quite nimbly from line to line.

Weizenbaum was astonished to discover that people were taking his little program seriously, pouring out their hearts to the computer. In fact, what he viewed as misuse of the computer radicalized Weizenbaum, who spent the next several years giving speeches and writing articles against artificial intelligence.

prets a set of rules. The inference engine applies the rules to the facts to make up new facts—thus, the computer has learned something new. Consider this simple example:

Fact: Kim is Hiroshi's wife.

Rule: If X is Y's wife, then Y is X's husband.

The computer—the inference engine—can apply the rule to the fact and come up with a new fact: Hiroshi is Kim's husband. Although the result of this simplistic example may seem of little value, it is indeed true that the computer now knows two facts instead of just one. Rules, of course, can be much more complex and facts more plentiful, yielding more sophisticated results. In fact, artificial intelligence software is capable of searching through long chains of related facts to reach a conclusion—a new fact.

Further explanation of the precise way computers learn is beyond the scope of this book. However, we can use the learning discussion as a springboard to the question that most people ask about artificial intelligence: Can a computer really think?

The Artificial Intelligence Debate

To imitate the human mind, a machine must be able to examine a variety of facts, address multiple subjects, and devise a solution to a problem by comparing new facts to its existing storehouse of data from many fields. So far, artificial intelligence systems cannot match a person's ability to solve problems through original thought instead of familiar patterns.

There are many arguments for and against crediting computers with the ability to think. Some say, for example, that computers cannot be considered intelligent because they do not compose like Beethoven or write like Shakespeare; the rejoinder is that neither do most ordinary human musicians or writers. You do not have to be a genius to be considered intelligent.

Look at it another way. Suppose you rack your brain over a problem, and then—Aha!—the solution comes to you all at once. Now, how did you do that? You do not know, and nobody else knows either. A big part of human problem solving seems to be that jolt of recognition, that ability to see things suddenly as a whole. Experiments have shown that people rarely solve problems by using step-by-step logic, the very thing that computers do best. Most modern computers still plod through problems one step at a time. The human brain beats a computer at the "Aha!" type of problem solving because the brain has millions of neurons working simultaneously. Now some scientists are taking that same approach with computers, in the form of neural networks.

Brainpower: Neural Networks

A microprocessor chip is sometimes referred to as the "brain" of a computer. However, a computer has not yet come close to matching the human brain, which has trillions of connections between billions of neurons. What is more, the most sophisticated conventional computer does not "learn" the same way the human brain learns. To understand this, let us consider an unconventional computer, one whose chips are actually

COMPUTING TRENDS

My Computer Life: The New Revolution

A compelling trend today is the availability of computer technology in most phases of everyday life. Here are some samples:

- **Couch potato bliss.** Video on demand means that a cable user can select a movie from the TV screen index. Unseen, the request is relayed to a central location where a robotic arm plucks the tape that holds the film from archival storage and feeds it to a disk drive, from which it travels back to your home screen.
- **The new yellow pages.** Your networked computer gives you fingertip access to buying books, gifts, clothing, music and videos, and so much more.
- **See and hear.** The multimedia arena offers sight and sound on an ever-broadening array of topics. Self-education at home is more dramatic than at any time in history.
- **Handy information.** Missed the news? Interested in the progress of a specific bill before Congress? Need quick medical or legal information? All this and more is as close as your connected computer.
- **Pocket communicator.** Part phone, part computer, your go-everywhere device—a personal digital assistant or possibly something even smaller—can alert you to appointments, store phone numbers and notes, send faxes, call your home or office computer, link up to electronic mail, and accept input in your own handwriting or by voice command.
- **ID card.** Wallet too fat? It will soon be much slimmer, as you use just a few chip-based cards for identification, credit, health care, membership, voting, work access, and more.
- **Automated house.** You will maintain computer control over house functions such as lighting, heating, air conditioning, and even cooking.
- **Virtual entertainment.** In the not-too-distant future, you will be able to don a head-mounted display and simulate rock and roll, country line dancing, or your choice of entertainment.

designed to mimic the human brain. These computers are called **neural networks,** or simply neural nets.

If a computer is to function more like the human brain and less like an overgrown calculator, it must be able to experiment and to learn from its mistakes. Researchers are developing computers with a few thousand brain-like connections that form a grid, much like a nerve cell in the brain. The grid enables the computer to recognize patterns rather than simply follow step-by-step instructions. For instance, a neural network with optical sensors could be "trained" to recognize the letter *A*. At best, today's neural networks consist of only a few thousand connections—still a far cry from the billions found in the human brain.

Meanwhile, scientists are getting rather good at developing related areas of artificial intelligence. We will focus on some of the more visible results of recent research in natural languages, expert systems, and robotics.

The Natural Language Factor

The language people use on a daily basis to write and speak is called a **natural language.** Natural languages are associated with artificial intelligence because humans can make the best use of artificial intelligence if they can communicate with the computer in their own language. Furthermore, understanding natural language is a skill thought to require intelligence.

Some natural language words—such as *horse*, *chair*, and *mountain*—are easy to understand because they represent a definable item. Other words, however—such as *justice*, *virtue*, *beauty*—are much too abstract to lend themselves to straightforward definitions. However, abstractness is just the beginning. Consider the word *hand* in these statements:

Raoul had a hand in the robbery.

Raoul had a hand in the cookie jar.

Raoul is an old hand at chess.

Raoul gave Kevin a hand with his luggage.

Raoul asked Laurie for her hand in marriage.

All hands on deck!

Look, Ma! No hands!

The word *hand* has a different meaning in each statement. So you can see that natural language abounds with inconsistency. In contrast, sometimes statements that appear to be different really mean the same thing, as in the following:

Denzel sold Kelly a pen for two dollars.

Kelly bought a pen for two dollars from Denzel.

Kelly gave Denzel two dollars in exchange for a pen.

The pen that Kelly bought from Denzel cost two dollars.

It takes very sophisticated software (not to mention enormous computer memory) to unravel all these statements and see them as equivalent. A key function of the AI study of natural languages is to develop a computer system that can resolve such problems.

Feeding computers the vocabulary and grammatical rules they need to know is a step in the right direction. However, as we saw earlier in regard to the language translation fiasco, true understanding requires more: Words must be taken in context. Humans begin acquiring a context for words from the day they are born. Consider the statement "Jack cried when Alice said she loved Pedro." From our own context, we could draw several possible conclusions: Jack is sad, Jack probably loves Alice, Jack probably thinks Alice does not love him, and so on. These conclusions may not be correct, but they are reasonable interpretations based on the context we supply. On the other hand, it would *not* be reasonable to conclude from the statement that Jack is a flight attendant or that Alice has a new refrigerator.

One of the most frustrating tasks for AI scientists is providing the computer with context. Scientists have attempted to do this on specific subjects and found the task daunting. For example, a computer scientist who wrote software so the computer could have a dialogue about restaurants had to feed the computer hundreds of facts that any small child would know, such as the fact that restaurants serve food and that you are expected to pay for it.

A less formidable task is to give a computer enough information to answer specific questions on a given topic. For instance, a stockbroker's computer does not need to know what a stock is, only if associated numbers indicate it is time to buy or sell. Such systems, which are categorized in a subset of artificial intelligence, are called expert systems.

Expert Systems

An **expert system** is software used with an extensive set of organized data that presents the computer as an expert on a particular topic. For example, a computer could be an expert on where to drill oil wells, what stock purchase looks promising, or how to cook soufflés. The user is the knowledge seeker, usually asking questions in a natural—that is, English-like—language format. An expert system can respond to an inquiry about a problem with both an answer and an explanation of the answer. The expert system works by figuring out what the question means and then matching it against the facts and rules that it "knows" (Figure 11-2). These facts and rules, which reside on disk, originally come from a human expert.

Expert Systems in Business

For years, expert systems were no more than bold experiments found only within the medical and scientific communities. These special programs could offer medical diagnoses, search for mineral deposits, or examine chemical compounds. In the early 1980s expert systems began to make their way into commercial applications. Today expert systems are slowly finding their place in big business. Consider these examples:

- Factory workers at The Boeing Company use an expert system to assemble electrical connectors for airplanes. In the old days workers had to hunt through 20,000 pages of cross-referenced specifications to find the right parts, tools, and techniques for the job—approximately 42 minutes per search. The expert system lets them do the same thing in about 5 minutes.

Figure 11-2 An expert system on the job. This expert system helps Ford mechanics track down and fix engine problems.

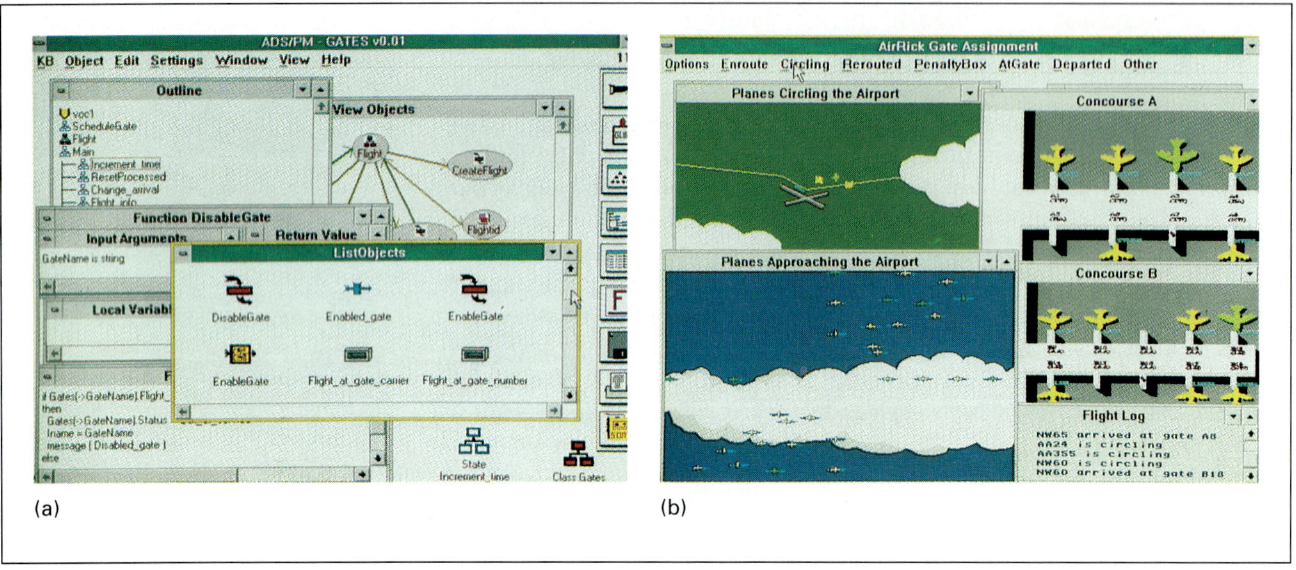

Figure 11-3 Airline-scheduling program produced with the aid of an expert system. This system offers a graphical user interface to help solve a complex airport-scheduling problem. (a) This screen illustrates the system's ability to display multiple views of objects in the knowledge-based system and the relationships between them. (b) Various screen windows show planes circling the airport, the number of planes circling the airport, gate information, and two concourses with planes at their gates.

- Employees at Coopers & Lybrand, a Big Eight accounting firm, use an expert system called ExperTax, which makes the knowledge of tax experts available to financial planners. The knowledge is, in fact, as close as their computers.
- About 400 flights per day land or take off from one of the 50 gates at the United Airlines terminal at O'Hare Airport in Chicago. Factors that complicate routing the traffic include the limitations of jumbo jets (which do not maneuver easily into some gates), weather, and heavy runway use, which can affect how quickly planes can get in and out. Airline employees used to track planes on a gigantic magnetic board. Now they keep track of gate assignments with an expert system that takes all factors into account (Figure 11-3).

The cost of an expert system can usually be justified in situations where there are few experts but great demand for knowledge. An expert system can be especially worthwhile where there is no margin for human failings, such as fatigue, stress, or sickness.

Building an Expert System

Some organizations choose to build their own expert systems to perform well-focused tasks that can easily be crystallized into rules. A simple example is a set of rules for a banker to use when making decisions about whether to extend credit. Very few organizations are capable of building an expert system from scratch. The sensible alternative is to buy an **expert shell**—a software package that consists of the basic structure used to find answers to questions. It is up to the buyer to fill in the actual

Personal Computers In Action

Robot Tales

Like computers before them, robots will soon be everywhere. Here are some examples.

- **My doctor the robot.** If you have orthopedic surgery, you may find that a key player alongside the surgeon is a robot. For example, to make room for a hip implant, a robotic arm drills a long hole in a thigh bone. Robotic precision improves the implant, reduces pain after surgery, and speeds healing.
- **Lending a hand.** Robots may soon be of significant use to the disabled. Researchers have already developed a robot for quadriplegics. The machine can respond to dozens of voice commands by answering the door, getting the mail, serving soup, or performing other tasks.
- **Road maintenance.** In California, road signs may soon say "Robots at Work." Robots use lasers to spot cracks in the pavement and dispense the right amount of patch material. Soon robots will also be painting the road stripes.
- **Robots making computers.** It seems most fitting that robots should be hard at work in factories that manufacture computers—and indeed they are. For example, in an IBM assembly plant, robots place memory boards inside computers, mount disk drives, screw in power supplies, and more.
- **Robots on display.** If you care to see robots in the workplace, here is your chance. At the General Motors manufacturing plant in Flint, Michigan, 216 state-of-the-art robots labor side-by-side with their human coworkers on an assembly line. One of the most advanced robots places car seats on a conveyor belt, using its electronic eye to match each seat with the appropriate car model. Tours are available for the public every Tuesday and Thursday.

- **Homer Hoover (see photo).** Robots as vacuum cleaners have always been the ultimate robot joke, but now we can stop laughing. A robot is being developed that can "see" its way around the house, vacuuming as it goes and carefully avoiding sucking up the cat.

knowledge on the chosen subject. You could think of the expert shell as an empty cup that becomes a new entity once it is filled—a cup of coffee, for instance, or a cup of apple juice.

In many cases the most challenging task of building an expert system is deciding who the appropriate experts are and then trying to pin down their knowledge. The person ferreting out the information, sometimes called a **knowledge engineer,** must have a keen awareness and the skills of a diplomat. Sometimes cameras and tapes are used to observe the expert in action.

Once the rules are uncovered, they are formed into a set of IF-THEN rules, which will probably run into hundreds or even thousands. Here is an example: IF the customer has exceeded a credit limit by no more than 20 percent and has paid the monthly bill for six months, THEN extend further credit. After the system is translated into a computerized version, it is reviewed, changed, tested, and changed some more. This repetitive process of revision could take months or even years. Finally, it is put into the same situations the human expert would face, where it should give equal or better service but much more quickly.

Robotics

Many people smile at the thought of robots, perhaps remembering the endearing R2D2 of *Star Wars* fame and its "personal" relationship with humans. But vendors have not made even a small dent in the personal robot market—the much-heralded domestic robots have yet to materialize. So, where are robots today? Mainly in factories.

Robots in the Factory

Most robots are in factories, spray-painting, welding, and assembling parts. The Census Bureau, after two centuries of counting people, has branched out and today is counting robots. About 15,000 robots existed in 1985, and double that number in 1990. What do robots do that merits all this attention?

A loose definition of *robot* is a type of automation that replaces human presence. A **robot** is more formally defined as a computer-controlled device that can physically manipulate its surroundings. Some robots, as we will see, can also manipulate themselves. Robots vary greatly in size and shape; each design is created with a particular use in mind. Often, a robot's job is a function that would be tedious or even dangerous for a human to perform. The most common industrial robots sold today are mechanical devices with five or six axes of motion so the machines can rotate into proper position to perform their tasks (Figure 11-4).

Figure 11-4 Industrial robots.
(a) These standard robots are used in the auto industry to spray-paint new cars. (b) This robot is not making breakfast. Hitachi uses the delicate egg, however, to demonstrate that its visual-tactile robot can handle fragile objects. Its sensors detect size, shape, and required pressure, attaining sensitivity almost equal to that of a human hand.

(a)

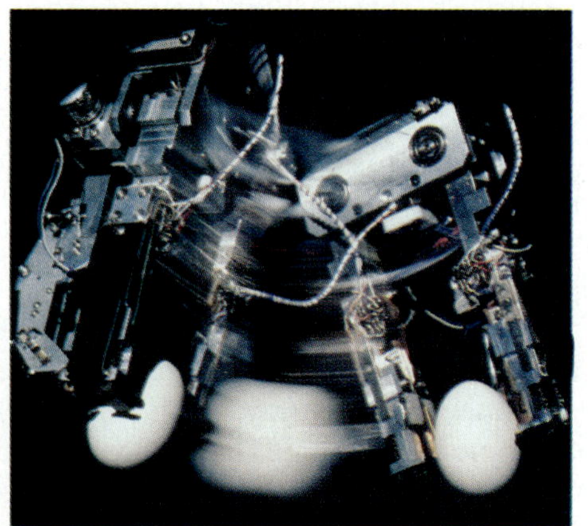

(b)

Color Graphics

Computers at their Best

Computer Art

The screen that opens this gallery was produced by photo imaging, a process that uses the computer to combine photos and sometimes artwork. The photos must first be scanned into the computer, where they can then be manipulated by the artist. Here, photos were added to artwork to produce a "message" computer graphic called *Car Crash*.

On these two pages we will recognize the artists by name.

1. Marc Yankus named this rendering *Pilgrim Road.*
2, 3, 4. These three abstract works were produced by Gregory MacNicol.
5. Bill Frymire won first prize in the annual Corel Draw (a software package) contest with this work.
6. John Fitzgerald leaves this scene untitled.
7. Joseph Maas developed a series of works based on what he calls *Glass Avenue.* This one is *Glass Avenue at Dusk.*

1

2

3

4

5

6

7

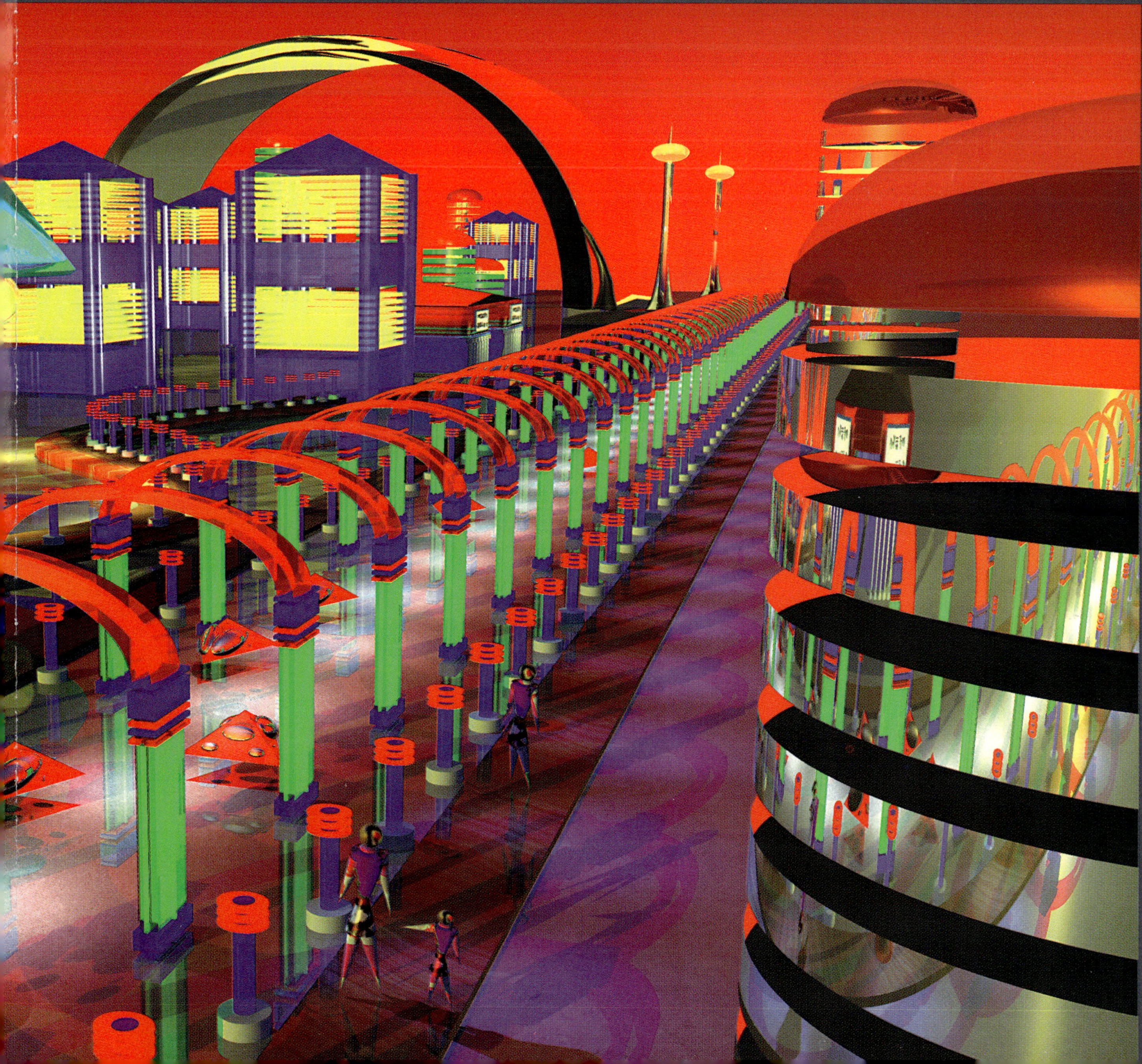

8

Whimsy and Imagination

The works assembled on these pages were chosen because they so clearly show the unfettered imaginations of the various artists.

8. Artist Tom Cushaw figuratively looks out the window.
9. Greg Buchman made this presentation of a ship sailing in a thunderstorm.
10. Steve Lyons won a prize for his version of *Horse Man.*
11. Called *Key Note,* this was produced by Joseph Maas.

9

10

11

12

12. Artist Lilla Rogers calls this bright montage *Red Bull on Big Red*.
13. This rendition of the letter A is just the first of a set of 26 letters.
14. As is often the case with artworks on canvas, this is untitled.
15, 16, 17. These screens were all created by Marc Yankus.

13

14

15

16

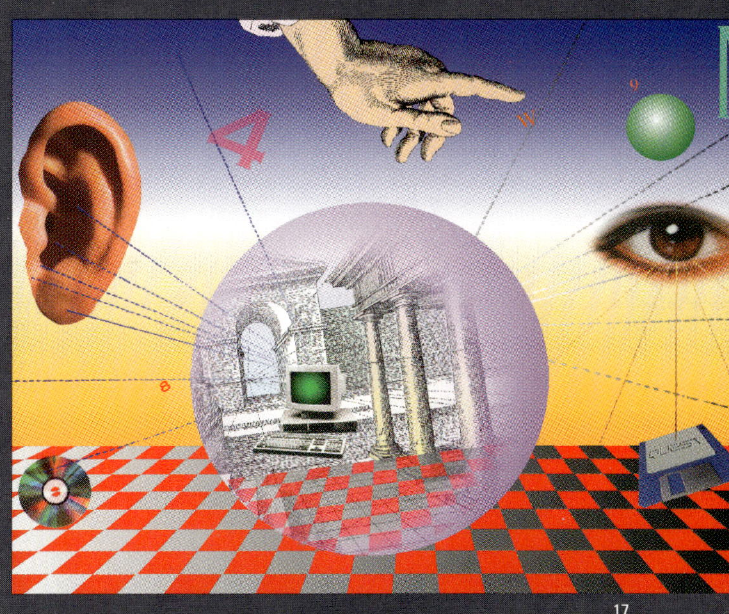

17

Commercial Applications

Whether the colorful work before your eyes is in a magazine, on a poster, or on television, chances are that it was created on a computer by a computer graphic artist. Here are some samples of their work.

18. This poster was created for the Miami Dolphins professional football team.
19. This design was created for the cover of *Art Direction* magazine.
20. This poster was designed to entice travelers to visit Venice.
21. A graphic artist has used his talents to advertise his own wares, proclaiming that his clients will be a "big fish" in his "small pond."
22. In a process called morphing, the computer is used to give the appearance of converting one photo to another. Here, Exxon wants to show the world what happens when you put a "tiger in the tank."
23. This simple but bright graphic is effective for selling Colgate toothbrushes.
24. A dramatic Academy Awards screen is prepared for the annual presentation.
25. This logo mock-up demonstrates the kinds of graphics available to foundations.
26. A graphic artist used a credit-card theme for the cover of a corporate annual report.

18

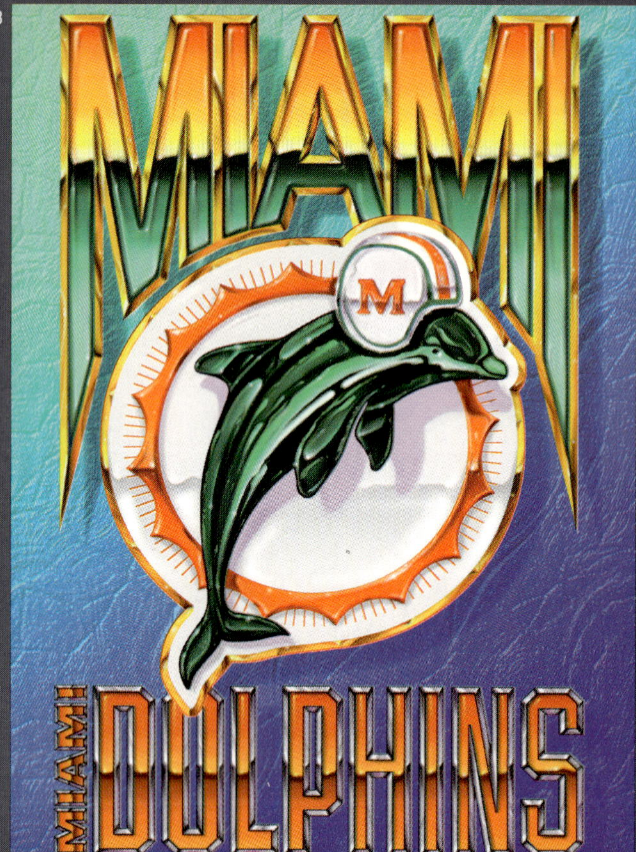

19

20

21

22

Colgate PRECISION

23

65TH
ANNUAL
ACADEMY
AWARDS

24

FOUNDATIONS
FOR THE
F·U·T·U·R·E

25

AT&T
Universal
VISA
MasterCard
AT&T

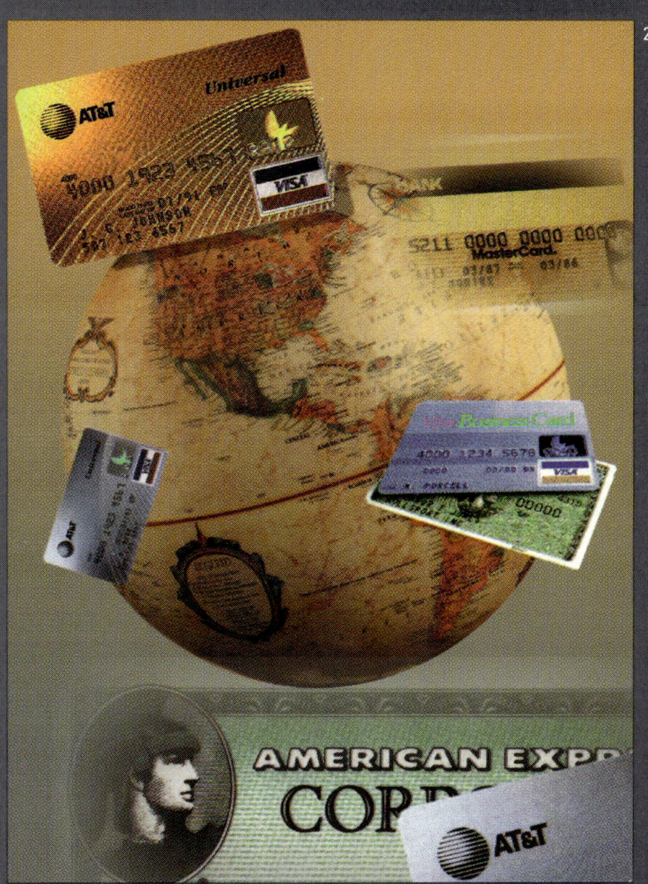

26

27

28

Photo Imaging

The opening gallery screen showed photos appended to computer-generated artwork. The works on this page show what can be done with photos alone. Begin with **27,** a photo of a building interior. Then consider **28,** which shows photos of strolling tourists, a statue, and a painting. These four photos have been scanned into the computer and manipulated to become **29,** a museum with artworks and tourists to view them. Note, in particular, the adjusted shape of the painting and the computer artist's addition of clouds in the skylight.

30. Here is the intriguing result of computer imaging four photos. The original photos were of trees, a sunset, a swan, and a red world logo.

31. The artist has produced various computer-manipulated versions of an original photo of a child.

29

30

31

(a)

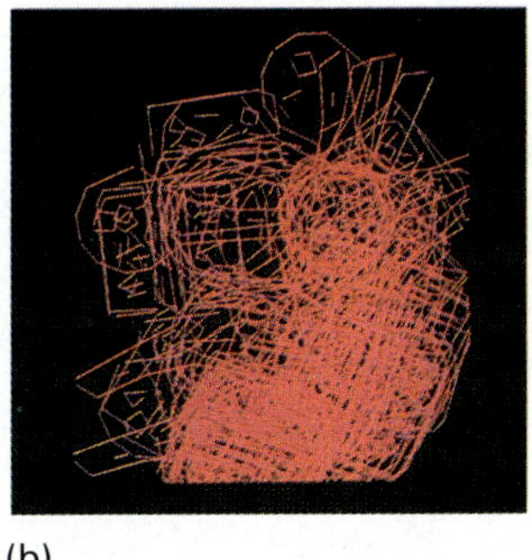
(b)

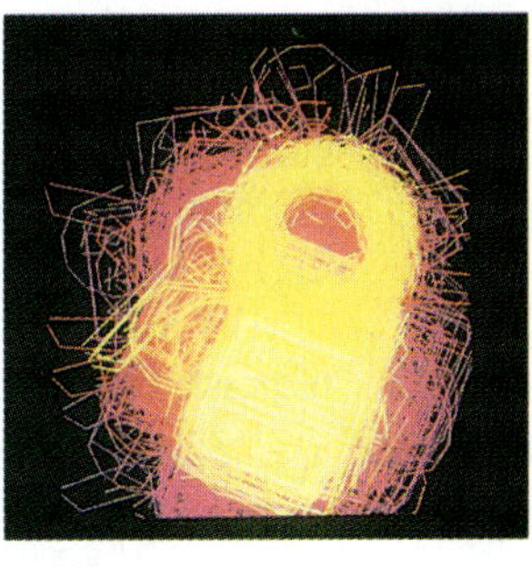
(c)

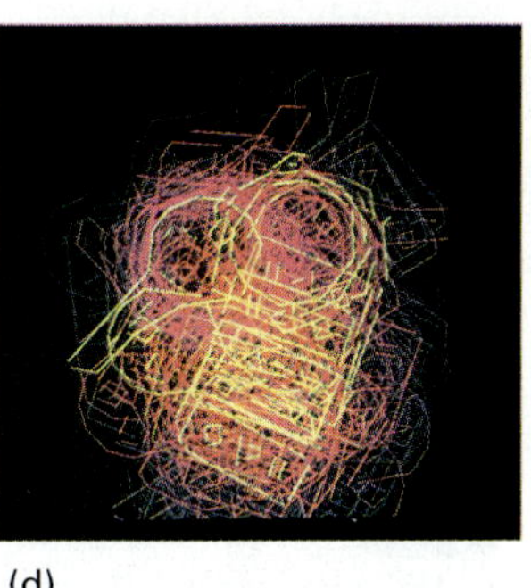
(d)

Figure 11-5 The seeing robot.
Robots "see" by casting light beams on objects and identifying them by matching their shapes to those of "known" objects. In this machine-vision sequence, (a) objects are seen by the robot, (b) the objects are matched to known shapes, (c) inappropriate shapes are eliminated, and (d) the objects are recognized.

We mentioned spray-painting and welding as jobs for robots. Robots that can perform these kinds of repetitive tasks are merely "dumb" robots. A more intelligent robot can adapt to changing circumstances. For example, with the help of a TV-camera eye, a robot can "see" components it is meant to assemble. It is able to pick them up, rearrange them in the right order, or place them in the right position before assembling them.

Robot Vision

Vision robots have been taught to see in living color—that is, they can recognize multicolored objects solely from their colors. This is a departure from the traditional approach, whereby robots recognized objects by their shapes (Figure 11-5) and from vision machines that see a dominant color only. For example, a robot in an experiment at the University of Rochester was able to pick out a box of Kellogg's Sugar Frosted Flakes from 70 other cereal boxes. Among the anticipated benefits of such visual recognition skills is faster supermarket checkout. You cannot easily barcode a squash, but a robot might be trained to recognize it by its size, shape, and color.

Field Robots

Just think of some of the places you would rather not be: inside a nuclear power plant, next to a suspected bomb, at the bottom of the sea, or in the middle of a chemical spill. Robots readily go all those places. Furthermore, they go there to do some dangerous and dirty jobs. These days robots "in the field"—called **field robots**—inspect and repair nuclear power plants, dispose of bombs, inspect oil rigs for undersea exploration, clean up chemical accidents, and much more. Space researchers look forward to the day when "astrobots" can be stationed in orbit, ready to repair faulty satellites.

Only a few years ago, there were just a handful of field robots commercially employed. Now there are thousands. Field robots may be equipped with wheels, tracks, legs, fins, or even wings (Figure 11-6).

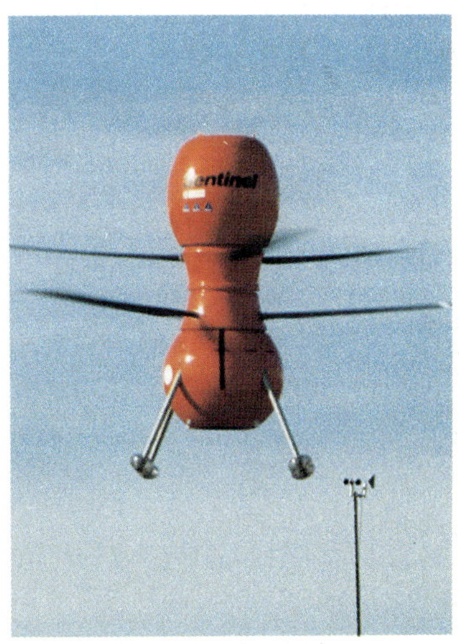

Figure 11-6 Flying robot.
Can a robot really fly? Yes. Flying robots have both military and civilian uses. This Sentinel robot can soar up to 10,000 feet to spy on an enemy or to inspect high-voltage wires or spot forest fires.

Commuting Is Getting Easier All the Time

How would you like to sit in the passenger seat reading the paper, or even in the back seat catching a few extra winks, while your car drives itself from your house to work? Yes, that's right: no human driver. Working models of this robotic car already exist.

It works this way. The on-board computer "learns to drive" by mimicking human drivers and matching what it sees through its electronic eyes. If the road curves to the left and the driver thus turns to the left, the computer learns to do the same thing. So far, the model car (a converted Army Humvee) does well on main roads, even in rainstorms. But it still gets lost and confused on off-the-road jaunts.

Enough computer power can be packed into a field robot to enable it to make most decisions independently. Field robots need all the power they can get. Unlike factory robots, which are bolted to the ground and do the same tasks over and over again, field robots must often contend with highly unstructured environments.

Although robots seem sophisticated, they cannot do many of the simple tasks that humans can do. Robots cannot yet tie shoelaces.

Virtual Reality

The concept of **virtual reality** is to immerse a user in a computer-created environment, so that the user physically interacts with the computer. This is made possible by sophisticated computers and optics that deliver to a user's eyes a three-dimensional scene in living color, complete with motion. The user's body movements can cause interaction with the virtual (artificial) world the user sees, and the computer-generated world responds to those actions. Sensors on the user's body send signals to the computer, which then adjusts the scene viewed by the user.

Travel Anywhere, But Stay Where You Are

At the University of North Carolina, computer scientists have developed a virtual reality program that lets a user walk through an art gallery. A user puts on a head-mounted display that focuses the eyes on a screen and shuts out the rest of the world. If the user swivels his head right, pictures on the right wall come in to view; similarly, the user can view any part of the gallery by just making head movements. This action/reaction presents realistic continuing changes to the user. Although actually standing in one place, the user feels as if he or she is moving and then must stop short as a pedestal appears in the path ahead. It is as if the user is actually walking around inside the gallery.

In another example scientists have taken data about Mars, sent back by space probes, and converted it to a virtual reality program. Information about hills, rocks, and ridges of the planet are used to create a Mars landscape, whose images are projected on the user's head screen.

Getting Practical

An embryonic technology such as virtual reality is filled with hype and promises. We must look to the practical commercial applications for real-world users to see where this technology might lead. Some applications under development include the following:

- Wearing a head-mounted display, consumers can browse for products in a "virtual showroom." From a remote location a consumer will be able to maneuver and view products along rows in a warehouse.
- Similarly, from a convenient office perch, a security guard can patrol corridors and offices in remote locations.
- Air traffic controllers may someday work like this: Microlaser scanner glasses project computer-generated images directly into the controller's eyes, immersing the controller in a three-dimensional scene

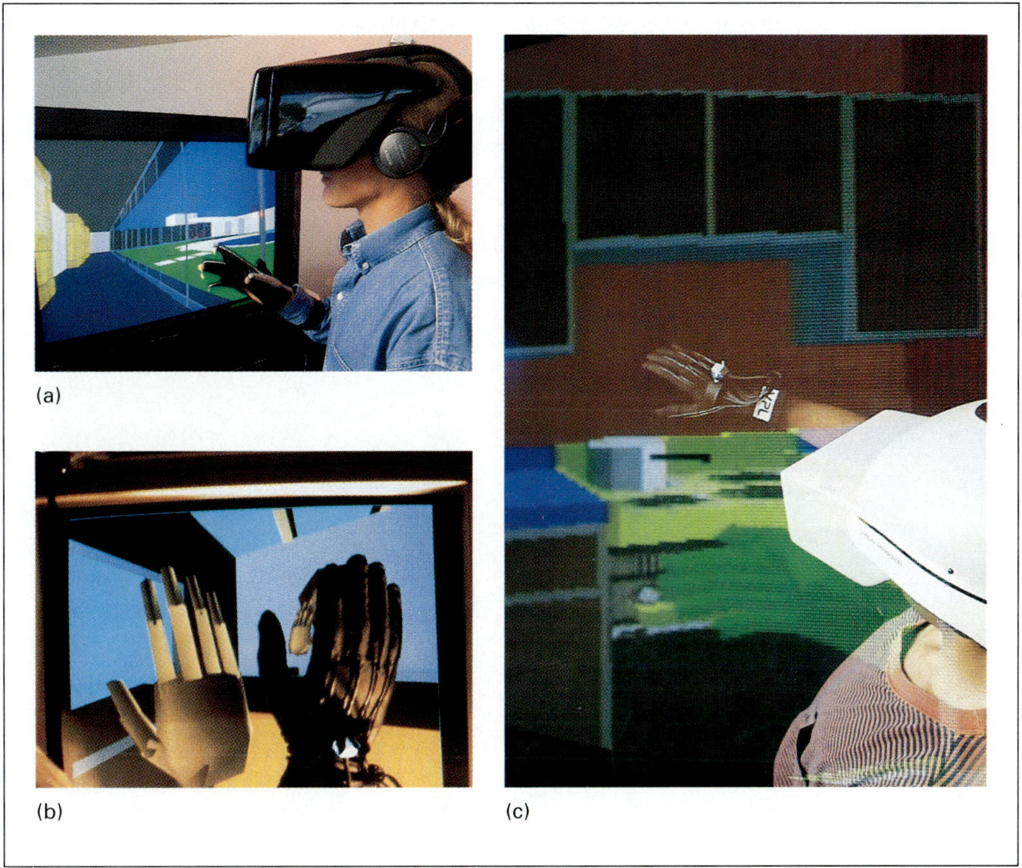

Figure 11-7 Virtual reality.
(a) Users can "tour" a building by physically reacting—a turn of the head shows a different scene. (b) The data glove in the foreground has fiber optic sensors to interact with a computer-generated world. (c) Virtual reality technology can be used to let people who are in wheelchairs design their own apartments.

showing all the aircraft in the area. To establish voice contact with the pilot of the plane, the controller merely touches the plane's image with a sensor-equipped glove (Figure 11-7).

- Using virtual reality headsets and gloves, doctors and medical students will be able to experiment with new procedures on simulated patients rather than real ones.

Any new technology has its drawbacks. In addition to rather clumsy physical equipment, today's virtual reality pioneers are faced with daunting costs. Many hurdles remain in the areas of software, hardware, and even human behavior before virtual reality can reach its full potential.

The immediate prospect for expert systems and robots is growth and more growth. We can anticipate both increased sophistication and more diverse applications. The progress in the more esoteric applications of artificial intelligence will continue to be relatively slow. No one need worry just yet that any computer can capture the wide-ranging sophistication of the human mind.

However, even today computer professionals must sometimes convince people that computers cannot "take over." Will intensified publicity about intelligent computers and robots revive these concerns? If so, the answer remains the same: People are in charge of computers, not the other way around.

Chapter **Review**

Summary and Key Terms

- **Artificial intelligence** (**AI**) is a field of study that explores how computers can be used for tasks that require the human characteristics of intelligence, imagination, and intuition. AI has also been described as the study of how to make computers do things that, at the present time, people can do better.
- *Artificial intelligence* is considered an umbrella term to encompass several subsets of interests, including problem solving, natural languages, expert systems, and robotics.
- In the early days of AI, scientists thought it would be useful just to stuff facts into a computer; however, facts are useless without the ability to interpret and learn from them.
- An early attempt to translate human languages via a computer using vocabulary and rules of grammar was a failure because the machine could not interpret context. This failure impeded the progress of artificial intelligence.
- Artificial intelligence applications are predicated on the computer's ability to learn—in particular, to improve performance based on past errors.
- A **knowledge base** is a set of facts and a corresponding set of rules about those facts. An **inference engine** accesses, selects, and interprets a set of rules. The inference engine applies rules to the facts to make up new facts.
- People rarely solve problems by using the step-by-step logic used by most computers. The brain usually beats computers at solving problems, because it has millions of neurons working simultaneously.
- Computers whose chips are designed to mimic the human brain are called **neural networks**.
- **Natural language**—the language people use on a daily basis to write and speak—is associated with artificial intelligence because humans can make the best use of artificial intelligence if they can communicate with the computer in their own language. Furthermore, understanding natural language is a skill thought to require intelligence.
- A key function of the AI study of natural languages is to develop a computer system that can resolve linguistic ambiguities.
- An **expert system** is software used with an extensive set of organized data that presents the computer as an expert on a specific topic. The expert system works by figuring out what the question means and then matching it against the facts and rules that it "knows."
- For years, expert systems were the exclusive property of the medical and scientific communities, but in the early 1980s they began to make their way into commercial applications.
- Some users buy an **expert shell**—a software package that consists of the basic structure used to find answers to questions. It is up to the buyer to fill in the actual knowledge on the chosen subject.
- A person working to obtain information from a human expert is sometimes called a **knowledge engineer.**
- A **robot** is a computer-controlled device that can physically manipulate its surroundings. Most robots are in factories.
- **Vision robots** recognize objects by their shapes or colors.
- **Field robots** do jobs in environments that are too dangerous or unpleasant for humans.
- **Virtual reality** immerses a user in a computer-created environment, so that the user physically interacts with the computer-produced three-dimensional scene.

Student Personal Study Guide

True/False

T F 1. An expert shell presents the computer as an expert on a specific topic.
T F 2. A human expert usually explains decision making to the robot replacement.
T F 3. Field robots are used mostly for farm assistance.
T F 4. Artificial intelligence is a broad field of study.
T F 5. An expert system is hardware that is an expert on some topic.
T F 6. Artificial intelligence software can rely on vocabulary and rules of grammar for language translation.
T F 7. Artificial intelligence is predicated on the computer's ability to produce knowledge it is given.
T F 8. A robot is computer-controlled.
T F 9. Natural language ambiguities have largely been solved.
T F 10. An inference engine is part of an expert system.

Multiple Choice

1. Computers whose chips are designed to mimic the human brain:
   a. neural nets | c. expert systems
   b. inference engines | d. AI
2. The person who extracts information from a human expert:
   a. system manager | c. system expert
   b. expert robot | d. knowledge engineer
3. Which is *not* a subset of artificial intelligence?
   a. chess | c. natural language
   b. robotics | d. expert systems
4. A robot that can recognize shapes and colors:
   a. vision robot | c. field robot
   b. knowledge robot | d. labor robot
5. A software package with which to build an expert system:
   a. expert shell | c. word processing
   b. neural network | d. natural language
6. A computer-controlled device that can manipulate its surroundings:
   a. expert system | c. inference engine
   b. robot | d. knowledge engineer
7. A robot that must react to changing surroundings:
   a. vision robot | c. field robot
   b. knowledge robot | d. labor robot
8. A set of facts and rules about these facts:
   a. natural language | c. AI
   b. expert shell | d. knowledge base
9. Interaction with a computer-created 3-D environment:
   a. inference engine | c. vision robot
   b. knowledge base | d. virtual reality
10. Which is *not* related to neural networks?
   a. simultaneous operations | c. mimic the brain
   b. recognize patterns | d. step-by-step process

Fill-In

1. The person who extracts what a human expert knows: ____________________.
2. The language people use on a daily basis: ____________________.
3. The study of how computers can do human tasks: ____________________.
4. Software that presents the computer as an expert on a topic: ____________________.
5. Software that accesses, selects, and interprets rules: ____________________.
6. Software that offers the structure needed to find answers to questions:

   ____________________.
7. A robot that can inspect a nuclear power plant: ____________________.
8. A set of facts and rules for an expert system: ____________________.
9. Computers that mimic the human brain: ____________________.
10. A robot that recognizes an object by shape or color: ____________________.

Answers

True/False: 1. F, 2. F, 3. F, 4. T, 5. F, 6. F, 7. F, 8. T, 9. F, 10. T
Multiple choice: 1. a, 2. d , 3. a , 4. a, 5. a, 6. b, 7. c, 8. d, 9. d, 10. d
Fill-In: 1. knowledge engineer, 2. natural language, 3. artificial intelligence, 4. expert system, 5. inference engine, 6. expert shell, 7. field robot, 8. knowledge base, 9. neural networks, 10. vision robot

Appendix Overview

Although the story of computers has diverse roots, the most fascinating part—the history of personal computers—is quite recent. The beginning of this history turns on the personality of Ed Roberts, whose foundering company took a surprising turn. Ed had already been burned once when he had borrowed heavily to produce microprocessor-based calculators, only to have the chip producers decide to build their own product—and sell it for half the price of Ed's calculator.

History and

APPENDIX

Industry

The Continuing Story of the Computer Age

Ed's new product was based on a microprocessor too—the Intel 8080—but it was a *computer*—a little computer. The "big boys" at the established computer firms considered computers to be industrial products; who would want a small computer? Ed was not sure, but he found the idea compelling. Ed's small computer and his company, MITS, were given a sharp boost by Les Solomon, who promised to feature the new machine on the cover of *Popular Electronics*. In Albuquerque, New Mexico, Ed worked frantically to meet the publication deadline, and he even tried to make the machine pretty, so it would look attractive on the cover (Figure A-1).

Figure A-1 The Altair.
The term *personal computer* had not even been invented yet, so Ed Roberts's small computer was called a "minicomputer" when it was featured on the cover of *Popular Electronics*.

Making a good-looking small computer was not easy. This machine, named the Altair, looked like a flat box. In fact, it met the definition of a computer in only a minimal way: It had a central processing unit (on the chip), 256 characters (a paragraph!) of memory, and switches and lights on a front panel for input/output. No screen, no keyboard, no storage.

But the Altair was done on time for the January 1975 issue of *Popular Electronics,* and Ed made plans to fly to New York to demonstrate the machine for Solomon. He sent the computer on ahead by railroad express. Ed got to New York, but the computer did not—the very first personal computer was lost! There was no time to build a new computer before the publishing deadline, so Roberts cooked up a phony version for the cover picture: an empty box with switches and lights on the front panel. He also placed an inch-high ad in the back of the magazine: Get your own Altair kit for $397. Ed, hoping for perhaps 200 orders, was astonished when 2000 orders came in.

Ed Roberts was an important player in the history of personal computers. Unfortunately, he never made it in the big time; most observers agree that his business insight did not match his technical skills. But other entrepreneurs did make it. In this appendix we will glance briefly at the early years of computers and then examine more recent history.

Figure A-2 **Charles Babbage's difference engine.**
This shows a prototype model. Babbage attempted to build a working model, which was to have been several times larger and steam-driven, but he was unsuccessful.

Figure A-3 **The Countess of Lovelace.**
Augusta Ada Byron, as she was known before she became a countess, was Charles Babbage's colleague in his work on the analytical engine and has been called the world's first computer programmer.

Babbage and the Countess

Born in England in 1791, Charles Babbage was an inventor and mathematician. When solving certain equations, he found the hand-done mathematical tables he used filled with errors. He decided a machine could be built that would solve the equations better by calculating the differences between them. He set about making a demonstration model of what he called a **difference engine** (Figure A-2). The model was so well received that in about 1830 he enthusiastically began to build a full-scale working version, using a grant from the British government.

However, Babbage found that the smallest imperfections were enough to throw the machine out of whack. Babbage was viewed by his own colleagues as a man who was trying to manufacture a machine that was utterly ridiculous. Finally, after spending its money to no avail, the government withdrew financial support.

Despite this setback, Babbage was not discouraged. He conceived of another machine, christened the **analytical engine**, which he hoped would perform many kinds of calculations. This, too, was never built, at least by Babbage (a model was later put together by his son), but the analytical engine embodied five key features of modern computers:

- an input device
- a storage place to hold the number waiting to be processed
- a processor, or number calculator
- a control unit to direct the task to be performed and the sequence of calculations
- an output device

If Babbage was the father of the computer, then Ada, the Countess of Lovelace, was the first computer programmer (Figure A-3). The daughter of English poet Lord Byron and of a mother who was a gifted mathematician, Ada helped develop the instructions for doing computations on the analytical engine. Lady Lovelace's contributions cannot be overvalued. She was able to see that Babbage's theoretical approach was workable, and her interest gave him encouragement. In addition, she published a series of notes that eventually led others to accomplish what Babbage himself had been unable to do.

Herman Hollerith: The Census Has Never Been the Same

The hand-done tabulation of the 1880 United States census took seven and a half years. A competition was held to find some way to speed the counting process of the 1890 United States census. Herman Hollerith's tabulating machine won the contest. As a result of his system's adoption, an unofficial count of the 1890 population (62,622,250) was announced only six weeks after the census was taken.

The principal difference between Hollerith's and Babbage's machines was that Hollerith's machine used electrical rather than mechanical power (Figure A-4). Hollerith realized that his machine had considerable commercial potential. In 1896 he founded the successful Tabulating Machine Company, which, in 1924, merged with two other companies to form the International Business Machines Corporation—IBM.

Watson of IBM: Ornery But Rather Successful

For over 30 years, from 1924 to 1956, Thomas J. Watson, Sr., ruled IBM with an iron grip. Cantankerous and autocratic, supersalesman Watson made IBM a dominant force in the business machines market, first as a supplier of calculators and then as a developer of computers.

IBM's entry into computers was sparked by a young Harvard professor of mathematics, Howard Aiken. In 1936, after reading Lady Lovelace's notes, Aiken began to think that a modern equivalent of the analytical engine could be constructed. Because IBM was already such a power in the business machines market, with ample money and resources, Aiken worked out a careful proposal and approached Thomas Watson. In one of those make-or-break decisions for which he was famous, Watson gave him $1 million. As a result, a computer named the Mark I was born.

The Start of the Modern Era

Nothing like the **Mark I** had ever been built before. It was 8 feet high and 55 feet long, made of streamlined steel and glass, and it emitted a sound during processing that one person said was "like listening to a roomful of old ladies knitting away with steel needles." Unveiled in

The Computer Museum

The Computer Museum in downtown Boston, Massachusetts, is the world's first and only museum devoted solely to computers and computing. The museum illustrates how computers have affected all aspects of life: science, business, education, art, and entertainment. Over half an acre of hands-on and historical exhibits chronicle the enormous changes in the size, capability, applications, and cost of computers over the past 40 years. Two mini-theaters show computer classics as well as award-winning computer-animated films.

The Computer Museum Store offers a large selection of such unique items as state-of-the-art silicon chip jewelry and chocolate "chips" as well as books, posters, cassettes, and more.

Figure A-4 Herman Hollerith's tabulating machine.
This electrical tabulator and sorter was used to tabulate 1890 census data.

Figure A-5 The ABC.
John Atanasoff and his assistant, Clifford Berry, developed the first digital electronic computer, nicknamed the ABC for Atanasoff-Berry computer.

1944, the Mark I was never very efficient. But the enormous publicity it generated strengthened IBM's commitment to computer development. Meanwhile, technology had been proceeding elsewhere on separate tracks.

American military officials approached Dr. John Mauchly at the University of Pennsylvania and asked him to build a machine that would rapidly calculate trajectories for artillery and missiles. Mauchly and his student J. Presper Eckert relied on the work of Dr. John V. Atanasoff, a professor of physics at Iowa State University. During the late 1930s Atanasoff had spent time trying to build an electronic calculating device to help his students solve mathematical problems. He and an assistant, Clifford Berry, succeeded in building the first digital computer that worked electronically; they called it the **ABC,** for **Atanasoff-Berry Computer** (Figure A-5).

After Mauchly met with Atanasoff and Berry in 1941, he used the ABC as the basis for the next step in computer development. From this association ultimately came a lawsuit, based on attempts to get patents for a commercial version of the machine Mauchly built. The suit was finally decided in 1974, when a federal court determined that Atanasoff had been the true originator of the ideas required to make an electronic digital computer actually work. (Some computer historians dispute this court decision.) Mauchly and Eckert were able to use the principles of the ABC to create the **ENIAC,** for **Electronic Numerical Integrator and Calculator.** The main significance of the ENIAC is that, as the first general-purpose computer, it was the forerunner of the UNIVAC I, the first computer sold on a commercial basis.

The Computer Age Begins

The remarkable thing about the Computer Age is that so much has happened in so short a time. We have leapfrogged through four generations of technology in about 40 years—a span of time whose events are within the memories of many people today. The first three computer "generations" are pinned to three technological developments: the vacuum tube, the transistor, and the integrated circuit. Each has drastically changed the nature of computers. We define the timing of each generation according to the beginning of commercial delivery of the hardware technology. Defining subsequent generations has become more complicated because the entire industry has become more complicated.

The First Generation, 1951–1958: The Vacuum Tube

The beginning of the commercial Computer Age may be dated June 14, 1951. This was the date the first **UNIVAC,** or **Universal Automatic Computer,** was delivered to a client, the U.S. Bureau of the Census, for use in tabulating the previous year's census. The date also marked the first time that a computer had been built for business applications rather than for military, scientific, or engineering use. The UNIVAC was really the ENIAC in disguise and was, in fact, built by Mauchly and Eckert, who in 1947 had formed their own corporation.

In the first generation, **vacuum tubes**—electronic tubes about the size of light bulbs—were used as the internal computer components

(Figure A-6). However, because thousands of such tubes were required, they generated a great deal of heat, causing many problems in temperature regulation and climate control. In addition, although all the tubes had to be working simultaneously, they were subject to frequent burnout—and the people operating the computer often did not know whether the problem was in the programming or in the machine.

Another drawback was that the language used in programming was machine language, which uses numbers. (Present-day higher-level languages are more like English.) Using numbers alone made programming the computer difficult and time-consuming. The UNIVAC used **magnetic cores** to provide memory. These magnetic cores consisted of small, doughnut-shaped rings about the size of pinheads, which were strung like beads on intersecting thin wires (Figure A-7). To supplement primary storage, first-generation computers stored data on punched cards. In 1957 magnetic tape was introduced as a faster, more compact method of storing data.

The Second Generation, 1959–1964: The Transistor

Three Bell Lab scientists—J. Bardeen, H. W. Brattain, and W. Shockley—developed the **transistor,** a small device that transfers electric sig-

Figure A-6 Vacuum tubes. Vacuum tubes were used in the first generation of computers. Vacuum tube systems could multiply two ten-digit numbers together in 1/40 second.

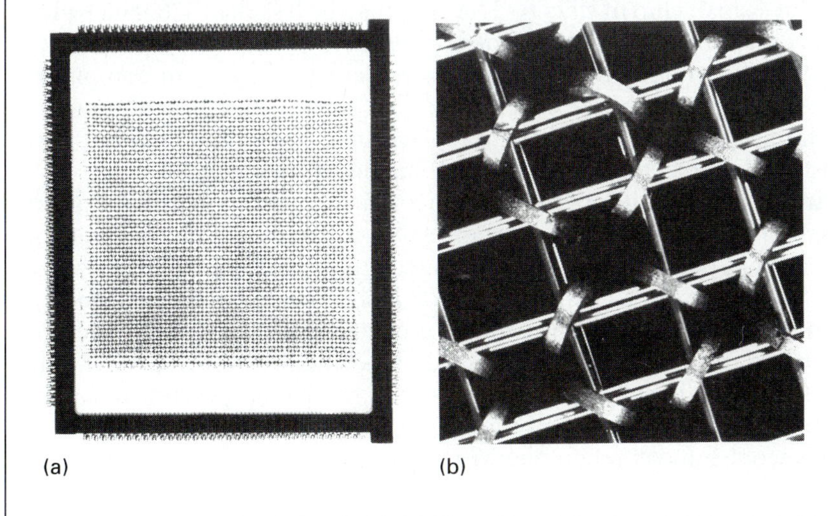

Figure A-7 Magnetic cores. (a) A 6- by 11-inch magnetic core memory. (b) Close-up of a magnetic core memory. A few hundredths of an inch in diameter, each magnetic core was mounted on a wire. When electricity passed through the wire on which a core was strung, the core could be magnetized as either off or on. These states represented a 0 (off) or a 1 (on). Combinations of 0s and 1s could be used to represent data. Magnetic cores were originally developed by IBM, which adapted pill-making machinery to produce them by the millions.

Watson Smart? You Bet!

Just as computers were getting off the ground, Thomas Watson, Sr., saw the best and brightest called to arms in World War II. But he did not just bid his employees a sad *adieu*. He paid them. Each and every one received one quarter of his or her annual salary, in twelve monthly installments. The checks continued to arrive throughout the duration of the war. Every month those former employees thought about IBM and the generosity of its founder.

The result? A very high percentage of those employees returned to IBM after the war. Watson got his brain trust back, virtually intact. The rest is history.

nals across a resistor. (The name *transistor* began as a trademark concocted from *trans*fer plus re*sistor*.) The scientists later received the Nobel prize for their invention. The transistor revolutionized electronics in general and computers in particular. Transistors were much smaller than vacuum tubes, and they had numerous other advantages: They needed no warm-up time, consumed less energy, and were faster and more reliable.

During this generation, another important development was the move from machine language to **assembly languages**—also called **symbolic languages.** Assembly languages use abbreviations for instructions (for example, L for LOAD) rather than numbers. This made programming less cumbersome.

After the development of symbolic languages came **high-level languages,** such as **FORTRAN** (1954) and **COBOL** (1959). Both languages, still widely used today (in updated forms), are more English-like than assembly languages. High-level languages allowed programmers to give more attention to solving problems. Also, in 1962 the first removable disk pack was marketed. Disk storage supplemented magnetic tape systems and enabled users to have fast access to desired data.

All these new developments made the second generation of computers less costly to operate—and thus began a surge of growth in computer systems. Throughout this period computers were being used principally by business, university, and government organizations. They had not filtered down to the general public. The real part of the revolution was about to begin.

The Third Generation, 1965–1970: The Integrated Circuit

One of the most abundant elements in the earth's crust is silicon, a nonmetallic substance found in common beach sand as well as in practically all rocks and clay. The importance of this element to Santa Clara County, which is about 30 miles south of San Francisco, is responsible for the county's nickname: Silicon Valley. In 1965 Silicon Valley became the principal site for the manufacture of the so-called silicon chip: the integrated circuit.

An **integrated circuit** (abbreviated **IC**) is a complete electronic circuit on a small chip of silicon. The chip may be less than 1/8 inch square and contain thousands or millions of electronic components. Beginning in 1965 integrated circuits began to replace transistors in computers. The resulting machines were now called third-generation computers. An integrated circuit was able to replace an entire circuit board of transistors, with one chip of silicon much smaller than one transistor.

Integrated circuits are made of silicon because it is a **semiconductor.** That is, it is a crystalline substance that will conduct electric current when it has been "doped" with chemical impurities implanted in its lattice-like structure. A cylinder of silicon is sliced into wafers, each about 6 inches in diameter, and the wafer is etched repeatedly with a pattern of electrical circuitry. Several layers may be etched on a single wafer. The wafer is then divided into several hundred small chips, each with a complete circuit so tiny it is half the size of a human fingernail, yet under a microscope it looks as complex as a railroad yard.

The chips were hailed as a generational breakthrough because they had desirable characteristics: reliability, compactness, and low cost. Mass-production techniques have made possible the manufacture of inexpensive integrated circuits.

The beginning of the third generation was trumpeted by the IBM 360 series (named for 360 degrees—a full circle of service), first announced April 7, 1964. The System/360 family of computers, designed for both business and scientific use, came in several models and sizes. The equipment housing was blue, leading to IBM's nickname, Big Blue.

The 360 series was launched with an all-out, massive marketing effort to make computers a business tool—to get them into medium-size and smaller business and government operations where they had not been used before. The result went beyond IBM's wildest dreams. The reported $5 billion the company invested in the development of the System/360 quickly repaid itself, and the system rendered many existing computer systems obsolete. Big Blue was on its way.

Software became more sophisticated during this third generation, permitting several programs to run in the same time frame, sharing computer resources. This approach improved the efficiency of computer systems. Software systems were developed to support interactive processing, which put the user in direct contact with the computer through a terminal. This kind of access caused the customer service industry to flourish, especially in areas such as reservations and credit checks.

Large third-generation computers began to be supplemented by minicomputers, which are functionally equivalent to a full-size system but are somewhat slower, smaller, and less expensive. These computers have become a huge success with medium-size and smaller businesses.

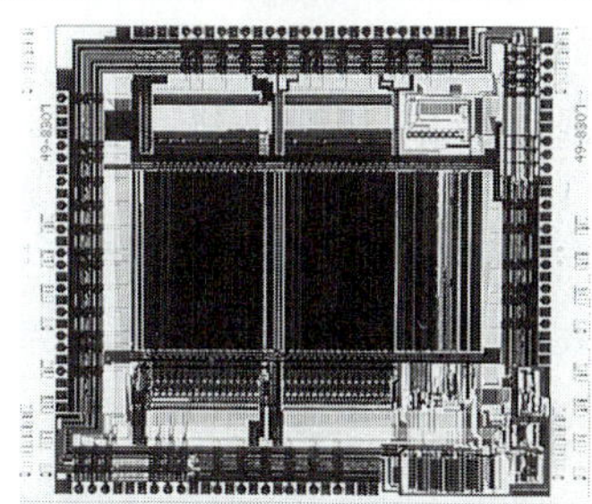

An Invention to Remember

There was a time when an engineer who was also an inventor could look forward to fame as well as fortune. Thomas Edison, for example, was one of the best-known people in the world before he was 35. Today's famous people, however, tend to come from the entertainment industry. So it is that we have lost the names of Jack Kilby and Robert Noyce, who invented the device that operates your watch, oven, calculator, and computer: the integrated circuit. Some have called it the greatest invention ever. Let us make Kilby and Noyce just a little bit famous.

Kilby and Noyce come from America's heartland, Kansas and Iowa, respectively. Both were interested in electronics. But there the similarities end. Jack Kilby flunked the entrance exam at MIT and received only a single job offer when he graduated with an engineering degree from the University of Illinois. Robert Noyce, on the other hand, did get into MIT and stayed around to get a Ph.D.

Kilby and Noyce worked independently, each coming out with the integrated circuit on a chip in 1959—Kilby at Texas Instruments, Inc., and Noyce at Fairchild Semiconductor. Kilby went on to develop the first hand-held calculator, and Noyce founded Intel Corporation to pursue the daring idea of putting the computer's memory on chips.

The Fourth Generation, 1971–Present: The Microprocessor

Through the 1970s computers gained dramatically in speed, reliability, and storage capacity, but entry into the fourth generation was evolutionary rather than revolutionary. The fourth generation was, in fact, an extension of third-generation technology. That is, in the early part of the third generation, specialized chips were developed for computer memory and logic. Thus, all the ingredients were in place for the next technological development, the general-purpose processor-on-a-chip, otherwise known as the **microprocessor,** which became commercially available in 1971.

Nowhere is the pervasiveness of computer power more apparent than in the explosive use of the microprocessor. In addition to the common applications of digital watches, pocket calculators, and personal computers, microprocessors can be anticipated in virtually every machine in the home or business—microwave ovens, cars, copy machines, television sets, and so on. Computers today are 100 times smaller than those of the first generation, and a single chip is far more powerful than ENIAC.

The Fifth Generation

The term *fifth generation* was coined by Japan to describe its goal of creating powerful, intelligent computers by the mid-1990s. Since then, however, it has become an umbrella term encompassing many research

Personal Computers In Action

The Software Entrepreneurs

Ever thought you'd like to run your own show? Make your own product? Be in business for yourself? Entrepreneurs are a special breed. They are achievement-oriented; like to take responsibility for decisions; and dislike repetitive, routine work. They also have high levels of energy and a great deal of imagination. But perhaps the key is that they are willing to take risks.

Entrepreneurs often have still another quality—a more elusive quality—that is something close to charisma. This charisma is based on enthusiasm, and it allows them to lead people and to form organizations, and give them momentum. Study these real-life entrepreneurs, noting their paths to glory and—sometimes—their falls.

Steve Jobs

Of the two Steves who formed Apple Computer, Steve Jobs was the true entrepreneur. Although they both were interested in electronics, Steve Wozniak was the technical genius, and he would have been happy to have been left alone to tinker. But Steve Jobs would not let him alone for a minute; he was always pushing and crusading. In fact, Wozniak had hooked up with an evangelist, and they made quite a pair.

When Apple was getting off the ground, Jobs wanted Wozniak to quit his job so he could work full-time on the new venture. Wozniak refused.

His partner begged and cried. Wozniak gave in. While Wozniak built Apple computers, Jobs was out hustling, finding the best marketing person, the best venture capitalist, and the best company president. This entrepreneurial spirit paid off in a spectacular way as Apple rose to the top of the list of microcomputer companies.

fields in the computer industry. Key areas of ongoing research are artificial intelligence, expert systems, and natural language—topics discussed in detail in Chapter 11.

Japan's original announcement of the fifth generation captivated the computer industry. Some view the fifth generation as a race between Japan and the United States, with nothing less than world computer supremacy as the prize. However, the Japanese budget has been cut significantly in recent years, and enthusiasm over the project has waned somewhat.

The Special Story of Personal Computers

Personal computers are the machines you can "get closest to," whether you are an amateur or a professional. There is nothing quite like having your very own personal computer. Its history is very personal too, full of stories of success and failure and of individuals with whom we can readily identify.

Bill Gates

When Bill Gates was a teenager, he swore off computers for a year and, in his words, "tried to act normal." His parents, who wanted him to be a lawyer, must have been relieved when Bill gave up the computer foolishness and went off to Harvard in 1974. But Bill started spending weekends with his friend Paul Allen, dreaming about personal computers, which did not exist yet. When the MITS Altair, the first personal computer for sale, splashed on the market in January 1975, both Bill and Paul moved to Albuquerque to be near the action at MITS. But they showed a desire even then to chart their own course. Although they wrote software for MITS, they kept the rights to their work and formed their own company. Their company was called Microsoft.

When MITS failed, Gates and Allen moved their software company to their native Bellevue, Washington. They employed 32 people in 1980 when IBM came to call. Gates recognized the big league when he saw it and put on a suit for the occasion. Gates was offered a plum: the chance to develop the operating system (a crucial set of software) for IBM's soon-to-be personal computer. Although he knew he was betting the whole company, Gates never hesitated to take the risk. He and his crew worked feverishly for many months to produce MS-DOS—Microsoft Disk Operating System. It was this product that sent Microsoft on its meteoric rise.

Mitch Kapor

Kapor did not start out on a direct path to computer fame and riches. In fact, he wandered extensively, from being a disk jockey to piano teacher to counselor. He had done some programming, too, but did not like it much. But, around 1978, he found he did like fooling around with personal computers. In fact, he had found his niche.

In 1983 Kapor introduced a software package called Lotus 1-2-3, and there had never been anything like it before. Lotus added the term *integrated package* to the vocabulary; the phrase described the software's identity as a combination spreadsheet, graphics, and database program. Kapor's product catapulted his company to the top of the list of independent software makers in just two years.

Champions of Change

Entrepreneurs thrive on change. Jobs, Wozniak, and Kapor all left their original companies to start new companies. Stay tuned for future breakthroughs from these and other personal computer entrepreneurs.

I Built It in My Garage

As we noted in the beginning of the chapter, the very first personal computer was the MITS Altair, produced in 1975. But it was a gee-whiz machine, loaded with switches and dials—and no keyboard or screen. It took two teenagers, Steve Jobs and Steve Wozniak, to capture the imagination of the public with the first Apple computer. They built it in that time-honored place of inventors, a garage, using the $1300 proceeds from the sale of an old Volkswagen. Designed for home use, the Apple was the first to offer an easy-to-use keyboard and screen. Founded in 1977, Apple Computer was immediately and wildly successful. When its stock was offered to the public in December 1980, it started a stampede among investors eager to buy in. Apple has introduced an increasingly powerful line of computers, including the Macintosh, which continues to sell well. (Figure A-8 shows early documentation for the first commercial Apple computer.)

The other major player in those early years was Tandy Incorporated, whose worldwide chain of Radio Shack stores provided a handy sales outlet for the TRS-80 personal computer. Other manufacturers who enjoyed more than moderate success in the late 1970s were Atari and Commodore. Their number was to grow.

APPLE COMPUTER CO

APPLE-1
OPERATION
MANUAL

APPLE COMPUTER COMPANY
770 Welch Road
Palo Alto, Calif. 94304

Figure A-8 Apple manual.
Shown here is a collector's item: the very first manual for operation of an Apple computer. Unfortunately, the early manuals were a hodgepodge of circuit diagrams, software listings, and handwritten notes. They were hard to read and understand and almost guaranteed to frighten away all but the most hardy souls.

The IBM PC Phenomenon

IBM announced its first personal computer in the summer of 1981. IBM captured the top market share in just 18 months and, even more important, its machine became the industry standard (Figure A-9). This was indeed a phenomenal success.

IBM did a lot of things right, such as including the possibility of adding memory. IBM also provided internal expansion slots, so that manufacturers of peripheral equipment could build accessories for the IBM PC. In addition, IBM provided hardware schematics and software listings to companies who wanted to build products in conjunction with the new PC. Many of the new products accelerated demand for the IBM machine.

Other personal computer manufacturers hurried to emulate IBM, producing "PC clones"—copycat computers that can run software designed for the IBM PC. Meanwhile, IBM has offered both upscale and downscale generations of its personal computer.

The story of personal computer history is ongoing, with daily fluctuations reflected in the trade press. The effects of personal computers are far-reaching, and they remain a key topic in the computer industry.

Semiconductor Drive

This street sign is in Silicon Valley, an area south of San Francisco. As its name indicates, Silicon Valley is noted for silicon chips, also known as semiconductors, and other related computer industries.

History is still being made in the computer industry, of course, and it is being made incredibly rapidly. A book cannot possibly pretend to describe all the very latest developments. Nevertheless, as we indicated earlier, the four areas of input, processing, output, and storage describe the basic components of a computer system—whatever its date.

Figure A-9 The IBM PC.
Launched in 1981, the IBM PC took just 18 months to rise to the top of the best-seller list.

Appendix **Review**

Summary and Key Terms

- Charles Babbage, is called "the father of the computer" because of his invention of two computation machines: the **difference engine** and the **analytical engine.** Countess Ada Lovelace helped develop instructions for carrying out computations on the analytical engine.
- The first computer to use electrical power instead of mechanical power was Herman Hollerith's tabulating machine, which was used in the 1890 census in the United States. Hollerith founded a company that became the forerunner of International Business Machines Corporation (IBM).
- Thomas J. Watson, Sr., built IBM into a dominant force in the business machines market. He also gave Harvard professor Howard Aiken research funds with which to build an electromechanical computer, the **Mark I,** which was unveiled in 1944.
- John V. Atanasoff, with assistant Clifford Berry, devised the first digital computer to work by electronic means, the **Atanasoff-Berry Computer (ABC).**
- The **ENIAC (Electronic Numerical Integrator and Calculator),** developed by John Mauchly and J. Presper Eckert at the University of Pennsylvania in 1946, was the world's first general-purpose electronic computer.
- The first computer generation began June 14, 1951, with the delivery of the **UNIVAC (Universal Automatic Computer)** to the U.S. Bureau of the Census. First-generation computers required thousands of **vacuum tubes.** The main form of memory was **magnetic core.**
- Second-generation computers used **transistors,** developed at Bell Laboratories. Compared to vacuum tubes, transistors were small, needed no warm-up, consumed less energy, and were faster and more reliable. During the second generation, **assembly languages,** or **symbolic languages,** were developed. They used abbreviations for instructions, rather than numbers. Later, **high-level languages,** such as **FORTRAN** and **COBOL,** were also developed. In 1962 the first removable disk pack was marketed.
- The third generation emerged with the introduction of the **integrated circuit (IC)**—a complete electronic circuit on a small chip of silicon. Silicon is a **semiconductor,** a substance that will conduct electric current when it has been "doped" with chemical impurities.
- With the third generation IBM announced the System/360 family of computers. During this period more sophisticated software was introduced that allowed several programs to run in the same time frame and supported interactive processing, in which the user has direct contact with the computer through a terminal.
- The fourth-generation **microprocessor**—a general-purpose processor-on-a-chip—grew out of the specialized memory and logic chips of the third generation. Microprocessors led to the development of microcomputers, expanding computer markets to smaller businesses and to personal use.
- In 1980 the Japanese announced a ten-year project to develop a fifth generation, radically new forms of computer systems involving artificial intelligence, expert systems, and natural language.
- The first microcomputer, the MITS Altair, was produced in 1975. However, the first successful computer to include an easy-to-use keyboard and screen was offered by Apple computer, founded by Steve Jobs and Steve Wozniak in 1977. IBM entered the microcomputer market in 1981 and captured the top market share in just 18 months.

Student Personal Study Guide

True/False

T F 1. The analytical engine embodied the five key concepts of a computer system.
T F 2. The ENIAC was the world's first electronic digital computer.
T F 3. The first generation was characterized by the vacuum tube.
T F 4. The transistor was faster and more reliable than the vacuum tube.
T F 5. Higher-level languages were developed during the second generation.
T F 6. Integrated circuits marked the advent of the third generation.
T F 7. Mauchly and Eckert produced the ENIAC.
T F 8. IBM's third generation computers were called the IBM PCs.
T F 9. First generation computers used transistors.
T F 10. Jobs and Wozniak invented the MITS Altair.

Multiple Choice

1. Aiken's computer at Harvard:
   a. ENIAC c. UNIVAC
   b. difference engine d. Mark I
2. The first microcomputer:
   a. MITS Altair c. Apple
   b. IBM PC d. Macintosh
3. The first electronic digital computer:
   a. ENIAC c. Macintosh
   b. ABC d. Mark 1
4. Second-generation technology:
   a. IC c. transistors
   b. microprocessor d. vacuum tubes
5. Father of the computer:
   a. Aiken c. Hollerith
   b. Atanasoff d. Babbage
6. A "doped" substance that will conduct electric current:
   a. semiconductor c. magnetic core
   b. vacuum tube d. analytical engine
7. Captured the personal computer market in just 18 months:
   a. Apple c. MITS
   b. IBM d. Microsoft
8. Babbage's assistant:
   a. Watson c. Lovelace
   b. Berry d. Eckert
9. A complete electronic circuit on a silicon chip:
   a. vacuum tube c. transistor
   b. magnetic core d. integrated circuit
10. The man who founded a company that became IBM:
    a. Atanasoff c. Aiken
    b. Watson d. Hollerith

Fill-In

1. The technology of the second generation: ________________ .
2. Built IBM into a dominant force in the business machine market: ________________ .

3. The Harvard professor who built the Mark I: ________________.
4. The first commercial computer, delivered in 1951: ________________.
5. The technology used for primary storage in the first generation: ________________.
6. The first personal computer for sale: ________________.
7. Inventor of the difference engine: ________________.
8. Considered the first programmer: ________________.
9. Atanasoff's computer: ________________.
10. Made a machine to tabulate the 1890 census: ________________.

Answers

True/False: 1. T, 2. T, 3. T, 4. T, 5. T, 6. T, 7. T, 8. F, 9. F, 10.F
Multiple choice: 1. d, 2. a, 3. b, 4. c, 5. d, 6. a, 7. b, 8. c, 9. d, 10. d
Fill-in: 1. transistor, 2. Thomas J. Watson, Sr., 3. Howard Aiken, 4. UNIVAC, 5. magnetic core, 6. MITS Altair, 7. Charles Babbage, 8. Ada Lovelace, 9. ABC, 10. Herman Hollerith

Appendix Overview

Number

APPENDIX

B

Data can be represented in the computer in one of two basic ways: as **numeric data** or as **alphanumeric data.** The internal representation of alphanumeric data—letters, digits, special characters—was discussed in Chapter 3. Recall that alphanumeric data may be represented using various codes; ASCII is a common code. Alphanumeric data, even if all digits, cannot be used for arithmetic operations. Data that is used for arithmetic calculations must be stored numerically.

Data stored numerically can be represented as the binary equivalent of the decimal value with which we are familiar. That is, values such as 1050, 43218, and 3 that we input to the computer will be converted to the binary number system. In this appendix we shall study the binary number system (base 2) and two related systems, octal (base 8) and hexadecimal (base 16).

Systems

Number Bases

A number base is a specific collection of symbols on which a number system can be built. The number base familiar to us is base 10, upon which the **decimal** number system is built. There are ten symbols—0 through 9—used in the decimal system.

Since society uses base 10, that is the number base most of us understand and can use easily. It would theoretically be possible, however, for all of us to learn to use a different number system. This number system could contain a different number of symbols and perhaps even symbols that are unfamiliar.

Base 2: The Binary Number System

Base 2 has exactly two symbols: 0 and 1. All numbers in the **binary** system must be formed using these two symbols. As you can see in column 2 of Table B-1, this means that numbers in the binary system become long quickly; the number 1000 in base 2 is equivalent to 8 in base 10. (When different number bases are being discussed, it is common practice to use the number base as a subscript. In this case we could say $1000_2 = 8_{10}$.) If you were to continue counting in base 2, you would soon see that the binary numbers were very long and unwieldy. The number 5000_{10} is equal to 1001110001000_2.

The size and sameness—all those 0s and 1s—of binary numbers make them subject to frequent error when they are being manipulated by humans. To improve both convenience and accuracy, it is common to express the values represented by binary numbers in the more concise octal and hexadecimal number bases.

Base 8: The Octal Number System

The **octal** number system uses exactly eight symbols: 0, 1, 2, 3, 4, 5, 6, and 7. Base 8 is a convenient shorthand for base 2 numbers because 8 is a power of 2: $2^3 = 8$. As you will see when we discuss conversions, one octal digit is the equivalent of exactly three binary digits. The use of octal (or hexadecimal) as a shorthand for binary is common in printed output of main storage and, in some cases, in programming.

Look at the column of octal numbers in Table B-1. Notice that, since 7 is the last symbol in base 8, the following number is 10. In fact, we can count right through the next seven numbers in the usual manner, as long as we end with 17. Note, however, that 17_8 is pronounced "one-seven," not "seventeen." The octal number 17 is followed by 20 through 27, and so on. The last double-digit number is 77, which is followed by 100. Although it takes a little practice, you can see that it would be easy to learn to count in base 8. However, hexadecimal, or base 16, is not quite as easy.

Base 16: The Hexadecimal Number System

The **hexadecimal** number system uses exactly 16 symbols. As we have just seen, base 10 uses the familiar digits 0 through 9, and bases 2 and 8

Table B-1 Number Bases 10, 2, 8, 16: First Values

Base 10 (decimal)	Base 2 (binary)	Base 8 (octal)	Base 16 (hexadecimal)
0	0000	0	0
1	0001	1	1
2	0010	2	2
3	0011	3	3
4	0100	4	4
5	0101	5	5
6	0110	6	6
7	0111	7	7
8	1000	10	8
9	1001	11	9
10	1010	12	A
11	1011	13	B
12	1100	14	C
13	1101	15	D
14	1110	16	E
15	1111	17	F
16	10000	20	10

use a subset of those symbols. Base 16, however, needs those ten symbols (0 through 9) and six more. The six additional symbols used in the hexadecimal number system are the letters A through F. So the base 16 symbols are: 0, 1, 2, 3, 4, 5, 6, 7, 8, 9, A, B, C, D, E, and F. It takes some adjusting to think of A or D as a digit instead of a letter. It also takes a little time to become accustomed to numbers such as 6A2F or even ACE. Both of these examples are legitimate numbers in hexadecimal.

As you become familiar with hexadecimal, consider the matter of counting. Counting sounds simple enough, but it can be confusing in an unfamiliar number base with new symbols. The process is the same as counting in base 10, but most of us learned to count when we were too young to think about the process itself. Quickly—what number follows 24CD? The answer is 24CE. We increased the rightmost digit by one—D to E—just as you would have in the more obvious case of 6142 to 6143. What is the number just before 1000_{16}? The answer is FFF_{16}; the last symbol (F) is a triple-digit number. Compare this with 999_{10}, which precedes 1000_{10}; 9 is the last symbol in base 10. As a familiarization exercise, try counting from 1 to 100 in base 16. Remember to use A through F as the second symbol in the teens, twenties, and so forth (. . . 27, 28, 29, 2A, 2B, 2C, 2D, 2E, 2F, 30, and so on).

Conversions Between Number Bases

It is sometimes convenient to use a number in a base different from the base currently being used—that is, to change the number from one base to another. Many programmers can nimbly convert a number from one base to another, among bases 10, 2, 8, and 16. We shall consider these conversion techniques now. Table B-2 summarizes the methods.

To Base 10 from Bases 2, 8, and 16

We present these conversions together because the technique is the same for all three.

Let us begin with the concept of positional notation. **Positional notation** means that the value of a digit in a number depends not only on its own intrinsic value but also on its location in the number. Given the number 2363, we know that the appearance of the digit 3 represents two different values, 300 and 3. Table B-3 shows the names of the relative positions.

Using these positional values, the number 2363 is understood to mean:

$$\begin{array}{r} 2000 \\ 300 \\ 60 \\ 3 \\ \hline 2363 \end{array}$$

Table B-2 Summary Conversion Chart

	To Base			
From Base	2	8	16	10
2	———	Group binary digits by 3, convert	Group binary digits by 4, convert	Expand number and convert base 2 digits to base 10
8	Convert each octal digit to 3 binary digits	———	Convert to base 2, then to base 16	Expand number and convert base 8 digits to base 10
16	Convert each hexadecimal digit to 4 binary digits	Convert to base 2, then to base 8	———	Expand number and convert base 16 digits to base 10
10	Divide number repeatedly by 2; use remainders as answer	Divide number repeatedly by 8; use remainders as answer	Divide number repeatedly by 16; use remainders as answer	———

Table B-3 Digit Positions

Digit	2	3	6	3
Position	Thousand	Hundred	Ten	Unit

This number can also be expressed as:

$(2 \times 1000) + (3 \times 100) + (6 \times 10) + 3$

We can express this expanded version of the number another way, using powers of 10. Note that $10^0=1$.

$2363 = (2 \times 10^3) + (3 \times 10^2) + (6 \times 10^1) + (3 \times 10^0)$

Once you understand the expanded notation, the rest is easy: You expand the number as we just did in base 10, but use the appropriate base of the number. For example, follow these steps to convert 61732_8 to base 10:

1. Expand the number, using 8 as the base:
   $61732 = (6 \times 8^4) + (1 \times 8^3) + (7 \times 8^2) + (3 \times 8^1) + (2 \times 8^0)$
2. Complete the arithmetic:
   $61732 = (6 \times 4096) + (1 \times 512) + (7 \times 64) + (3 \times 8) + (2 \times 1)$
   $= 24576 + 512 + 448 + 24 + 2$
3. Answer: $61732_8 = 25562_{10}$

The same expand-and-convert technique can be used to convert from base 2 or base 16 to base 10. As you consider the following two examples, use Table 1 to make the conversions. (For example, A in base 16 converts to 10 in base 10.)

Convert $C14A_{16}$ to base 10:

$$\begin{aligned} C14A_{16} &= (12 \times 16^3) + (1 \times 16^2) + (4 \times 16^1) + (10 \times 16^0) \\ &= (12 \times 4096) + (1 \times 256) + (4 \times 16) + (10 \times 1) \\ &= 49482 \end{aligned}$$

So $C14A_{16} = 49482_{10}$.

Convert 100111_2 to base 10:

$$\begin{aligned} 100111_2 &= (1 \times 2^5) + (1 \times 2^2) + (1 \times 2^1) + (1 \times 2^0) \\ &= 39 \end{aligned}$$

So $100111_2 = 39_{10}$.

From Base 10 to Bases 2, 8, and 16

These conversions use a simpler process but more complicated arithmetic. The process, often called the *remainder method*, is basically a series of repeated divisions by the number of the base to which you are converting. You begin by using the number to be converted as the dividend; succeeding dividends are the quotients of the previous division. The converted number is the combined remainders accumulated from the divisions. There are two points to remember:

1. Keep dividing until you reach a zero quotient.
2. Use the remainders in reverse order.

Consider converting 6954_{10} to base 8:

Division	Remainder
8⌊6954	
8⌊869	2
8⌊108	5
8⌊13	4
8⌊1	5
0	1

Placing the remainders backward, $6954_{10} = 15452_8$.

Now use the same technique to convert 4823_{10} to base 16:

Division	Remainder
16⌊4823	
16⌊301	7
16⌊18	13 (=D)
16⌊1	2
0	1

The remainder 13 is equivalent to D in base 16. So $4823_{10} = 12D7_{16}$.

Convert 49_{10} to base 2:

Division	Remainder
2⌊49	
2⌊24	1
2⌊12	0
2⌊6	0
2⌊3	0
2⌊1	1
0	1

Again placing the remainders in reverse order, $49_{10} = 110001_2$.

To Base 2 from Bases 8 and 16

To convert a number to base 2 from base 8 or base 16, convert each digit separately to three or four binary digits, respectively. Use Table B-1 to make the conversion. Leading zeros—zeros added to the front of the number—may be needed in each grouping of digits to fill out each to three or four digits.

Convert 4732_8 to base 2, converting each octal digit to a set of three binary digits:

4	7	3	2
100	111	011	010

So $4732_8 = 100111011010_2$. Notice that leading zeros were sometimes needed to make three binary digits from an octal digit: for octal digit 3, 11 became 011 and, for octal digit 2, 10 became 010.

Now convert $A046B_{16}$ to base 2, this time converting each hexadecimal digit to four binary digits:

A	0	4	6	B
1010	0000	0100	0110	1011

Thus $A046B_{16} = 10100000010001101011_2$.

From Base 2 to Bases 8 and 16

To convert a number from base 2 to base 8 or base 16, group the binary digits from the right in groups of three or four, respectively. Again use Table 1 to help you make the conversion to the new base.

Convert 111101001011_2 to base 8 and base 16:

In the base 8 conversion, group the digits three at a time, starting on the right:

111	101	001	011
7	5	1	3

So $111101001011_2 = 7513_8$.

For the conversion to base 16, group the digits four at a time, starting on the right:

1111	0100	1011
F	4	B

$111101001011_2 = F4B_{16}$.

Sometimes the number of digits in a binary number is not exactly divisible by 3 or 4. You may, for example, start grouping the digits three at a time and finish with one or two “extra” digits on the left side of the number. In this case just add as many zeros as you need to the front of the binary number.

Consider converting 1010_2 to base 8. By adding two zeros to the front of the number to make it 001010_2, we now have six digits, which can be conveniently grouped three at a time:

001	010
1	2

So $1010_2 = 12_8$.

Glossary

Access arm A mechanical device that can access all the tracks of one cylinder in a disk storage unit.

Accumulator A register that collects the result of computations.

Active badge A badge that, imbedded with a computer chip, signals the wearer's location by sending out infrared signals, which are read by computers distributed throughout the building.

Active cell The cell currently available for use on a spreadsheet. Also called the current cell.

Address A number used to designate a location in memory.

Address register A register that tells where instructions and data are stored in memory.

AI *See* Artificial intelligence.

ALU *See* Arithmetic/logic unit.

America Online (AOL) A major information utility that offers a variety of services.

Analog transmission The transmission of computer data as a continuous electric signal in the form of a wave.

Analytical engine A mechanical device of cogs and wheels, designed by Charles Babbage, that embodied the key characteristics of modern computers.

Analytical graphics Traditional line graphs, bar charts, and pie charts used to illustrate and analyze data.

ANSI American National Standards Institute.

AOL *See* America Online.

Applications software Programs designed to perform specific tasks and functions.

Arithmetic/logic unit (ALU) The electronic circuitry in a computer; it executes all arithmetic and logical operations.

Arithmetic operation Mathematical calculation the ALU performs on data.

Artificial intelligence (AI) The field of study that explores computer involvement in tasks requiring intelligence, imagination, and intuition.

ASCII (American Standard Code for Information Interchange) A coding scheme using 7-bit characters to represent data characters.

Assembler program A translator program used to convert assembly language programs to machine language.

Assembly language A second-generation language that uses abbreviations for instructions.

Atanasoff-Berry Computer (ABC) The first electronic digital computer, designed by John V. Atanasoff and Clifford Berry, in the late 1930s.

ATM *See* Automated teller machine.

Audio-response unit A device that converts data in main storage to sounds understandable as speech to humans. Also called a voice synthesizer or a voice-output device.

Automated teller machine (ATM) An input/output device connected to a computer used by bank customers for financial transactions.

Automatic reformatting In word processing, automatic adjustment of text to accommodate changes.

Auxiliary storage Storage, often disk, for data and programs; separate from the CPU and memory. Also called secondary storage.

Axis A reference line of a graph. The horizontal axis is the x-axis. The vertical axis is the y-axis.

Backup system A method of storing data in more than one place to protect it from damage or loss.

Bar code Standardized pattern (Universal Product Code) of vertical marks that identifies products.

Bar code reader A stationary photoelectric scanner that reads bar codes by means of reflected light.

Bar graph A graph made up of filled-in columns or rows that represent the change of data over time.

BASIC (Beginner's All-purpose Symbolic Instruction Code) A high-level programming language that is easy to learn and use.

Batch processing A data processing technique in which transactions are collected into groups, or batches, for processing.

BBS *See* Bulletin board system.

Binary system A system in which data is represented by combinations of 0s and 1s, which correspond to the two states off and on.

Biometrics The science of measuring individual body characteristics; used in some security systems.

Bit A binary digit.

Block copy command In word processing, the command used to copy a block of text into a new location.

Block delete command In word processing, the command used to erase a block of text.

Block move command In word processing, the command used to remove a block of text from one location in a document and place it elsewhere.

Boldface Printed characters in darker type than the surrounding characters.

Booting Loading the operating system into memory.

Branch In a flowchart, the connection leading from the decision box to one of two possible responses. Also called a path.

Bulletin board system (BBS) Telephone-linked personal computers that provide public-access message systems.

Business graphics Graphics that represent data in a visual, easy-to-understand format.

Business-quality graphics program A program that allows a user to create professional-looking business graphics. Also called a presentation graphics program.

Bus line Electrical path that transports data from one place to another inside the computer.

Bus network A type of local area network that assigns a portion of network management to each computer but preserves the system if one node fails.

Byte A string of bits (usually 8) used to represent one data character—a letter, digit, or special character.

C A sophisticated programming language invented by Bell Labs in 1974.

Cache A small amount of very fast memory that stores data and instructions that are used frequently, resulting in improved processing speeds.

CAD/CAM *See* computer-aided design/computer-aided manufacturing.

Cathode ray tube (CRT) The most common type of computer screen.

CD-ROM *See* Compact disk read-only memory.

Cell The intersection of a row and a column in a spreadsheet. Entries in a spreadsheet are stored in individual cells.

Cell address In a spreadsheet, the column and row coordinates of a cell.

Cell contents The label, value, formula, or function contained in a spreadsheet cell.

Centering The word processing feature that places a line of text midway between the left and right margins.

Centralized data processing Keeping hardware, software, storage, and computer access in one location.

Central processing unit (CPU) The electronic circuitry that executes stored program instructions. It consists of two parts: the control unit and the arithmetic/logic unit.

CGA (color graphics adapter) An early color screen standard with 320 by 200 pixels.

Change agent A systems analyst who, acting as a catalyst, overcomes the reluctance to change within an organization.

Character A letter, number, or special character (such as $).

Client An individual or organization contracting for systems analysis.

Clip art Illustrations stored on disk that are used to enhance a graph or document.

Clustered-bar graph A bar graph comparing several different but related sets of data.

Coaxial cable Bundles of insulated wires within a shielded enclosure that can be laid underground or undersea.

COBOL (COmmon Business-Oriented Language) An English-like programming language used primarily for business applications.

Command A name that invokes the correct program or program segment.

Compact disk read-only memory (CD-ROM) Optical data storage technology using disk formats identical to audio compact disks.

Compare operation An operation in which the computer compares two data items and performs alternative operations based on the comparison.

Compiler A translator that converts the symbolic statements of a high-level language into computer-executable machine language.

CompuServe A major information utility that offers a variety of services.

Computer A machine that accepts data (input) and processes it into useful information (output).

Computer-aided design/computer-aided manufacturing (CAD/CAM) The use of computers to create two- and three-dimensional pictures of manufactured products.

Computer conferencing A method of sending, receiving, and storing typed messages within a network of users.

Computer Fraud and Abuse Act A law passed by Congress in 1984 to fight computer crime.

Computer Matching and Privacy Protection Act A law that regulates comparison of records held by different branches of the government.

Computer literacy Awareness, knowledge of, and interaction with computers.

Computer programmer A person who designs, writes, tests, and implements programs.

Computer system A system that has one or more computers as components.

Concurrent licensing A software licensing agreement in which a customer is permitted to use only a limited number of copies of a software product simultaneously.

Concurrently With reference to the execution of computer instructions, in the same time frame. *See also* Multiprogramming.

Conditional replace A word processing function that asks the user whether to replace copy each time the program finds a particular item.

Connector A symbol used in flowcharting to connect paths.

Consortium A joint venture to support a complete computer facility to be used in an emergency.

Control unit The circuitry that directs and coordinates the entire computer system in executing stored program instructions.

Copy protection A software or hardware block that makes it difficult or impossible to create unauthorized copies of software.

CPU *See* Central processing unit.

CRT *See* Cathode ray tube.

Current cell The cell currently available for use on a spreadsheet. Also called the active cell.

Current drive The disk drive currently being used by the computer system. Also called the default drive.

Cursor A flashing indicator on the screen; it indicates where the next character will be inserted. Also called a pointer.

Cursor-movement keys The keys on the computer keyboard that allow the user to move the cursor on the screen.

Custom software Software specifically tailored to user needs.

Cut and paste In word processing, removing a block of text from one location and placing it in another location.

DASD *See* Direct access storage device.

Data The raw material to be processed by a computer.

Database A collection of interrelated files stored together with minimum redundancy.

Database management system (DBMS) A set of programs that create, manage, protect, and provide access to a database.

Data collection device A device that allows direct data entry in such places as factories and warehouses.

Data communications The process of exchanging data over communications facilities.

Data communications system A computer system that transmits data over communications lines, such as public telephone lines or private network cables.

Data Encryption Standard (DES) The standardized public key by which senders and receivers can scramble and unscramble their messages.

Data item Data in a relational database table.

Data point A single value represented by a bar or symbol in a graph.

DBMS *See* Database management system.

DDP *See* Distributed data processing.

Debugging The process of detecting, locating, and correcting mistakes in a program.

Decision box The standard diamond-shaped box used in flowcharting to indicate a decision.

Default drive The disk drive to which commands refer in the absence of any specified drive. Unless instructed otherwise, an applications program stores files on the memory device in the default drive. Also called the current drive.

Default settings Settings automatically used by a program unless the user specifies otherwise.

Demodulation The process of converting a signal from analog to digital.

DES *See* Data Encryption Standard.

Desk-checking A programming phase in which the logic of the program is mentally checked to ensure that it is error-free and workable.

Desktop publishing The use of a personal computer, special software, and a laser printer to produce very high-quality documents that combine text and graphics. Also called electronic publishing.

Desktop publishing program A software package for designing and producing professional-looking documents. Also called a page composition program or a page makeup program.

Diagnostic message A message that informs the user of programming-language syntax errors.

Difference engine A machine designed by Charles Babbage to solve polynomial equations by calculating the successive differences between them.

Digital transmission A data transmission method that sends data as distinct electrical (on or off) pulses.

Digitizer A graphics input device that converts images into digital data that the computer can accept.

Direct access The immediate access to a record in secondary storage, usually on a disk. Also called random access.

Direct access storage device (DASD) A storage device in which a record can be accessed directly.

Direct-connect modem A modem connected directly to the telephone line.

Disaster recovery plan A method of restoring data processing operations if those operations are halted by major damage or destruction.

Disk drive A device that allows data to be read from a disk and written on a disk.

Diskette A single magnetic disk on which data is recorded as magnetic spots. Available in both 5¼-inch format and 3½-inch format.

Disk pack A stack of magnetic disks assembled together.

Displayed value 1. The calculated result of a formula or function in a spreadsheet cell. 2. A number in a cell; it is displayed according to a user-specified format.

Distributed data processing (DDP) A data processing system in which processing is decentralized, with the computers and storage devices in dispersed locations.

Documentation 1. A detailed written description of the programming cycle and specific facts about the program. 2. The instruction manual for packaged software.

Dot-matrix printer A printer that constructs a character by activating a matrix of pins to produce the shape of a character on paper.

Download The transfer of data from a mainframe or large computer to a smaller computer.

Downsizing The process of shifting mainframe computer applications to smaller computers that are often a local area network of personal computers.

DRAM *See* Dynamic RAM

Dynamic RAM (DRAM) Memory chips that are periodically regenerated, allowing the chips to retain the stored data.

EFT *See* Electronic Fund Transfer.

EGA (enhanced graphics adapter) A color screen standard with 640 by 350 pixels.

Electronic fund transfer (EFT) Paying for goods and services by using electronically transferred funds.

Electronic mail (e-mail) The process of sending messages directly from one terminal or computer to another. The messages may be sent and stored for later retrieval.

Electronic spreadsheet An electronic worksheet used to organize data into rows and columns for analysis.

E-mail *See* Electronic mail.

Emulation software Software that permits a personal computer on a network to imitate a terminal.

Encryption The process of encoding communications data.

End-user A person who buys and uses computer software or who has contact with computers.

ENIAC (Electronic Numerical Integrator and Computer) The first general-purpose electronic computer, which was built by Dr. John Mauchly and J. Presper Eckert, Jr., and was first operational in 1946.

Equal to (=) condition A logical operation in which the computer compares two numbers to determine equality.

Erase head The head in a magnetic tape unit; it erases any previously recorded data on the tape.

Ethernet A popular local area network using a bus topology.

E-time The execution portion of the machine cycle.

Expansion slots The slots inside a computer that allow a user to insert additional circuit boards.

Expert shell Software having the basic structure to find answers to questions; the questions can be added by the user.

Expert system A software package that presents the computer as an expert on some topic.

Exploded pie chart A pie chart with a "slice" that is separated from the rest of the chart.

External modem A modem that is separate from the computer, allowing it to be used with a variety of computers.

Facsimile technology (fax) The use of computer technology to send digitized graphics, charts, and text from one facsimile machine to another.

Fair Credit Reporting Act Legislation passed in 1970; it allows individuals access to and the right to challenge credit records.

Fax board A circuit board that fits inside a personal computer and allows the user, without interrupting other applications programs, to transmit computer-generated text and graphics.

Federal Privacy Act Legislation passed in 1974; it stipulates that no secret personal files can be kept by government agencies and that individuals can have access to all information about them that is stored in government files.

Fiber optics Technology that uses light instead of electricity to send data.

Field A set of related characters. In a database, also called an attribute.

Field name In a database, the unique name describing the data in a field.

Field robot A robot that is used on location to inspect nuclear plants, dispose of bombs, clean up chemical spills, and so forth.

Field type A category describing a field; it's determined by the kind of data the field will accept. Common field types are character, numeric, date, and logical.

Field width In a database, the maximum number of characters that can be contained in a field.

Fifth generation A term coined by the Japanese; it refers to new forms of computer systems involving artificial intelligence, natural language, and expert systems.

File 1. A repository of data. 2. A collection of related records. 3. In word processing, a document created on a computer.

Flash memory Nonvolatile memory chips.

Floppy disk A flexible magnetic diskette on which data is recorded as magnetic spots.

Flowchart The pictorial representation of a step-by-step solution to a problem.

Font A complete set of characters in a particular size, typeface, weight, and style.

Font library A variety of type fonts stored on disk.

Format The specifications that determine the way a document or worksheet is displayed on the screen or printer.

Formula In a spreadsheet, an instruction to calculate a value.

FORTRAN (FORmula TRANslator) The first high-level language, introduced in 1954 by IBM; it is scientifically oriented.

4GL *See* Fourth-generation language.

Fourth-generation language A nonprocedural language. Also called a 4GL or a very high-level language.

Freedom of Information Act Legislation passed in 1970; it allows citizens access to personal data gathered by federal agencies.

Freeware Software that is free.

Full justification In word processing, making both the left and right margins even.

Function A built-in spreadsheet formula.

Function keys Special keys programmed to execute commonly used commands.

GB *See* Gigabyte.

Gigabyte (GB) One billion bytes.

Grammar/style program Software that checks a document for common grammar and writing errors.

Graphical user interface (GUI) A software feature that uses screen icons invoked by pointing and clicking a mouse.

Graphics Pictures or graphs.

Greater than (>) condition A comparison operation that determines if one value is greater than another.

Groupware Software that allows teams of workers on a network to swap information and collaborate on projects.

GUI *See* Graphical user interface.

Hacker A person who gains access to computer systems illegally, usually from a personal computer.

Halftone A reproduction of a black-and-white photograph; it is made up of tiny dots.

Hard copy Printed paper output.

Hard disk An inflexible disk, usually in a pack, often in a sealed module.

Hard magnetic disk A metal platter coated with magnetic oxide and used for magnetic disk storage.

Hardware The computer and its associated equipment.

High-level languages English-like programming language that is easier to use than older symbolic languages.

Host computer The central computer in a network.

Icon A small picture on a computer screen; it represents a computer activity.

Impact printer A printer that forms characters by physically striking the paper.

Inference engine In artificial intelligence systems, software that accesses, selects, and interprets a set of rules.

Information Processed data; data that is organized, meaningful, and useful.

Information center A company unit that offers employees computer and software training, help in getting data from other computer systems, and technical assistance.

Information system (IS) A set of business systems, usually with computers among its components, designed to provide information for decision making.

Information systems manager The person who runs the information systems department.

Information utilities Commercial consumer-oriented communications systems, such as America Online, CompuServe, and Prodigy.

Initialize Set the starting values of storage locations in a program.

Ink-jet printer A printer that sprays ink from jet nozzles onto the paper.

Input Raw data that is put in to the computer system for processing.

Input device A device that puts data in machine-readable form and sends it to the processing unit.

Integrated package A set of software that typically includes related word processing, spreadsheet, database, and graphics programs.

Interactive Data processing in which the user communicates directly with the computer, maintaining a dialogue.

Internal font A font built into the read-only memory of a printer.

Internal modem A modem on a circuit board; it can be installed in a computer by the user.

Internal storage The electronic circuitry that temporarily holds data and program instructions needed by the CPU. Also called memory, main memory, primary memory, primary storage, and main storage.

Internet A loosely organized collection of networks.

IS *See* Information system.

Iteration The repetition of program instructions under certain conditions. Also called a loop.

I-time The instruction portion of the machine cycle.

Joystick A graphics input device that allows fingertip control of figures on a CRT screen.

Justification Aligning text along left or right margins or both.

K *See* Kilobyte.

Kerning Adjusting the space between characters to create wider or tighter spacing.

Keyboard A common input device similar to the keyboard of a typewriter.

Kilobyte (K) 1024 bytes.

Knowledge-based system A collection of information stored in a computer and accessed by natural language.

Knowledge engineer A computer professional who extracts information from a human expert to design an expert system based on that information.

Label In a spreadsheet, data consisting of a string of text characters.

LAN *See* Local area network.

Laptop computer A small portable computer that can weigh less than 10 pounds. Also called a notebook computer.

Laser printer A printer that uses a light beam to transfer images to paper.

LCD *See* Liquid crystal display.

Leading The vertical spacing between lines of type.

Legend The text beneath a graph; it explains the colors, shading, or symbols used to label the data points.

Less than (<) condition A logical operation in which the computer compares values to determine if one is less than another.

Licensed software Software that costs money and must not be copied without permission of the manufacturer.

Light pen A graphics input device that allows the user to interact directly with the computer screen.

Line graph A graph made by using a line to connect data points.

Link A physical data communications medium.

Link/load phase The phase during which prewritten programs may be added to the object module by means of a link/loader.

Liquid crystal display (LCD) The flat display screen found on some laptop computers.

Load module The output from the link/load step.

Local area network (LAN) A network designed to share data and resources among several computers.

Logical field A field used to keep track of true and false conditions.

Logical operations Comparing operations. The ALU is able to compare numbers, letters, or special characters and take alternative courses of action.

Logic error A flaw in the logic of a program.

Loop The repetition of program instructions under certain conditions. Also called iteration.

Machine cycle The combination of I-time and E-time.

Machine language The lowest level of language; it represents information as 1s and 0s.

Magnetic core A flat doughnut-shaped piece of metal used as an early memory device.

Magnetic disk An oxide-coated disk on which data is recorded as magnetic spots.

Magnetic-ink character recognition (MICR) A method of machine-reading characters made of magnetized particles.

Magnetic tape A medium with an iron-oxide coating that can be magnetized. Data is stored on the tape as extremely small magnetized spots.

Magnetic tape unit A data storage unit used to record data on and retrieve data from magnetic tape.

Mainframe A large computer that has access to billions of characters of data and is capable of processing data very quickly.

Main memory The electronic circuitry that temporarily holds data and program instructions needed by the CPU. Also called memory, primary memory, primary storage, main storage, and internal storage.

Main storage The electronic circuitry that temporarily holds data and program instructions needed by the CPU. Also called memory, main memory, primary memory, primary storage, and internal storage.

Mark The process of defining a block of text before performing block commands.

Mark I An early computer; it was built in 1944 by Harvard professor Howard Aiken.

Master file A semipermanent set of records.

MB *See* Megabyte.

Megabyte (MB) One million bytes.

Megahertz (MHz) Millions of machine instructions per second.

Memory The electronic circuitry that temporarily holds data and program instructions needed by the CPU. Also called main memory, primary memory, primary storage, main storage, and internal storage.

Menu An on-screen list of command choices.

MHz *See* Megahertz.

MICR *See* Magnetic-ink character recognition.

Microcomputer The smallest and least expensive class of computer. Also called a personal computer.

Microcomputer manager A person who manages microcomputers. Also called personal computer manager.

Microprocessor A general-purpose processor on a chip; it was developed in 1969 by an Intel Corporation design team headed by Ted Hoff. Also called a logic chip.

Microsecond One-millionth of a second.

Microwave transmission The line-of-sight transmission of data signals through the atmosphere from relay station to relay station.

Millisecond One-thousandth of a second.

Minicomputer A computer with storage capacity and power less than a mainframe's but greater than a personal computer's.

MITS Altair The first microcomputer kit; it was offered to computer hobbyists in 1975.

Model A type of database, each type representing a particular way of organizing data. The three database models are hierarchical, network, and relational.

Modem The term short for *mo*dulate/*dem*odulate. A modem converts a digital signal to an analog signal or vice versa. Used to transfer data over analog communication lines between computers.

Modulation The process of converting a signal from digital to analog.

Monochrome A computer screen that displays information in only one color.

Monolithic Description of a chip because a single unit of storage comprises the circuits on a chip.

Mouse A hand-held computer input device whose rolling movement on a flat surface causes corresponding movement of the cursor on the screen.

Multimedia The multiple sight/sound experience available from a computer that has certain hardware (CD-ROM drive, sound card, speakers) and software.

Multiple-range graph A graph that plots the values of more than one variable.

Multiprogramming A mainframe computer operating system feature under which different programs from different users compete for the use of the central processing unit.

Multitasking A feature of an operating system, in which several programs can compete concurrently for the use of the central processing unit.

Nanosecond One-billionth of a second.

Natural language A programming language that resembles human language.

Network A computer system that uses communications equipment to connect two or more computers and their resources.

Network manager A person designated to manage and run a computer network.

Neural network Computer chips designed to mimic the human brain.

Node A device—such as a personal computer, hard disk, printer, or another peripheral—that is connected to a network.

Nonimpact imprinter A printer that prints without striking the paper.

Nonprocedural language A language that states what task is to be accomplished but does not state the steps needed to accomplish it.

Notebook computer A small portable computer that can weigh less than 10 pounds. Also called a laptop computer.

Object module A machine-language version of a program; it is produced by a compiler or assembler.

Object-oriented programming (OOP) Building a new program from standardized, pre-coded program modules.

OCR-A A standard typeface for optical characters.

OCR devices *See* Optical-character recognition devices.

Office automation The use of technology to help achieve the goals of the office.

OMR devices *See* Optical-mark recognition devices.

Online Processing in which terminals are directly connected to the computer.

OOP *See* Object-oriented programming.

Operating environment An operating system environment in which the user does not have to memorize or look up commands.

Operating system A set of programs through which a computer manages its own resources.

Optical-character recognition (OCR) device An input device that uses a light source to read special characters and convert them to electrical signals to be sent to the CPU.

Optical disk Storage technology that uses a laser beam to store large amounts of data at relatively low cost.

Optical-mark recognition (OMR) device An input device that uses a light beam to recognize marks on paper.

Optical read-only memory (OROM) Optical storage media that cannot be written on but can be used to supply software or data.

Optical-recognition system A system that converts optical marks, optical characters, handwritten characters, or bar codes into electrical signals to be sent to the CPU.

OROM *See* Optical read-only memory.

Output Raw data that has been processed into usable information.

Output device A device, such as a printer, that makes processed information available for use.

Packaged software Software that is packaged and sold in stores.

Page composition Adding type to a page layout.

Page composition program A software package for designing and producing professional-looking documents. Also called a page makeup program or a desktop publishing program.

Page layout In publishing, the process of arranging text and graphics on a page.

Page makeup program A software package for designing and producing professional-looking documents. Also called a page composition program or a desktop publishing program.

Pagination In word processing, including page numbers on printed output.

Pan To move the cursor across a spreadsheet.

Parallel processing Using several processors in the same computer at the same time.

Pascal A structured, high-level programming language named for Blaise Pascal, the 17th-century French mathematician.

Path In a flowchart, the connection leading from the decision box to one of two possible responses. Also called a branch.

Peer-to-peer network A network in which personal computers are physically cabled together.

Pen-based computer A small portable computer that accepts handwritten input on a screen. Also called personal digital assistant.

Peripheral equipment Hardware devices attached to a computer.

Personal computer Generally, the least-expensive class of computer. Also called a microcomputer.

Personal computer manager The manager in charge of personal computer use. Also called a microcomputer manager.

Personal digital assistant (PDA) A small portable computer that accepts handwritten input on a screen. Also called a pen-based computer.

Picosecond One-trillionth of a second.

Pie chart A pie-shaped graph used to compare values that represent parts of a whole.

Pixel A picture element on a computer display screen. Pixels are the individual points of light that make up screen images.

Point A typographic measurement equaling approximately 1/72 inch.

Pointer A flashing indicator on a screen that shows where the next user—computer interaction will be. Also called a cursor.

Point-of-sale (POS) terminal A terminal used as a cash register in a retail setting. It may be programmable or connected to a central computer.

Portable computer A self-contained computer that can be easily carried and moved.

POS terminal *See* Point-of-sale terminal.

Presentation graphics program A program that allows a user to create professional-looking business graphics. Also called a business-quality graphics program.

Primary memory The electronic circuitry that temporarily holds data and program instructions needed by the CPU. Also called memory, primary storage, main storage, internal storage, and main memory.

Primary storage The electronic circuitry that temporarily holds data and program instructions needed by the CPU.

Also called memory, primary memory, main storage, internal storage, and main memory.

Printer A device for generating output on paper.

Print preview In word processing, a feature that permits viewing the page to be printed on the screen before actual printing.

Procedural language A language used to present a step-by-step process for solving a problem.

Process box In flowcharting, a rectangular box that indicates an action to be taken.

Processor The central processing unit (CPU) of a computer.

Prodigy A major information utility that offers a variety of services.

Program A set of step-by-step instructions that directs a computer to perform specific tasks and produce certain results.

Programmable read-only memory (PROM) chips ROM chips that can be changed by ROM burners.

Programmer/analyst A person who performs systems analysis functions in addition to programming.

Programming language A set of rules that can be used to tell a computer what operations to do.

PROM chips *See* Programmable read-only memory chips.

Prompt A signal that the computer or operating system is waiting for data or a command from the user.

Pseudocode An English-like way of representing structured programming control structures.

Public-domain software Software that is free.

Pull-down menu A command menu system in which the click of an initial choice causes a list of subcommands to be "pulled down" like a window shade under the initial selection.

Ragged right margin The nonalignment of text at the right edge of a document.

RAM *See* Random access memory.

Random access The immediate access to a record in secondary storage, usually on a disk. Also called direct access.

Random access memory (RAM) The memory that provides temporary storage for data and program instructions.

Range A group of one or more cells, arranged in a rectangle, that a spreadsheet program treats as a unit.

Raster scan technology A process that forms an image on a computer screen by beaming electrons on a phosphorus-backed screen, causing it to glow.

Read To bring data outside the computer into memory.

Read-only memory (ROM) Memory that can be read only and remains after the power is turned off. Also called firmware.

Read/write head An electromagnet that reads the magnetized areas on magnetic media and converts them into the electrical impulses that are sent to the processor.

Real-time processing Processing in which the results are available in time to affect the activity at hand.

Record A collection of related fields.

Reformatting The readjustment of visual aspects of a word processing document, including the accommodation of additions and deletions.

Register Temporary storage area associated with the CPU that accepts, holds, and transfers instructions or data.

Relation A table in a relational database model.

Relational database A database in which the data is organized in a table format consisting of columns and rows.

Relational model A database model that organizes data logically in tables.

Relational operator An operator (such as <, >, or =) that allows a user to make comparisons and selections.

Resolution The clarity of a video display screen or printer output.

Reverse video The feature that highlights on-screen text by switching the usual text and background colors.

Ring network A circle of point-to-point connections of computers at local sites, with no central host computer.

Robot A computer-controlled device that can physically manipulate its surroundings.

ROM *See* Read-only memory.

ROM burner Used to change instructions on ROM chips; these chips are known as programmable read-only memory (PROM) chips.

Sans serif typeface A typeface that is clean, without the small marks of a serif typeface.

Satellite transmission Data transmission from earth station to earth station via communications satellites.

Scanner A device that reads text and images directly into the computer.

Screen A television-like output device that can display information.

Scrolling A word processing feature that allows the user to move to and view any part of a screen document in 24-line chunks.

SDLC *See* Systems development life cycle.

Sealed module A sealed disk drive containing disks, access arms, and read/write heads. Also called a Winchester disk.

Search and replace function A word processing function that finds and changes each instance of a repeated item.

Secondary storage Additional storage, often disk, for data and programs; it is separate from the CPU and memory. Also called auxiliary storage.

Security A system of safeguards designed to protect a computer system and data from deliberate or accidental damage or access by unauthorized persons.

Semiconductor A crystalline substance that conducts electricity when it is "doped" with chemical impurities.

Semiconductor storage Data storage on a silicon chip.

Serif typeface A typeface in which each character includes small marks that make the eye travel easily from one character to the next.

Server The central computer in a network; it is responsible for managing the LAN.

Shareware Software that is given away free, although the maker hopes that satisfied users will voluntarily pay for it.

Shell An operating environment layer that separates the operating system from the user.

SIMM *See* Single in-line memory module.

Single in-line memory module (SIMM) A board containing memory chips that can be plugged in to a computer expansion slot.

Single-range bar graph A graph that plots the values of only one variable.

Site license A license permitting a customer to make multiple copies of a piece of software.

Soft copy Computer output displayed on a screen.

Soft font A font that can be downloaded from disk files in a personal computer to a printer.

Software Instructions that tell a computer what to do.

Software piracy Unauthorized copying of computer software.

Source data automation The use of special equipment to collect data and send it directly to a computer.

Source document Data, on paper, to be prepared as input to a computer.

Source module A program as originally coded, before being translated into machine language.

Source program listing The printed version of a program as the programmer wrote it.

Speaker dependent A data input method in which a speech recognition system "learns" the voice of a speaker.

Speaker independent A data input method in which a speech recognition system can recognize commands from any speaker.

Speech recognition The process of presenting input data to the computer through the spoken word.

Speech recognition device A device that accepts the spoken word through a microphone and converts it into digital code that can be understood by a computer.

Speech synthesis The process of enabling machines to talk to people.

Spelling checker program A word processing program that checks the spelling in a document.

Spreadsheet An electronic worksheet divided into rows and columns that can be used to analyze and present business data.

Stacked-bar graph A bar graph in which all data common to a given row or column appears stacked in one bar.

Star network A network consisting of one or more smaller computers connected to a central host computer.

Start/stop symbol An oval symbol used to indicate the beginning and end of a flowchart.

Storage register A register that temporarily holds data that is taken from memory or about to be sent to memory.

Style The way a typeface is printed, for example, in *italic.*

Submenu An additional set of options related to a prior menu selection.

Supercomputer The largest and most powerful category of computers.

Supermicro A multiuser, multitasking microcomputer that has a high-speed microprocessor, increased memory, and hard-disk storage.

Supermini A minicomputer at the top end of capacity and price.

Surge protector A device that prevents electrical problems from affecting data files.

SVGA (super VGA) A superior screen standard with 800 by 600 pixels or 1024 by 768 pixels.

Syntax The rules of a programming language.

Syntax errors Errors in the use of a programming language.

System An organized set of related components established to perform a certain task.

System software The operating system; the underlying computer software.

Systems analysis The process of studying an existing system to determine how it works and how it meets user needs.

Systems analyst A person who plans and designs individual programs and entire computer systems.

Systems design The process of developing a plan for a system, based on the results of a systems analysis.

Systems development life cycle (SDLC) A model for developing a computer system.

Tape drive The drive on which reels of magnetic tape are mounted when their data is ready to be read by the computer system.

Telecommuting The home use of telecommunications and computers as a substitute for working outside the home.

Teleconferencing A system of holding conferences by linking geographically dispersed people through computer terminals or personal computers.

Terminal A device that consists of an input device, an output device, and a communications link to the main terminal.

Text block In word processing, a continuous section of text in a document.

Thesaurus program With a word processing program, this program provides a list of synonyms and antonyms for a word in a document.

Title The caption on a graph that summarizes the information in the graph.

Token passing In a ring network, the node possessing the token is permitted to send a message.

Topology The physical layout of a local area network.

Touch screen A computer screen that accepts input data by letting the user point at the screen to select a choice.

Trackball A ball used as an input device; it can be hand manipulated to cause a corresponding movement of the cursor on the screen.

Transaction file A file that contains all the changes to be made to a master file: additions, deletions, and revisions.

Transaction processing The technique of processing transactions one at a time in the order in which they occur.

Transistor A small device that transfers electrical signals across a resistor.

Translator A program that translates programming language into machine language.

Transponder A device in a communications satellite that receives a transmission from earth, amplifies the signal, changes the frequency, and retransmits the data to a receiving earth station.

Twisted pairs Wires twisted together in an insulated cable. Twisted pairs are frequently used to transmit information over short distances. Also called wire pairs.

Typeface A set of characters—letters, symbols, and numbers—of the same design.

Type size The size, in points, of a typeface.

Underlining Underscoring text.

UNIVAC (UNIVersal Automatic Computer) The first computer built for business purposes.

Universal Product Code (UPC) A code number, unique to a product, represented on the product's label in the form of a bar code.

Update To keep files current by changing data as appropriate.

Upload To send a file from one computer to a larger computer.

User A person who uses computer software or has contact with computer systems.

User friendly Refers to software that is easy for a novice to use.

User involvement The participation of users in the systems development life cycle.

Vacuum tube An electronic tube used as a basic component in the first generation of computers.

Value In a spreadsheet, data consisting of a number representing an amount, a formula, or a function.

Variable 1. A storage location in memory. 2. On a graph, the items that the data points describe.

Vertical centering A word processing feature that adjusts the top and bottom margins so that text is midway between the top and the bottom of the page.

Very high-level language A nonprocedural language. Also called a 4GL or a fourth-generation language.

VGA (video graphics adapter) A common screen standard with 640 by 480 pixels.

Videoconferencing Computer conferencing combined with cameras and wall-size screens.

Virtual reality A system in which a user is immersed in a computer-created environment, so that the user physically interacts with the computer-produced three-dimensional scene.

Virus A set of illicit instructions that passes itself on to other programs in which it comes in contact.

Vision robot A robot that can recognize an object by its shape or color.

Voice input The process of presenting input data to the computer through the spoken word. Also called speech recognition.

Voice mail A system in which the user can dictate a message into the voice mail system, where it is digitized and stored in the recipient's voice mailbox. Later the recipient can dial the mailbox, and the system delivers the message in audio form.

Voice-output device *See* Voice synthesizer.

Voice synthesizer A device that converts data in main storage to sounds understandable as speech to humans. Also called an audio-response unit or a voice-output device.

Volatile Refers to the loss of data in semiconductor storage when the current is interrupted or turned off.

WAN *See* Wide area network.

Wand reader An input device that scans the special letters and numbers on price tags in retail stores.

Weight The variation in the heaviness of a typeface; for example, type is much heavier when printed in **boldface.**

"What-if" analysis An approach, using spreadsheets, to experiment with different figures to determine potential outcomes.

Wide area network (WAN) A network of geographically distant computers and terminals.

Winchester disk A sealed disk drive containing disks, access arms, and read/write heads. Also called a sealed module.

Wire pairs Wires twisted together in an insulated cable. Wire pairs are frequently used to transmit information over short distances. Also called twisted pairs.

Word processing Computer-based creation, editing, formatting, storing, and printing of text.

Word wrap A word processing feature that automatically starts a word at the left margin of the next line if there is not enough room for it on the previous line.

Workgroup computing Every aspect of a group of workers using computer technology to meet a common goal.

Worksheet A spreadsheet.

Workstation A personal computer attached to a LAN.

Worm A program that transfers itself from computer to computer over a network and then plants itself as a file on the target computer's disk.

WORM *See* Write once, read many.

Write once, read many (WORM) Describes media that can be written on only once; then it becomes read-only media.

x-axis The horizontal reference line of a graph; it usually represents units of time.

y-axis The vertical reference line of a graph; it usually represents values or amounts, such as dollars, staffing levels, or units sold.

Credits

Photo Credits
Frontispiece: © John Wilkes/Photonica.

Table of contents
viii Intergraph.
viii Visual Data Research System.
viii © Rob Crandall/Picture Group
ix © Mark Marinello.
x © John Storey.
xii © Blair Seitz/Photo Researchers, Inc.
xii © Terry Vine/TS Images.
xiii © Ed Lallo/Gamma-Liaison International.
xiv ©Peter Menzel.
xv © Frank Herholdt/TS Images.
xvi PV Wave.
xvi © Jay Freis/Image Bank.
xvii © Brownie Harris/The Stock Market.
xvii ©Alan Levenson/TS Images.
xviii Visual Data Research Systems.
xviii © Peter Beck/The Stock Market.
xix Intergraph.
xix Workstation Technologies.
xix ©Peter Menzel.

Chapter openers ©Ted Kurihara.

Part 1 opener © Tori Butt.

Chapter 1
1.1.a ©Laima Druskis/Stock Boston.
1.1.b ©Sue Ann Miller/TS Images.
1.1.c ©Bruce Ayres/TS Images.
1.1.d ©Daniel Bosler/TS Images.
1.2 © Rysard Horowitz
1.3.a "Glass Planets" © Kai Krause/HSC Software Corporation.
1.3.b ©Diane Fenster.
1.4 ©Charles Harbutt.
1.5 ©Joe Sohn/Uniphoto.
1.6 Image produced by NCSA using Wavefront's Visualizer™
1.7 Dr. R.W. Kohl.
1.8 ©John Madere/The Stock Market.
1.9 © Phillip Saltonstall.
1.10 David Umberger, Purdue News Service.
1.11 Courtesy of Brøderbund Software, Inc.
1.12 Sandia National Labs/Livermore.
1.13 ©Scott Camazine/Photo Researchers, Inc.
1.14 ©Chris Sorensen.
Margin Note: Courtesy of Apple Computer Company.
PCA ©Francois Gohier.

Chapter 2
2.CT Courtesy of NEC Corporation.
Margin Note: International Business Machines.
PCA.1 Courtesy of Software Toolworks; Courtesy of International Business Machines.
PCA.2 Courtesy of Zagat-Axxis.
PCA.4 Courtesy of Software Marketing Corporation.
PCA.5 ©Robert Holmgren.
2.2.1-4 Courtesy of International Business Machines.
2.2.5,6 Courtesy of Intel Corporation.
2.3a ©Peter Steiner.
2.3b Recognition Equipment, Inc.
2.3c Courtesy of AT&T.
2.4a © Bachmann/The Stock Solution.
2.4b Courtesy of Texas Instruments.
2.5a ©Uniphoto.
2.5b Courtesy of Unisys Corporation.
2.5c Courtesy of BASF Corporation.
2.5d ©Terry Wild Studio.
2.6a Photo by Paul Shambroom, Courtesy of Cray Research, Inc.
2.6b U.S. Department of Energy/Mark Marten/Photo Researchers, Inc.
2.6c Courtesy of Digital Equipment Corporation.
2.6d ©Christopher Harris/Uniphoto.
2.7 Courtesy of San Diego Supercomputer Center.
2.8a ©Marion Stirrup/AlaskaStock Images.
2.8b ©Jim Cambon/TS Images.
2.8c Courtesy of Compaq Computer Corporation.
2.9a,b Courtesy of GRID Systems Corporation.
2.10 ©Steven Underwood.
2.13a Lotus Development Corporation.
2.13b Produces with 35mm Express™from BPS.
2.14a Courtesy of Texas Instruments.
2.14b Courtesy of Intel Corporation.
2.15 Jim Folts/Benjamin/Cummings.

Part 2 openers:
© Rick Reinhard, © FPG, © Greg Pease/TS Images.

Chapter 3
Margin Note: Courtesy of Intel Corporation.
Margin Note: ©Jeff Schultz/AlaskaStock Images.
PCA ©Hank deLespinasse/Reportage Stock.
3.4a ©Fred Bodin.
3.4b Courtesy of Intel Corporation.

Chapter 4
Margin Note: ©Bruce Jaffe/Gamma Liaison.
PCA Courtesy of ADAM, Inc., Marietta, GA.
4.1 box Courtesy of Unisys Corporation.
4.1a ©Lawrence Migdale/TS Images.
4.1b Courtesy of McDonalds Corporation.
4.1c Courtesy of International Business Machines.
4.2a ©David Mallory Jones/Uniphoto.
4.2b ©David Bishop/PhotoTake, NYC.
4.2c Courtey of Lotus Development Corporation.
4.3 Courtesy of Microsoft Corporation
4.7 Courtesy of International Business Machines.
4.8 ©Philip Gould.
4.9 a Courtesy of International Business Machines.
4.9 b ©Richard Tauber.
4.9 c Sun Microsystems, Inc.
4.11.a ©Alan L. Detrick.
4.11.b ©Jon Reis/PhotoLink.
4.12a Kai Krouse/KPT Texture Explorer.
4.12b ©Lloyd R. Hill.
4.12c San Diego Super Computer Center.
4.12d ©Charles Altschul/CCI.
4.13 a-c Created by Ken Bringhurst in Strata Vision 3e. Courtesy of Strata, Inc.
4.14a ©Hank Morgan/Science Source/Photo Researchers, Inc.
4.14b ©Berenguier/Jerrican/Photo Researchers,Inc.
4.15, 4.16 Courtesy of Hewlett-Packard Company.
4.17a Logitech, Inc.
4.17b ©Terry Wild.
4.18 ©Ed Kashi.

Chapter 5
MAC Courtesy of SyQuest Corporation.
Margin Note: ©Rick Smolan, "From Alice to Ocean." Screen shots from the Apple CD. Used with permission.
5.3 Courtesy of International Business Machines.
5.4a Unisys Corporation.
5.5a ©Frederick D. Bodin
5.5b BASF Systems Corporation.
5.5c KAO Infosystems Company.
5.7a,c Ancodyne, Inc.
5.9 Courtesy of Quantum Corporation.
5.10 Courtesy of Pionerr Communications of America, Inc.
5.12a,b,c Courtesy of Microsoft Corporation.

Chapter 6
Margin Note: Courtesy of In-Flight Phone Corporation.
PCA Courtesy of Prodigy Services Company.
6.1 Courtesy of Unisys Corporation.
6.2b ©Frederick D. Bodin.
6.2c Courtesy of Inmac.
6.3a National Wire and Cable Corporation.
6.3b,c Courtesy of Inmac.

6.6 Courtesy of International Business Machines.
6.7 ©HMS Images/The Image Bank.
6.8 Courtesy of AT&T.
6.9c Courtesy of America Online, Inc.
6.10 ©Louis Psihoyos/Matrix.
6.11 ©J. Barry O'Rourke/The Stock Market.

Part 3 opener
© Alain McLaughlin and The Monterey Bay Aquarium.

Chapter 7
CT Jim Folts/Benjamin/Cummings.
Margin Note:Department of the Navy.
PCA ©Chuck Savage/Uniphoto.

Chapter 8
CT © David Burnett/ Digital Originals™
Margin Note: Courtesy of ©IDG Books Worldwide, Inc.
8.4 Courtesy of Microsoft Corporation.
8.5a Lotus Development Corporation
8.5b Courtesy of Borland International.
8.5c Courtesy of Aldus Corporation.

Part 4 opener © Ted Soqui.

Chapter 9
CT © Bob Daemmrich/Stock Boston.
PCA © Greg Buchman/The Big Pixel.
9.1a ©Richard Gross/The Stock Market.
9.1b ©Gabe Palmer/Mugshots/The Stock Market.
9.1c Courtesy of Hewlett Packard Corporation.
9.1d Courtesy of Compaq Computer Corporation.
9.2 ©Howard Grey/TS Images.
9.3 Courtesy of Lotus Development Corporation.

Chapter 10
PCA Misco, Inc.
10.3 Courtesy of Eyedentify, Inc.

Chapter 11
Margin Note (2 photos)©Hank Morgan/Rainbow.
PCA ©Andy Freeberg/Discover Magazine.
11.2 ©Ed Kashi/Phototake.
11.3a,bCourtesy of Aion Development Corporation.
11.4a ©Andy Sacks/TS Images.
11.4b Courtesy of Japan Airlines.
11.5a-d©Thinking Machines Corporation.
11.6 Courtesy of Control Data Corporation.
11.7a ©P. Howell/Gamma-Liaison.
11.7b Courtesy of VPL Research.
11.7c ©David Sutton.

Historical Appendix
H1 Reprinted from POPULAR ELECTRONICS, January 1975/ ©1975 Ziff-Davis Publishing. Company.
H2 IBM Archives.
H3 Culver Pictures.
H4 IBM Archives.
H5 Iowa State University of Science and Technology.
H6-7b IBM Archives.
H9 Courtesy of Inmac, Santa Clara, CA
Margin Note:1 ©Marjorie Nichols/The Computer Museum, Boston
Margin Note:.2 IBM Archives.
Margin Note:3 Courtesy of Intel.
Margin Note:4 Computer Museum, Boston.
PCA © Steve Jobs/Reportage Stock.
PCA.2 ©Matthew McVay/Stock Boston.
PCA.3 Courtey of EFF. Photo by Seth Resnick

Graphics Gallery
opener © Cynthia Satloff.
1 © Marc Yankus.
2-4 © Gregory MacNicol.
5 ©Bill Frymire.
6 © John Fitzgerald.
7 © Joseph Maas/Paragon 3.
8 ©Tom Cushwa.
9 © Greg Buchman/The Big Pixel.
10 ©Steve Lyons.
11 ©Joseph Maas/Paragon 3.
12 ©Lilla Rogers.
13,14 © Annie Higbee.
15-17 © Marc Yankus.
18 Created in Fractal Design Painter by John Taylor Dismukes at Capstone Studios, L.A.
19 © Marc Yankus.
20 © Peter McCormick, courtesy of CorelDraw.
21 ©Gary Preister/CorelDraw.
22 Courtesy of Pacific Data Images.
23 Intergraph.
24 HSC Software/KAI'S Powertools.
25 Chris Purcell/CorelDraw.
26 © Mark Yankus.
27-30 ©Katrin Eisman.
31 XAOS.

Multimedia gallery
opener: ©Rick Smolan/Against All Odds.
2 Courtesy of Microsoft Corporation.
2, btm: © Sigma Designs.
3, 1–3 Courtesy of Microsoft Corporation.
4, 5 & 17–19 Courtesy of Discovery Communications.
6, 7 Courtesy of Brøderbund Software, Inc.
23 Courtesy of E Book, Inc.
26–28 Courtesy of Bureau Development, Inc.
all others: Courtesy of Microsoft Corporation.

Buyer's Guide
1 ©Fredrik D. Bodin.
2 Courtesy of International Business Machines.
3 Courtesy of Apple Corporation.
4.1 Courtesy of International Business Machines.
4.2 Courtesy of NEC.
5 Courtesy of Microcomputer Accessories.
6 Courtesy of International Business Machines.
7 ©John Curtis.
8.1 Courtesy of BASF Corporation.
8.2 Microscience International Corporation.
9,10 Courtesy of Hewlett Packard.
11.1 Courtesy of QMS Corporation.
11.2,3 Courtesy of Eastman/Kodak.
12 Courtesy of Sparc.
13 Courtesy of Edstrom.
14 ©John Curtis.
15 Courtesy of Inmac.
16 ©Richard Tauber.

Index

NOTE: Page numbers in italics indicate illustrations or tables separated from accompanying text.

A

B

E

F

G

H

N

O

P

T

U

V

W

Y

Z